TEN BAD DATES WITH DE NIRO

10 BAD DATES WITH DE NIRO

A BOOK OF ALTERNATIVE MOVIE LISTS

edited by Richard T. Kelly
illustrated by Andrew Rae

The Overlook Press
New York

TEN BAD DATES WITH DE NIRO

This paperback edition first published in the United States in 2009 by

The Overlook Press, Peter Mayer Publishers, Inc.
141 Wooster Street
New York, NY 10012
www.overlookpress.com

Copyright © 2007 Richard T. Kelly
Each individual list is © 2007 by its author
Illustrations copyright © 2007 by Andrew Rae

Published in the UK by Faber & Faber Ltd.

First published in hardcover in 2008 by The Rookery Press

Cataloging-in-Publication Data is on file at the Library of Congress

Printed in the United States of America
1 3 5 7 9 8 6 4 2
ISBN 978-1-58567-971-3

For Cordelia

Contents

List of Contributors

GILBERT ADAIR has published novels, essays, translations, children's books and poetry. His most recent novel is *A Mysterious Affair of Style*, a sequel to *The Act of Roger Murgatroyd*. The acclaimed author of *The Postmodernist Always Rings Twice*, he has also written screenplays, including *The Dreamers* – from his own novel – for Bernardo Bertolucci. His favourite film is *La Sortie des usines Lumière* (1895). 'After that it was all downhill.'

KALEEM AFTAB is the author of *Spike Lee: That's My Story and I'm Sticking to It*. He writes for the *Independent* and also produces films. His favourite film is *Pakeezah* (1971).

GEOFF ANDREW is Head of Film Programming at London's National Film Theatre, Contributing Editor of *Time Out London*, and the author of numerous books on the cinema, including studies of the films of Nicholas Ray, and monographs on Kiarostami's *10* and Kieslowski's *Three Colours* trilogy. His favourite film is (probably) *L'Atalante* (1934).

ANDREW BENBOW was seven years old when his life was changed by seeing a trailer for *Stars Wars* on *Spot On* (the New Zealand equivalent of the UK's *Blue Peter*). His favourite film is *Orphée* (1950).

ANNE BILLSON is a novelist, film critic and photographer who has lived in London, Tokyo and Croydon. Her books include *Suckers*, an upwardly mobile vampire novel, and *Stiff Lips*, a ghost story set in Notting Hill. She now lives in Paris, where she is writing another vampire novel. Her favourite film is *Night of the Demon* (1957).

CHRISTOPHER BRAY is the author of *Michael Caine: A Class Act*, and is at work on a book on Sean Connery. He writes about books, movies and music for the *Daily Telegraph*, the *New Statesman* and the *New York Times*. His favourite film is *To Have and Have Not* (1944).

JONATHAN CARTER, having helped to launch *Hotdog* with James Brown, became Film Editor on *Sleazenation* and contributed to various UK/US publications and radio shows. He is currently a producer commissioning video content for the BBC's online cultural magazine *Collective*, and is finishing a novel in a bid for freedom. His favourite film is *Mirror* (1974).

MAVIS CHEEK lives in the English countryside. She is the author of thirteen novels, most recently *The Sex Life of My Aunt*, *Patrick Parker's Progress*, *Yesterday's Houses*, and *Amenable Women*. Her favourite film, were she to be chained to a rock with a film carved into it, would be *Brief Encounter* (1945); though when feeling glum she prefers *Bridget Jones's Diary* (2001), mainly for the drunk-in-pyjamas-singing-'All By Myself' scene.

IAN CHRISTIE is a film historian and broadcaster, currently professor at Birkbeck College, where he is developing London Screen Studies. His books have been on Eisenstein, Powell and Pressburger, Scorsese and Gilliam; and he has worked on the exhibitions *Spellbound* at the Hayward and *Modernism* at the V&A. His favourite film is *A Matter of Life and Death* (1946), ideally programmed with Len Lye's *Rainbow Dance* (1936).

ETHAN COEN AND JOEL COEN are the men responsible for *Blood Simple* (1984), *Raising Arizona* (1987), *Miller's Crossing* (1990), *Barton Fink* (1991), *The Hudsucker Proxy* (1994), *Fargo* (1996), *The Big Lebowski* (1998), *O Brother, Where Art Thou?* (2000), *The Man Who Wasn't There* (2001), *Intolerable Cruelty* (2003), *The Ladykillers* (2004) and *No Country for Old Men* (2007).

KIERON CORLESS is the deputy editor of *Sight and Sound* magazine and has written for *Time Out London*, *Vertigo*, the *Independent*, and others. He has served as a jury member at the Bucharest and Lisbon international film festivals. His favourite film is *Performance* (1970).

MARK COUSINS is a film-maker, author, TV presenter and festival director. His documentary film subjects include Mikhail Gorbachev, Neo-Nazism and the cinema of Iran. He has directed the Edinburgh Film Festival and Cinema China. *The Story of Film* was translated into ten languages, including Mandarin. A film he craves to see again is *Nippon konchuki* (1963).

PAUL DALE is an award-winning writer and 1970s-bespoke dandy, the best-dressed film journalist currently working in Scotland. As well as editing the film section of *The List* (a *Time Out* for Edinburgh and Glasgow) his writings on film for marginal and mainstream publications have won him fans and detractors in equal measure. His favourite film is *The Wages of Fear* (1953).

CHRIS DARKE's writing has appeared in *Film Comment*, *Sight and Sound*, the *Independent*, and *Cahiers du cinéma*. He is also the author of *Light Readings: Film Criticism and Screen Arts*, and a monograph on Godard's *Alphaville*. His favourite film is *La Jetée* (1962).

PAUL FARLEY is a writer and broadcaster. He has published three widely acclaimed collections of poetry – most recently *Tramp in Flames* (Picador) – as well as a study of Terence Davies' *Distant Voices, Still Lives*. He lives in north Lancashire. One favourite film is *La Vie Rêvée des Anges* (1998).

MIKE FIGGIS is the director of *Stormy Monday* (1988), *Internal Affairs* (1990), *Liebestraum* (1991), *Mr Jones* (1993), *The Browning Version* (1994), *Leaving Las Vegas* (1995), *One Night Stand* (1997), *Loss of Sexual Innocence* (1999), *Miss Julie* (1999), *Timecode* (2000), *Hotel* (2001) and *Cold Creek Manor* (2003). He has written *Projections 10* and *Digital Film-making* for Faber. His favourite film is *Weekend* (1967).

LIZZIE FRANCKE was Artistic Director of the Edinburgh Film Festival from 1997–2001. She is the author of *Script Girls: Women Screenwriters* in Hollywood and a contributor to the

Guardian and *Sight and Sound* among others. She is currently, for her sins, a film producer. Her favourite film, if put on the spot, is *Vertigo* (1958).

GRAHAM FULLER has been the film columnist for *Interview* magazine for sixteen years, and also contributes to *Sight and Sound* and *Film Comment*. He is the editor of *Potter on Potter* and *Loach on Loach* (Faber). His favourite film is unquestionably *A Canterbury Tale* (1944).

RYAN GILBEY is film critic of the *New Statesman*. He is also the author of *It Don't Worry Me* and a study of *Groundhog Day* in the BFI Modern Classics series. His favourite film is *McCabe and Mrs Miller* (1971).

DAVID HARE has written over twenty stage plays, among them *Plenty*, *The Secret Rapture*, *Racing Demon*, *The Absence of War*, *Skylight*, *Amy's View*, *Via Dolorosa*, *The Permanent Way*, *Stuff Happens* and *The Vertical Hour*. He has adapted into English plays by Pirandello, Brecht, Chekhov, Schnitzler, Lorca and Gorky. His television films include *Licking Hitler*. He has written screenplays for many feature films, most recently *The Hours*. His favourite film is *The Battle of Algiers* (1966).

KEVIN JACKSON was appointed Visiting Professor of English at University College, London in 2007. Editor of *Schrader on Schrader* for Faber, his recent publications include *Lawrence of Arabia*, *The Pataphysical Flook*, and *The Book of Hours* (all 2007). *Lawrence of Arabia* (1963) is probably his favourite film, too.

RICHARD T. KELLY is the author of *Alan Clarke* (1998), *The Name of this Book is Dogme 95* (2000), *Sean Penn: His Life and Times* (2004), and the novel *Crusaders* (2008). His favourite film is *Lancelot du Lac* (1974).

EDWARD LAWRENSON is a freelance writer based in London. His favourite film is *Hail the Conquering Hero* (1944).

DANNY LEIGH is the author of the novels *The Greatest Gift* and *The Monsters of Gramercy Park*, and has written on film (and occasionally the world beyond) for numerous newspapers and magazines. His favourite film is *Seconds* (1966).

JAMES LITTLE is a fan of anything that involves sitting on the sofa, with a special predilection for Asian cinema, particularly horror, and a hatred of remakes. His favourite film is *One Flew Over the Cuckoo's Nest* (1975).

KEVIN MACDONALD is a film-maker best known for the documentaries *Touching the Void* and *One Day in September*, and the feature film *The Last King of Scotland*. He is also the co-editor of *Imagining Reality: The Faber Book of Documentary*. His favourite film is *Singin' in the Rain* (1951).

GEOFFREY MACNAB contributes regularly to the *Independent*, *Screen International* and the *Guardian*. His books are *J. Arthur Rank and the British Film Industry*, *Searching for Stars*, *Key Moments in Cinema* and *The Making of Taxi Driver*. His favourite film is *Barry Lyndon* (1975).

DEMETRIOS MATHEOU is the film critic of Glasgow's *Sunday Herald* and also writes about film for the *Sunday Times*, the *Independent on Sunday* and *Sight and Sound*. He is currently writing a book for Faber on South American cinema. His favourite film is *The Philadelphia Story* (1940).

SAUL METZSTEIN is the director of the feature films *Late Night Shopping* and *Guy X*. His favourite film is *The Conformist* (1970).

JAMES MOTTRAM contributes regularly to *The Times*, the *Independent* and *Scotland on Sunday*. He has written four books, including *The Making of Memento* and *The Sundance Kids* for Faber. He lives in north London and his favourite film is *Blue Velvet* (1986).

ANDREW O'HAGAN was born in Glasgow in 1968. He is the author of the novels *Our Fathers*, *Personality*, and *Be Near Me*, has won the James Tait Black Memorial Prize for Fiction and the E.M. Forster Award from the American Academy of Arts and Letters, and has been short-listed for the Booker Prize. He is a contributor to the *London Review of Books* and the *New Yorker*. His favourite film (this week) is *Badlands* (1973).

GEORGE PELECANOS is a screenwriter, independent film producer, award-winning journalist, and the author of a bestselling series of novels set in and around Washington, DC. His most recent novel was *The Night Gardener* and he has also recently been working as a producer, writer and story editor on the highly acclaimed HBO series *The Wire*. His favourite film is *The Wild Bunch* (1969).

NEV PIERCE is the editor of *Total Film* (www.totalfilm.com), definitively the best magazine in the world named *Total Film*. His favourite movie is *Fight Club* (1999), when it's not *It's a Wonderful Life* (1946).

DBC PIERRE was born in Australia and raised in Buñuel's Mexico City. His debut novel *Vernon God Little* won the Man Booker Prize, the Whitbread First Novel Award and the Bollinger Everyman Wodehouse Award for Comic Writing in 2003. His second novel was *Ludmila's Broken English*. He lives in Cambridgeshire. His favourite film is *Eraserhead* (1977).

ANTHONY QUINN is the film critic of the *Independent*. His favourite film is *The Lady Eve* (1941).

TIM ROBEY is the deputy film critic for the *Daily Telegraph*. He contributes regularly to *Sight and Sound*, and is co-editor of *The DVD Stack*. His favourite film is *The Thin Red Line* (1998).

RAFAELA ROMAYA is a designer and typographer. She has worked at Faber & Faber and Macmillan Publishers, and is currently finishing a book on film title credits and design. She lives in Kent, and her favourite film is *A Matter of Life and Death* (1946).

MARK SALISBURY writes about films for a variety of publications. Until its recent, sad demise, he was London Correspondent of *Premiere* magazine and is a former editor of *Empire*. He's written and/or edited several books including *Burton On Burton* (Faber). His favourite film is *A Matter of Life And Death* (1946).

STEVEN SODERBERGH is the director of *sex, lies and videotape* (1989), *Kafka* (1991), *King of the Hill* (1993), *The Underneath* (1995), *Gray's Anatomy* (1996), *Schizopolis* (1996), *Out of Sight* (1998), *The Limey* (1999), *Erin Brokovich* (2000), *Traffic* (2000), *Ocean's Eleven* (2001), *Full Frontal* (2002), *Solaris* (2002), *Ocean's Twelve* (2004), *Bubble* (2005), *The Good German* (2006), and *Ocean's Thirteen* (2007).

GORDON SPIERS saw too many monster, sci-fi and horror films at a tender age, though he is now a well-adjusted family man. His favourite film (the first DVD he bought, months before owning a player) is *Raising Arizona* (1987).

JAMES SPIERS is an expatriate raised on a questionable diet of US fare, now insulated by Tivo and BBC America. His favourite film ('Here I... am') is *Manhunter* (1986.)

LESLEY THORNE is a literary agent who also handles film and TV for Aitken Alexander Associates Ltd. She lives in London with her husband and son. Her favourite film is *Vertigo* (1958).

MATT THORNE was born in Bristol in 1974 and is the author of six novels including *Eight Minutes Idle* (Winner of an Encore Award, 1999) and *Cherry* (long-listed for the Man Booker Prize, 2004). He has also written three children's books and has co-edited two anthologies. His favourite film is *La Maman et la putain* (1973).

DAVID THOMPSON makes arts documentaries for the BBC, specialising in film subjects (from Jean Renoir to Quentin Tarantino). In collaboration with Matthew Sweet he recently made *Silent Britain*, a celebration of the strengths and glories of British silent cinema. He is also co-editor of *Scorsese on Scorsese* and editor of *Altman on Altman*. His favourite film (if his arm is twisted) is *L'Atalante* (1934).

JASON WOOD is a writer and film programmer. Recent publications include *Nick Broomfield: Documenting Icons*, *The Faber Book of Mexican Cinema* and *Talking Movies*. His writing also appears in *Time Out*, *Sight and Sound* and *Vertigo*. As he likes a bit of a cavort, his favourite film is *Performance* (1970).

Introduction

RICHARD T. KELLY

The French have a euphonious word to describe the love of movies – *cinéphilia* – which also manages to sound uncomfortably like a clinical condition. But then the association isn't so far-fetched. We've all met people who profess to be 'mad about films' and do indeed rave about them in semi-lunatic fashion. Even the Oscar-winning maestro Bernardo Bertolucci has been heard to speak wryly of 'the disease of *cinéphilia*'. One widespread symptom of same is that an awful lot of movie-lovers keep lists (or once kept them) as a log of their evolving tastes, of their post-show arguments in the pub, and their special interests in particular actors, directors, genres, themes, areas of seeming trivia . . . These can develop into extraordinary close fascinations with minute aspects of cinema: there's just something about the medium that encourages this kind of train-spotting. A further symptom is that most film fans – guiltily or otherwise – seem to get a kick out of reading other people's lists too. Hence this book.

As its title will suggest, *Ten Bad Dates with De Niro* is not a set of critical judgements on what are the all-time cinematic greats, with *Citizen Kane* and *La Règle du Jeu* at the top, *Ishtar* and *Howard the Duck* at bottom. Nor is it a compendium of trivia or miscellany – no lists of Hitchcock's cameos in his own movies, or actors who turned down parts in *Star Wars*, or digital watches sported by extras in historical dramas, or the 'Ten Biggest Flops of All Time'. It is essentially a symposium and celebration of viewing pleasures, private passions and cinematic lost causes: of films that have rightly earned obsessive dialogue-spouting fans, of gems that have been unfairly neglected or lost, and, yes, movies deeply

flawed but still weirdly riveting. We are speaking perhaps of 'cult
movies', though that term doesn't mean what it used to, not in
the era of DVD and YouTube. Repertory cinemas and late-night
double-features are the stuff of nostalgia now. The availability and
repeatability of movies is legion, and the history of cinema is an
ever-more dauntingly broad subject to get one's head around. This
book simply offers an array of partial but passionate selections of
dearly beloved movies, by film writers, film-makers, screenwriters,
novelists, poets – *cinéphile* scribes of all stripes.

The lists are ordered in thematic chapters, with brief explanations
from each author as to his or her special interest in the given area,
and a sense of the criteria behind the choice of Ten: whereupon the
lists unfold in ascending order. We hope you will be amused,
informed, and provoked into argument by these lists. If so, then
please come and join the discussion at *www.tenbaddates.com*. I welcome corrections, suggestions, criticisms, feedback of all kinds.

I

Losing it at the Movies

Pure Emotional Responses to Cinema

ANNE BILLSON: 'It's Only a Movie . . .' Ten Films (Non-Horror) that Traumatized Me When I Was Younger

DBC PIERRE: Ten Films to Avoid on Medication (or Within Reach of a Cutlery Drawer)

NEV PIERCE: My Love Wears Forbidden Colours – Ten Films It's Painful to Like

A ROUNDTABLE: The Crying Game – Ten Confessions of Uncontrollable Movie Tears

'It's Only a Movie . . .'

Ten Films (Non-Horror) that Traumatized Me When I Was Younger

ANNE BILLSON

What were my parents *thinking*? How come they never realized that films deemed suitable for Family Viewing were often, in fact, subversive Freudian swamps that would give me bad dreams for months to come? How come they let me stay up late to watch so many unsuitable films on television? And how come they never noticed how *upset* I was getting?

I must have sensed any hint of distress on my part would only have resulted in heavy parental censorship, and toned down my reactions accordingly. The only film I was actively forbidden to watch was the first TV screening of *Psycho*. I got sent to bed shortly after Janet Leigh arrived at the motel, though I do remember thinking, as I reluctantly climbed the stairs, that the motel manager seemed a likeable sort of chap, and that he and Janet were bound to get together later on.

Otherwise, I had carte blanche to watch any old film that took my fancy. And I watched as many as I could, and of course, some of them gave me nightmares – though not necessarily the films you'd expect. Horror movies didn't worry me unduly; I was impressed by an early screening of *Night of the Demon* (GB 1957, dir. Jacques Tourneur) but I can't say it lodged in my subconscious to fester there like a scrap of decaying offal between the teeth – not like some films I could tell you about. But Italian neo-realism, now, that's another story . . .

10. *Roma Ore 11* / *Rome Eleven O'Clock* (Italy 1952, dir. Giuseppe De Santis)

A whole gaggle of unemployed Italian girls are applying for a secretarial job, but there are so many of them, and they're so desperate, that the staircase on which they're queuing collapses – resulting in rubble, screams, horrible injuries. You'll have to excuse me if my memory of this drama (apparently based on a real incident) from the director best known for *Bitter Rice* is a little hazy. It took me forty years to find out precisely which late-night film about the collapsing staircase had given me such terrifying nightmares, and I still haven't managed to set up a repeat viewing. Kids, eh? But it just goes to show – there's nothing scarier than Italian neo-realism.

9. *Swiss Family Robinson* (US 1960, dir. Ken Annakin)

Many of my younger friends will cite *Chitty Chitty Bang Bang* – specifically the Child Catcher – as one of the most disturbing viewing experiences of their childhood, though by the time it came out in 1968 I'd already graduated to 'grown-up' films like the James Bonds and *Modesty Blaise*. But not before I'd been traumatized by this jolly Disney desert island adventure. I was okay with the pirates, I was even okay with the ostrich abuse and the dog-versus-tiger fight, but oh, the anaconda attack in the swamp! What Freudian rumblings do you suppose were even then stirring in my innocent seven-year-old brain that made me fret over it for such a long time afterwards? And what were anacondas doing on a tropical island in the Pacific anyway? This is possibly the only film I ever saw that truly scarred me for life, in that I'm still an ophiophobe. I then read the book on which the film was based, only to be further traumatized by a colour plate of a donkey being crushed to death in the coils of a giant snake. Who the hell thought this stuff was suitable for small girls?

8. *The Lost Weekend* (US 1945, dir. Billy Wilder)

I can only assume my parents thought that letting me watch this film noir about a dipsomaniac writer would put me off alcohol for life. Or maybe writing, I don't know – though it did add the term *delirium tremens* to my vocabulary at an unusually tender age. It's bad enough when Ray Milland gets locked up in a ward full of raving alcoholics, but when he later imagines he's seeing a bat biting the head off a mouse, and the mouse's blood starts running down the wall . . . well, the only reason I didn't start screaming along with Milland was that I didn't want to get sent to bed.

7. *Sammy Going South* (GB 1963, dir. Alexander Mackendrick)

I can vaguely see why my parents thought a film about a small boy who treks 4,500 miles across Africa and has incredible adventures along the way might have been a suitable cinema treat for their nine-year-old. But I wonder whether they began to question their judgement once the film got going. It kicks off with Sammy's parents being killed in a bomb blast, and then it's downhill all the way, the nadir reached when our young traveller is picked up by a Syrian peddler who exhibits what one can only, in retrospect, call paedophiliac intent. As if this guy isn't scary enough, he gets even scarier when a rock explodes in his face, leaving him blind and horribly disfigured. Sammy manages to escape – only to fall into the clutches of a diamond smuggler played by Edward G. Robinson, an actor whose very appearance I found terrifying ever since a television screening of . . .

6. *The Red House* (US 1947, dir. Delmer Daves)

. . . in which Robinson lives with his sister and adopted daughter in a house in the woods, the setting for a spooky melodrama with intimations of incest and necrophilia. Spoiler Alert! I daresay my childhood antennae might already have picked up on all that psychological sickness and so sent out the appropriate alarms, but what really upset me was the ending, in which Robinson, who has been unmasked as a mentally unbalanced killer, drives his car into an ice-house at the edge of a lake and, slowly but surely, sinks bug-eyed into the water. Once seen, never forgotten, and truly the stuff of nightmares, though of course I never told my parents about them.

5. *Bambi* (US 1942, dir. David Hand)

No list of childhood trauma would be complete without an animated feature from Uncle Walt – though the scariness of the villainesses in *Snow White*, *The Sleeping Beauty* and *101 Dalmatians* was tempered by my nerdling appreciation of their operatic stylishness and bad-girl fashion sense. To tell you the truth, I was so young when I first saw *Bambi* that for years I couldn't remember much about it, though I did vaguely recall being upset. So, aged thirty, I

went to see it again. My boyfriend and I were the only childless adults
in the auditorium. As soon as the film started I felt something primal
welling up inside me. Long before Bambi's mother bit the dust, I was
sobbing convulsively. I even sobbed through the funny bits. I sobbed
so noisily that small children turned to stare at me, bemused by this
bawling adult in their midst. (And yes, I was probably weeping for my
lost childhood, as well, but we won't go into that.)

4. *Kiss Me Deadly* (US 1955, dir. Robert Aldrich)

Admittedly, the version I saw on the BBC all those years ago did-
n't include the scene in which Cloris Leachman is tortured to
death with pliers, but in any case *Kiss Me Deadly really* engaged
my childish imagination. It evidently didn't trouble me that the
nominal hero Mike Hammer (Ralph Meeker) was a thug just as
vicious and unprincipled as the bad guys, but I was seriously
spooked by the mysterious box everyone was chasing: the way it
made a scary 'oooh-wheee-oooh' noise and let out a blast of white
heat every time someone lifted the lid. I dread to think what this
symbolized in my carefree infant psyche.

3. *Le Boucher / The Butcher* (France 1970, dir. Claude Chabrol)

After that early exposure to horrifying Italian neo-realism, sub-
titles held no terror for me. Our French teacher had already taken
us to see Eric Rohmer movies about droopy young people who
talked a lot, and so I trotted off happily on my own to see my first
Chabrol, expecting more of the same: a bit dull and talky, maybe,
but good for my French. And what did I get? Blood from a murder victim dripping on to a pupil's brioche at a school picnic.
Aaagh! Thus was I introduced to this French director's two major
auteurial motifs: food and death.

2. *The Charge of the Light Brigade* (GB 1968, dir. Tony Richardson)

I was no longer a child capable of being traumatized by any old thing;
I was an adolescent, and I fancied David Hemmings, so I made my
dad take me to see this unofficial adaptation of Cecil Woodham-

Smith's *The Reason Why*. I knew it was going to end in tears – I'd read the Tennyson poem, for heaven's sake – but since David was playing the hero, I confidently assumed he was to be spared, perhaps a little roughed up, but in sufficiently good shape to see out the closing credits with Vanessa Redgrave, even if she was a head taller than him. Imagine my shock, then, when, *before the charge has even started*, David gets hit by a stray piece of shrapnel, shrieks like a girl, and dies, bleeding from the mouth. Not only that, but the breakdown in communications leading to the suicidal charge itself is nearly all *his fault*. Welcome to the wonderful world of grown-ups.

1. *The Wizard of Oz* (US 1939, dir. Victor Fleming)

Quite frankly, how could a child see this film and *not* be severely traumatized by it? If it's not the wicked witches, it's the creepy Munchkins, or the flying monkeys, or the Wizard himself, or that garish Technicolor, or the supposedly 'good characters' like The Tin Man or Glinda, who to a child seem every bit as sinister as the evil ones. But if I had to pick one scene in particular, it's the tornado. Even now, when it's particularly windy, I catch myself worrying that my roof is going to blow away or, worse, the entire building will be ripped from its foundations, swept up spinning into the air, and set down in a place of perpetual nightmare populated by flying monkeys and creepy little people who sing like Pinky and Perky. I can't think of anything worse, unless maybe it's a witch flying past the window on the way there.

Ten Films to Avoid on Medication (or Within Reach of a Cutlery Drawer)

DBC PIERRE

Each of us has been indelibly scarred by cinema; not only by its content, but by the scattergun pellets of individual concepts, faces, voices, settings, music, and, most especially, moods. A film is a petite life, and deserves to walk and suffer harm and pay taxes. Here I would like to explore a deep passion of mine associated with life, and hence cinema in its role as a tiny life.

Kismet. Fortune's wheel, and how it delivers the coincidence of mood and cinema into our lives in ominous ways. Specifically: the violent effect of chancing upon the wrong film at the wrong time. This is cinema to beware of.

The list is an advisory service, and should be consulted prior to deploying unfamiliar motion pictures. Masterpieces form part of the list, as does crap, and I don't sully either by identifying which I think are which. I do not say to you that these are films to avoid – indeed, some are unspeakably beautiful. I do, however, try to impart a sense of why each motion picture, in its own way, should not be watched within reach of any stabbing blade, or under the influence of heavy drugs of any ilk, or from within any institution providing purely palliative care, or in an active phase of any of the following afflictions: bipolar disorder, schizophrenia, antisocial personality disorder, slipped disc, alcoholism, spastic mega colon, or any condition, disease, disorder or bent capable of rendering throbbing pain. I can reliably report that the only medication proven safe to accompany any of the listed films is amitriplyline hydrochloride, and then only if you are a new user.

If any of these film choices seem incongruous under the light of a chirpy day, forgive me; for I chanced upon them in the dark of a life, within reach of that blade, under the influence of those substances. I bear the scars as I write, and live each moment with the certainty that they will outlive the flesh on my bones.

Let me expand upon the concept behind this list. Theoretically, a motion picture is crafted to be a beginning and end unto itself, a whole; that is, it undertakes to transport the viewer into the mood where its works will be done. It is, of course, impossible to know what mood inhabits a viewer before the film begins. And so – I say – viewers are imagined, for the purposes of this theory, as entering the process in a neutral frame of mind, a zero value.

But therein lies the danger. Because outrageous inner and outer conflicts, undiagnosed instabilities of character or mind, coincidences of mood that might lead to exponential effects, or moods of an opposite nature to those contrived by the film – none of these is taken into account.

My observation, then, is this: that while tolerances governing the emotional effectiveness of cinema, and the ability of a viewer to adapt and filter content, and the occurrence of day-to-day emotional coincidences, are broad and generally non-threatening within an average lifetime . . .

Every so often a film takes you apart.

Here are ten of them.

10 *Titanic* (US 1998, dir. James Cameron)

A Night to Remember (GB 1958) is still better, and cost less than the catering on Cameron's film. Such an observation might seem trivial and pedantic as you read it now, but mark my words: it's an awareness that burrows and itches, arousing anything from persistent irritation to moderate rage and – when added to the fanfare accompanying *Titanic*'s release – actual swelling. A work not to be taken lightly, or viewed while drunk, or Scottish, as base rules. But probably safe under the influence of America.

9 *Auch Zwerge haben klein angefangen* / *Even Dwarfs Started Small* (West Germany 1971, dir. Werner Herzog)

Even on cannabis, or lightly depressed, Herzog's second work, in which a collection of German dwarves and midgets run amok at an asylum in Spain to very strange music, can unhinge you. And the last minute of action proves Werner is actually aiming at this, which does nothing for your paranoia. The film's effect can be emulated by spending ninety minutes on acid at a kindergarten sports day in Lübeck. Watch the real thing, though, and you'll never come back.

8 *Fierce Creatures* (GB 1997, dir. Fred Schepisi and Robert Young)

View this and recall that the force behind it, John Cleese, was once widely hailed as a genius. This work is an invoice for the cost of a man's sanity; watching the sums add up on screen is a devastating business, and will forever wreck your faith in any right to the pursuit of happiness.

7 *The Piano* (Australia/France 1993, dir. Jane Campion)

(Advisory for men) A beautiful production with a haunting post-modern piano theme attributed to a very plain girl who chooses to remain speechless in a past century where she has a shit life in some mud in New Zealand. She ends this highly phlegmy, gluti-nous, man-indicting work by tying the piano to her leg and hav-ing it hoisted over the side of a rowing boat at sea. This film can bring long-term frustration; not in your hard-earned delight that the girl is finally plummeting to the seabed, but in your inability to express this glee, or indeed anything much, because it makes you one of the bastards targeted by the film.

6 *On Golden Pond* (US 1981, dir. Mark Rydell)

If you didn't sleep through this coral-filter of a yarn about famous old Americans playing old Americans getting too old beside a lake, you're in danger of severe dismay; not from the work's inher-ent stupor, but the certainty that you'll never actually remember how the action went, or if, indeed, there was any, and hence enter an anxiety loop about your own declining cognitive powers. Avoid sedatives.

5. *Gorillas in the Mist* (US 1988, dir. Michael Apted)

One of the ugliest motion pictures you can see, a rage-inducer that can clash badly with stimulants; even coffee and tea. The story of an earthy American college woman who can't keep a boyfriend and unleashes atrocities upon African natives who kill gorillas due to poverty. Her portrayal as a heroic crusader touched by justified obsession will rile you for life, as will the highly inflammatory absence of any ending where she gets nailed by a gorilla.

4. *The Other Side of the Mountain* (US 1975, dir. Larry Peerce)

This film carries a general advisory for Depression tinged with Political Correctness Fatigue. From the heart of the emotionally manipulative seventies, the most emotionally manipulative work I can think of: based on the true story of a champion skier who

becomes crippled and ends up in sunny activities rooms pretending that eating crisps with her knuckles is a big step forward. Then
the tragedies begin. This one slaps you sideways, I doubt even a
rugby club or stag party would survive it.

3. *Mondo Cane* (Italy 1962, dir. Paolo Cavara, Gualtiero Jacopetti, Franco E. Prosperi)

Legendary Italian documentary that scours the globe for the most
distasteful customs and occurrences, then runs overwrought violin music to them, with narration by an American who has clearly spent twenty years on lithium in Sicily. As you watch, you can't
help but feel this is what they showed to Malcolm McDowell in
A Clockwork Orange in order to straighten him up. Severe advisory against acid use, I mean it.

2. *La Strada / The Road* (Italy 1954, dir. Federico Fellini)

Fellini's tale about a dimwit embarking on a road trip for no good
reason with some bastard in an Italian prototype of the Reliant
Robin, and getting a bloody good slapping along the way, is a masterpiece. And therein lies its danger; you can't even escape into
humour. It's art. This is cinema you can't admit the effects of,
even to yourself. I tell you as a friend: the scornful tirade above is
because I cried. Avoid gin or brandy. Close your eyes as soon as
Richard Basehart appears.

1. *Vredens Dag / Day of Wrath* (Denmark 1943, dir. Carl Dreyer)

The ultimate accompaniment to death; a work that starts bleak-
ly, then plunges downhill in one of Scandinavia's more pessimistic
dialects. Moreover, from the first frame you know which way it's
headed. The opening scene is all you need to feel a weight of mud
bulldozed on to your grave. And Dreyer's undoubted brilliance is
deployed through a muffled monochrome fog, making the thing
even more nightmarish. When your cries for help are over, and
you finally pick the day, line up your razor and pills to this one.
And rest in peace.

My Love Wears Forbidden Colours

Ten Films It's Painful to Like

NEV PIERCE

You know you're not supposed to. Something inside tells you it's wrong, or else the sniggers and scowls of real film aficionados – heads swivelling, eyebrows raised – underline the clear stupidity of your taste. And yet, and yet . . . you can't help yourself. So you learn, gradually, to hide your true nature, keep your desires hidden, your longings suppressed. Maybe it's just you. Maybe these feelings will go away. Maybe your heart will stop raging against your head and you'll be able to join the gang in its comfort-blanket dismissal of these tacky movies. But you know you can't. You know, deep down, you'll *always* have these feelings. And, one day, you'll have to speak out . . .

10. *Top Gun* (US 1986, dir. Tony Scott)

A late Cold War-era recruitment ad for Reaganite America, Tony Scott's chrome blockbuster makes *Sands of Iwo Jima* look like *The Battle of Algiers*. Tom Cruise is insufferably cocky, the sexual and global politics are Neanderthal, and Kenny Loggins's driving theme-tune 'Danger Zone' is an offence against God and Man. I can watch this film again and again and again . . . And ever since Quentin Tarantino's cameo monologue in *Sleep With Me* (1994) where he espouses a theory of sub-textual gay love between Maverick (Cruise) and Iceman (Val Kilmer), it's even possible to feel a little right-on in celebrating *Top Gun*: 'It is a story about a man's struggle with his own homosexuality . . . It is!'

9. *I Know What You Did Last Summer* (US 1997, dir. Jim Gillespie)

It would be a shock to find anyone who claims to know their horror hailing writer Kevin Williamson's follow-up to *Scream* as better than *The Exorcist* or *Halloween*. In fact, it's a claim so ridiculous only an idiot would make it. I am that idiot. The slick, icky tale of a hook-brandishing windbreaker-wearing fisherman seeking revenge on four photogenic teens is generally regarded as a routine slasher-picture notable only for the key supporting role given to Jennifer Love Hewitt's breasts. I've been championing it since release, and it's only after writing the last sentence that I realize, tragically, why . . .

8. Alien³ (US 1992, dir. David Fincher)

Even Fincher despises this movie, whose birth was as bloody and unpleasant as the titular beast's chest-bursting offspring. In its day the most expensive film ever entrusted to a first-time director, this 60-million-dollar production was shot without a finished script (at one stage pages were faxed through for scenes on a set that had already been torn down) and Fincher was in constant conflict with Fox over his vision for the picture. But amid the doom and gloom and borderline incoherence, there's a film of some worth, boldly breaking with the first sequel *Aliens* (indeed killing off all its surviving characters apart from Ripley during the *credits*) and replacing James Cameron's wham-bam aesthetic with a creepy, Gothic ambience. There's also a touching exploration of mortality and lost love in Ripley's pain over the death of her surrogate daughter Newt, and her brief intimacy with ill-fated physician Charles Dance. Fincher still wants to burn the negative . . . but there's a thoughtfulness to his debut feature that shouldn't to be dismissed.

7. Bad Boys II (US 2003, dir. Michael Bay)

The first *Bad Boys* was a *Beverly Hills Cop* knock-off and the sequel was yet brasher and crasser, bloody and loud, arguably racist, certainly sexist, hypocritical and – in one played-for-laughs scene involving a big-breasted corpse – absolutely foul. That this exuberantly violent, fascistic action picture received a 15 certificate a year after Ken Loach's exquisite *Sweet Sixteen* was given an 18 for its bad language (you can desecrate corpses, but don't you dare swear!) shows how Hollywood-biased our censor – and media – has become. Proving the aforementioned point: I don't remember feeling as much pure enjoyment – Explosions! Car chases! Gun battles! – in a cinema that year; though I left wanting to take a shower.

We'd Like to Thank the Academy: The Ten Most Richly
Deserved Oscars, p 36

6. *Forces of Nature* (US 1999, dir. Bronwen Hughes)

Ben Affleck appears an easy person to hate – on screen, at least, given the vitriol aimed at him for the likes of *Pearl Harbor*, *Paycheck* and *Gigli* (all surely more the responsibility of – I don't know – the *director* than the star?). The critical lashing for *Forces of Nature*, one of his first above-the-title gigs after the Oscar success of *Good Will Hunting*, showed just how much people can hate others who are young and successful. Affleck is teamed with cutesy klutz Sandra Bullock on a cross-country trek to his wedding, and issues of commitment and cold-feet are touched on with surprising maturity. Despite that slow-motion bit in the rain . . .

5. *Hannibal* (US 2001, dir. Ridley Scott)

A money-spinning sequel that no one but Thomas Harris's bank manager really wanted – sure, Scott's resurrection of Dr Lecter was attacked for its OTT noggin-lopping, and for Anthony Hopkins's apparent slide into pantomime villainy. If *The Silence of the Lambs* was considered art, this was idiocy, yet it is precisely these 'flaws' that make the movie so delicious: a *Grand Guignol* cartoon, shorn of *Lambs*' solemnity, spiced with a sly sense of its own absurdity. Michael Mann's *Manhunter* (1986) remains the best adaptation of Harris's compulsive schlock, but *Hannibal* is the most fun.

4. *Hook* (US 1991, dir. Steven Spielberg)

The teaming of Spielberg and Robin Williams was too much for all manchild-loathing critics, but *Hook*'s high concept (may I say hook?) – 'What if Peter Pan Grew Up?' – is still compelling, and the message about rediscovering your inner sprog is actually rather sweet. The world's most commercially successful director has made some terrible films – *The Color Purple*, *The Terminal* – but *Hook* has been unfairly skewered. It's an unpretentious and charming family film, and Dustin Hoffman makes the definitive Captain Hook. Although, yes, the dayglo skate-chic restyling of the 'Lost Boys' is hard to stomach.

18

3. A *Beautiful Mind* (US 2001, dir. Ron Howard)

Howard's biopic of genius/schizophrenic mathematician John
Nash was ripped to shreds by some critics, damned as conde-
scending drivel, a movie-of-the-week dressed up for Oscar. And
there's little point disputing that it is grossly manipulative, sim-
plistic, and sentimental; nor that Howard has made some hero-
ically bad pictures. Anyone who sat through *The Grinch* – even
if paid to review it – has probably earned the right to bear a lifelong grudge, even to bear arms against this man. So, it's with a
degree of no little self-loathing that I type: I liked *A Beautiful
Mind* . . . Whether it's accurate or admirable or not, Howard
made mental illness cinematic, while the love-conquers-all message – trite as it may be – was given heft by Russell Crowe's
lunatic-with-a-heart and the exquisite Jennifer Connelly as his
long-suffering, Oscar-guaranteed wife.

2. *Jeepers Creepers* (US 2001, dir. Victor Salva)

Should a film-maker's past and personal mistakes influence your
opinion of their work? In 1988 Victor Salva served time for sexually abusing the twelve-year-old male lead of his movie
Clownhouse. His 1995 Disney movie *Powder* was protested
against because of that criminal record (it also wasn't very good)
and his commercial breakthrough *Jeepers Creepers* is about a
demonic winged killer terrorizing two teenagers. I found it
astonishingly unsettling, scary and intense; with an uncanny
feeling for predation. And that was before I knew the history of
its director, who was charming, funny and thoughtful in two
interviews I conducted with him. It is presumably a hard thing
to carry the weight of one's mistakes so publicly – if not so hard
as the weight suffered by victims of abuse. After I wrote about
Salva's criminal record in an article for the BBC, he (perhaps
understandably) stopped returning my emails. I still don't know
if I did the right thing in mentioning a crime for which he paid
time in prison – or whether it's right to read into his kids-in-
peril horror picture an echo of prior transgressions. And I still
don't know that I like loving the movie.

1. *Love Actually* (GB/US 2003, dir. Richard Curtis)

Could a picture be more manipulative? Set in the run-up to Christmas, soundtracked with its own ironically dire cover of 'Love Is All Around' so as to recall Curtis's chart-hogging *Four Weddings and a Funeral*, and with enough story-strands to appeal to every demographic, *Love Actually* unsurprisingly copped some critical hate. But only the truly guileless could create a movie offering up such bulls-eyes to the cynics . . . *Love Actually* succeeds because Curtis is heartfelt, faults and all. Okay, so there's too much crammed in, it's cartoonish in places, and Curtis the director doesn't rein in the extravagances of Curtis the writer quite enough. But there are some beautiful scenes, from the glorious fantasy of Hugh Grant's PM demolishing the visiting US President, to Colin Firth proposing to his cleaner in broken Portuguese (how could any woman ever leave him?). And the moment which still reduces me to an embarrassed, snivelling wreck: when Emma Thompson's cheated-on wife hugs her big brother (Grant), her face turned from the camera. The movie may not be as textured or deftly hewn as the Robert Altman pictures its structure begs comparison to, but this beat of emotional truth is every bit as convincing as anything that gets dubbed 'Altman-esque'. There's much more to this movie than marketing.

The Crying Game

Ten Confessions of Uncontrollable Movie Tears

A ROUNDTABLE

A lot of film critics do it at festivals. Directors sometimes do it while they're watching the movie get born before their eyes. Some of us do it on aeroplanes, probably because the altitude gets to us. And we all do it happily at home on the sofa, don't we? But crying in a movie theatre? That can be an awkward old experience, whether one is in company (in which case you have to hope your friends feel likewise, or tolerate your maudlin side) or sat all alone (in which case pray there are no mean kids sitting nearby).

Crying over a movie can feel like real heartache, though there's often an undeniable pleasure in it. The many teenagers who paid a dozen times to watch Leonardo DiCaprio die in *Titanic* weren't just masochists: clearly something about the sadness was beautiful and delightful to them. Critics can sometimes be a bit snooty about what makes them cry: it seems to help to have the word 'Enfants' in the title (*Les Enfants du Paradis*, *Au Revoir les Enfants*). But as with the things that make us laugh, good taste doesn't always apply.

Literary critic George Steiner has argued that the greatest moment in dramatic tragedy is the word 'Adieu' at the end of Racine's *Bérénice*. Forget the ghosts and gore of *Hamlet* or *Macbeth*: here are two people who love one another but know they will never meet again. Separation, too, is the cause of many a tear in the selections below. The ordering of the ten is purely random. *Eh bien, préparez vos mouchoirs*. (RTK)

10. *A Cry in the Dark* (Australia/US 1988, dir. Fred Schepisi)

MATT THORNE

This is the true-life story of Australian mother Lindy Chamberlain, who claimed that her ten-week-old daughter had been snatched by a wild animal while camping near Ayers Rock, but who was subsequently charged with murder. Schepisi's tear-jerker was called *Evil Angels* in the US, but its European title makes more sense, both for the film's action and for the experience of watching it. When I was a teenager in Bristol, *A Cry in the Dark* acquired a reputation as the perfect date-movie, because you could comfort your girlfriend after watching it. Unfortunately, my girlfriend was the one comforting me after watching Meryl Streep wail, 'The dingo's got my baby!' I went back four times, trying to work out how such a silly film could have such an impact. Streep may have given far more distinguished performances, but I still think this is her most affecting.

9. *The Day of the Dolphin* (US 1975, dir. Mike Nichols)

SAUL METZSTEIN

Although I'm Jewish, my Scottish upbringing has resulted in a certain Presbyterian stoicism – I've only ever cried at one film, Mike
Nichols's *The Day of the Dolphin*. The sight of the trained-to-speak
dolphins pleading 'Ma!' and 'Pa!' as they are sent into exile by their
trainer – thus preventing them from being used and abused by *bad
people* – was enough to send the five-year-old me into floods of tears.
My brother and my sister also wept inconsolably (which must have
made the whole outing huge fun for my parents). Something like
twenty-five years later, at the Edinburgh Film Festival, I was handed an unexpected opportunity to achieve cathartic 'closure' to this
episode, when I was introduced to the film's writer, Buck Henry. So
I confided in him that *The Day of the Dolphin* was the only film that
had ever made me cry. Henry looked me straight in the eye, and told
me quite matter-of-factly, 'You *must* be brain-damaged.'

8. *Breaking the Waves* (Denmark 1996, dir. Lars von Trier)

TIM ROBEY

It's when we feel most like children that we cry in the movies –
for this writer, in everything from *E.T.* to *Babe: Pig in the City*. If
there's one director guaranteed to treat us like infants, for better
and worse, it's Lars von Trier, which perhaps explains the suscep-
tibility I have to even the most brazenly manipulative gambits of
his best film, *Breaking the Waves*. Watching Emily Watson's Bess
pursue her selfless, confused, excruciating path to obliteration is
like having another child – a sibling, maybe – snatched away from
us, and her martyrdom, unlike, say, Falconetti's in Dreyer's *The
Passion of Joan of Arc* (1928) has a dumb, affectless quality that
creates a virtual bypass of the intellect. For many viewers, Trier
doesn't get away with those heavenly bells at the end, groping for
a crude transcendence, indulging Bess's faith. But the majesty and
compassion of the gesture, the first time I saw it, wiped me out
like no film has before or since.

7. *Schindler's List* (US 1993, dir. Steven Spielberg)

KIERON CORLESS

I've a sneaking suspicion I bawled my eyes out during *The Sound of Music*, though the one I most definitively remember from my early years is *E.T.* But the most tears shed? Well, I'm ashamed to say that has to be *Schindler's List* – by a long, long way, in fact. So Spielberg wins at both ends, which says much about his powers of manipulation even in the teeth of great resistance. By the time *Schindler's List* was released, my attitude to the whole Spielberg/Lucas axis of bloated Hollywood film-making was one of fiercely *cinéphile* resentment. When a friend insisted on our seeing it, I entered the cinema in a mood of indifference. About halfway through, round the point where the list is being put together and Ben Kingsley's eyes are shining with gratitude, the tears began to flow. And not just a few sporadic drops – more like a series of powerful waves breaking, which continued throughout, impossible to hold back. My companion was similarly afflicted, as were many others in the audience. Afterward I felt so emotionally drained it took me days to recover, during which time I thought about the film constantly. Spielberg is truly an evil genius.

6. *The Darkest Light* (GB 1999, dir. Simon Beaufoy & Billie Eltringham)

RICHARD T. KELLY

You might have missed this British film co-directed by the writer of *The Full Monty*. Set in rural North Yorkshire, it mainly concerns cattle farmer Tom (Stephen Dillane), his daughter Catherine (Keri Arnold), and her younger brother Matthew (Jason Walton), who is gravely ill with leukaemia and undergoing chemotherapy. In the course of a lively family evening meal the mood is suddenly punctured when Matthew, in mounting terror, starts pulling tufts of hair from his head. Like a shot Tom wrenches the boy from his seat and carries him out to the shearing shed: he knew this moment was coming. There he takes up clippers and shaves Matthew's head clean. The boy's vulnerable scalp is a terribly plangent sight. Then another marvellous stroke: Tom gets on to his knees, says, 'Your turn', and gives the clippers to his son, who gratefully gets to work. I don't think I ever saw anything so sadly lovely in a cinema. Certainly the tears squirted out of me, and I had to force myself not to think back to that scene for the rest of this very fine movie.

5. *The Champ* (US 1979, dir. Franco Zeffirelli)

LESLEY THORNE

Forget *Rocky*, if boxing movies have a true champion weepy it is Zeffirelli's remake of *The Champ*. Jon Voight stars as an ageing fighter down on his luck, struggling to look after his son T.J. (Ricky Schroder) whose mother is busy sailing yachts with her new husband. The worst bit is where T.J., who has already witnessed his father receiving a clearly fatal blow in a fight (surely not appropriate for an eight-year-old?), then has to watch him draw his final breath in a backroom. As everybody tries to drag the boy away from the bloodied and bruised body – just when you think you can't take it any more – he lifts up his father's fist and screams, '*Champ, champ, please, champ!*' But it's too late. I don't know what they did to that child to produce such snotty realistic tears, but frankly I don't want to think about it. Even worse, just to rub the salt in, the kid has to go back to his disinterested mother at the end. I first saw this film when I was the same age as T.J. and have yet to recover.

4. *True Grit* (US 1969, dir. Henry Hathaway)

CHRISTOPHER BRAY

The first time I remember weeping in a cinema is actually the first time I remember being in a cinema. (Apparently at the age of two or three I wept all the way through *The Sound of Music*, an incident my father has always recalled as the night he knew I would make a fine movie critic.) Cut to a few years later – my eighth birthday so, of course, we go to see a movie my elder brother wants to watch: *True Grit*. I'm all ready to be bored, but Kim Darby is such a boyish-looking girl that I find it easy to side with her against big John Wayne and his refusal to get involved in other people's fights. Half an hour in, I feel a clutch in my throat as she steers her horse through a deep, fast-moving river, and a still-wavering Wayne says, 'By god, she reminds me of me!' An hour later, now committed to bringing killer Ned Pepper into custody, Wayne tells his opponent to 'Fill your hand, you son of a bitch!' and rides straight at him.

Well, that was thirty-seven years ago, and for more than a few of those years I have known that scene, that movie, to be belli- cose, peacenik-baiting junk. But just remembering it and describ- ing it these past few minutes, my eyes have watered all over again.

3. *Whale Rider* (New Zealand 2002, dir. Niki Caro)

MIKE FIGGIS

My father would weep copiously during films on TV – Bing Crosby movies, usually after a few drinks and Sunday lunch. So I've always had a certain resistance, knowing that I'm susceptible to the same emotional manipulation. Whenever I feel it coming on, I do stiffen up the sinews. But I've sometimes made myself cry writing a sad scene. And I've lost it a few times on the set, when actors do great emotional work and they start crying – Elisabeth Shue on *Leaving Las Vegas*.

I can't remember the first time it happened but more recently I did lose it. It was in the ArcLight in Los Angeles, a brand new state-of-the-art cinema with expensive tickets, great seats, good sound, and a hip audience. The film? *Whale Rider*. The scene? Where the little girl Paikea makes the speech thanking her grand- father – so moving and 'real' that it took one by surprise, so no time for sinew-stiffening. And not just me but the entire audience, hunching their shoulders and trying to repress those funny little animal sounds that come with a good weep. I wondered how it would be if we all just let go and made big noises, howling, sobbing.

2. *Under the Skin* (GB 1997, dir. Carine Adler)

LIZZIE FRANCKE

Cinema introduced me to death. The *Bambi* experience is proba- bly commonplace – aged five I wept as everyone does when

'Murther' was felled by the hunter's bullet. A stronger grasp on mortality came to me a few years later when, while on a children's adventure holiday in Yorkshire – my first time away from my parents – I watched the musical remake of *Scrooge* (1971). As Albert Finney was summoned by an apparition to peer into the deep, black hole of his future grave, I teetered on the edge of my own brink. These weren't just tears, or even sobs, but a hysteria that took hours (and a promise by my parents that they would come from London to collect me) to abate. A musical had brought me the news that death is terminal, the final darkness.

Years later I realized I had become a professional mourner – someone who actively sought those films most prominently concerned with the *la condition humaine*. *Breaking the Waves*, *The Ice Storm*, *Rosetta*, *The Time of Drunken Horses* all had me keening. But the hardest experience of all was *Under the Skin* in which Sam Morton gives a visceral portrayal of a woman mourning her mother. I went with a dear friend who had just that day been told she had only months to live. In that screening we wept copiously, clung together for dear life. It was typical of my friend's wit and great fortitude that as the credits rolled she looked at me, laughed and said, 'People are going to think we're mad. The film's not that sad.' But then, ultimately, no film can be.

1. *The Searchers* (US 1956, dir. John Ford) and others

GRAHAM FULLER

The Ritz, an unlovely, long-gone deco cinema in Shoreham-by-Sea, Sussex: I wept at *Bambi* and *Shane*, the first two films I saw, at age five. They must have been reruns because it was 1961. They remain masterpieces of separation anxiety (not that Bambi's mother's death would faze my four-year-old daughter years later). I can still see Alan Ladd's buckskins glowing yellow as he headed up into the mountains, and I can still hear Brandon de Wilde calling 'Come back, Shane . . .' 'Shane will come back, won't he, Dad?' I asked. 'I expect he'll come back for a cup of tea,' my father replied, but I doubted it. Then . . . not a tear for twenty-three years, until I saw the home movie of Harry Dean Stanton and Hunter Carson, father and son, dancing in *Paris, Texas*. And only the odd moistening since, at films I can't remember. But when, in *A Canterbury Tale*, Alison (Sheila Sim) picks up her and her missing lover's hats in the dilapidated caravan and the moths fly out, and when Ethan (John Wayne) turns away into the desert at the end of *The Searchers*, I'm in serious trouble. But only for a second, you understand.

2

Quality Counts

Arguments, Judgements, and Personal Views on the 'Best' and 'Worst' in Cinema

IAN CHRISTIE: Heartbreaking Works of Staggering Genius? – Ten of the Unlikeliest Films Ever Judged 'The Best of All Time'

MIKE FIGGIS: Ten Great Films

TIM ROBEY: We'd Like to Thank the Academy – The Ten Most Richly Deserved Oscars

KIERON CORLESS AND CHRIS DARKE: Judged by Ten Under Riviera Sun – The Ten Dodgiest Decisions of the Cannes Festival Jury

RICHARD T. KELLY: Don't Believe the Gripes – Ten So-Called 'Turkeys' that are Actually Terrific

DAVID HARE: Ten Great Films Which Defy Genre

STEVEN SODERBERGH: One Great Film (Greater Even Than Is Widely Supposed

Heartbreaking Works of Staggering Genius?

Ten of the Unlikeliest Films Ever Judged 'The Best of All Time'

IAN CHRISTIE

The history of 'Ten Best' movie lists – to which this book aspires to be both a contribution and an alternative – probably started with a 1952 invitation from *Sight and Sound* magazine to critics around the world to send in their picks of the all-time greats, which were then aggregated to produce a World Top Ten. The British Film Institute's august organ has continued this exercise every ten years, the most recent appearing in 2002. And a fascinating series they have proved, running from the post-war list in which silent classics still held sway, followed by the coronation of Welles's *Citizen Kane* as the official Greatest Film in 1962 – a position it has retained for the last forty-five years.

Lumping together individual Ten Best lists is always likely to produce a cosy – or at least classical – consensus, with the eccentrics and the nay-sayers safely marginalized by their inability to agree with each other. But what about the crazy choices that may surface as individual critics (and, increasingly, film-makers) sit down to compose their lists? What, we wondered, were the most unlikely nominations for 'Best Film'?

Immediately, doubts crowd in. How serious was one (English) critic in 1969 when he put at the top of his list the 1932 Bela Lugosi horror flick *White Zombie*? Probably not very. Of course, tastes change: youthful firebrands often lose interest in snook-cocking and develop more refined tastes, to the embarrassment of their earlier selves. For that reason I've preserved the anonymity of critics in the citations given below, though directors' enthusiasms are fearlessly revealed.

The following then claims to be the first list of unlikely choices as 'best film' in the annals of published lists. And *not*, please note, a list of worst films, or 'films we love to hate', or 'turkeys', which is another form of inverted canon-making, originally popularized by

Michael Medved (who started out as a connoisseur of rubbish and then became the voice of Christian conservatism in US criticism). Most of these are fine films in their own ways – they are simply strange choices as the best of all time. But, to paraphrase Jean Renoir (whose *La Règle du Jeu* of 1939 is a perennial runner-up to *Citizen Kane*), those who did the choosing all had their reasons.

10. *The Ballad of Cable Hogue* (US 1970, dir. Sam Peckinpah)

Usually, neither westerns (other than John Ford's *The Searchers*) nor comedies (apart from Chaplin's) fare well in Ten Best lists. Peckinpah's amiably sardonic take on entrepreneurial spirit in the Old West topped the list of a Japanese critic in the 1992 *Sight and Sound* poll: an interesting choice, rather than the 'official' Peckinpah masterpiece, *The Wild Bunch*. And there's certainly plenty to admire in this rare meeting of tough-man Peckinpah and the dodgy sub-genre of 'comedy western', including superb performances from Jason Robards, Stella Stevens and L.Q. Jones.

9. *Why Did Bodhi-Dharma Leave for the East?* (Korea 1999, dir. Yong-Kyun Bae)

A gently meditative film set in a Buddhist monastery, and top dog of a Belgian critic's Ten Best list in 1992. More recently described in a DVD review as 'One of those movies where you have no idea what is happening even after it is halfway over.' Which, presumably, is just what an introduction to Zen Buddhism is aiming at; and Bae seems to have achieved with stunning simplicity. Peckinpah it certainly ain't.

8. *Brother's Keeper* (US 1992, dir. Joe Berlinger & Bruce Sinofsky)

Documentaries are rarely remembered in Ten Best lists, other than by film-makers, although it will be fascinating to see if they enjoy a higher profile in 2012 given the spate of recent feature documentary successes. Perhaps surprisingly, this doc about a small town's response to a mystery death was chosen by Ethan Coen in *Time Out*'s 2002 poll: the reason being, perhaps, that it carried (in the words of Roger Ebert) 'an impact and immediacy that most fiction films can only envy'.

7. *Maciste all'inferno / Maciste in the Inferno* (Italy 1925, dir. Guido Brignone)

Famously chosen by Federico Fellini in the 1992 *Sight and Sound* poll as his personal all-time favourite, this is one of the oddest of a cycle of 'strong-man' epics spawned by *Cabiria* (1914). In that picture the character of Maciste (played by ex-docker Bartolomeo Pagano) had all but stolen the show as the hero's burly side-kick. In his own movies he escaped Ancient Rome to become a modern super-hero, ever ready to stage a daring rescue – even when the baddies are, as in this case, literally from hell. Fellini paid tribute to his childhood inspiration in *Intervista* (1987) and, one could argue, in the fantasy sequences of most of his great movies.

6. *Around the World in 80 Days* (US 1956, dir. Michael Anderson)

The US Academy thought Mike Todd's globe-circling spectacle good enough to win Best Picture in 1956, and Jackie Chan's selection of it as his favourite in 1992 may not be unconnected with his starring in a 2004 remake. As with *The Sound of Music* and *The Rocky Horror Picture Show*, there's little point in trading niceties: you either buy the whole caboodle or you don't. But showman Todd's extended demo for his widescreen process Todd-AO counts as one of the greatest logistical feats of film history (more cameos, more costumes, more extras, et cetera), and it remains a ripping yarn.

5. *Mask of the Demon / Black Sunday* (Italy 1960, dir. Mario Bava)

Horror movies rarely (if ever) reach Top Ten lists, although they probably figure on many long-lists before being reluctantly dropped as the final cut looms. But back in 1969 horror was newly fashionable, Roger Corman in the US and Bava in Italy leading a new wave. So alongside *White Zombie*, noted above, another Young Turk writing in *Cinema* in 1969 boldly chose Bava's masterpiece, in which the hypnotic *belle dame sans merci* Barbara Steele returns from the dead to wreak lurid revenge on her descendants. Ravishing stuff, and fully deserving to be on *some* kind of list.

4. *F for Fake / Vérités et mensonges* (France/Iran/West Germany 1974, dir. Orson Welles)

Welles's last completed film was chosen by writer-director James Toback (*Fingers*, *The Pick-Up Artist*) for his *Time Out* Top Ten in 2002. You can see the logic of tricksy Toback paying tribute to Welles, and without choosing either *Kane* or *The Magnificent Ambersons*. (Indeed I've been there myself, having once picked Welles's *Chimes at Midnight* over the more obvious contenders for a Ten Best.) *F for Fake* may not be the most impressive film of those Welles managed to complete, but its ingenious 'now-you-see-it-or-do-you?' texture reflects the great man's lifelong fascination with illusion, filtered here through the stories of two master con-men: the art forger Elmyr de Hory, and his biographer, Clifford Irving.

3. *Abraham Lincoln* (US 1930, dir. D.W. Griffith)

Griffith's penultimate feature (and his first talkie after a lifetime of silents) makes a decidedly odd choice of 'Best' in that Griffith's 'official' masterpieces of the 'teens have been Top Ten perennials (*Broken Blossoms* gradually edging out the now-suspect *Birth of a Nation*). But *Lincoln* was the choice of a Serbian critic in 1992, and now that this hitherto highly inaccessible film has become available on DVD its considerable virtues may be more widely appreciated. Walter Huston certainly gives Raymond Massey and Henry Fonda stiff competition as the best screen Lincoln; but that is another list . . .

2. *Sweet Movie* (Canada/France/West Germany 1974, dir. Dusan Makavejev)

Makavejev's *W.R. – Mysteries of the Organism* (1971) was an unlikely art-house hit, a disarming combination of in-your-face sex and intellectual high-concept. But its sequel went *much* further, breaking just about every taboo in its fearless carnival of capitalism, communism and highly explicit copulation (including a notorious chocolate-bath scene). It thus became one of the 'unseeable' scandal movies of the 1970s. Undaunted, Wayne Wang (usually associated with milder fare) put it at the top of his list in the *Time Out* poll of 2002, the same year that he directed Jennifer Lopez in *Maid in Manhattan*. Perhaps this choice tells us something about the sort of movies he'd *really* like to be doing?

1. *National Lampoon's Animal House* (US 1978, dir. John Landis, scr. Harold Ramis, Douglas Kenney, Chris Miller)

Does the movie that launched a thousand gross-out comedies of similar (if lesser) ilk deserve such recognition? Can time turn drivel – even *inspired* drivel, enlivened by the late John Belushi – into a classic? Why has Harold Ramis's *Groundhog Day* never appeared in anyone's Ten Best list? And does a movie of such tasteless energy and invention as *Animal House* need excuses made on its behalf? The answers to these and other redundant questions were provided by film-maker Michael Tolkin (writer of *The Player*) when he chose *Animal House* in the 1992 *Sight and Sound* poll, 'because a good list needs a sick comedy': sound advice that we hereby follow.

Ten Great Films

MIKE FIGGIS

This is not sequential: no one film is more important than any other. Next week the list would be different. It's more to do with the film-makers themselves, these examples of their work.

10. *The Hill* (GB 1965, dir. Sidney Lumet, scr. Ray Rigby, from the play by Rigby & R.S. Allen)

I watch parts of this every time it's on cable. It's theatrical inasmuch as the drama takes place most of the time in a confined space (a British military prison camp) and the director of photography Ossie Morris uses very wide lenses to great effect. I'd love to hear what Morris thought of this venture. I met him once, at my interview for the National Film School, and we got on very badly – he was quite rude about the home movie I'd submitted, and I thought he was old-school. But he's damn good. Sean Connery is magnificent, but so is the entire ensemble. It's about to come out on DVD and I will buy a copy.

9. *Bonnie and Clyde* (US 1967, dir. Arthur Penn, scr. David Newman & Robert Benton)

Like a fine wine, it just gets better and better. Everything about it works for me, it epitomises good film-making. And it still has the power to shock.

8. *Week End* (France 1967, dir./scr. Jean-Luc Godard)

It's not rated as his best but it's my favourite. It's funny, sexy, provocative, shocking and weird. What more can one ask of a film?

7. *Dogme number 1: Festen / The Celebration* (Denmark 1998, dir. Thomas Vinterberg, scr. Vinterberg & Mogens Rukov)

I must check it out again to see if it still works, but I think it will. I found *Festen* almost unbearably emotional to watch, and it felt like a masterpiece of ensemble creativity. By far the best of the Dogme 95 crop, in my opinion. But it could have worked just as well on 35mm as it did on digital video.

6. *Notorious* (US 1946, dir. Alfred Hitchcock, scr. Ben Hecht)

A master-class in script-plotting and genre. *Notorious* gets to the point so quickly and its two stars are entirely believable as being nuts about each other within such a short space of time. It seems to sum up the ability of film to telegraph ideas. Fabulous ensemble work, and genius camera. For Hitchcock it was either this or *Shadow of a Doubt*, and *Notorious* came out tops this week.

5. *Repulsion* (GB 1965, dir. Roman Polanski, scr. Polanski & Gérard Brach)

So creepy that I'd love to watch it again. But I get very frightened by this genre, and I believe there's an interesting point proven here – namely that in the hands of a master such as Polanski the genre is almost *too* disturbing. I think any middle-of-the-road hack can frighten an audience with cinema tricks, but to *disturb* you need to be special. Hard to choose one Polanski: *Chinatown* and *Knife in the Water* loom large, particularly the wide-angle stuff in *Knife* – another master-class in the use of the camera.

4. *La Femme d'à côté / The Woman Next Door* (France 1981, dir. François Truffaut, scr. François Truffaut & Suzanne Schiffman & Jean Aurel)

My favourite Truffaut – his penultimate film, which was given a lukewarm reception at the time of its release. Gérard Depardieu is on form and he and Fanny Ardant are entirely believable as lovers. This kind of film defines the huge gap between European cinema and American film: I can't imagine an American version of this story that would work. I particularly love the scene where the lovers kiss for the first time after their discovery that they are neighbours. It sets up the tragedy perfectly. A master's hand in evidence all the way through.

3. *Invasion of the Body Snatchers* (US 1956, dir. Don Siegel, scr. Daniel Mainwaring, from a magazine serial by Jack Finney)

It could be used as a template for low-budget cinema, and it works on so many levels. It also has one of the best, creepiest screen kisses of all time.

2. *Cet Obscur Objet du Désir / That Obscure Object of Desire* (France/Spain 1977, dir. Luis Buñuel, scr. Buñuel & Jean-Claude Carrière from the novel *La femme et le pantin* by Pierre Louÿs)

Again, it's hard to choose one Buñuel, but this one has the edge for me. An amazing revelation in the (expedient) use of two actresses to play the same part. His humour is always in evidence, along with the constant atmosphere of cool detachment as he microscopically dissects the human condition. He has never been replaced, although David Lynch sometimes gets close.

1. *Persona* (Sweden 1966, dir./scr. Ingmar Bergman)

Well there had to be one Bergman. Despite not really having much of a sense of humour (they say he started off in Swedish comedy . . . well, there you go, Sweden) this one is amazing. Nothing I read about Bergman endears him very much, but it's a mark of his genius that it doesn't really matter if his ego was somewhat vast, or that the films tended to be endlessly autobiographical.

We'd Like to Thank the Academy

The Ten Most Richly Deserved Oscars

TIM ROBEY

Oscars have always been the pet whipping-boy of the serious-minded film buff. Just consider that the Academy of Motion Picture Arts and Sciences is the organization that thought *Forrest Gump* was the best picture of 1994, that rewarded Robert Zemeckis for said work and yet never gave a Best Director stat-uette to Hitchcock, Kubrick, Altman, Welles, Buñuel . . . the injustices are so many they're hardly worth listing. Nevertheless, across seventy-nine years of Academy Awards, the voting members have had time to get a few things right.

What we're celebrating here are those rare instances when a deserving artist is credited for exactly the right film, not with some consolation Oscar to make up for past losses. We hereby snub Best Picture and Best Director as the categories which, by general reck-oning, have made the greatest number of mistakes over the years. We set aside Best Foreign Film too, where there have been many worthy winners – as indeed the odds would favour, if one shoved all of non-Anglophone cinema into one competing category. It's in the technical fields that Academy voting tends to be sharpest. Half of these choices come from the 1970s, when there was great work to reward almost every year and Oscar's strike-rate soared accordingly. So now, the envelope; and the winners are:

10. Eiko Ishioka, Best Costume Design, *Bram Stoker's Dracula* (US 1992, dir. Francis Coppola)

'We will let the costumes be the set,' decreed Coppola as production began on his love-it-or-hate-it camp-revamp: a philosophy that presumably came as a disappointment to his Oscar-nominated art directors, yet paid off thanks to the startlingly outlandish gambits, colours and materials furnished by Ishioka (who made her name outside Japan on Paul Schrader's *Mishima* (1985) and the Broadway play *M. Butterfly*). Every garb is a stunner, from Dracula's blood-red wolf-like body-armour, to Lucy's suitably risqué funeral shroud with its lizard headdress, to the meek, virginal, minty pallor of Mina's Victorian gowns. This must be one of the most eclectically clothed pictures ever made, and yet each one of Ishioka's designs could somehow belong only to Coppola's mad and operatic smorgasbord. This Dracula is dressed up to its dripping canines.

9. Jack Cardiff, Best Colour Cinematography, *Black Narcissus* (GB 1947, dir./prod. Michael Powell & Emeric Pressburger)

The Colour Cinematography Oscar was first awarded to *Gone With the Wind* (1939), for which Ernest Haller and Ray Rennahan certainly got their dues. But Cardiff's win for this visual high watermark of the Powell/Pressburger canon proved that AMPAS wasn't blind in this category to achievements made outside the Hollywood studios. Honours for the film's chromatically lush Himalayan fantasia – created in the Pinewood backlot – were rightly split on awards night with The Archers' regular production designer Alfred Junge, but how Cardiff achieved the delicate hues of his airy, Vermeer-styled interiors – with a camera weighing 600 pounds and requiring light to be poured in from all directions – remains one of the mysteries of this sacred art.

8. H.R. Giger & Co., Best Visual Effects, for *Alien* (US 1979, dir. Ridley Scott)

Probably the most triumphant of the many decisions made on *Alien* was the idea of hiring Giger, a Swiss conceptual artist little known at the time, to provide the design for the creature itself, which he based on an existing painting called *Necronom IV*. Fellow Oscar-winners Carlo Rambaldi (the *giallo* expert who later worked on David Lynch's *Dune*), Brian Johnson, Nick Allder and Denys Ayling helped Giger create not just one of cinema's most fearsome baddies, but an entire lifecycle for the dreadful creature: every stage of reproduction, pupation, 'birth', growth and awesome adulthood is worked out in convincing organic terms. The credit certainly doesn't go to Giger alone, since the chest-burster set-piece and spaceship effects exhibit the best kind of pre-CGI ingenuity in the workshop.

7. Vivien Leigh, Best Actress, for *A Streetcar Named Desire* (US 1951, dir. Elia Kazan)

Twelve years after Leigh's first Oscar for playing one flighty Southern belle, she was caught up in Scarlett fever all over again. Jessica Tandy had originated the plum role of Blanche DuBois on Broadway, but wasn't considered a big enough star to carry the film opposite the then barely known Marlon Brando. Bette Davis and Olivia de Havilland were again in the running, but Leigh clinched it after starring in the Olivier-directed London run of the play, in which the foundations of her monumental, flibbertigibbet performance were presumably laid down. Elia Kazan exploited two things: Leigh's uneasiness about being the sole addition to the Broadway cast, and the friction between her expertly assembled mannerisms and Brando's Method rage. The result was one of the most unforgettably neurotic star turns in cinema.

6. Charlie Kaufman, Michel Gondry & Pierre Bismuth, Best Original Screenplay, *Eternal Sunshine of the Spotless Mind* (US 2004, dir. Gondry)

Hailed all over the place as the best American film of 2004,

Eternal Sunshine was hard done by at the Oscars, with nominations for the script, Kate Winslet, and no one else. Still, this was easily the most, as well as the best, original screenplay of that year, and having failed to win for either *Being John Malkovich* or *Adaptation* it was Kaufman's award to lose. It's as close to a perfect script as makes no difference, in its illumination of sad and desperate emotional truths through a playful prism of ideas, the opportunities it gives to a gifted director and cast, the beautiful, glancing structure and an unmistakably Kaufman-esque love of odd, off-kilter language. It's hard to imagine him ever improving on it, which is why we hereby privilege it over *All About Eve*, *Annie Hall*, and – yes – *Citizen Kane*.

5. Eugen Shüfftan, Best Black-and-White Cinematography, for *The Hustler* (US 1961, dir. Robert Rossen)

Shüfftan started out as a visual effects technician for Fritz Lang, and gave his name to a famous process that became the industry standard for using miniature backgrounds before matte photography. He helped to make Franju's *Les yeux sans visage* (1960) the oneiric marvel it is, and a year later conjured an intoxicating world of smoky Harlem pool halls in Rossen's existential classic. Shüfftan's subtle lighting makes the onlookers as interesting to watch as the central combat, and the starker contrasts of Paul Newman and Jackie Gleason's climactic showdown are a textbook illustration of drama heightened almost wholly through a choice of bulbs, the scorching spotlights etching their duel with shadow and despair.

4. Verna Fields, Best Editing, *Jaws* (US 1975, dir. Steven Spielberg)

Academy voters jealous of the mega-hit Spielberg was enjoying after a notoriously fraught shoot were determined to give all available credit to his veteran editor Verna Fields. She won and Spielberg wasn't even nominated, pushed out by Fellini for *Amarcord*. But *Jaws* remains one of the most remorselessly brilliant editing jobs in suspense cinema, cueing up underwater, shark-POV shots with the quailing distress of about-to-be-chomped swimmers in sequence after traumatic sequence.

Together, Spielberg and Fields kept that pesky mechanical shark out of view until they absolutely had to show it. And when an additional shock was required – Ben Gardner's head popping out through the rotten hull of his fishing boat – they went and shot it in Fields's swimming pool.

3. Ken Adam, Best Art Direction, for *Barry Lyndon* (GB 1975, dir. Stanley Kubrick)

Adam should have won for his two most famous creations, both absurdist fantasies of Cold War megalomania: the war room in *Dr Strangelove* (1964) and Blofeld's volcano hideout in *You Only Live Twice* (1967). But he was hardly any less deserving for his non-pareil fusion of architectural styles to re-create Thackeray's eighteenth century in *Barry Lyndon*. Long-standing tension between the director and designer, who tended to want to outdo each other in perfectionism, reached a peak in this production, thanks to Kubrick's insistence on filming almost everything on location, while the director's reluctance to travel meant Adam had to find examples of Austrian baroque in rural Ireland. For Lady Lyndon's mansion, which needed to pre-date other buildings from the period, he combed England and used four different sixteenth- and seventeenth-century castles to create a composite exterior. It all fits superbly.

2. Christopher Walken, Best Supporting Actor, for *The Deer Hunter* (US 1978, dir. Michael Cimino)

Previously audiences had enjoyed their best glimpse of Walken as Diane Keaton's weird brother in *Annie Hall*, but he became an instantly celebrated character actor from these Russian roulette scenes onwards. Walken is always a joy to watch, but never since has he been quite so electrifying, so tragic, so alive, or cast such a crucial pall of psychic damage over a film. His Nick is a tortured angel on a downslide. It's the intensity of his playing in the internment sections that locates them at the harrowing heart of the movie, as we witness a man's very soul cracking open under unthinkable duress. Some fine actors vied for the prize that year

(Richard Farnsworth, Bruce Dern, John Hurt and Jack Warden) but it would have been heresy had Walken not topped the poll.

1. Walter Murch, Best Sound, for *Apocalypse Now* (US 1979, dir. Francis Ford Coppola)

Murch revolutionized the aural possibilities of cinema in the Movie Brat era, and never more so than with his epic, immersive soundscape here. As an editor he was able to shape large sections of the film using sound, whether as an associative device (whirring helicopters become the ceiling fan in Willard's hotel room), as a way of putting bats (or more often jungle crickets) in the main character's belfry, and of course as a hair-raising accompaniment to Coppola's wild spectacles. The 'Ride of the Valkyries' sequence stands out as a mighty layer-cake of sonic elements – music, choppers, AK47s, mortars, grenades, footsteps, dialogue, screaming – and not one gets drowned out in Murch's mix, exquisitely orderly in its grasp of chaos.

Judged by Ten Under Riviera Sun

The Ten Dodgiest Decisions of the Cannes Festival Jury

KIERON CORLESS AND CHRIS DARKE

Once asked if she would rather win an Academy Award or a Best Actress prize from the Cannes Film Festival, Jodie Foster replied, 'You kiddin' me?' Okay: the Cannes prizes may not be in the same Hollywood power-league as the Oscars, but they are thought by the cognoscenti to convey a finer appreciation of what is best in world cinema. That said, controversies over the judging at Cannes occur so regularly that some cynics believe the festival more or less cooks them up for publicity. But then the various disputes discussed below don't exactly cast Cannes authorities in a glowing light, suggestive as they are of incompetence, lack of foresight and even – whisper it – corruption. Sometimes the prizes handed out have been attributed to bureaucratic interference or political pressure; at other times to the outcome of friction between jury members, ideological differences, professional or personal rivalries or breaches of protocol. The President of the Jury – usually an eminence of world cinema – is nearly always influential.

10. *La Dolce Vita* (Italy 1960, dir. Federico Fellini): Palme d'Or, *jury de* Georges Simenon

Strong-willed Belgian novelist Simenon was directed by the festival authorities to give at least one award to the United States. Simenon had other ideas: he had struck up a friendship with Fellini and his wife in the course of the festival, and was determined that *La Dolce Vita* should receive a big prize. American novelist Henry Miller, a largely disengaged juror more interested in playing tennis, agreed to vote as directed by Simenon. This sufficed to get *La Dolce Vita* the Palme d'Or, and years later Fellini would declare that it was to Simenon he owed his career.

9. *Le Salaire de la peur* / *The Wages of Fear* (France 1953, dir. Henri-Georges Clouzot): Grand Prix, *jury de* Jean Cocteau

One of the oddest couples ever to sit together on a Cannes jury was the mercurial Cocteau and Hollywood's star gangster Edward G. Robinson. These were the days when national sensitivities could strongly impact on the festival, and eagerly awaited in competition was Clouzot's tense thriller, starring the well-known leftist Yves Montand, about a group of roughnecks extinguishing an oil-well fire. Cocteau went so far as to tell a newspaper how highly he rated the film: to his diary he confided that he had only agreed to the presidency in order to secure Clouzot a prize. But the *Herald Tribune* accused *The Wages of Fear* of depicting the oil business as gangster capitalism, of being a communist film, insulting to America. Cocteau told his diary that this was neither the US delegation's attitude nor Edward G. Robinson's, but added: 'I can see that Robinson is afraid of something – which is natural.' Despite the off-stage clamour, Cocteau got his way.

8. *La Maman et la putain* / *The Mother and the Whore* (France 1973, dir. Jean Eustache): Grand Prix Spécial, *jury de* Ingrid Bergman, 1973

At festival number 25 two supremely controversial films left a trail of scandals, punch-ups and jury recriminations in their wake. Eustache's *La Maman* and Marco Ferreri's *La Grande Bouffe* shocked partly because of their subject matter – Ferreri's film depicting a group of well-heeled *roués* eating and screwing themselves to death, Eustache's showing a scabrously explicit *ménage à trois* – but also for the glee with which the film-makers seemed to invite trouble off-screen too. Ferreri's producer caused a particular stir by accusing Ingrid Bergman of favouritism towards a Hollywood film and of having a relationship with a studio executive. Small wonder, then, that Bergman made no secret of her lack of appetite for *La Grande Bouffe*. Meanwhile actress Jeanne Moreau reportedly attended the festival solely to protest the presence of the 'abomination' that was *La Maman et la putain*. But Eustache came away with a jury prize, and he and Ferreri also shared the FIPRESCI critics' award.

7. Multiple prizes for blacklisted Americans: *jury de* Marcel Pagnol, 1955

The Cold War was much rehearsed at Cannes during the mid-fifties. The USSR was keen that Cannes act as a shop window for Soviet expertise in cinema, and their delegation threw legendary parties. Then the activities of the House Un-American Activities Committee (HUAC) impinged on Cannes in 1955 when the jury gave prizes to a number of film-makers whose lives had been changed by the 'Hollywood Blacklist'. Jules Dassin, exiled in Europe, shared a prize for *Rififi* and blacklisted actress Betsy Blair won for Delbert Mann's *Marty*, which also took the Palme d'Or. (Elia Kazan, who had testified to HUAC, also won for *East of Eden*.) But the decisions discomfited certain Americans present and led to behind-the-scenes manoeuvres, as Dassin later recalled: 'Some guy from the American Embassy was assigned to come and visit and talk to me and it looked as though he wanted to give me my passport back. That would have fixed things, but you know the manner in which they wanted to fix things, so it didn't happen . . .'

6. *Jury de* Joseph Losey, 1972

Picture the scene: director Losey is presiding over the jury, and who should be bringing his film *The Visitors* into competition that year but Elia Kazan? The two men had a history, as they say: colleagues and friends in the New York theatre thirty years earlier, Kazan had named names for HUAC while Losey had refused, eventually leaving America to pursue his career in Britain. Swedish actress Bibi Andersson, also a juror that year, recalled that Losey was 'violently, persistently, and most absolutely against *The Visitors* and never let up attacking it'. Tarkovsky, Fellini, Elio Petri – all had prizes on awards night, but for Kazan came there none.

5. *Skupljaci perja / I Even Met Happy Gypsies* (Yugoslavia 1967, dir. Aleksandar Petrovic): Grand Prix Spécial (ex-aequo), *jury de* Alessandro Blasetti

This year's scandal – it does have the feel of an annual rite – concerned sex, money, and jurors Shirley MacLaine and Claude Lelouch. During festival fortnight MacLaine embarked on a torrid and widely reported affair with actor Bekim Fehmiu: unfortunately he also happened to be the lead in Aleksandar Petrovic's competition film. After much agonized deliberation, MacLaine was allowed to remain on the jury. But then Lelouch was pressured to resign when it was discovered that he was a member of a group negotiating French distribution rights to the Petrovic picture, which – *somehow* – went on to share the Special Jury prize with Joseph Losey's *Accident*.

4. *Chronique des années de braise / Chronicle of the Years of Fire* (Algeria 1975, dir. Mohammed Lakhdar-Hamina): Palme d'Or, *jury de* Jeanne Moreau

1975 was made tense by bombings and death threats connected to the presence in the main competition of this controversial Algerian picture, screened amid strict security. According to critic and juror

So Good They Made it Thrice: The Ten Greatest Movie Trilogies,
P 79

Pierre Mazars, the Right thought 'the producers of the Algerian film were pulling the strings' while the Left saw 'the hand of vengeful *pieds noirs*'. No one was charged with the bombings and Mazars recalled no direct pressure on the jury, no 'starlet in my bed, or a case of champagne'. Fellow juror Anthony Burgess remembered things differently: 'We were given an anonymous warning that a bomb would go off in the great *salle* if [*Chronique*] did not win.' Even on prize-giving night there was a string of bomb alerts, and the Algerian delegation and Cannes representatives received anonymous death threats. But Lakhdar-Hamina got his prize, one that he claimed 'recognizes the existence of the Third World'.

3. Helen Mirren in *Cal* (GB 1984, dir. Pat O'Connor): Best Actress, *jury de* Dirk Bogarde

Another dark tale of alleged jury arm-twisting, this time centred on the figure of Mirren, now an Oscar-laurelled *grande dame*, but back in 1984 still a relative unknown internationally. When Bogarde's jury decided to award her performance as a policeman's widow in *Cal*, the festival authorities were less than pleased that Best Actress was going to someone they'd never heard of. Bogarde later went on the record to say that he was summoned into a side-room, where the powers-that-be announced their displeasure in the clearest terms. '*Elle est nulle, elle est nulle*' was their verdict on Mirren's talents. But they'd picked the wrong guy to lean on: Bogarde dug his heels in and Mirren had her prize.

2. *Apocalypse Now* (US 1979, dir. Francis Ford Coppola): Palme d'Or (ex-aequo), *jury de* Françoise Sagan

On virtually the final day of the 1979 festival Coppola flies into Cannes to show a 'work-in-progress' print of his desperately long-awaited and grandly conceived Vietnam epic. The film is in competition. The media feeding-frenzy around the screening is unprecedented, viewers are blown away, and *Apocalypse Now* seems a shoo-in for the Palme d'Or. There's only one small problem, we later learn – the jury, presided over by novelist Sagan, has already decided to give the big Palme to another epic masterpiece,

Volker Schlondorff's *The Tin Drum*. The two films eventually share the top prize, but months later Sagan gives an interview in which she maintains that pressure was exerted from outside the jury room to ensure Coppola was properly rewarded for his time.

1. *Fahrenheit 9/11* (US 2004, dir. Michael Moore): Palme d'Or, *jury de* Quentin Tarantino

Those 'cheese eating surrender monkeys' from 'Old Europe' gave the Bush White House the fat middle finger with their award to Moore's vitriolic documentary. At the opening press conference juror Benoît Poelvoorde jokingly claimed that the intention was to 'make sure that the worst film wins'. Some claimed he got what he wanted. President that year was the shy and retiring Tarantino, his cohort included actresses Kathleen Turner, Tilda Swinton and Emmanuelle Béart and directors Jerry Schatzberg and Tsui Hark. Tarantino strenuously – and disingenuously – denied any political considerations behind the award but with a field that included Wong Kar-Wai's *2046* and Walter Salle's *Motorcycle Diaries*, Moore's Palme was seen by some as the triumph of political polemic over cinematic craft.

Don't Believe the Gripes
Ten So-Called 'Turkeys' that Are Actually Terrific

RICHARD T. KELLY

They call it *schadenfreude*. Ever since the escalating budgets and on-set problems of studio movies began to get reported gleefully in newspapers, the public has developed a relish for the prospect of a film's failure – the date of its premiere is duly marked in all diaries as an invitation to a beheading. Most of the ten films below cost more to make than they should have, it's true. But we the viewers shouldn't act as if that money had been earmarked for spending on schools and hospitals instead. Worse films have cost more, only to be redeemed at the box-office by less demanding crowds. All of these movies are worth your time, so long as they are first met on the terms intended by their makers and decreed by those genres within which they are cast. Comedy, admittedly, is much the hardest of those in which to salvage a movie's reputation once it's been widely written off as garbage. Pity the fool reduced to arguing, 'No, but, see, you just didn't *appreciate* the joke first time, watch it again and you'll laugh like a drain.' But, reader, this fool must.

10. *Waterworld* (US 1995, dir. Kevin Reynolds, scr. Peter Rader & David Twohy)

So it's *Mad Max* at sea. What's your problem with that? But yes, Kevin Costner's run of middle-of-the-road hits had become a little wearying, and movie crews working on water almost inevitably come to grief. *Waterworld*'s beleaguered shoot in Hawaii soon acquired an air of siege. The results look like no other picture. Costner's terse uningratiating hero and Dennis Hopper's sunburnt villain provide doses of pawky humour. The early 'Battle of the Atoll' is a ripping set-piece, and the athletically choreographed in-camera action looks better with each passing CGI-ridden year. But none of this can match the wit of those who got in first with epitaphs such as 'Fishtar', 'Kevin's Gate', or 'Waterworld Ate My Hamster'. (That last one is a joke, but only just.)

9. *Tough Guys Don't Dance* (US 1987, dir. Norman Mailer, scr. Mailer, from his novel)

Few of the twentieth century's great writers got to direct screen versions of their own books, and were he not so legendarily hard-wearing then Norman Mailer might have wished he hadn't bothered. Nicolas Roeg had been circling Mailer's 1984 novel, a *roman noir* set in Provincetown, written double-quick after the years Mailer had lost on his Egyptian epic *Ancient Evenings*. It's a mark of Mailer's obsessions with Marilyn Monroe and strong grass that he hinged his plot on two dyed-blonde female heads severed and stored in a woodland locker reserved for the hero's stash. Having dabbled in celluloid during the late sixties Mailer seized the chance to make *Tough Guys* himself with finance from Cannon Films in return for trying to script Godard's *King Lear*. The results are clunky at times, but offer some heroic efforts to convey the authentic Mailer mood by a cast of flawed stars and unsung character actors, led by Ryan O'Neal and Isabella Rossellini.

8. *Hudson Hawk* (US 1992, dir. Michael Lehman, scr. Daniel Waters & Steven E. de Souza from a story by Bruce Willis and Robert Kraft)

It was partly due to his smirk that Bruce Willis, ex-bartender at New York's Café Central, became a star. Those resistant to his wiseacre charm waited for that smirk to be dispelled. *Hudson Hawk*, Willis's 'vanity project' wherein he played a cat-burglar blackmailed into stealing Da Vinci artworks, stepped nicely into the crosshairs. The previously bullet-proof Joel Silver produced but the shoot in Budapest was a nightmare: Richard E. Grant, funny as a maniacal villain ('I'll torture you so slowly you'll think it's a career') lamented his hateful experience at length in a book. But Willis was only trying what Mike Myers would later achieve more crudely – reviving a certain kind of late-sixties hipster-adventure-pic. The acid-test scene comes early when we see that Willis synchronizes his heists to the timings of old show tunes, which he proceeds to sing. If the first of these ('Swingin' on a Star!') doesn't please you, turn off the DVD: nothing thereafter can come to any good.

7. *Legend* (US 1985, dir. Ridley Scott, scr. William Hjortsberg)

Scott's box-office failures are usually more intriguing than his hits. *Legend* was meant as an 'adult fairytale' with a princess, a forest-dwelling hero, and a satanic villain. But the definition of adult soon proved an issue: 'You can't have the villain fuck the princess,' was an early script comment from a Fox executive. In the midsummer of 1984 Scott had his sylvan forest constructed on the 'James Bond' sound-stage at Shepperton Studios: part-planted, part-hand-carved, populated by real animals. It would all look luscious on film, but its very crowded density led to a fire that burned down the famous stage. Scott then lost his nerve over the length and music, and the failure of the release-version marked an early career setback for its young star Tom Cruise. But as in all of Early Scott, there is visual brilliance here, and in the design of Darkness (Tim Curry, made to stand thirteen-feet-tall in horns and stilt-hooves, his skin furnace-red), Scott and make-up wizard Rob Bottin gave birth to a positively Miltonic vision.

6. *Sorcerer* (US 1977, dir./scr. William Friedkin, based on the Clouzot movie *Les Salaire de la Peur*)

This remake of *The Wages of Fear* is one of those ill-fated movies upon which Peter Biskind feasted for the long cautionary tale that is his bestselling *Easy Riders, Raging Bulls*: how a director flushed with success blows $22.5 million obeying a whim. Steve McQueen was the intended leading man but as usual he wouldn't work without Ali McGraw. In stepped Roy Scheider, briefly a global star after *Jaws*. On its release, Friedkin's track record (*The French Connection*! *The Exorcist*!) and the sheer scale of the thing (Three continents! Two years in the making!) were boldly and vainly trumpeted to tempt reluctant crowds. But *Sorcerer* is a ter-rific picture. Friedkin may be a sometimes wilfully incoherent storyteller but he is a brilliant picture-maker. Cutting to an elec-tronic score by Tangerine Dream, he laid down a template for the future of music video, and Michael Mann's subsequent career is not quite imaginable without this movie.

5. *Bitter Moon* (France/GB 1992, dir./scr. Roman Polanski)

Avant-garde pornographer Georges Bataille achieved a service-able definition of the Absurd when he noted that all matters we take seriously have the potential to be taken deeply unseriously a split second later. In 1992 sex was being taken *very* seriously by scholars of gender and media, because of – rather than despite – such 'texts' as *Basic Instinct* and Madonna's book *Sex*. It was Polanski's bad luck to release the mordant *Bitter Moon*, wherein Hugh Grant and Kristin Scott-Thomas have their holiday cruise and bourgeois illusions spoiled by meeting the disabled Peter

Coyote, the luscious Emmanuelle Seigner, and the sorry tale of how their *amour* soured into boredom and cruelty ('Everyone has a sadistic streak'). In proposing that the heights of passion are sometimes banal and silly, Polanski was only being his inimitable self, but his movie got drowned in emissions of critical contempt. Had he kept a straight face – maybe resolved his plot by an ice-pick under a bed – *Bitter Moon* could have become a key text for all those sex-crazed sages of academe.

4. *One From the Heart* (US 1982, dir./scr. Francis Ford Coppola)

In 1979 Coppola acquired the nine-acre site of Hollywood General Studios for 7.2 million dollars and rechristened it Zoetrope. As he told Lillian Ross for the *New Yorker*, he wanted to make a movie celebrating three old loves of his: show tunes, stagecraft, and remote-control toys. Tom Waits wrote him the songs, he built a stylized Las Vegas on his new lot (Dean Tavoularis's sets costing 6 million dollars alone) and he rehearsed and cut the film with fancy new video technology. Gene Kelly was the film's dance consultant. It was only a slender story of two lovers in a rut, travel agent Frannie (Teri Garr) and junkyard mechanic Hank (Frederic Forrest). They both have whirlwind flings, Frannie with waiter Raul Julia, Hank with tightrope walker Nastassja Kinski (then the girl of the moment), but are finally reconciled. The film went 11 million dollars over budget and its distribution changed hands from MGM to Paramount to Columbia, before it tanked with audiences and Coppola yanked it from cinemas, his mogul dream already facing disillusion. 'Sometimes I wonder', he told Lillian Ross, 'whether it's worth it in such a cynical and frightened world?' But it was, maestro, it was.

3. *Heaven's Gate* (US 1980, dir./scr. Michael Cimino)

It was a bad moment for *Heaven's Gate* – possibly the first of the many to come – when its supervising executive at United Artists, the newly appointed Steven Bach, decided to keep a diary of his job. Bach's agonies led to the book *Final Cut*, an account of the spiral of this anti-capitalist immigrant-centred western into insane overspend, leading in turn to the ignominious sale of the studio

founded by Chaplin, Griffith, Fairbanks and Pickford. Bach's book
is superb, Cimino's foolish profligacy and obnoxiousness very evident. But the danger is that no one is prepared to sit through the
four-hour version of the film any more; whereas nobody I know
who *has* seen that version has failed to comment on its brilliance.

2. *Mary Reilly* (US 1996, dir. Stephen Frears, scr. Christopher
Hampton from the novel by Valerie Martin)

A *Jekyll and Hyde* movie comes along every year, and they're all the
goddamn same. The only one to conjure the third-person enigma of
Stevenson's classic is *Mary Reilly* – a moody re-imagining of the tale
in which the tentative romance of a troubled physician (John
Malkovich) and his Irish scullery maid (Julia Roberts) is menaced by
the good doctor's laconic thug of an assistant. Roberts traded in her
famous piano-key smile for a convincing, flinching display of suppressed courage and desire, though for a fee of 8 million dollars she
might have cracked the accent (she had managed by the time she
did *Michael Collins* for Neil Jordan). Hampton's script is a work of
Stevenson scholarship into which he injects doses of imagery from
Baudelaire's *Les Fleurs du Mal* (sadness as a tide, the urge to be 'both
knife and wound'). But after an interrupted shoot, dispiriting inser-
tions of blood and butchery, and wrangles over the ending, Frears
and Hampton endured a horrible test screening in a San Diego
shopping mall, possibly the least likely spot on earth where Mary's
bleak, dark radiance could flower.

1. *Ishtar* (US 1987, dir./scr. Elaine May)

I like to imagine a parallel universe wherein May's comedy is considered an endlessly quotable classic, hailed by the worthier critics for its accurate reflection of US foreign policy in the Middle
East, MP3 files of its adeptly terrible songbook keenly swapped.
None of that is ever going to happen on this planet; but such are
the virtues discussed on rare occasions when two or more *Ishtar*
fans are gathered. The rest of the world believes that May wasted
Columbia's money on some imbecile script allowing Dustin
Hoffman and Warren Beatty to insult the audience as klutzy New

York songwriters who dream of being Simon and Garfunkel. The duo wind up in Morocco, buffeted between leftist guerrilla Isabelle Adjani and CIA man Charles Grodin. This colossal commercial failure, funnily enough, is a heartening comedy *about* failure. Watch Beatty trying earnestly to talk Hoffman out of a suicide jump: 'It takes a lotta *nerve* to have nothing at your age . . . Most guys would be *ashamed*. But you've got the guts to just say, "To hell with it." You say you'd rather have *nothing* than settle for less.' The stricken look of dawning love on Hoffman's face upon hearing this is worth your money alone.

Ten Great Films Which Defy Genre

DAVID HARE

It's as simple as this: genre has almost destroyed cinema. The audience is bored. It can predict the exhausted UCLA film-school formulae – acts, arcs and personal journeys – from the moment they start cranking. It's angry and insulted by being offered so much Jung-for-Beginners, courtesy of Joseph Campbell. It's now impossible to imagine a gangster picture, romantic comedy, biopic, war picture, goblin epic or detective thriller which could come anywhere near the vitality and reach of non-genre pictures like *Amores Perros* (Mexico 2000, dir. Alejandro González Iñárritu) or *Talk to Her* (Spain 2002, dir. Pedro Almódovar).

All great work is now outside genre.

10. *All the King's Men* (US 1949, scr./dir. Robert Rossen, from the novel by Robert Penn Warren)

The story of a well-intentioned American populist who turns into a monster, its mix of drink, high-octane private life and social fraud makes this one of the most far-reachingly toxic movies ever made. It has the almost unknown effect of making politics seem a heady, complex and attractive profession. As 'Willy Stark', Broderick Crawford is superb.

9. *La Strada / The Road* (Italy 1954, dir. Federico Fellini, scr. Fellini, Tullio Pinelli)

The ultimate story about people who seek to buy other people, *La Strada* is also a vision of a lost Italian geography which doesn't belong anywhere, which no longer exists even while it's being filmed: nostalgia for a vanished world, rooted in the yearning fantasy music of Nino Rota.

8. *Die Ehe der Maria Braun / The Marriage of Maria Braun* (West Germany 1979, dir. Rainer Werner Fassbinder, scr. Peter Märthesheimer & Pea Fröhlich)

How to survive in post-war Germany after you've lost the love of your life. Nobody rivals Fassbinder as the genre-buster of his day. His seemingly improvised camera-work and lighting has a power way beyond the over-tended, cut-lawn look of modern cinema. This is the film of his I like most – sassy and free-spirited, with a standout performance in the title role from Hanna Schygulla. Who else could make scenes of business life so gripping?

7. *Idi i Smotri / Come and See* (USSR 1985, dir. Elem Klimov, scr. Klimov & Ales Adamovich)

The Nazi invasion of Byelorussia, as witnessed by young Flor (Aleksei Kravchenko). Any fool can decide where to put a camera, but it's terrifying how few film-makers can actually *stage*. The burning of a church and the villagers therein is as great as anything in Eisenstein, but its impact comes from Klimov's staging as much as his montage. Too good to be called a war picture, and too smart to succumb to the clichés of an anti-war picture, *Come and See* is really a process picture. Magnificent in its unlikeliness.

6. *Vertigo* (US 1958, dir. Alfred Hitchcock, scr. Samuel Taylor & Alec Coppel, from the novel *D'Entre Les Morts* by Pierre Boileau & Thomas Narcejac)

The story of a detective who becomes weirdly fascinated by the wife of one of his clients. Again, if you set out to make a film on this subject – memory as erotic obsession – chances are you wouldn't do it this way. A film which is never quite as you remember it, and which you can never wholly grasp, however often you watch it.

5. *Un Condamné à mort s'est échappé* / *A Man Escaped* (France 1956, dir. Robert Bresson, scr. Bresson from a memoir by André Devigny)

A French Resistance activist dreams of escaping a Nazi prison. You might argue that this one does follow a formula: after all, it's an escape picture. But who would recognize the formula in Bresson's unique manifestation, with Mozart, of all people, providing the backing track?

4. *Room at the Top* (GB 1959, dir. Jack Clayton, scr. Neil Paterson from the novel by John Braine)

Young men are always on the make, but this film defies genre with ostensible miscasting. At first you can't understand what the three principals – Laurence Harvey, Donald Wolfit and Simone Signoret – are doing in the same film. A Lithuanian, a ham Shakespearean and a Frenchwoman in what's meant to be British social realism. But their presence slowly gives this film an alien drive, an otherness which transcends more conventional British cinema.

3. *Tokyo Monogatari* / *Tokyo Story* (Japan 1953, dir. Yasujiro Ozu, scr. Ozu & Kogo Noda)

The simplest plot: some ageing parents want to visit their grown-up children in Tokyo. There aren't really any villains, and there most certainly aren't any heroes. The villain is age and the passage of time, the inevitability of decline. A masterpiece.

2. *Le Souffle au Coeur* / *A Murmur of the Heart* (France/Italy/ West Germany 1971, dir./scr. Louis Malle)

Malle looks ever more brilliant with the passage of the years: a singular humanist, an observer – in short, an artist. All his work (okay, except *Black Moon*) is worth revisiting: *Vanya on 42nd Street* is definitive. You might call this one his 'incest picture', but that tag would tell you nothing about the film itself – an account of adolescent sexuality which is warm and authentic in equal parts. Plus: a sex scene which is actually sexy.

1. *Sommarlek / Summer Interlude* (Sweden 1951, dir. Ingmar Bergman, scr. Bergman & Herbert Grevenius)

A talented young ballet dancer (Maj-Britt Nilsson) looks back to a relationship she had years ago on an island she visits in a break from rehearsal. Yes, Ingmar Bergman will go on to do 'greater' things, but there's a poetic simplicity about this film which is unequalled. Youth is caught in the frame – the very *essence* of youth, and the beauty of its transience. This is heart-breaking stuff, the purest expression of cinema as the fleeting medium.

One Great Film (Greater Even Than Is Widely Supposed)

STEVEN SODERBERGH

Let me just say that I'm sick of people digging up obscure master-pieces designed to make me feel like a philistine; or, worse, argu-ing that an acknowledged masterpiece isn't in fact a masterpiece at all but the beneficiary of some collective cultural hypnosis. I'm going in the opposite direction: I'm going to call attention to a classic that, in my opinion, is even better than we all think it is.

1. *Chinatown* (US 1974, dir. Roman Polanski, scr. Robert Towne)

If you really analyse a great film, it can teach you how to make a film, and *Chinatown* may be the best blueprint of all. It has: a compelling and/or entertaining subject, explored through a well-constructed narrative (Robert Towne brilliantly fictionalises the true story of Los Angeles' battle for a water supply);[1] a great cast, doing career-defining work (Nicholson and Dunaway both look and act better than they've ever looked or acted);[2] an appropriately distinctive visual scheme (the sets, costumes and photography are painfully evocative, and Polanski *never* puts the camera in the wrong place);[3] and, most crucially, smart editing and scoring (the macro-editing has just the right press and release, the micro-editing is seamless except when it's not supposed to be; and Goldsmith's melancholy score – a last-minute addition – wraps the whole film in an intoxicating perfume of dread).[4]

Of course, it also follows that bad films contain the reverse DNA, showing you what *not* to do. But in general I like to watch good films, because bad films make me sad. Actually, *Chinatown* makes me sad too, mostly because it reminds me that I began watching and making films at a time when the movies really were just as great as they seemed to be. Oh well. At least I wasn't imagining things.[5]

1 This is a good moment to comment on the cottage industry that has sprung up around 'How To' screenwriting manuals. I think of this because Towne's script is often cited as a great template (which it is), but, invariably, with no understanding or acknowledgement of the role film editing has in shaping a finished work. So any discussion that omits this issue shows a palpable lack of experience in the actual making of films on the part of the scriptwriting teacher/author.

2 I'm not kidding, Nicholson and Dunaway are fucking *spectacular* in this. His smile and her cheekbones? Come *on*.

3 Like I say, there's everything you need to know to direct a movie here. There's a huge difference between being economical and being cheap, and Polanski shows you the difference, over and over again. You might not notice he basically shoots the whole film with one lens; and check out the multiple-destination camera moves, which are invariably hidden within the actors' moves. Plus, there's nobody better at knowing when to pull the camera off the dolly and go handheld.

4 This is a good moment to say that, currently, I think editing on a micro-level has never been better, and editing on a macro-level has never been worse. I leave it to you to decide why this is.

5 Oh no. I've officially become a bitter, nostalgic fuck. How did this happen?

3

The Phantom Picture House

Movies You Can't See, Won't See or Will Never, Ever Get to See

GILBERT ADAIR: *Un Salon des Refusés* – Ten Films Difficult to Pick Up

NEV PIERCE: The Age of Ignorance – Ten Great Films I Haven't Seen

KEVIN JACKSON: The Greatest Movies Never Made – Ten Sadly Unrealized Masterworks

Un Salon des Refusés
Ten Films Difficult to Pick Up

GILBERT ADAIR

The films listed below – in anti-chronological order, the natural direction of memory – all belong to what, in the nineteenth century, the French termed a *salon des refusés*. What they have in common is that they have all been *refused* – refused by the public, by critics, in one instance by the director himself. Deemed irrelevant, embarrassing, ideologically suspect, unworthy of their creators, they have all been mercilessly expunged from the history of the cinema. There is, however, something else which they have in common. Jean Cocteau writes somewhere of having chanced to notice, in the pages of a mail-order catalogue, a peculiarly shaped item which was categorized only and tantalizingly as 'an object difficult to pick up'. Each of these films is just such an object.

10. *Lolita* (France/US 1997, dir. Adrian Lyne)

The rejection, by British and American reviewers, of Adrian Lyne's *Lolita* as a seamy travesty not merely of Nabokov's novel but of Kubrick's earlier adaptation has always struck me as a serious miscarriage of film-critical justice. Heaven knows, I have no axe to grind for Lyne. But, apart from a misjudged opening sequence in a fey and wispy David Hamiltonesque style (how is it that Hamilton's photographs, even if motionless, nevertheless leave one with the impression that they are somehow in slow-motion?), his *Lolita* is rather more faithful to the spirit of the novel than Kubrick's, more lusciously erotic, also more tender and poignant. As for Dominique Swain in the title-role, she gives (I weigh my words) a quite extraordinary performance, and the wreck of her career by the near-universal contempt with which the film was greeted is something of a tragedy. Though there is, for an actor or actress, nothing more mortifying than a scattered smattering of applause, I'd still like to offer Swain a lonely, belated Bravo!

9. *Times Square* (US 1980, dir. Allan Moyle)

I was apparently the only critic in the world who liked *Times Square*. Its director, a Canadian, seems to have vanished from circulation, and its young female star, Robin Johnson, a fifteen-year-old newcomer whom I praised in my original review as 'charisma incarnate', remains as unknown today as she was when the film was made. What I recall, nevertheless, is a *folie à deux* not unworthy of comparison with Rivette's *Céline et Julie vont en bateau* and culminating in a weird, Feuilladesque shot of Johnson, a black garbage bag worn as a punky waistcoat and a highwayman's domino mask painted on her face, perched atop a neon-lit cinema marquee overlooking Times Square. Or did I imagine this film?

8. *Roberte* (France 1979, dir. Pierre Zucca)

Here is a real rarity – a scabrous fantasy of sado-masochistic erotomania, directed by the late Zucca, based on a novel by Pierre Klossowski, the Nietzschean philosopher (also the brother of Balthus), and featuring the septuagenarian Klossowski himself and his hardly less ancient spouse and muse, Denise Morin Sinclair, as the Groucho Marx and Margaret Dumont of unintentional humour. It's a film which, as they say, has to be seen to be believed. And not the least adornment of the chronicle (to paraphrase the lyrical blurb on the last page of Nabokov's *Ada*) is the delicacy of pictorial detail, the amazing dialogue, Barbet Schroeder as a lecherous Swiss Guard, Juliet Berto as a boy, and much, much more.

7. *Sextette* (US 1979, dir. Ken Hughes)

I once described *Sextette* as 'the most chivalrous film in the history of the cinema', its extreme fascination deriving less from the age of its star, Mae West (who turned eighty-six in 1979), than from the fact that *the film pretends not to notice it*. Though poor, hapless Timothy Dalton is her romantic lead, and though they share a few discreetly erotic exchanges, this isn't a

May–December (or May–Mae) love story. Corseted to within an inch of her life, the actress sashays across the screen as though her (always moot) sex appeal were absolutely intact. *Sextette* thus offers the unique spectacle of Mae West living, as Oscar Wilde died, 'beyond her means'.

6. *Seven Women* (US 1966, dir. John Ford)

Ford's last work (excepting *Young Cassidy*, co-directed with Jack Cardiff), has tended to be dismissed as one of this great director's worst. For me it's one of his best, maybe the best of all. About a group of female missionaries stranded in a very backlot-y China, it's a silent film with a soundtrack, a black-and-white film in colour, an old film even in the year of its release. It's also – unexpectedly if unmistakably – feminist. The Japanese director whose name has traditionally been linked with Ford's is, of course, Kurosawa. *Seven Women*, by contrast, is a profoundly Mizoguchian film.

5. *It's a Mad, Mad, Mad, Mad World* (US 1963, dir. Stanley Kramer)

As everyone is aware, there exists a special brand of American stupidity, as also of its physically externalized equivalent, ballooning American obesity, and both are combined in that least appetizing of sub-genres, epic slapstick. Back in 1963 I found watching *It's a Mad, Mad, Mad, Mad World* (with its hideous gallery of has-beens – Mickey Rooney, Ethel Merman, Phil Silvers et al.) an unfunny, unendurable ordeal. Watching it anew in 2007, what I discovered was an astounding parable *avant la lettre* of the obscenity, the unspeakable vulgarity, of Bush's America. Paradoxically, this film was much more prophetic than Kramer's naively post-apocalyptic *On the Beach* (1959).

4. *My Son John* (US 1952, dir. Leo McCarey)

Even in the paradoxical Paris of the fifties, when left-wing cinephiles tended to idolize right-wing cineastes (Ford, Vidor, Fuller), a line was drawn at McCarey's *My Son John*. Certainly, this drama, not so much mawkish as downright *mawk*, of an elderly, cloyingly wholesome couple (Dean Jagger and Helen Hayes) discovering to their horror – and the film's – that their only son (Robert Walker, who died before completion of the shoot) has become a member of the Communist Party is, at one level, a loathsome artefact. (But then, at the same level, so is *The Birth of a Nation*.) And it would be tempting to propose that therein lies precisely the source of its enduring interest. Except that it isn't so. *My Son John* is actually, inexplicably, a very moving film. Go figure, as the Americans say.

3. *Deux Sous de violettes* (1951, dir. Jean Anouilh)

Deux Sous de violettes means 'Two Pennyworth of Violets' and the film in question was written and directed by the once fashionable dramatist Anouilh. Considering that twee title, as also Anouilh's current reputation as a purveyor of bittersweet whimsy, one could scarcely be less prepared for such an orgy of (literally) breathtaking misanthropy, of sheer, unrelenting nihilism. Which is why, despite the fact that, visually, it's of scant interest, most of its shots being as grubby as factory windows, I nevertheless regard it as still worthy of attention. Put simply, I've always preferred films *by* someone to films *for* everyone.

2. *Två människor* / *Two People* (Sweden 1945, dir. Carl Th. Dreyer)

This is a unique case, a good, even very good, film which was actually repudiated by its own director. That director was Dreyer, a fact that should, but doesn't, go without saying, since many of his admirers have never heard of *Two People*. Why, then, did Dreyer refuse to talk about this haunting, intense, proto-Bergmanesque chamber piece on the theme of plagiarism? Perhaps simply because it's not one of the greatest films ever made – and the greatest films ever made were, after all, Dreyer's speciality.

1. *The Sin of Nora Moran* (US 1933, dir. Phil Goldstone)

Directed by a producer of exploitative films (though doubts have

arisen as to whether Goldstone actually was the director), and
starring Zita Johann, Miss Flash-in-the-Pan of 1933, *The Sin of
Nora Moran* is 'the one about' a loose woman sacrificing herself to
save the career of her politician lover. A typical B-movie dud, you
might suppose. In fact, piling flashbacks on flash-forwards, dream
sequences on sequences which may or may not be dreams, its narrative structure is of a confounding subtlety and complexity, sur-
reality and sophistication, closer to David Lynch, let's say, than to
Michael Curtiz. Recently rediscovered, then restored and now,
seemingly, neglected all over again, *The Sin of Nora Moran* is a
real UFO: an Unidentified Filmic Object.

The Age of Ignorance

Ten Great Films I Haven't Seen

NEV PIERCE

There are people who think of cinema as a competition. They *collect* movies rather than watch them – there's *nothing* they haven't
seen. They know so much more than the everyday Joe, who can
enjoy his Friday Night Flick without caring if it's lifted its style
from the Movie Brats or its substance from Scandinavia.
Undoubtedly it is a fine thing to be informed, to have a depth of
knowledge and a respect for film history: an art critic should know
his Picasso from his Goya; a film critic his Cameron from his
Kurosawa. But if a film transports you, then the creative fuel of
the film-maker shouldn't be an issue. You can't contextualize
everything; you can't *watch* everything. Next time you're with a
film snob who's boasting about his knowledge of Werner Herzog
or Satyajit Ray, ask which are the best scenes in *Fitzcarraldo* (it's
the steamboat down the rapids; I haven't seen it) and *Apur Sansar*
(it's the wedding with the lunatic groom; I haven't seen it).
Memory and experience are slippery things, and imagining the
scenes may be as vivid as watching the movies (which are now
like half-remembered dreams, from many years ago).
  So, below is a list of ten great films I haven't seen and brief

reasons – both valid and pathetic – why not. Some readers may be appalled that the editor of a national film magazine (for what that's worth) hasn't seen such established classics. If you'd like, think of it as a confession, or the beginning of a film buff's perverse pub game (points for each classic you *haven't* seen!), but I'd rather you consider it a *Jerry Maguire*-style manifesto for the passion of the fan over the pinched superiority of the *cinéphile* ('My God, he's seen *Jerry Maguire* but hasn't seen *Persona*!'). You can love films without having seen them all. You can enjoy the ride without knowing who taught the driver. Movies are for you as much as anybody. Film is about emotion, not statistics.

10. *Double Indemnity* (US 1944, dir. Billy Wilder)

Wilder's classic of duplicity and death sees the Austrian émigré mastering yet another genre, with the wily Edward G. Robinson investigating fellow insurance agent Fred MacMurray over the murder of Barbara Stanwyck's other half. Ingeniously engineered and oiled with Wilder's trademark wit, it's one of the bleakest and best of the noir explosion ignited by the Second World War. I know all this. It's alive in my mind. Why spoil it?

9. *Otto e Mezzo* / 8 1/2 (Italy 1963, dir. Federico Fellini)

Because even Fellini's admirers would suggest this is more self-indulgent than *La Dolce Vita* (1960): a thought that makes me want to vomit.

8. *Duck Soup* (US 1933, dir. Leo McCarey)

Why not? Honestly? Those glasses and moustache masks you can buy from joke shops. Of course, blaming Groucho Marx for giggling, moustachioed David Brent-types at fancy-dress parties is as blinkered as blaming Einstein for the atom bomb, but no one asked that this list be reasonable.

7. *Nashville* (US 1975, dir. Robert Altman)

Shelley Duvall.

6. *Scener ur ett äktenskap / Scenes From a Marriage* (Sweden 1973, dir. Ingmar Bergman)

Knowledge of Bergman's *oeuvre* is the foundation of the Serious Film Critic. If you've seen each of his films, you receive a Distinguished Service Cross from the London Film Critics' Circle and a visit from Death. Yes, I have seen one Ingmar Bergman film: *The Seventh Seal*. It was both diverting and impressive and a tad precious and pretentious, and I learnt not to dare question its genius in discussion after being branded an idiot (I am, but for so much more important reasons). So, Bergman remains the great unwatched and *Scenes From a Marriage* an arbitrary choice, as it's arguably the apex of his output (I am in no position to judge, obviously) and the title suggests a film even more self-important than *The Seventh Seal*. There's a strong chance I will one day regret this aversion to the great Swede (which stems from being raised on Hollywood and disgusted by film snobs), but if I ever really want to watch a painful dissection of love and relationships, I can always set up a camera at home.

5. *The Birth of a Nation* (US 1915, dir. D.W. Griffith)

If I love it, I'm a racist. If I hate it, I'm a fool. Where's the win in watching this film?

4. *Eraserhead* (US 1977, dir. David Lynch)

That hair . . . That director . . . The subject matter of child-rearing, death and mutation . . . Even thinking about *Eraserhead* makes me feel queasy, troubled and upset. A singular vision hailed as the greatest ever cult movie; a masterpiece, no doubt. One day I *will* watch it. But not yet . . . not yet . . .

3. *The Birds* (US 1963, dir. Alfred Hitchcock)

Like a novel half-read, lost and never missed, *The Birds* festered on VHS in my front room for years, tape stopped twenty minutes in due to an interruption I can't now recall (children, the postman, football?). And twenty minutes was enough to realize I would never care about Tippi Hedren enough to mind if anyone tortured her, whether it be birds or a porcine sadist with a camera.

2. *Bicycle Thieves / Ladri di biciclette* (Italy 1948, dir. Vittorio De Sica)

Man needs bike for job. Man has bike stolen. Man searches for bike. Pass the popcorn . . .

1. *Shichinin no samurai / Seven Samurai* (Japan 1954, dir. Akira Kurosawa)

This is a source of genuine regret and an admission of embarrassment and sorrow: I have never seen a film by Akira Kurosawa. The excuses are both practical and – this may be overstating it – spiritual. First, you try persuading your other-half that a three-hour Japanese-language epic is preferable to *Changing Rooms*. Second, well . . . the real reason is deeper than that. I grew up watching Scorsese movies and became infected by his passion for cinema and excited by his love for Kurosawa; I've seen *The Magnificent Seven* and dreamt the original to be better; I've read of the director's simpatico relationship with Toshiro Mifune and the poetry and majesty of the rain-drenched final fight sequence of his most iconic action picture. The hype and reverence around *Seven Samurai*, *Yojimbo*, *Ikiru* et al. have turned them into almost holy relics; convinced me that viewing them on the box, with the distractions of home, the phone, the family, will be doing them a grave disservice. And the longer the omission goes on, the more importance the films possess. So, like a man who won't go to church because he's a sinner (when in reality that's a key reason for going), I avoid *Seven Samurai* because of the power and glory I've invested in the experience; I wait for a revival season at the NFT and the miracle of some free time. For the meantime, Kurosawa is sacred in my imagination.

The Greatest Movies Never Made
Ten Sadly Unrealized Masterworks

KEVIN JACKSON

'Heard melodies are sweet, but those unheard are sweeter.' (Keats)

The curse of every artist who needs a patron – and in today's movie world that usually means the CEO of a major production company – is that one works at the patron's whim. And even when patrons are not fickle, they may fall out of favour, or be summarily axed, or simply fail in tenacity or power. So it is almost more normal for a film to fall at the first or second hurdle than to make it all the way into distribution, and the true chronicle of unmade films is too vast to record. This personal list of ten great unmade films is confined to those projects which came tantaliz-ingly close to production, sometimes to the point of having actors cast, sets designed, caterers booked. (I know of at least one recent example of the last: a film of Robert Irwin's novel *Exquisite Corpse*.) The history of production would only need to have been a little different for the history of cinema to look *very* different.

10. Francis Ford Coppola's 'Megalopolis'

Unlike most of the titles on this list, *Megalopolis* may one day be completed. Perhaps. Coppola has been developing the project for well over a decade now, and it is rumoured that hours of second unit footage already exist. Performers known or believed to have read for parts include Nicolas Cage, Russell Crowe, Robert De Niro, Paul Newman, Kevin Spacey and Parker Posey. Coppola has offered some vague descriptions of the film as being somewhat like an Ayn Rand novel (to be precise *The Fountainhead*), and taking the form of a science-fiction drama set in the present day, about an architect who dreams of rebuilding New York. It is also said that the film links contemporary New York with ancient Rome at the time of the Catiline Conspiracy. But sceptical souls have cast doubt on it ever reaching a screen.

The Mighty Apoplexies of Pacino: Ten Scenes Where 'Shouty Al'
Shows Up, p 96

9. David Lean's 'Mutiny on the Bounty'

To be pedantic, this thwarted project would have taken the form of two films: *The Lawbreakers* and *The Long Arm*, both scripted by Lean's most trusted writer, Robert Bolt. In the summer of 1977, Bolt received an unexpected summons to the island of Bora Bora in the South Pacific, where Lean had settled in his long retreat from directing that began with the critical massacre of *Ryan's Daughter* (1970). He had fallen in love with the islands of Polynesia, and felt compelled to convey their beauty in a new film; the full story of the *Bounty*, which he had rediscovered in Richard Hough's study *Captain Bligh and Mister Christian*, seemed the ideal vehicle. Dino De Laurentiis had agreed to finance both films, even though the production costs included the hugely expensive task of building a full-sized replica of the *Bounty*. Both Lean and De Laurentiis declared themselves ecstatic with Bolt's writing: the first script detailed the events leading up to the mutiny, while the second would show its various consequences. But De Laurentiis began to repent his involvement when it became clear that the films would cost almost twice as much as he had first calculated, and he put the project into turnaround. Not long after, Bolt suffered a major stroke, which threatened to leave him permanently disabled and incapable of writing, though he eventually managed a partial recovery. A much pared-down version of the two scripts was eventually directed by Roger Donaldson in 1984, but this film had none of the epic sweep Lean and Bolt had originally conceived.

8. Stanley Kubrick's 'Napoleon'

Riding high on the critical success of *2001: A Space Odyssey* (1968), Kubrick believed that he had MGM in the palm of his hand, and was finally in a position to make 'the one film I've always wanted to make, the life of Napoleon'. He was almost right: Napoleon came so close to being shot that some filmographies – such as that in Joseph Gelmis's *The Film Director as Superstar* (1970) – actually list it as a completed work. Cynics were not slow to point out the reasons why Kubrick might have found the Corsican such an appealing subject, but their quips were blunted by the director's own willingness to confess how much he identified with Bonaparte, even down to copying the undiscriminating manner in which Napoleon wolfed his food. Kubrick planned to start shooting in the winter of 1969 – three months on location, four in studio – using as many as 40,000 infantrymen and 10,000 cavalry. Jack Nicholson, still a hungry young actor, was the unconventional choice for the title role. By August 1969, however, corporate changes at MGM meant that Kubrick no longer had approval for his grandiose scheme, and he went on to develop the much more modestly budgeted *A Clockwork Orange*, from the novella by Anthony Burgess. One of the few concrete survivals from this busy period is Burgess's novel *Napoleon Symphony*, dedicated to Kubrick.

7. Bernardo Bertolucci's 'Red Harvest'

Ever since the late 1960s Bernardo Bertolucci had been telling people that one of his dream projects would be a film based on Dashiell Hammett's 1929 novel. He came closest to achieving the dream in the early 1980s, when Jack Nicholson and Debra Winger were both attached to the project. It soon fell through, partly because of a complication concerning rights to the book. But perhaps it would have been a rather redundant project anyway, since the essential plot of *Red Harvest* has turned up, only lightly disguised, in everything from Kurosawa's *Yojimbo* (a samurai version) to *A Fistful of Dollars* to *Mad Max Beyond Thunderdome* to *Miller's Crossing* to *Last Man Standing* . . .

6. Alfred Hitchcock's 'Kaleidoscope'

In 1966 the novelist Howard Fast received an urgent phone call from Hitchcock: 'My God, Howard! I've just seen Antonioni's *Blow-Up*. These Italian directors are a century ahead of me in terms of technique! What have I been doing all this time?' Anxious to bring himself up to Swinging Sixties speed, Hitchcock asked Fast to sketch out a treatment for a film to be called 'Kaleidoscope: the story of a deformed serial killer' (who also

became gay as the treatment developed). Hitchcock was delighted with Fast's writing, and soon sketched out a shot list that
included over 450 camera positions. He also shot about an hour's
worth of experimental colour rushes, some of which have since
been broadcast as part of a BBC *Reputations* on Hitchcock, and
which show just how radical a stylistic change 'Kaleidoscope'
would have been. But MCA/Universal were disgusted by Fast's
script, and cancelled the project. For the first time in his career,
Hitchcock was so wounded by the rejection that he burst into
tears.

5. John Waters's 'A Confederacy of Dunces'

Attempts to make a film of John Kennedy Toole's remarkable
comic novel began as early as 1980, when a young executive at
20th Century Fox, Scott Kramer, began to hawk early copies
around to his peers, few of whom were bright enough to see the
funny side of a book about a corpulent, flatulent, terminally sloth-
ful misanthrope and medievalist – Ignatius J. Reilly. Those who
have attempted scripts over the years include Buck Henry, Harold
Ramis and Stephen Fry; actors cast for the role have included
John Belushi, John Candy, and Chris Farley, all of whom died
before cameras could turn over – hence the legend of a
Confederacy 'Curse'. Fans of the novel most lament the failure of
John Waters to realize his version, since the man who devised
Pink Flamingos and *Hairspray* would undoubtedly have made
something memorable of a book still considered 'unfilmable'. At
the time of writing, there are rumours of a *Confederacy* to be
directed by David Gordon Green from a script by Kramer and
Steven Soderbergh; but it would not be wise to grow impatient
over this.

4. Robert Bresson's 'Genesis'

The most dearly cherished project of Bresson's later years was a
lavish adaptation of the Book of Genesis. It was the unlikely
patronage of Dino De Laurentiis (that man again) which first
made this ambitious plan seem possible in the late sixties, but

Bresson abandoned it, only to take it up again and again until the very end of his life. He once remarked that one of the problems with the subject matter was that – as had never been the case in his previous dealings with amateur human 'models' – he couldn't make his animal performers do as they were told.

3. Martin Scorsese's 'Gershwin'

Paul Schrader wrote a brilliant screenplay for this highly ambitious biopic of the great American composer. Schrader's idea was to alternate between lavish production numbers of Gershwin's works and thematically related scenes from his short life, using the device of having Gershwin mull over key events on a psychoanalyst's couch. The project was eventually cancelled because of the difficulty and expense of securing rights; and because of doubts as to whether the all-important younger audience would know or care about a composer of Gershwin's vintage.

2. Alexander Korda's 'Revolt in the Desert'

Attempts to bring the story of T.E. Lawrence's Arabian exploits to the screen began while Lawrence was still alive. Confused as ever about his attitude to fame, Lawrence initially acquiesced in the idea, or even encouraged it, but later declared himself bitterly opposed. A meeting with Alexander Korda, whom he found surprisingly civil, settled the matter: Korda agreed that no film would go into production while Lawrence was still alive. Lawrence's accidental death in 1935 set off a competition between rival producers that was to last almost three decades, until Sam Spiegel finally made it possible for David Lean to direct the epic tale. In the interim, it was almost always Korda who was the front-runner, with his brother Zoltan usually slated as director. Leslie Howard was the leading contender for the title role, though many other names were mooted, from Walter Hudd to Dirk Bogarde. A curious detail: those who knew Lawrence well said that, of all the actors considered for the role, it was Howard whose voice most closely resembled the original.

1. Michael Powell's 'The Tempest'

Michael Powell's grand farewell to the cinema, like Shakespeare's
to the stage, was to have been *The Tempest* – a play he had always
adored. James Mason, whom he had just directed in *Age of
Consent*, agreed to play Prospero; Michael York was cast as
Ferdinand, Mia Farrow as Ariel, and Topol as Caliban ('I always
felt I understood Caliban better than anyone else except Roger
Livesey', said Powell). André Previn, Farrow's husband at the
time, was asked to write the score. Powell's adaptation of
Shakespeare's text was fairly free-handed; at one point, Mason
asked him whether the scene with Galileo showing Prospero a tel-
escope was Shakespeare. No, came the reply, it's Powell. (This
scene was later dramatized for a BBC documentary about Powell
by David Thompson.) It all sounded most promising, especially
when the Greek royal family became briefly involved as producers, but in the event this *Tempest* couldn't be financed as no suitable patron was found for Powell's dream swansong.

4

Take Two, or Even Three

Remakes, Recycles and Return Visits

MARK COUSINS: So Good They Made It Thrice – The Ten
Greatest Movie Trilogies

NEV PIERCE: Even Better than the Real Thing – Ten Remakes
that Improve on the Originals

ETHAN COEN AND JOEL COEN: Ripe for Remake – Five Films
We'd Like to See Remade

So Good They Made It Thrice

The Ten Greatest Movie Trilogies

MARK COUSINS

The world of commercial cinema has, for many years, suffered from sequel-itis: if a film does well at the box office, a follow-up is produced to cash in on that success. With some of the following trilogies there was an element of cash-in – but, in each case, the second and third films extend the story or world of the first film in some meaningful way. In Satyajit Ray's and Bill Douglas's films, we see what happens when Apu and wee Jamie begin to grow up. And in the *Star Wars* trilogy, we chart a series of reversals of fortune in the battle between The Force and the Dark Side.

Some would say that Peter Jackson's *The Lord of the Rings Trilogy* should be on the list. These are certainly amongst the most commercially significant movies of the millennium to date; and, at a time when film is tending toward realism, they were unapologetically works of high fantasy. But your compiler found them tedious and repetitive, and so exercised his prerogative to ignore them.

10. *The Golden Heart Trilogy* by Lars von Trier

After years of boring works of empty formalism, modern cinema's great shape-shifter discovered emotion and goodness, and made *Breaking the Waves* (1996), *Dogme number 2: The Idiots* (1998) and *Dancer in the Dark* (2000). In retrospect, part of the impact of the first of these was how completely it took us by surprise. Influenced by the piety of Dreyer's films, it used handheld video imagery and hard sex to tell its story of a woman who suffers and goes to heaven, to the sound of bells. The mix of formal vivacity, thematic conservatism, and lachrymose scenes worthy of Douglas Sirk's *Imitation of Life* (1956) was not exhausted by one movie so, alas, two years later, *The Idiots* was born. *Dancer in the Dark* was another impossibly eccentric stew – Björk, Catherine Deneuve on the sidelines in a housecoat, hundreds of cameras, a completely implausible story in which Björk is put to death by the state – that made many want to boo and cheer at the same time. How could Trier be so inventive and yet so stupid at the same time? A question impossible to answer – but these violently unresolved films were a sign of his brilliance.

9. *Star Wars* Episodes IV–VI by George Lucas

Back in 1977 the box-office takings of Lucas's 'space opera' were big enough to transform the industry: as director Paul Schrader put it, *Star Wars* 'ate Hollywood'. But, to be fair, its visual and sonic excitements created a wondrous cosmology, one that sutured many of us to the love of cinema for the rest of our lives. *The Empire Strikes Back* (1980) was even better, the first movie remade as a film noir. *The Return of the Jedi* (1983) showed signs that enough was enough, that there was no more juice in the trilogy's engine – warnings that its creator studiously ignored in producing *Episode 1: The Phantom Menace*, and its two restless, unfeeling sequels.

8. *The Qatsi Trilogy* by Godfrey Reggio

These trippy, non-narrative films, made way before Google Earth but with some of the same God's-eye-view fascination, were executive-produced by George Lucas but can be thought of as the anti-*Star Wars* trilogy. *Koyaanisqatsi: Life Out of Balance* (1982) and *Powaqqatsi: Life in Translation* (1988) were dazzling works of global village humanism – landscape and urban vistas from a director who spent fourteen years in prayer and partial silence whilst studying with the Christian Brothers. These were state-of-the-planet films and, in their vast New Mexico manner, seemed to portray what the earth itself was thinking and saying. *Naqoyqatsi: Life as War* (2002) was equally sincere but struck some as platitudinous. Their scores, by Philip Glass, influenced cinematic documentary for a generation.

7. *The Evil Dead Trilogy* by Sam Raimi

The Evil Dead (1981), *II – Dead by Dawn* (1987), *III – Army of Darkness* (1992). Infamous, nocturnal, resplendent devilry, way ahead of most of the baroque horror trash of the 1980s because the camera seemed to have an outboard motor attached, as did the director's imagination.

6. *The Three Colours Trilogy* by Krzysztof Kieslowski

This high-concept trio – based on the themes of Liberty, Equality and Fraternity and on the *Bleu* (1993), *Blanc* (1994) and *Rouge* (1994) of the French flag – sound windy and pretentious on paper. Steven Spielberg, or even, one suspects, Andrei Tarkovsky, would have been wrong-footed by such a brief. Surely too preachy, too abstract? But Kieslowski and his screenwriter Krzysztof Piesiewicz never seem as if they are sailing towards any Great Conclusions. Instead, in the case of *Bleu* for example, they show a composer (Juliette Binoche) coping after the deaths of her husband and child. And in sound and vision they capture the world she inhabits: the apparitions, the welling of memory, the lapses in consciousness wrought by grief. The relationship between liberty and that grief is never spelled out, but we sense that Binoche escapes into music. This trilogy lets us escape into cinema.

5. *The Godfather Trilogy* by Francis Ford Coppola

The Godfather (1971), *Part II* (1974), *Part III* (1990). What Rembrandt would have made, if he had made movies.

4. *The Red Curtain Trilogy* by Baz Luhrmann

The 'new wave' of Australian and New Zealand films that emerged in the early 1990s was clearly a distinct reaction against the traditional masculinity of Antipodean culture. High-camp and sequinned, the dance-themed *Strictly Ballroom* (1992) was the showiest of the lot, as if its maker were pulling up a curtain and screaming, 'Ta-dah!' Its success led in 1996 to *Romeo + Juliet*: a thrilling variety show of MTV, Rodriguez/Leone gun-opera, the Village People, CNN and achingly beautiful Shakespearean line readings by Leonardo DiCaprio and Clare Danes. Five years later, Luhrmann lifted the curtain once more, this time on a bohemian world of Parisian *fin de siècle* poets and courtesans in *Moulin Rouge*. His fast, furious bricolage now even included

a smidgen of Bollywood. It shouldn't have worked but it did, sublime-
ly. Luhrmann's uniquely gendered trilogy drew most of its effects from
the display and artifice of the stage, yet presented them in a way that
was made for the movie screen.

3. *The Apu Trilogy* by Satyajit Ray

It started with *Pather Panchali* (1955), a crisp and luminous film
about a Bengali boy that was more modern and compelling even
than its model – the Italian neo-realist classic *Bicycle Thieves*
(1948). In *Aparajito* (1956), ten-year-old Apu goes to school, does
well, and so leaves for college in Calcutta. By the time of *The
World of Apu* (1959), he has graduated and we follow him into the
vale of tears of a tragic marriage, and doubts about life itself. The
novel by Bibhutibhushan Bandyopadhyay provided the storyline,
Soumitra Chatterjee and the sublime Sharmila Tagore brought
the characters to life, and maestro director Ray rendered them on
celluloid, just as vividly as Sergei Eisenstein at his best.

2. *The Bill Douglas Trilogy*

My Childhood (1972), *My Ain Folk* (1973), *My Way Home* (1978).
Eisenstein was also a touchstone for this trilogy of medium-length
films about a boy growing up in an unfeeling post-war mining village in Eastern Scotland. Bill Douglas used his own life as inspiration, hardly moved his camera, and made scenes that nearly
clanged with grimness. Yet the framing is exquisite: these are
movies of still lives. And when Jamie – in Egypt on national service, years after we've first met him – puts his head on the shoulder of another soldier, so hinting at love, the moment is amongst
the most moving in all cinema.

1. *The Koker Trilogy* by Abbas Kiarostami

In 1987 Tehrani film-maker Kiarostami made *Where is the Friend's
House?* in Koker, northern Iran. Three years later, a devastating
earthquake in the Koker killed 50,000 people. Kiarostami went
back and made *And Life Goes On . . .* (1992), in which a film

director searches for the boy-actors from the first movie. Two
years after that, the director revisited Koker once more to direct
Through the Olive Trees (1994), its subject the making of a single
scene in *And Life Goes On* . . .

This may sound impossibly self-referential: but the result is, yes,
the greatest trilogy in movie history. The second film shows us
that the flow of life is unstoppable, even after tragedy strikes.
Whilst it was being made, one of the extras fell in love – and the
whole of the third film is about the very moment when that love
emerged. The second film doesn't tell us whether those boys survived the original earthquake, yet in the third film, seven years
on, we glimpse them briefly – grown, pubescent – and the recognition is thrilling. *The Koker Trilogy* is full of the human details of
Iranian life. Its unique structure suggests that such detail can be
endlessly unfolded, and metaphysically revealing.

Even Better than the Real Thing

Ten Remakes that Improve on the Originals

NEV PIERCE

Remakes: the only things lower than sequels . . . Often created to
exploit a brand, pushed by studios looking for safe bets where an
audience is pre-sold. But for all the critical carping about regurgitat-
ing old ideas, if a remake is talent-driven then there's no reason it
can't be great – rebuilding the idea for a different age, fuelled by the
fears of a new generation. Citing ten remakes better than the movies
they're based on, though – it's hard. Originally this list had rules: the
films needed to be 'pure' remakes, rather than alternative adaptations of source material. Then I discovered *The Thing from Another
World* was based on a novella, and remembered *His Girl Friday* was
originally a play. So, in the tradition of Hollywood fair-dealing . . .

10. *The Departed* (US 2006, dir. Martin Scorsese)

Infernal Affairs was a polished, over-praised Hong Kong cop drama whose lack of John Woo-style gunplay could be confused for depth. It owed a debt to *Heat*, yet somehow *The Departed* owes a debt to no one. William Monahan lifts the structure from Andy Lau's thriller and then layers on Irish Catholic guilt, profanity and plenty of opportunity for Scorsese to deliver what he does like no other: violence, bloody and true. Jack Nicholson destroys the scenery and Leonardo DiCaprio has the angrier, flashier role of the doppelgänger cop/criminal pairing at the picture's centre. But it's Matt Damon who delivers the best performance as the sly ingratiating rat prepared to do anything to rise to the top. *The Departed* is about ambitions. And it fulfils them admirably.

9. *Vanilla Sky* (US 2001, dir. Cameron Crowe)

'LoveHateDreamsLifeWorkPlayFriendshipSex'. Crowe's 'cover version' of *Abre los ojos / Open Your Eyes* was criticized by some for simply translating the script, but he brings much more to the Spanish crit-hit. Alejandro Amenábar's original was ingenious but chilly; Crowe infuses warmth and accessibility, not least by casting Tom Cruise as the whiz-kid publisher whose life is too good to be true. The man with the million-watt smile keeps it hidden for much of the movie and for all the criticism the actor receives off-screen, it's hard to think of any A-list star quite so prepared to mess with his image: sexually violent, self-loathing, rich beyond his wildest dreams, but never quite satisfied . . . There's something daring and intriguing about Cruise's willingness to play such a character and suggest everything is not quite right behind the mask.

8. *Dawn of the Dead* (US 2004, dir. Zack Snyder)

This is another cheat: Snyder's unheralded zombie remake isn't actually better than George A. Romero's seminal shocker. But against all expectations it really is bloody good. The first UK press screening was crammed with twenty- and thirty-something hacks ready to tear up the joint (or, you know, use really *cutting* sarcasm) if one of their favourite genre classics was desecrated. Instead they laughed, winced and cheered at an amped up, MTV-take on a ghastly resurrection. Here the dead don't walk, they run . . . But for all the frenetic action and gore, there are characters you care about at *Dawn*'s heart, from Ving Rhames's God-fearing security guard to Sarah Polley's tough totty.

7. *Scarface* (US 1983, dir. Brian De Palma)

Blood, yucks and vulgarity: De Palma's garish, defiantly brutal gang-banger is in its way as mannered and of-its-time as Howard Hawks's 1932 original. But Al Pacino is more charismatic than Paul Muni and with no Hays Code to restrict him the modern *Scarface* is excess-all-areas: greed is good, more is more . . . If Michael Corleone was villainy with an old-school sheen, Tony Montana is out there, coarse and unrepentant; the Me Generation's gangster – he wants it all, he wants it now, and he'll kill anyone who gets in his way.

6. *Ocean's Eleven* (US 2001, dir. Steven Soderbergh)

George Clooney trumps Frank Sinatra in Steven Soderbergh's whip-smart re-mix. The 1960 caper was essentially an excuse for the Chairman of the Board to kick back with pals in Las Vegas, but while there's the same camaraderie in this new Rat Pack (Brad Pitt, Matt Damon, Don Cheadle et al.), Soderbergh also delivers slick set-pieces and an understated sense of menace, thanks to Andy Garcia's casino boss. The sequel to the remake was widely (and incorrectly) judged to be as self-indulgent and messy as the original, but the ker-ching-generating *Ocean's* movies not only allow Soderbergh the freedom to deliver more experimental fare – they're also the most enjoyable adult franchise around.

5. *Heat* (US 1995, dir. Michael Mann)

If at first you don't succeed . . . Dissatisfied with his original take on this based-on-fact story of career cop versus career criminal, Mann revisited his 1989 TV movie *LA Takedown* with rather amplified ambitions, replacing Scott Plank (*The Princess and the Call Girl*) with Al Pacino (um, *The Godfather: Part II*) and Alex McArthur (*Desperado: The Outlaw Wars*) with Robert De Niro (I dunno . . .

The Godfather: Part II?). The result was suitably superior, with Mann putting his lately acquired experience on the action set-pieces of *The Last of the Mohicans* (hey, another remake . . .) to good use for *Heat*'s blistering gun-battles, while building effectively on the theme of driven cop and brooding robber as two-sides-of-the-same-coin.

4. Invasion of the Bodysnatchers (US 1978, dir. Philip Kaufman)

A Cold War classic revisited, with post-Watergate conspiracy fear replacing reds-under-the-beds paranoia. Don Siegel's 1956 original remains a gripping UFO noir, but Philip Kaufman's big city reworking now feels more immediate, particularly if you live in London – where its scenes of metropolitan dislocation and blank-eyed, emotionally stunted automatons are repeated daily on the Tube. The pod-people are taking over . . . Donald Sutherland is superb as the last of the free spirits, while there's an effective dig at 1970s self-help culture in the form of Leonard Nimoy's pop-psychologist.

3. The Fly (US 1986, dir. David Cronenberg)

In the era of AIDs an appalling disease destroys eccentric scientist Jeff Goldblum after he falls for exclusive-hungry journo pickup Geena Davis. Having invited her back to his apartment to see something extraordinary, he reveals his experiment in teleportation and she falls for the kooky scientist shtick. Before you can say 'safe sex', she's pregnant and he's conducting ill-advised self-experimentation that sees him fuse with a housefly at a molecular-genetic level. Cronenberg's first real mainstream hit, *The Fly* is as gory and unsettling as anything he's directed, rooted in his fascination with infection and bodily malfunction, as Goldblum falls apart – nails, ears, penis – bit by gooey bit. Horrendous and compelling: a distant world away from the woman-in-peril sci-fi schlock of the 1958 Vincent Price original.

2. The Thing (US 1982, dir. John Carpenter)

Howard Hawks was the producer (and, most agree, unaccredited director) of Christian Nyby's *The Thing From Another World* (1951).

The superior remake was definitely the work of John Carpenter, six years after he had riffed on Hawks's *Rio Bravo* in *Assault on Precinct 13*. Carpenter took the Cold War fear-infused sci-fier and re-booted it. The bloke-in-a-suit alien of the original bore a strong resemblance to a carrot with a furrowed brow. Carpenter's alien takes refuge inside the flesh of its human prey ('Man is the Warmest Place to Hide', as the poster put it). The concept encouraged some ground-breaking special effects – including a horrific moment when a stricken man's chest cavity turns into a set of jagged jaws. And in contrast to the paranoid vigilance at the end of Hawks's picture – 'Keep watching the skies!' – Carpenter concludes with one of the bleakest final beats in horror history, our hero Kurt Russell in the gathering dark with one fellow survivor: 'Why don't we just wait here for a little while . . . see what happens?'

1. *His Girl Friday* (1940, dir. Howard Hawks)

Hawks wasn't shy of remakes himself, with *El Dorado* a self-confessed reworking of his own *Rio Bravo* and this, the definitive screwballer, a take on Lewis Milestone's 1931 hit *The Front Page*. The crucial change was from Hildebrand to Hildegard, a gender-switch for the story's hard-boiled 'newspaperman' (Rosalind Russell). Perhaps this gives a proto-feminist worth to the material; it certainly lends more edge to the relationship between Hildy and her editor (Cary Grant): he's her ex-husband. So, a rat-tat-tat romance revolves around the original's madcap tale of journos tracking an escaped killer. Few remember *The Front Page*. Everyone should remember *His Girl Friday*. 'Walter, you're wonderful, in a loathsome sort of way . . .'

Ripe for Remake

Five Films We'd Like to See Remade

ETHAN COEN AND JOEL COEN

5. *Guess Who's Coming to Dinner* (US 1967, dir. Stanley Kramer)

This has already been remade as a comedy – some sort of

intentional travesty of the Stanley Kramer film. A pity. This is one movie that would benefit from the Gus Van Sant treatment: a shot-by-shot remake that would reinforce the stiffness of the original and further petrify its already passé social commentary. The result would have the lofty irrelevance of high art.

4. *Koyaanisqatsi* (US 1982, dir. Godfrey Reggio)

We have not seen the original but suspect it could be interestingly remade with Cameron Diaz and Ashton Kutcher.

3. *Harley Davidson and the Marlboro Man* (US 1991, dir. Simon Wincer)

Nothing wrong with the underrated original, but since this Don Johnson/Mickey Rourke star-pairing took place in the near future, it could be remade now (about the time when the first was speculatively set) with the same cast and the same short-term futurism: an exercise in kicking a can down the road. Further remakes with the same cast at fifteen-year intervals would constitute a mind-bending variation on the *7-Up* series.

2. *Out 1: Spectre* (France 1972, dir. Jacques Rivette)

Rivette's original was four hours long. Come on.

1. *The Godfather, Part III* (US 1990, dir. Francis Ford Coppola)

Be clear, this would not be 'Godfather IV' but a remake of III, which, let's not kid ourselves, was not so hot. If the remake were successful, one could waltz back through the other 'II', making for a hell of a lot of *Godfather*s. Arriving at 'Godfather I' or, as it was myopically called at the time, *The Godfather*, it is simply not possible to imagine anyone but Chris Walken playing the Sterling Hayden part. Indeed, if the director were feeling his artistic oats, Chris Walken could play all the parts.

5

That Thing They Do

Actors and Acting

RICHARD T. KELLY: Twisted Christopher – Ten Inimitable
Walken Line-Readings

TIM ROBEY: The Mighty Apoplexies of Pacino – Ten Scenes
Where 'Shouty Al' Shows Up

DEMETRIOS MATHEOU: Ten Bad Dates with De Niro – Lessons
from Bobby in How *Not* to Treat a Lady

DANNY LEIGH: They Could Have Been Contenders – Ten Great
Performances by Frequently Derided Actors

RYAN GILBEY: Maestros Who Got into Make-Up – Ten Directors
Who Acted, with Honour

JAMES MOTTRAM: O Brothers, Here Art Thou – The Coen Bros'
Ten Most Memorable Minor Characters

Twisted Christopher

Ten Inimitable Walken Line-Readings

RICHARD T. KELLY

Few actors ever strike us as totally unique in the way they do that voodoo they do. Regrettably, those who clearly are one-offs in this world then risk being widely imitated, by fans as well as peers. Sometimes it's a physical tic that inspires this odd form of flattery, sometimes a manner of speech. 'I learn my lines by saying them over and over', Christopher Walken once remarked to this writer, 'and it seems to me that whenever it *sounds* right, it's right.' But Walken's version of 'right' is entirely his own. He is seldom caught attempting naturalism – only greater or lesser variations on what comes naturally to him and him alone, a glorious singularity that has spawned a thousand mimics. But no one compares to Walken: he is one of the all-time glories of American cinema, in whatever project he picks to showcase his nimble moves, phenomenal hair, and peculiar diction. As to the snippets of dialogue below – just try to imagine how they looked on the page before Walken arrived at his 'choices'.

10. 'Sometimes when I'm driving – on the road, at night – I see two headlights coming toward me – fast, I have this sudden impulse to turn the wheel quickly . . .'
As Duane Hall in *Annie Hall* (US 1977, dir./scr. Woody Allen)

Walken grew up in showbusiness, was a child performer then a dancer in musicals until the age of twenty-five, whereupon movie parts begun to trickle in. Ten years into that career he was still only fodder for a one-scene Woody Allen gag about someone else's neurosis (which could be considered a bit rich). But Walken surely convinces as Annie Hall's wan brother, the suicide-fixated motorist to whom Allen's Alvy Singer gives the widest berth at a Hall family dinner, only to discover that Duane will be his ride home for the night. Credit to Allen for making use of the talent, albeit partially. Walken's next movie was *The Deer Hunter*, whereupon everything changed.

9. 'I don't know the O'Doyles but – they can bite it *hard*.'
As Morty in *Click* (2006, dir. Frank Coraci, scr. Steve Koren &
Mark O'Keefe)

In the thirty years since *Annie Hall* Walken has been generous
with his comedic chops, including a half-dozen hosting stints on
NBC's *Saturday Night Live* wherein he and Adam Sandler shared
a few skits. In *Click* Walken plays the Grim Reaper disguised as a
lab boffin who gifts harassed suburban family guy Sandler with a
magical remote control. When Sandler wonders aloud if he will
now be the envy of his gadget-proud neighbours, Walken's eyes
dissimulate pleasure, his smile slight but delighted as he offers the
opinion above. The part was otherwise child's play for Walken,
permitting him both to sing a little (Irving Gordon's 'Be
Anything But be Mine'), and dance (George Clinton's 'Give Up
the Funk').

8. 'You *amuse* me, Mr Bond.'
As Max Zorin in *A View to a Kill* (1985, dir. John Glen, scr. Richard
Maibaum & Michael G. Wilson from the story by Ian Fleming)

Playing the Bond baddy is a risky step for a real actor: you're rarely
made to look handsome, and you're liable to get hoary old lines
like this one, in the obligatory early face-off with 007 en route to
be being ingeniously killed. Walken's trick was to utter it while
lifting his eyebrows as well as the corners of his mouth – as if genuinely amused, but more genuinely keen to let Roger Moore know
he wasn't feeling at all threatened. He bucked another trend by
managing to look sharp in a white suit and damn-near-white
blond hair. All in all, duties were discharged with honour, though
the role would light Walken's way to more frictionless essays in
summer-movie villainy.

7. 'See, most people that drive through here – they see *farms* –
houses and fields and . . . shit. I see money. Everywhere I go I
see money. I see things that can move, anything that can move's
got my name writ on it. "Brad Whitewood! Please *hooold* for
delivery!"'

THAT THING THEY DO

As Brad Whitewood Snr. in *At Close Range* (US 1986, dir. James Foley, scr. Nicholas Kazan)

A transitional moment for Walken, this. Previously (barring his stupendous cameo as a dancing pimp in *Pennies From Heaven*) he tended to look a little wraith-like on screen: hollow-cheeked, haunted, somewhat cerebral. Suddenly he was acting from the hips, or even further below the waist, and amusing himself in the process. He didn't do a great deal of prep for this part as a Pennsylvania tractor thief, other than getting his hair good and bushy (with highlights), then driving to the location from New York in a pick-up truck with Sean Penn (cast as Brad Jr., 'Little Brad'). The accent Walken settled on for 'Big Brad' owed more to Tupelo than Philly, most exuberantly in readings like the one above. 'Somebody called him a hillbilly Lucifer,' Walken later told *Film Comment*. 'He was sort of the dark side of the moon of Elvis.'

6. 'If any of you – are tired of getting ripped off by guys like that [Shoots Artie Clay's corpse three times] – you come with me, I'm at the Plaza Hotel. You're welcome, you're all *welcome*! [Shoots Clay's corpse again] Enjoy!'
As Frank White in *King of New York* (US 1990, dir. Abel Ferrara, scr. Nicholas St John)

Walken's collaboration with Ferrara has run to four pictures and is clearly valuable to both men, as well as a legion of fans. This viewer can't get into those pictures, partly because of scenes such as the one above, which at least offers something of a model for scarily irredeemable behaviour executed with panache.

5. 'Put it on *straight*, punk.'
As Bruno Buckingham in *Wild Side* (US 1995, dir. Donald Cammell & China Kong, scr. Cammell)

The 'it' in question is a Trojan condom that high-rolling financier Buckingham insists his traitorous chauffeur (Steven Bauer) fit him with, so that he can then sodomize the guy in front of the woman he loves (Anne Heche), in order to prove to her that . . . well, actually, it's a hard one to put in a nutshell. But Buckingham is a loose cannon and a sexual tyrannosaurus, so it's no accident he should resort to his crotch to inflict punishment as readily as pleasure. In fact he withdraws at the last from carrying out the threat, but only after Bauer has trembled spread-eagled for some moments while Walken dances about, brandishing a gun and a cigar, lashing the victim with his own Calvin Klein pants, and yelling a load of sexualized gibberish ('You're lucky 'cos you're *peachy*! You're lucky 'cos you're *fucky*'). The hair here, by the way, is a glossy black bob.

4. 'I respect you as an Englishman, but not if you're a . . . communist *poof*. You're not a *poof*, are you?'
As Robert in *The Comfort of Strangers* (Italy/GB 1990, dir. Paul Schrader, scr. Harold Pinter from the novel by Ian McEwan)

A case of what Freudians call 'projection', for the moneyed Venetian Robert is half in love with Rupert Everett's Colin, yet wholly committed to cutting his throat. The marriage of McEwan and Pinter produced a character of colossal perversity, apparently warped by an appalling childhood. Schrader added spice by calling on Walken's suavity and draping him in Armani. This was a role that seemed to really interest Walken (as it had intrigued Al Pacino, who nearly played it).

3. 'Five long years, he wore this watch – up his ass. Then – he died of dysentery, he give me the watch. I hid this uncomfortable hunk of metal up my ass two years. Then . . . after seven years, I was sent home to my family. Now – little man? I give the watch to you.'
As Captain Koons in *Pulp Fiction* (US 1994, dir. Quentin Tarantino, scr. Tarantino & Roger Avary)

This is merely the pay-off on a four-minute monologue, but a clear instance of why actors flocked to Quentin Tarantino in the mid-1990s as they had to Woody Allen for two decades previous: he offered original dialogue, and pages of it. Walken had sat and listened to Dennis Hopper expound in the Tarantino-scripted *True Romance* (1993). Now he got to play at leisure himself, delivering a carefully preserved – and yet somehow soiled – token of affection to the boy version of Bruce Willis from his POW dad.

2. 'The *ice* is gonna *break*.'
As John Smith in *The Dead Zone* (US 1983, dir. David Cronenberg, scr. Jeffrey Boam from the novel by Stephen King)

A regular name for a seemingly regular guy – hardly tailor-made for Walken. But this is maybe his greatest, most affecting performance: a schoolteacher too decent to sleep with his fiancée, who drives off instead to a car-wreck that casts him into a five-year coma. He awakens with his love and livelihood lost; what he has gained is the curse of second sight. In time he will use it to battle a sinister populist politician, but the true core of the film is Johnny's thwarted love for Sarah (Brooke Adams), now married with a baby son. He gets close to her again, but not close enough. (In one oddly touching moment we see Walken sat pensively amid kids' toys.) Weepy and pained thereafter, he becomes a tutor and surrogate father to the shy son of a wealthy man. Seized by a vision of the boy's death under a frozen lake he goes to the father and demands he postpone a planned game of ice hockey. When Dad won't listen, Johnny raises his cane, smashes it down upon a side-table heavy with ornaments, and dispenses altogether with the soft-spoken approach.

1. 'Two *mice* – fell in a bucket of *cream*, Frank. Which one am I?'
As Frank Abagnale in *Catch Me if You Can* (US 2002, dir. Steven Spielberg, scr. Jeff Nathanson from the book by Frank Abagnale Jr. & Stan Redding)

After a few lean years devoted largely to Abel Ferrara, Walken very wisely got onboard what turned out to be one of Spielberg's best pictures, playing a fluent liar who serves to convince his son (Leonardo DiCaprio) that anything can be believed if said with an earnest mien or a husky catch in the throat. We first see him as his boy sees him: a successful businessman, twirling his fair French wife

(Nathalie Baye) round the parlour, one of life's lucky guys – hence his fondness for the tale of the hapless mouse who churned cream into butter. But Frank is on a collision course with the IRS. While Junior brazenly forges his way into jobs as a pilot, doctor and lawyer, Frank will soon be riding the train and wearing a postman's uniform. If it is a rueful thing to see DiCaprio trying to impress his father with the facade of having 'made it', it is highly poignant to observe Walken's sorrow once he has very quickly spotted the strings at this particular puppet-show. The man is still full of surprises, no question.

The Mighty Apoplexies of Pacino

Ten Scenes Where 'Shouty Al' Shows Up

TIM ROBEY

All paid-up Pacino fans require him to lose his rag and turn into Shouty Al at least once in a movie. This can be facilitated in a number of ways: with an abusive tirade, some good fiery inspirational rhetoric, or just a plain old-fashioned wobbly. Pacino, like Jack Nicholson, has always seemed to pick scripts that offer such wig-out moments, and he invariably turns them into blistering dramatic high points. There's majesty in his rage, a showman's instinct for ramming the point home with unpredictable emphases, sudden surges of volume and a general *Sturm und Drang* exhibitionism. Here are ten of the best.

10. 'FUCK Caspar Gomez and FUCK the FUCKING DIAZ brothers! Fuck 'em all! I bury those cock-a-roaches!'
As Tony Montana in *Scarface* (US 1983, dir. Brian De Palma, scr. Oliver Stone)

Has anyone ever put more 'f's into 'fuck'? Tony Montana is a rarity among Pacino characters in being so savagely inarticulate: he hardly needs words of more than one syllable. Listen to him stumble over 'cockroaches' as if it's the first time he's ever said it. This particular explosion is pivotal – Tony's soon-to-be-ex boss Robert

Loggia certainly isn't expecting such an earful, and the balance of power shifts abruptly the second Pacino gets out of his seat. His face distorts with an obscene lust for power, and a contempt for his rivals: you know he would never do anything so civilized as actually bury an enemy, unless they happened to be alive at the time and his chosen ground was wet cement.

9. 'You think you're merely sending this splendid footsoldier back home to Oregon with his tail between his legs, but I say you are executin' his SOUL!'
As Frank Slade in *Scent of a Woman* (US 1992, dir. Martin Brest, scr. Bo Goldman, from the novel *Il Buio e il Miele* by Giovanni Arpino)

There's plenty of Shouty Al to choose from here: all those 'Hoo-hahs', and more pungent ham when Frank Slade is contemplating suicide ('I'm in the dark here! Y'understand? *I'm in the dark!*'). But it's his big speech to Chris O'Donnell's prep school disciplinary committee that really gives those bellowing lungs a workout. Like many an Oscar-winning bit of grandstanding, it's ripe for parody, and the film's punishing length and tidal wave of smarmy codswallop have only helped it mature. A certified guilty pleasure.

8. 'If you deny me, FIE UPON YOUR LAW!'
As Shylock in William Shakespeare's *The Merchant of Venice* (US/Italy/Luxembourg/GB 2004, dir./scr. Michael Radford)

Radford's film is only really worth watching for Act IV, when Pacino's Shylock comes damn near greatness in the trial scene. The whole court is expecting a 'gentle answer', but one look at the Jew's scrunched, intransigent expression, his 'lodged hate', should warn them it isn't coming. He only wants his bond, his pound of flesh. 'It is mine.' Antonio, played with touching and tragic resignation by Jeremy Irons, is the only one who realizes there's no use arguing with him. But still they argue. Pacino's Shylock unleashes a hot contempt for the whole society that would buy him off and then mock him for accepting. He was born to conjure here with the word 'fie'.

7. 'Run at thunder, girl! Thunder can't hurt! Harmless noise! BULLSHIT! You deceitful old fuck! Altobello, you fuck!'
As Michael Corleone in *The Godfather, Part III* (US 1990, dir. Francis Coppola, scr. Coppola & Mario Puzo)

Michael's bizarre Lear-on-the-Heath-style breakdown, precipitated by some kind of minor stroke, might have had more force if it wasn't taking place in a rather poky Manhattan kitchen. It's a pretty wretched scene, actually – despite the famous 'Just when they thought I was out, they pull me back in!' line, referenced ad nauseam in *The Sopranos*. Still, Pacino gives Michael's free-associative ravings some serious welly, and his gaping agony as he slumps into a chair is obviously meant to foreshadow the silent screaming on the opera house steps at the end. Coppola's real touch too much? A clumsy jump-cut before Michael, still out of his mind, starts exclaiming 'Fredo! Fredo!' for good measure.

6. 'Attica! Attica!'
As Sonny in *Dog Day Afternoon* (US 1975, dir. Sidney Lumet, scr. Frank Pierson)

Probably the most famous scene in the movie, and an idea Pacino improvised out of thin air, repeatedly invoking the 1971 Attica, NY prison riots in which some thirty-nine inmates were shot dead by overzealous guards. The charge Sonny gives the crowd here is extraordinary. This has got to be one of Pacino's greatest performances – perhaps the greatest – because you never sense him retreating into solo showmanship. He's feeding off everything: the actors playing the cops, the onlookers, the whole hubbub. He makes Sonny's desperation heroic without it ever seeming staged or self-righteous. Shouty Al, at his combustible best, was born here.

5. 'I'm angry. I'm very angry, Ralph. You know, you can ball my wife if she wants you to. You can lounge around here on her . . . sofa, in her ex-husband's dead-tech, postmodernistic bullshit house if you want to. But you do not [slams TV] get to watch [slam!] MY . . . FUCKING TELEVISION SET!'

As Detective Vincent Hanna in *Heat* (US 1995, dir./scr. Michael Mann)

It's all in the slamming. Hanna might actually be Pacino's single angriest character, a man so ruthlessly dedicated to his job that he has watched everything else in his life curdle and collapse. His discovery that bitter wife Diane Venora has taken a new lover (Xander Berkeley) leads to this seething, cathartic outburst. Berkeley spends the scene looking as if he's trying to crawl down the gap between sofa cushions, as well he might. It's not even a very nice telly.

4. 'We claw with our fingernails for that inch, because we know, when we add up all those inches, that's gonna make the FUCKIN' difference between WINNIN' and LOSIN'! Between LIVIN' and DYIN'!'
As Tony D'Amato in *Any Given Sunday* (US 1999, dir. Oliver Stone, scr. Stone & John Logan)

The mother of all sports-movie pep talks, this is known to its fans as the 'Peace by Inches' speech, and it has Pacino impersonators across America posting their renditions on YouTube. A near five-minute motivational marathon to the post-rock crescendo of Paul Kelly's score, the scene starts with coach Pacino – sporting arguably the worst haircut of his life – sounding like an exhausted husk. 'I don't know what to say, really . . . I made every wrong choice a middle-aged man could make.' It has the feel of a practised slow-burn, a wheezy, intentionally laborious way of hauling his team's morale from the pit of despondency to the brink of victory.

3. 'I will not go down THAT WAY. I choose to FIGHT BAACK! I choose to RISE, not fall! I choose to LIVE, not die! And I know that what's within me is also WITHIN YOU!'
As Mayor John Pappas in *City Hall* (US 1996, dir. Harold Becker, scr. Ken Lipper, Paul Schrader, Nicholas Pileggi, Bo Goldman)

On paper at least, this funeral oration over a child's coffin is much the grisliest scene in Becker's watchable but overblown picture.

Sick buckets ought to be passed down the aisles to help grievers cope with the sheer gushiness of the Mayor's rhetoric – there's some guff about Pericles, and something else about the dead boy being 'as pure and as innocent as the driven snow . . .' Somehow, though, Pacino rescues it. He makes Pappas a pretentious preacher, a demagogue. There's a throwaway arrogance to the speech's build-up, as if he doesn't even respect the words he's uttering. And then watch him grab the crowd, conducting and channelling his anger through symmetrical hand movements, thrusting it at them. He turns an incredibly hokey monologue into performance art.

2. 'You never open your mouth until you know what the shot is. You fucking child.'
As Ricky Roma in *Glengarry Glen Ross* (US 1992, dir. James Foley, scr. David Mamet, from his play)

It's a wonder Kevin Spacey isn't stretchered off set whimpering after the demolition his milquetoast office manager suffers here. Pacino's Roma, his back to Spacey after he's blabbed a costly bit of information, lets his eyes flick right, then left. He turns. And, elaborately planting hands on hips to assume the stance of an alpha male confronting a gamma, he slowly lets rip. This fury is a contained, burning thing. He barely needs raise his voice – the shouting's all in his eyes, in the palpable heat coming off his face. Spacey has never before or since been so entirely dealt with, dismantled. The scene is perfectly capped by Jack Lemmon, leaning in the doorway after Pacino's exit ('You *are* a shithead, Williamson'), though Lemmon is in for a nasty surprise on that score.

1. 'He's laughing his SICK, FUCKING ASS off! He's a TIGHT-ASS! He's a SADIST! He's an ABSENTEE LANDLORD! Worship that? NEVER!'
As John Milton in *The Devil's Advocate* (US 1997, dir. Taylor Hackford, scr. Jonathan Lemkin & Tony Gilroy, from the novel by Andrew Neiderman)

This Satanic vaudeville is succulent, Parma-grade Pacino ham, the

Get the Look: The Ten Best Male Movie Outfits, p 127

standout scene in the single most entertaining performance of his
career. You'd barely know Keanu Reeves and Connie Nielsen were
in the same room as Pacino's Milton struts around his baroque, fire-
lit inner sanctum, spewing bile at God's very own 'private, cosmic
gag reel'. 'It's the goof of all time – look, but don't touch,' he carries
on, with an extraordinary, impish step backwards, licking his lips
and rubbing his fingers together. 'Touch – but don't taste!' Another
gleeful pause. 'Taste – but don't swallow . . .' And then he claps his
hands and laughs, shifting his weight from one foot to the other and
back as he works himself up into an apoplexy. Listen closer, and you
can almost hear choirboys being spit-roasted in the hearth.

Ten Bad Dates with De Niro

Lessons from Bobby in How *Not* to Treat a Lady

DEMETRIOS MATHEOU

Robert De Niro is exceptional amongst A-List movie stars, in that
he could never be thought of as a romantic lead. His characters
tend to live amongst men, often as gangsters, or alone, inside their
own heads. And when they try to love, they are clueless and cruel.
Watch De Niro try to kiss a woman – and it always looks like an
effort – in any of his movies: he fumbles, unsure, before hoover-
ing up their faces. It's not a pretty sight.

Sometimes I think this is wholly deliberate: De Niro is, after
all, a fabulous comedian. At the same time, it could well be that
a reticent man is attracted instinctively to characters with an
innate inability to connect. His smile says it all: creasing his
whole face, it denotes pleasure and pain simultaneously, as though
he has no idea, himself, what he's feeling.

That half of the scenes here involve Scorsese is of no surprise:
not just because of the quality of their collaborations, but because
together actor and director have so brilliantly essayed male inad-
equacy, especially in the domestic arena. The order is informed by
the extremes of violence, but also by how important the victim is,
supposedly, to De Niro's character. My top spot may seem occu-

pied by the least heinous act of all, but it reflects the essential iso-
lation that informs De Niro's monstrously bad boyfriends.

10. The courting of Betsy (Cybill Shepherd) in *Taxi Driver* (US
1976, dir. Martin Scorsese)

'I don't believe I've ever met anyone quite like you,' says posh and
proper campaign worker Betsy when first confronted with the
eccentric charm of Travis Bickle. Travis is in with a real chance
here, but blows it on their first date: a dirty movie double-bill is
hardly the most romantic option Manhattan has to offer. Betsy
gamely gives it a go, but lasts barely a minute into *Swedish
Marriage Manual*, before storming off. The disappointment probably lights the tinderbox in Travis, consequently left alone to ask
the mirror, 'Are you talking to me?'

9. The courting of Rita (Diahnne Abbott) in *The King of
Comedy* (US 1983, dir. Martin Scorsese)

'Rita. Every king needs a queen!' Sadly, for Rita, her would-be lord
and aspiring king of comedy is Rupert Pupkin. In reality a talentless
fantasist and celebrity stalker, Pupkin's self-delusion suckers Rita into
a second date at comedy legend Jerry Langford's summer house – only
Langford (Jerry Lewis) knows nothing about an invitation. 'Anybody
tell you you're a moron?' Langford asks the pest as he throws them
out. 'You know, Jerry, ordinarily I never allow anyone to speak that
way about Rita.' What a punch-line, adding insult to humiliation.

8. The marriage to Francine (Liza Minnelli) in *New York, New
York* (US 1977, dir. Martin Scorsese)

A big-band-era account of the disintegration of a showbiz marriage, this features the De Niro male at his most irksome. Sax
player Jimmy Doyle is brash, eccentric and self-centred, a clown
one moment, a cad the next; the film's unintentional mystery
being why on-the-rise singer Francine Evans (Liza Minnelli) puts
up with him for so long. 'Will you go away?' she asks, at their first
meeting. 'I don't want to,' he replies, 'I want to stay here and

annoy you.' And boy, he is very annoying. Avoiding the truism that wary fathers melt on first sight of their child, Jimmy doesn't even look at his newborn before walking. Typical.

7. The ill-use of Ada (Dominique Sanda) and others in *1900 / Novecento* (Italy/France/West Germany 1976, dir. Bernardo Bertolucci)

De Niro's Alfredo has a way with women: whether masturbating one with a rifle butt, and complaining that 'not even an elephant could make you come', or fleeing another's bed when she has an epileptic fit, without a backwards glance. Is it that the young landowner is really in love with his peasant chum Olmo (Gérard Depardieu)? Or is he simply too indolent and apathetic to care for anyone? His wife, the beautiful and compelling Ada, fares no better: enthusiastically courted, then neglected – sexually and emotionally – the moment she marries him. At least she has the good sense to abandon Alfredo to his rebellious workers.

6. The marriage to Caroline (Ellen Barkin) in *This Boy's Life* (US 1993, dir. Michael Caton-Jones)

It's the 1950s, when people still wait till their wedding night before sleeping together. This modesty proves disastrous for attractive divorcée Caroline Wolff, whose second husband – and hoped-for father figure for her tearaway son – is Dwight. A petty-minded loser whose constant retort is 'Shut your goddamn pie-hole', the awful Dwight's correctives for zero self-esteem are many and start, inauspiciously, in bed. 'I want to see your face,' suggests Caroline. 'Oh no, I don't like that way,' Dwight declares, 'I don't like to see the face.' 'You mean, never?' 'Look. You can get it doggy style or lying on your side. Those are your only choices. This is my house and I get to say. Got it?'

5. The beating of Vickie (Cathy Moriarty) in *Raging Bull* (US 1980, dir. Martin Scorsese)

Arguably De Niro's greatest performance, as real-life boxer Jake La Motta, also sees him at his most macho, brutish and tragicomic. Having won his coveted world title, La Motta's bloated ego has manifested itself in paranoia and a paunch. In the film's central sequence, an offhand comment by his brother Joey leads to the unstable boxer becoming convinced of in-house infidelity. 'Why did you fuck Joey?' he asks of Vickie, before breaking the door down and giving her a two-slap. 'Get off me, you fat pig,' she retorts defiantly. But after he's punched Joey into submission, Jake aims a championship jab at his wife and she's out for the count.

4. The killing of Melanie (Bridget Fonda) in *Jackie Brown* (US 1997, dir. Quentin Tarantino)

Louis and Melanie, ex-con and surfer girl, are sort of an item, hanging out together, stoned, while waiting on arms dealer Ordell to tell them what to do. Louis seems harmless, barely awake most of the time, accepting Melanie's offers of sex as casually as one would a cup of tea and a biscuit. But as soon as they commit a crime (or think they have) he loses his cool – and Melanie makes the mistake of taunting her lover. 'Loooisssh. Have you lost your car?' He warns her to be quiet. Melanie's next, only and last word has barely left her lips when Louis shoots her dead. 'See, just where I said it was.'

3. The rape and assault of Lori (Illeana Douglas) in *Cape Fear* (US 1991, dir. Martin Scorsese)

Max Cady has studied at the Hannibal Lecter school of seduction: why give a tender kiss on the cheek, when you can bite it off? The newly released rapist wants revenge on lawyer Sam Bowden (Nick Nolte). And he warms up, in the only way he knows, with the lawyer's work colleague Lori. Befriending her in a bar, Cady could not be more charming; once in the bedroom, the handcuffs come out, the killer smile segues to a grimace and the poor woman is beaten, mutilated and raped.

2. The rape of Deborah (Elizabeth McGovern) in *Once Upon a Time in America* (US 1984, dir. Sergio Leone)

Brooklyn gangster Noodles has a flaw worse than bootlegging, extortion and murder: he's a serial rapist. But surely he will treat the love of his life differently? It appears time for Noodles and Deborah to consummate a lifelong attraction. He hires an entire restaurant by the sea for them alone; musicians play; the night is magical. But Deborah announces that she intends to leave New York to pursue her acting career. In any case, she suggests, 'You'd lock me up and throw away the key.' Noodles shrugs. 'Yeah, I guess so.' As they are being driven back to Brooklyn she kisses him, out of love, with a promise for the future. But the sulking Noodles turns romance to assault and, despite her rending cries, rapes her. This is the most heartbreaking scene in any De Niro movie.

1. The abandonment of Edie (Amy Brenneman) in *Heat* (US 1995, dir. Michael Mann)

Having wooed this young, lonely graphic designer in the hills above the shimmering lights of LA, brooding bank robber Neil McCauley asks her, right now, to skip town with him for a new life. He seems ready, finally, to commit to a relationship. But can he? He's already hinted at the answer, over an impromptu coffee with the cop on his tail (Al Pacino). 'Don't let yourself get attached to anything you are not willing to walk out on in thirty seconds flat,' he intones, 'if you feel the heat around the corner.' A little later McCauley drives through the night, his lover beside him, 'home free'. But, imperceptibly rearranging the muscles of his face, De Niro moves from serenity to anger, pleasure, acceptance, resolve. 'I've got to take care of something,' he says, veering the car. And then he leaves her – open-mouthed, in shock – at what will moments later be his final crime scene.

They Could Have Been Contenders

Ten Great Performances by Frequently Derided Actors

DANNY LEIGH

In the course of a career certain actors come to represent an informal seal of quality for a project, a subtle guarantee of excellence. Others are less blessed. Instead, their fate is to become a byword for the ill conceived, their very presence in a cast enough for the eyes to skip ahead to the next title in the video shop. It may, in the final and most brutal analysis, be a lack of acting chops that does for them or, perhaps, an off-camera reputation so vivid it ends up overshadowing their talents. Either way, and however unjustly, their fate is to be scorned; to exist as a punch-line.

Yet the most unlikely figures often have at least one sublime performance inside them. Occasionally it comes at the outset of a career, before the tabloids and turkeys. Sometimes, it's a casting masterstroke later down the line that provides a clear view of a long-forgotten (or hitherto un-glimpsed) talent. Either way, there's something particularly heart-warming about it when it happens. Here are what I hope are the most unexpected examples, and thus the most oddly inspiring.

10. Oliver Reed as Bill Sykes in *Oliver!* (GB 1968, dir. Carol Reed)

By the time of his death in 1999, such was Reed's status as Great British Inebriate that it's easy to imagine the younger (or more forgetful) among those chuckling at his latest soused TV appearance only having the vaguest idea what had made him famous in the first place. After all, although fellow carouser George Best had at least secured a European Cup before lurching into retirement, Reed's acting career had always seemed (to him more than anyone) an adjunct to his drinking. Yet for all that, there was always a fine actor behind the debauchery – and while some may claim his role opposite (and underneath, and on top of) Alan Bates in Ken Russell's *Women in Love* (1969) as the pinnacle, it's perhaps in the much-loved Dickensian musical *Oliver!* that we see him at his swaggering best. Cast as the thuggish Sykes, Reed could have simply delivered a display of panto hammery before striding off to the pub, but instead – maybe through familial loyalty to the director, his uncle Carol Reed – opened a rich vein of glowering menace, the result a bristling portrait of a fist of a man that lent the film as a whole an invaluable realism.

9. Melanie Griffith in *Body Double* (US 1984, dir. Brian De Palma)

Another inspired performance from another actor undone less by any lack of talent than by a very tabloid-friendly personal life. Now seemingly a long-term victim of the famed lack of roles available to older women, Griffith's gifts have become obscured by a propensity for the eccentric off-screen; there was, however, a point at which a stellar career seemed all but inevitable. Between her debut in Arthur Penn's fine 1975 thriller *Night Moves* and her commercial zenith in 1988's *Working Girl*, Griffith was cast by Brian De Palma in his glassy thriller *Body Double* (her presence perhaps the ultimate accessory for a director so famously Hitchcock-fixated, given that her mother is Tippi Hedren). Griffith's role as the adult movie star Holly Body in De Palma's porno-*Vertigo* was, on paper, little more than a stack of clichés, and yet Griffith invests the character with genuine poignancy, her Monroe breathiness giving voice to both jaded pragmatism and touching artlessness.

8. Adam Sandler as Barry Egan in *Punch Drunk Love* (US 2002, dir. Paul Thomas Anderson)

The road to Hollywood from comedy institution *Saturday Night Live* has been well-travelled ever since John Belushi stuffed his cheeks with mashed potato in *Animal House* (1978). It has, however, rarely brought those trekking down it much in the way of respect – not least Adam Sandler, whose tightly wound, boorishly sardonic everyman (typically dumped by a girlfriend inside ten minutes of the credits) featured in a slew of critically reviled comedies throughout the 1990s. The spirit of full disclosure demands I admit a fondness for several of these – but even without any such a bias, it would take a churl not to acknowledge the brilliance of Sandler's performance in *Punch Drunk Love*. Tweaking the salient features of his stock character – cranking up the stifled rage and self-loathing, losing the wisecracking –

Sandler entered the soul of Barry Egan, an epically repressed salesman of novelty bathroom accessories whose moment-to-moment
existence teeters on the point of collapse throughout the film,
only saved by the prospect of a romance with the winsome Emily
Watson. 'Your face is so beautiful I wanna smash it with a sledge-
hammer,' he announces – and, at that exact point in time, no
sweeter declaration of love could you ever imagine.

7. David Bowie in *Merry Christmas Mr Lawrence / Furyo* (GB
1983, dir. Nagisa Oshima)

Perhaps the most derided actor here – which, on a list including
Robin Williams and Sylvester Stallone – is no small feat.
Somehow, it's as if every atom of credibility that Bowie ever
accrued as a musician vaporizes the second he appears on-screen,
his chilly artifice seeming, oddly, forever out of place on film, the
most artificial medium of them all. And yet there have, here and
there, been diverting performances: a brief cameo in *Twin Peaks:
Fire Walk With Me* (1992), for instance, that (while objectively
terrible) enhanced the film's deeply unhinged mood; and here, in
Oshima's account of a battle of wills in a Japanese prisoner-of-war
camp, circa 1942. Called upon to play the brittle and headstrong
British officer Jack Celliers, Bowie's turn vindicated the decision
to cast him (one evidently made in the confidence that his diffident charisma would for once suit the character), and was also
tribute to his own perseverance. So often guilty of misjudging all
sense of tone in his movie appearances, here Bowie was just a cog
in a greater whole, and much the better for it.

6. Jerry Lewis in *The King of Comedy* (US 1983, dir. Martin
Scorsese)

By the early 1980s, the frantic shtick of Jerry Lewis had turned
radioactive. Eisenhower-era America's unrivalled clown prince, a
new generation had long since decreed him an unwanted throwback, his belligerent zaniness and damp-eyed mugging for charity
telethons laughable in only the worst sense of the word. So what
better time to deliver a dramatic performance of astonishing power

and clarity? The chance came with *The King of Comedy*, a black-hearted, oracular dissection of celebrity culture before it even had a name, in which De Niro's monstrous would-be comic Rupert Pupkin stalks and then kidnaps his idol, chat show host Jerry Langford – essayed to sour perfection by Lewis (cast only after the role was turned down by, among others, his estranged former partner Dean Martin). His jowly features set in a rictus of displeasure, the role of Langford finally gave us a Lewis who seemed authentic, plausible, a man for whom comedy was nothing but a chore.

5. Mickey Rourke as Jim Olstad in *The Pledge* (US 2001, dir. Sean Penn)

It seems unreasonable for the sins of an entire decade to be visited on one man – but after the 1980s finally staggered to a conclusion, Mickey Rourke came to embody in the public mind all that was ludicrous about the era just passed. Driven ever deeper into weird semi-notoriety as his star faded (an undefeated stint as a professional boxer, a surfeit of cosmetic surgery, a detour into 'erotic thrillers'), it was with an air of out-of-the-wilderness authenticity that Rourke returned to something approaching active service at the end of the 1990s – and it was in *The Pledge*, Sean Penn's drama of obsession and regret, that Rourke delivered the most startling performance of his comeback. On paper merely a fleeting cameo, Rourke appears as the janitor father of a murdered eight-year-old girl whose killer is being pursued by Jack Nicholson's retired cop. Enjoying a smoke in his cupboard office, Olstad/Rourke is, at first, a mask of cool detachment, the Motorcycle Boy of *Rumble Fish* in greying adulthood – but then, in a blink, he crumples at a sudden rush of memories, overcome by tears and bone-deep grief as he tries to explain what his daughter meant to him. Running just ninety seconds from beginning to end, the scene is an astonishing howl of pain – and a glimpse of what might have been had infamy not got in the way.

4. Terence Stamp in *The Limey* (US 1999, dir. Steven Soderbergh)

Sometimes an actor's very limitations suit a movie so perfectly that each of them prospers from the association. So it proved with the casting of Stamp in Soderbergh's nimble revenge thriller, wherein he stars as Wilson, a trimly middle-aged ex-con newly arrived in LA from London to investigate his daughter's death. An instantly recognizable presence since his emergence in Peter Ustinov's *Billy Budd* (1963), thanks to his glacial good looks and unknowable demeanour, Stamp came to find those same traits something of a straitjacket, as he drifted from film to film playing Manhattan art dealers, Sicilian princes and General Zod (nemesis of Superman), but always, ultimately, playing Stamp. Yet in Soderbergh's likeable concoction, the role of Wilson seemed as exquisitely tailored as if it had been designed on Savile Row, his deadpan suavity and cold-eyed stoicism playing to all of Stamp's strengths while also allowing him the sly pleasure of relentlessly using rhyming slang around a string of befuddled Americans.

3. Robin Williams in *The Fisher King* (US 1991, dir. Terry Gilliam)

To leaf, flinching, through the filmography of Robin Williams is to invite kinship with Brando's Colonel Kurtz in *Apocalypse Now*, staring into the abyss and softly whispering: 'The horror . . . the horror.' But it's not simply bad taste in scripts that has led to Williams appearing in so many clunkers; truth be told, his own pathological gurning and free associating is part of what makes them so hard to embrace. As such, Williams working with a director like Gilliam – so possessed by the baroque – should have yielded nothing but a migraine. Oddly, however, the two men find a hugely fruitful equilibrium. Cast as homeless savant Parry, driven into madness by tragedy and now determined to retrieve the Holy Grail from a townhouse on New York's Upper East Side, Williams suddenly has a context and dramatic heft for his mania, while Gilliam's boundless imagination ensures the film is big enough to also hold that of his star. Some readers will inevitably prefer Williams's more restrained turns in *Dead Poets Society* or *Good Will Hunting* but, for me at least, those performances work only because they deny Williams his real identity – only in *The Fisher*

King has a film succeeded because of, and not despite, its essential Williamsness.

2. Madonna in *Desperately Seeking Susan* (US 1985, dir. Susan Seidelman)

A case study in unfulfilled ambition, Madonna's twenty years of trying to parlay her mega-stardom into movie stardom have brought out little in those observing other than mean spirits. And yet it all started so well, and with such serendipity – a casting made on the cusp of her musical fame, in a low-budget comedy poised between sweet-natured sass and the trashy tang of its location in pre-gentrification Manhattan. Starring as free spirit Susan (genuinely selfish enough not to be 'kooky'), Madonna brought an inscrutable charm to every scene she appeared in, perfectly offsetting co-star Rosanna Arquette's good-girl transparency in this yarn of mistaken identity. Drying her armpits under the hand-dryer of a nightclub toilet she was, briefly, the most alluring woman on earth. By the time the film was released in 1985, it benefited immeasurably from its star having broken big as a singer in the interim – sadly, it was downhill from then on for her film career, but at least she, and we, would always have Susan.

1. Sylvester Stallone in *Cop Land* (US 1997, dir. James Mangold)

Something of the last resort hung about the involvement of Stallone in James Mangold's deftly low-key *Cop Land*. Stallone's most successful alter-ego Rocky Balboa had, by the late 1990s, been mothballed for almost a decade; in his place, while Bruce Willis and John Travolta re-invented themselves under the direction of Quentin Tarantino, Stallone had instead bumbled in car-go-boom blockbusters and a couple of notably ill-advised comedies. But if the whiff of opportunism marked Stallone's conversion to indie cinema, his performance was revelatory. The role was Freddy Heflin, the hard-of-hearing sheriff of a dormitory town for New York cops and their families; cops who openly

regard him as a sap. And Freddy, for his part, takes their conde-
scension without complaint – until he stumbles upon his heroes'
involvement in a tangle of corruption and murder. With Stallone
appearing opposite the likes of Harvey Keitel and Robert De
Niro, the film should have presented the cruel spectacle of an
elephant dancing among ballerinas – instead, it was Stallone's
wounded pathos and gravity that gave this darkly cynical picture
its heart, the fact he never appeared in anything like it again
only adding to the novelty.

Maestros Who Got into Make-Up

Ten Directors Who Acted, with Honour

RYAN GILBEY

I seek out acting performances by directors in the same way that
I scrutinize author photos on book jackets. It's the Wizard of Oz
factor – the curtain tugged back to reveal that the mighty Oz is
just a mortal like us. Except that film directors who act have submitted willingly to the exposure – they want us to see them
revealed more nakedly than ever before. Here a note of
masochism is introduced, especially when the director is clearly
shy or ill-at-ease (cf. Mike Nichols, below).

Not that the performance is always a revelation. One director
narrowly excluded from this list, David Cronenberg, has played
leads in *Nightbreed* and *Last Night*, and numerous cameos in films
including *Extreme Measures* and *To Die For* (he's the hit man sent
to kill Nicole Kidman). But as an actor he is muted, measured,
almost shockingly normal: letting slip nothing of the tempera-
ment that wrote and directed *Shivers* aka *Orgy of the Blood
Parasites* (1975).

Usually, though, directors acting is like when the teachers
you've feared all year suddenly put themselves in the stocks at the
school fete, there to be pelted with wet sponges: a sensation that
may be explained by the high proportion of directors in this list
appearing as tyrants or bullies, as if toying with the popular image

of the megalomaniac brandishing a riding crop and loudhailer.
Why do they do it? Is it an act of penance for having made so
many actors suffer? Or is it the control-freak sensibility in full
bloom, needing to be not just puppet-master but puppet too? I
don't care as long as I can watch.

Film-makers sometimes insert into the cast other directors
who have influenced them, as a kind of inbuilt homage; thus
Wim Wenders cast Nicholas Ray in *The American Friend* (see
below) alongside Sam Fuller and Jean Eustache, while Jean-Luc
Godard persuaded Fritz Lang to play himself in *Le Mépris*.
Cameron Crowe narrowly failed to get Billy Wilder to play Tom
Cruise's mentor in *Jerry Maguire*. Steven Spielberg gave some
viewers their first and only taste of François Truffaut by directing him in *Close Encounters of the Third Kind*, and Jonathan
Demme pays regular tribute to his own former boss and benefac-
tor, Roger Corman, by giving him minor parts. Demme also
accommodated some adorable director-cameos in his *Something
Wild* (1987) – John Waters as a crooked car salesman, John
Sayles as a macho motorcycle cop. But my favourite Sayles performance is as the man who sacks Dolly Parton from her job as
a dance teacher in the glorious *Straight Talk*. Am I allowed to say
that I like Sayles in that brief appearance more than I like most
of his films?

Martin Scorsese, as the toxic back-seat racist in *Taxi Driver*, was
disqualified from consideration here, as were any other directors
who (rather cockily) cast themselves in their own films. All of the
following are fully fledged performances rather than walk-ons,
with one exception – Gus Van Sant, in a cameo that says more
about this director's fleeting, mid-career sell-out than any amount
of scathing broadsides.

10. Nicholas Ray in *Der Amerikanische Freund / The American
Friend* (West Germany 1977, dir. Wim Wenders)

Wenders engineered a touching reunion here for Ray and Dennis
Hopper, who worked together on *Rebel Without a Cause* more
than twenty years earlier. A clearly exhausted Ray is Derwatt, an

exiled artist in an eye-patch, who jabs his finger, spins weirdly in his chair and utters cryptic messages like 'Close the doors and they'll come in through the windows.' Two years later, Wenders and Ray co-directed *Lightning Over Water*, a documentary shot virtually from the latter's deathbed.

9. Barbet Schroeder in *Céline et Julie vont en bateau / Celine and Julie Go Boating* (France 1974, dir. Jacques Rivette)

I didn't see Rivette's time-hopping fantasy until after Schroeder's perverse little comedies like *Maîtresse* and *Single White Female* (those films make me think he could have been a soul-mate to Almodóvar with a little more luck and wisdom). But in his turn as the powder-faced figure overseeing the attempted murder of a child, he looked every bit as sinister and depraved as his own work suggested he would. He's an occasional Rivette collaborator, from the mammoth *Out 1: Spectre* all the way to *Don't Touch the Axe*.

8. Pier Paolo Pasolini in *Requiescant*, aka *Kill or Pray* (Italy 1966, dir. Carlo Lizzani)

Pasolini turns up sporadically as a priest-cum-freedom fighter in this curious Marxist western, but he's here more for the symbolism of his casting than for his acting abilities. Not that he doesn't cut the mustard – he brings gravitas to the most functional line of dialogue, and seems to relish his final speech to the vengeful, trigger-happy hero whom he wants to recruit for the peasant cause. 'It pleased you to kill, didn't it?' he asks after the protagonist has slaughtered the villain. 'You had fun, like a little boy with a fly.' Worth seeking out for a glimpse of those classic Pasolini cheekbones, which could slice a loaf of bread.

7. Gus Van Sant in *Jay and Silent Bob Strike Back* (US 2001, dir. Kevin Smith)

Something went wrong with Van Sant in the late 1990s. Sandwiching his most boldly experimental work – the frame-for-frame *Psycho* remake – were two unspeakably banal tales of educational excellence against the odds, *Good Will Hunting*, which gave him his first taste of official commendation, and *Finding Forrester*. But in his cameo in Kevin Smith's ragbag comedy, he shows some flair for irony and self-deprecation. He plays himself, holed up on the brazenly commercial endeavour, *Good Will Hunting 2: Hunting Season*, but too busy counting his money to give Ben Affleck the most basic direction (which explains a lot about Van Sant, Affleck and *Good Will Hunting*).

6. Mark Rydell in *The Long Goodbye* (US 1973, dir. Robert Altman)

This director is poison behind the camera and dynamite in front of it. As the ghoulish kingpin Marty Augustine in Altman's jazzy Chandler adaptation, he does some twisted things. He forces everyone in the room, henchmen included, to strip down to their underwear, which is pretty gay. (You get to see a young Arnold Schwarzenegger in his knickers.) And he breaks a Coke bottle in his girlfriend's face just to scare the bejeesus out of Elliott Gould. That miniature portrait of magnificent barbarity was almost as painful as the experience of watching Rydell's own films – *For the Boys*, say, or *On Golden Pond*.

5. Erich von Stroheim in *La Grande Illusion* (France 1937, dir. Jean Renoir)

He is probably prized more as the butler in *Sunset Boulevard*, but von Stroheim's Von Rauffenstein, a real good egg, is crucial to the compassion of Renoir's wartime masterpiece. Kindness from movie characters whom experience tells you ought to be mean always makes me sob. So the first meeting between Von Rauffenstein and the French prisoners of war is upsetting enough. 'What a lovely fellow,' I found myself thinking. 'If I ever become a POW, here's hoping . . .' Well, you can see where that's going. And if I'm ever shot during my escape attempt, and comforted on my deathbed by the man responsible, I hope he's the spit of von Stroheim, right down to the monocle and neck-brace.

4. Mike Nichols in *The Designated Mourner* (US 1997, dir. David Hare)

Meryl Streep once told me (if only all sentences could begin that way!) that Nichols felt so awkward and humble about acting in this film of Wallace Shawn's play that he did everything he could to obstruct his friends' attempts to see it. 'But isn't he marvellous in it?' she cooed. Yes, he is. He had already played Jack – a philistine who watches as society is stripped of all traces of art and intellect – on stage in London, and the movie is just a filmed play, three actors sitting behind a table for the duration. But that 'just' is misleading. Nichols is variously arrogant, serene, maddening and heartbreaking. I'd watch him here over any of the films he has directed.

3. John Huston in *Chinatown* (US 1974, dir. Roman Polanski)

All hope of goodness, mercy and humanity are extinguished in Noah Cross from the moment we meet him, yet the sordid magic of Huston's performance lies in the way he lets this rankness float on the smooth surface of the character like scum. That, and the way he insists on pronouncing J.J. Gittes's surname as 'Gits', as though a fragment of English vernacular has strayed into his sunny Californian vocabulary. Also, when you look at him, and this is a terrible thing to say, he makes you believe that he really has had sex with his daughter.

2. Werner Herzog in *Julien Donkey-Boy* (US 1999, dir. Harmony Korine)

Ewen Bremner put in some real donkeywork in the lead, but the wonder of Herzog's performance is that it appears to require no effort whatsoever; insanity seeps out of his pores as naturally as sweat. Whether hosing down his son while exhorting him to 'Quit that moody brooding!', leaping in one swift movement to a standing position from lying down, or holding court on the subject of talking birds – he upstages casually not only his co-stars but the entire film. Two special moments of genius: Herzog barking at

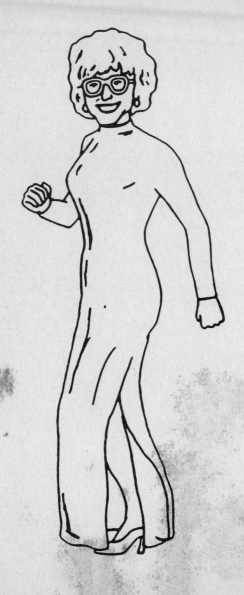

I Feel Pretty: Ten Great Thespian Turns in Drag, p 131

Bremner, 'If I were so stupid, I would slap my own face'; and the dinner table scene in which he interrupts Bremner's poem ('I don't like that artsy-fartsy stuff') to describe, in a tone of sober derangement, the ending of *Dirty Harry*. It makes you want to hear him describe every key scene in cinema history.

1. Sydney Pollack in *Husbands and Wives* (US 1992, dir. Woody Allen)

One of cinema's most sore and sour double-acts is Pollack and Judy Davis as the recently separated couple who remain palpably in each other's hair. With his big stupid coat and clunky glasses and enormous face, Pollack blunders around the screen being oafish and beastly, like a panicked ogre. But he's still achingly human. It's typical Woody Allen to write a middle-aged man who falls for an astrology-obsessed aerobics teacher, and to undermine that relationship in the script. But Pollack makes us feel that it's real, from his initial rhapsodizing about this new squeeze to the horrific scene in which he drags her, kicking and screaming, from the party at which she has embarrassed him by failing to be intellectual.

O Brothers, Here Art Thou

The Coen Bros' Ten Most Memorable Minor Characters

JAMES MOTTRAM

Nestling somewhere above a cameo but below a substantial supporting role, the 'minor character' is a function that Joel and Ethan Coen have turned into a fine art. In the Coens' hands these aren't merely serviceable figures to help shift the plot along, but fully rounded gems that reflect the distinctive tone and texture of the sibling duo's celluloid universe. Frankly, this list could have been compiled from *The Big Lebowski* alone, with its castration-threatening nihilists, 'vaginal' artists, pornographers and iron-lung-dwelling TV writers. But in cherry-picking the best from across the Coens' entire *oeuvre*, judging each on its ability to make a dramatic impression in just a handful of

scenes, one realizes that these fiercely inventive film-makers have
been playing this game ever since their debut feature.

10. Wheezy Joe (Irwin Keyes) in Intolerable Cruelty (2003)

Even in this, their least idiosyncratic effort, the Coens manage to
conjure up a deliciously off-kilter character. In what is a classic
set-up, anticipation in the audience is built by the way of meeting
an asthma-suffering assassin by the name of 'Wheezy Joe', hired by
divorce lawyer Miles to bump off the duplicitous gold-digger
Marylin. But after receiving a faceful of mace from his employer
(now desperate to stop the hit), Joe starts wheezing and, in the
confusion, pops his gun in his mouth and points his inhaler at
Miles. Full marks for execution.

9. Buzz (Jim True-Frost) in The Hudsucker Proxy (1994)

'The name is Buzz, I got the fuzz . . . I make the elevator do what she
duzz!' Lift operator at Hudsucker Industries, the crew-cut-sporting
Buzz is another in a longline of fast-talking pip-squeaks in the world
of the Coens, rhyming his way from floor to floor like a screwball
comedy cousin to Barton Fink bellhop Chet. Yet, employed in a building dominated by a clock tower, Buzz proves to be an intricate cog in
the works after he designs a prototype drinking straw called the 'Buzz-
Sucker' and becomes an unwitting pawn in Hudsucker chief Sidney
J. Mussberger's plot to bring down hick hero Norville Barnes.

8. George 'Babyface' Nelson (Michael Badalucco) in O Brother, Where Art Thou? (1999)

While the Coens had previously drawn from reality – left-wing
playwright Clifford Odets inspired Barton Fink – this was the first
time they featured a true-life person. That said, their take on this
original gangster was more myth than anything, perpetuating the
apocryphal story that Nelson hated his derogatory nickname while
adding for good measure a morbid dislike of cows. Joining the likes
of Mickey Rooney and Richard Dreyfuss as actors who have played
the psychopathic Babyface, Badalucco's rocket-fuelled performance

echoes Nelson's prediction that he's 'gonna go off like a Roman candle' when he reaches the electric chair.

7. Mink (Steve Buscemi) in *Miller's Crossing* (1990)

Cast because he could read the lines faster than any other actor, Buscemi here makes his debut for the Coens. You have to stay alert, though, because he appears on screen for a total of only 52 seconds. It feels far longer: partly because his weasel-like character Mink is integral to the rumpus at the core of this gangster classic but mainly because Buscemi speaks like he's try-ing to shoehorn five scenes into one. Spraying out words as if he had a tommy-gun lodged in his throat, he turns Mink into the quintessential Coen motormouth.

6. Leonard Smalls (Randall Tex Cobb) in *Raising Arizona* (1987)

Like the grenades on his jacket that ultimately cause his untimely demise, this *Mad Max*-inspired 'lone biker of the Apocalypse' lands in the Coens' madcap sophomore film with an explosive force. He even blows up a bunny upon his arrival, so it's easy to see why this 'warthog from hell', hired by furniture magnate Nathan Arizona to retrieve his stolen child from kidnappers Nicolas Cage and Holly Hunter, has a tattoo that reads 'Mama Didn't Love Me'. In reality, former boxer Cobb, reputedly very difficult to work with, couldn't even ride a bike, but he was evidently well cast: Joel Coen called him 'less an actor than a force of nature'.

5. Freddy Riedenschneider (Tony Shalhoub) in *The Man Who Wasn't There* (2001)

Granted, this may be a re-run of Shalhoub's rapid-patter Capitol Pictures producer from *Barton Fink*, but arriving in a film where the laconic central character, 1950s barber Ed Crane, speaks less than an under-oath monk, the effect is spellbinding. The sort of defence lawyer you'd want if you were facing the electric chair for murder – 'I litigate,' he says, 'I don't capitulate' – Riedenschneider talks as much as he eats in his brief scenes. Evidencing the Coens' ability to write dialogue where not one syllable is wasted, Shalhoub barely draws breath throughout.

4. Brandt (Philip Seymour Hoffman) in *The Big Lebowski* (1998)

Forget *Capote*, Hoffman's finest hour came for the Coens, as the smarmy Smithers-like flunky to the titular tycoon. A perfect reminder of every pain-in-the-ass PA you've ever met, Brandt is a man of sweaty palms and obsequious gestures: when we first meet him he 'has his hands clasped in front of his groin' says the script. The tone is set as he enthusiastically shows The Dude (Jeff Bridges) around his employer's lair, patriotically pointing out a framed picture of the Big Lebowski and Nancy Reagan, 'the first lady of the nation, yes, yes?'

3. Jack Lipnick (Michael Lerner) in *Barton Fink* (1991)

Head of Capitol Pictures, the company that locks the eponymous left-wing playwright into writing a Wallace Beery wrestling picture, Lipnick is an epitome of old-school Hollywood. Brilliantly channelled through veteran actor Lerner, as he tells his new recruit to give him 'that *Barton Fink* feeling', Lipnick is an amalgam of Jack Warner's boorishness, the girth of MGM's Louis B. Meyer and the crudity of Columbia's Harry Cohn. 'Bigger and meaner than any other kike in this town,' as he delicately phrases it, when he's not lounging by his pool Lipnick even dresses like Warner in his military uniform.

2. Visser (M. Emmet Walsh) in *Blood Simple* (1984)

Heaven knows what rock he came out from under, but this Texan private eye is the most repellent of all Coen characters, slithering his way through their debut feature like a slug leaving a trail of slime across your patio. By his own admission, Visser belongs on all fours. 'Gimme a call whenever you wanna cut off my head,' he tells his paymaster, a cuckolded husband who has been muttering darkly about killing the messenger. 'I can crawl around without it.' Even his name has a reptilian hiss to it, while his car is an aptly chosen

VW bug. His eventual fate, to be skewered to a windowsill with a knife like an insect pinned to a board, is fitting to say the least.

1. Jesus Quintana (John Turturro) in *The Big Lebowski* (1998)

Never mind Robert De Niro's bar-room bow in *Mean Streets* – how about arriving to the sound of the Gypsy Kings' version of 'Hotel California', in an all-in-one purple polyester tunic, no less? Our introduction to Turturro's hot-shot bowler is arguably the finest entrance scene in American cinema. Ritualistically licking the ball before rolling, Quintana – a convicted pederast, we're told – not only destroys all-comers on the lanes, but all other Coen creations. Like he says, 'Nobody fucks with the Jesus.' The role was written especially for Turturro after the brothers saw him play a Hispanic on stage. And he rolls a perfect strike.

6

What *Are* You Wearing?

Wardrobe, Cosmetics and Personal Style

Get the Look

The Ten Best Male Movie Outfits

CHRISTOPHER BRAY

'Do we look the way we are?' Miss Jean Brodie asks her crème de la crème girls. 'Or are we the way we look?' Who knows? Doubt is one of life's keystones, and it would take sharper eyes than mine – even Kant's or Schopenhauer's or Wittgenstein's – to demarcate phenomenon from noumenon. The movies, less given to abstract thought, have no such reservations. Appearance, they teach us over and over again, is destiny. Only look like X, and Y shall be your fate. Such certainties cannot but reassure (if only for the duration of the movie). Out of that reassurance grows romance: if I looked like X, I could do that. Which is a way of saying that in a cinema the guys and gals up there on the screen aren't the only ones doing the acting. There is just as much pretending going on down in the auditorium. Like the performers we pay to watch, we go to the movies to become other people. And it may be that the fantasies last longer for us than for those who make their living by them.

10. Sean Connery as James Bond in *Dr No* (GB 1962, dir. Guy Hamilton)

Thirty-five years since first seeing *Dr No*, for instance, I am still hoping that I will one day look as good in a tuxedo and dress shirt as Connery does in that picture. Yet he is the best part of a head taller than I am, and considerably leaner, so there is no question that the rounded shawl-collar his tuxedo boasts would do nothing for me. Nor would the skinny, straight-across-the-neck bow-tie he favours grant me any. Thankfully, anyone can get away with a cocktail cuff (the turned-back but still flyaway grace note to the sleeve that Messrs Turnbull & Asser recommended Mr Bond sport). And for several years I have.

9. Jeff Bridges as Jack Baker in *The Fabulous Baker Boys* (US 1989, dir. Steve Kloves)

No such decadence about the evening clothes Bridges wears for a goodly part of this picture. Threadbare, moth-eaten and likely dandruff-dusted, this tux-and-tie just might have seen better days. Then again, like the Baker Boy himself, they might not. For clothes really do maketh the man here, and Bridges's achievement in the movie (as so often) is to make us dream about being less than we already are. This downward mobility reached what we ought perhaps call its nadir (but may think of as its zenith) in *The Big Lebowski*, wherein Bridges contrives to look good in tatty Ts and track pants. In front of a pony-tail and behind some ZZ Top face-fuzz. And with a Bud belly to boot!

8. Marlon Brando as Stanley Kowalski in *A Streetcar Named Desire* (US 1951, dir. Elia Kazan)

All such dressing down has its origins in the bowling gear and labourer's kit Brando wore here. After *Streetcar* I doubt that any serious actor has begun work on any performance without feeling the weight of Brando's example on their shoulders. Indeed, the fact that so many of those shoulders are muscled and oiled and precision-sculpted is down to his example. Little wonder the cap-sleeved, spray-on undershirt he sloughs off in his first scene in the picture made fashionable an item of clothing that had been in the doldrums since Clark Gable appeared vestless in *It Happened One Night* two decades earlier. Nor that even the most bookish guy has fantasized about having a body like the young Brando.

7. Robert De Niro as Jake La Motta in *Raging Bull* (US 1980, dir. Martin Scorsese)

One way of reading *Raging Bull* is to see the picture as De Niro's homage to the early Brando. *The Godfather, Part II* had given Bobby the chance to show he could imitate the master so well Brando might no longer be number one. But as Jake La Motta, De Niro was licensed to strut the *Streetcar* stuff – even wearing one

garment less than Brando's Stanley. Despite the pasta and pista-
chio pounds he piled on for the movie's closing sections, the over-
riding memory of De Niro in *Raging Bull* is of a Renaissance Christ
(wearing silk trunks in place of a loincloth) with a body ripped to
perfection and a soul being torn to pieces: you wouldn't want to
be him, but boy would you like to look like him.

6. Jude Law as Dickie Greenleaf in *The Talented Mr Ripley* (US
1999, dir. Anthony Minghella)

Alas, the results of Brando's influence have not always been so
happy. Not the least of the absurdities of Matt Damon's performance as Tom Ripley is his pumped and preened physique. Patricia
Highsmith's Tom never rippled like that. How much better the
movie would have been had Jude Law played the lead – though
then we wouldn't have got to see Jude sashay around southern
Italy in a litany of linens, each entry suppler and softer than that
last. The pork-pie hat he wears to sing 'Americano' may, as
Anthony Lane pointed out at the time of the film's release, be a
steal from the cover of Sinatra's *Come Fly With Me*, but that
detracts nothing from its rakish insouciance. Indeed, it reassures
would-be dandies that dandies proper borrow from one another,
too.

5. Alain Delon as Jef Costello in *Le Samourai* (France/Italy
1967, dir. Jean-Pierre Melville)

Where, after all, would the Delon of *Le Samourai* be without
Bogart's example? Sans his overcoat and fedora, most likely (as
would the wartime heroes of Melville's *L'Armée des Ombres*,
most of whom anachronistically sport that stylized armour, too).
Yet there is no denying that Delon, blade-thin and angular as a
cubist cut-up, takes the trench coat look to new heights of elegance. Square of shoulder and cinched of waist, he would look
like a noir abstraction were it not for the arc of his raised collar,
the weighty curve of his Borsalino brim. The world would be a
better place, one often thinks, if everyone went to the movies
dressed like this.

4. Humphrey Bogart as Harry 'Steve' Morgan in *To Have and Have Not* (US 1944, dir. Howard Hawks)

Bogie himself was never much of a clothes-horse. In *The Maltese Falcon* John Huston had him wear a boxy double-breasted pin-stripe number that, by broadening his beam, contrived to make a less-than-tall actor seem shorter still. The white tux he wears as the host of Rick's in *Casablanca* is cut a treat, but it sits uneasy on the shoulders of so instinctively insolent a star. Which is why his sole outfit in *To Have and Have Not* – baggy, off-white, duck can-vas khakis, long-gauge blazer, open-necked shirt and jauntily set peaked cap – makes for the only Bogart look that counts: a styl-ized slovenliness that would look ragged were it not so relaxed, so certain that there is no other way to be.

3. Marcello Mastroianni as Guido Anselmi in *Otto e Mezzo* / 8 1/2 (Italy 1963, dir. Federico Fellini)

Such bravado is in evidence, too, in the Mastroianni of *Otto e Mezzo*. Battered of hat, crumpled of shirt, and draped in a suit (Armani? Cerruti?) a size too big for him, he ought to look like a down-and-out as he drudges through Fellini's dreamscape. In fact, he looks like part of the dream, a man utterly at ease in a world whose rules he doesn't so much ignore as refuse to acknowledge. Certainly nobody in the history of movies has worn old man's braces as well as Mastroianni's troubled movie-maker, nobody hung an overcoat from his forearm with such penetrating languor.

2. Johnny Depp as Captain Jack Sparrow in *Pirates of the Caribbean: The Curse of the Black Pearl* (US 2003, dir. Gore Verbinski)

But I'm not sure even Marcello could have got away with looking like the Depp of the *Pirates* pictures. This dreadlocked tatterde-malion is an affront to pretty much every contemporary hygiene regulation, yet such is the raffish camp of Depp's creation that one would join the great unwashed at the drop of a tricorn hat. Puff-sleeved and frock-coated, Jack Sparrow may not have a look that many of us could borrow, but it is always pleasant to spend time in the company of people who seem relaxed in their own skin.

1. Cary Grant as Roger Thornhill in *North by Northwest* (US 1959, dir. Alfred Hitchcock)

Note the word 'seem' above. As the man himself once pointed out, 'Everybody wants to be Cary Grant. Even I want to be Cary Grant.' Twenty years since his death, everybody still feels the same way. Certainly an awful lot of people I know would give an awful lot for the suit Grant wears in *North by Northwest*. It was made for him by Kilgour of Savile Row, and I have it on authority from one of their cutters that the reason so many men adore this suit is simply because it fits Grant so tightly. There isn't any give in it – not enough to survive a day in our air-conned office, let alone a day involving several rounds of fisticuffs and flight from the unwanted attentions of a machine-gun-firing crop-dusting plane. Still, no matter what it is put through, this suit comes out looking dandy. Truly, they don't make 'em like that any more.

I Feel Pretty

Ten Great Thespian Turns in Drag

RYAN GILBEY

The pleasures involved in watching a drag act in a movie are numerous and complex. On one level, it recalls the unselfconscious freedoms of childhood. Let me take you back now to the playroom of your youth. I understand you've got plans, but come with me anyway – it won't take more than a moment. Do you remember how, back then, all it took to change your identity was a plunge into the dressing-up box? You could never tell what you might find there. Perhaps you'd pull out a hat or a waistcoat. Or if you were very lucky, a beautifully ruffled evening dress with puckered sleeves and matching elbow-length gloves . . .

If playfulness and liberty are the predominant factors in our

enjoyment of drag, there is also, I think, a slightly unsavoury element similar to seeing our faces distorted in warped funhouse mirrors. Several of the actors on the list below are there for that reason.
I'm sure we've all sat daydreaming about what Sylvester Stallone or
Donald Pleasence or Matt Damon look like in women's clothing –
there's no point pretending otherwise. And for the actors themselves, the transformation can open them up to new experiences.
'The dress was hell to be inside,' Gael García Bernal once told me
on the subject of wearing a Gaultier-designed sequinned spectacular
for Pedro Almodóvar's *Bad Education*. 'But when I was Zahara, all
the men treated me differently. They pulled my chair out for me,
they asked if I was tired. They treated me like a girl.' I pointed out
that he must get treated like that anyway, being a star on a film set?
'Ah, but as a man you cannot allow yourself to exploit that.
Whereas when you're a woman, there's an attractiveness that you
can use to your advantage.' You can see that knowingness at its most
vivid in Johnny Depp's entry on this list.

Rules employed in the selection meant restricting the list to
only those performers whom we are meant to accept as characters
temporarily posing in the opposite sex. So it was with heavy heart
that I had to leave Divine out in the cold, since in his films for
John Waters he was playing women – Edna Turnblad in *Hairspray*
or Babs Johnson in *Pink Flamingos*. Eva Mattes was shown the
door for the same reason, despite her scorching performance as a
surrogate Fassbinder in *A Man Like Eva*. The standard Hollywood
examples of drag-as-acting-exercise, such as *Mrs Doubtfire* and *To
Wong Foo, Thanks for Everything, Julie Newmar*, were excluded by
dint of being too obvious and uninspiring. An exception is
Tootsie, hardly obscure, but certainly a screwball masterpiece.

10. Iggy Pop in *Dead Man* (US 1995, dir. Jim Jarmusch)

If you think there's nothing shocking left for Iggy Pop to do on
God's earth, you haven't seen him in a frilly frock and bonnet,
which is more disturbing than his appearance as a rat-faced
mutant in *Tank Girl*. He plays Sally, a trapper who reads from the
Bible to his campfire compadres in Jarmusch's trippy western.

9. Donald Pleasence in *Cul-de-Sac* (GB 1966, dir. Roman Polanski)

Stuck in a Holy Island retreat with his young wife (Françoise Dorléac), the shaven-headed Pleasence is cracking up long before the arrival of a gangster on the run. If the three main characters form a kind of unconsummated love triangle, Pleasence is its most sexually indistinct participant, appearing rather poignantly in Dorléac's nightdress and make-up. Lionel Stander mistakes him for his late wife and later gives him a sound spanking.

8. Matt Damon in *The Good Shepherd* (US 2006, dir. Robert De Niro)

It's Damon's blasé approach to drag, as much as how utterly strange he looks in it, that merits his inclusion here. From beneath the wig, dress and make-up that he assumes for a university production of *HMS Pinafore*, his essential Matt Damon-ness – that deceptive, preppy blankness that lends itself to 'undercover' roles like *The Talented Mr Ripley*, *The Departed* and this – is undiminished. We also get to see him in the dressing room, still in drag but without the squeaky stage voice.

7. Sylvester Stallone in *Nighthawks* (US 1981, dir. Bruce Malmuth)

This fun thriller is book-ended by scenes of Stallone dragging up to fight crime. In the first instance his disguise snares muggers preying on vulnerable women. More spectacularly, the film subverts the standard woman-in-peril scene at the end by having psychopathic Rutger Hauer creep up on what he, and we, think is Lindsay Wagner in a dressing gown doing the washing-up – only for the supposed damsel in distress to spin round at the last second, revealing an armed Stallone in blonde wig and full beard. In the cold light of day it sounds like a bad episode of *Punk'd* but in fact it's a rather wonderful moment.

6. Stephen Dorff in *I Shot Andy Warhol* (US/GB 1996, dir. Mary Harron)

An unexceptional, pocket-sized actor, Dorff grew in stature, and most people's estimation, when he stepped into the high heels of the pre-op transsexual Candy Darling – an example of drag making an actor appear more interesting. Dorff's pinched, doll-like face and breathy readings of lines like 'I have always found that socially unacceptable people make the best lovers because they are more sensitive' made you forget his humdrum, Gap-billboard good looks.

5. Bugs Bunny in *What's Opera, Doc?* (US 1957, dir. Chuck Jones)

The wiseacre wabbit makes no secret of his drag-act aspirations. Between 1939 and 1996, he crossed the gender divide more than forty times in shorts. In *The Wabbit Who Came to Supper* (1942), he shaves his pits and appears in lingerie. For the out-of-circulation anti-Japanese wartime short, *Bugs Bunny Nips the Nips* (1944), he was a geisha. In *Napoleon Bunny-part* (1956), he's a fetching Josephine. But he is on top form in the excellent *What's Opera, Doc?*, donning helmet and swishing blonde pigtails as a coquettish Brünnhilde in this Wagner pastiche. Now in semi-retirement, Bugs can reputedly be found working the cloakroom at Madame Jo Jo's in the midweek lull.

4. Dustin Hoffman in *Tootsie* (US 1982, dir. Sydney Pollack)

Hoffman has never been better than as Michael Dorsey, the out-of-work actor who drags up to land a female part on a hospital soap. But this is more than just a playful, adventurous performance – it's an uncanny synthesis of actor and role. Hoffman was already notorious as a pernickety perfectionist, so playing one allowed him to riff on his persona while bringing emotional authenticity to the film's screwball set-up. Just as importantly, he made a damn fine woman: his Dorothy Michaels is a mumsy, homespun fusspot who becomes not just a mouthpiece for everything Michael couldn't say as a man, but a weirdly autonomous character in her own right. So much so that the euphoria of the climax, in which Dorothy becomes Michael on live television, is also a kind of comedown, since it means saying goodbye to Dorothy for good – arguably as painful a departure as the estrangement of Elliott and *E.T.* in another of 1982's best films. Most sublime moment among many goes to Bill Murray, as Michael's flatmate, waking up to see his unexpectedly altered chum and asking blearily: 'Mom?'

3. Paul Reubens in *Pee-Wee's Big Adventure* (US 1985, dir. Tim Burton)

As the whey-faced child-man Pee-Wee Herman, Reubens seems to be in drag even when he isn't, which makes it doubly weird when he poses as the wife of an escaped convict to get past a police roadblock. What a peach he looks too. A burly cop asks him to step out of the vehicle. 'Is there a problem, Officer?' purrs Pee-Wee. 'No, Ma'am, I just wanna get a look at you in that pretty outfit.' Pee Wee gives a twirl, cackling away gleefully, and shoots back one of his playground catchphrases: 'Why don't you take a picture? It'll last longer!' The real pay-off occurs when he gets back in the car and receives a look from his roughneck companion that seems to say: 'I'm going to have you, Pee-Wee Herman. It's not going to be pretty, it will take all night, but by the morning you'll be a man reborn.' Something along those lines, anyway.

2. Roman Polanski in *Le Locataire* / *The Tenant* (France/US 1976, dir. Roman Polanski)

As Trelkovsky, the mousey little nobody who begins turning into the woman who lived in his Paris apartment before him, Polanski is frail and contrite – until the process of possession extends to his wardrobe. He goes out to buy a wig, a horrible, raggedy brown number, and can't even wait until he gets home to try it on. Back at his flat, he caresses and coos over the heels he's bought, and parades in front of the mirror in a black floral number, rubbing his (non-existent) breasts. You couldn't say he's attractive exactly, but something about his cheerful belief in his own prettiness is rather winning. When Trelkovsky climbs into his glad rags at the end of the film and hurls himself out of his top-floor window, not once but twice, it should not be taken as a comment on the wisdom or otherwise of dragging up.

1. Johnny Depp in *Before Night Falls* (US 2000, dir. Julian Schabel)

Depp has form in this area – he played the cross-dressing title character in *Ed Wood*, while for the *Pirates of the Caribbean* movies his make-up box is apparently bigger than his trailer. He's never been more alluring, though, than in his brief turn as the jailbird transvestite Bon-Bon. You don't see his face at first. But there are plenty of other delights to take in: the vanilla wig that bounces with every step, the dusky feather boa, the garter belt hoisted up his thigh, all nicely offset by the inky black armpits. Depp sashays through the prison yard like a seductive tornado, turning every head, causing eyes to pop out on stalks, making grown men pant like dogs, both on-screen and in the audience. He gets two unforgettable close-ups – one of his face, with his lipstick mouth locked in a lemon-sucking pout, his blonde hair clashing with his black lashes and stubble. Then there's the tight shot of his behind, underwear snagged between his cheeks. That arse has Tardis-like dimensions, perfectly compact on the outside but roomy enough within to smuggle the hero's manuscript out of the slammer.

Manicure Madness

Ten Shining Examples of Notable Nail Varnish

ANNE BILLSON

My fingernails tend to be characterized by creeping cuticles and the chipped remains of last week's nail lacquer, but when did you last see such realism on a movie screen? On the rare occasions when chipped nail varnish does crop up, it's a signifier of clueless adolescence, drug addiction or sociopathy (and I swear none of these descriptions apply to me). Some of cinema's most dastardly villains sport nails of extraordinary length (hello there, Ming the Merciless, Fu Man Chu, David Lo Pan and Casanova Frankenstein) but the best, most impeccable cinematic manicures are more moderate affairs.

10. *Wild at Heart* (US 1990, dir. David Lynch)

There are several directors on this list who seem to me to be nail fetishists, and Lynch is one of them. Who can forget Isabella Rossellini's red fingernails digging into Kyle MacLachlan's pasty bottom as she fellates him in *Blue Velvet*? Or Patricia Arquette's contrasting good girl/bad girl nail colour in *Lost Highway*? Or Elena Harring's red nails adding the finishing touch to the lesbian love scene in *Mulholland Dr.*? Most extreme, though, are Diane Ladd's coral-coloured nails as she makes kitty-cat claws at Harry Dean Stanton, or slathers red lipstick all over her face in *Wild at Heart*, Lynch's decadent parody of *The Wizard of Oz*. If only it had been green lipstick, the resemblance to the Wicked Witch of the West would have been complete.

9. *Death on the Nile* (GB 1978, dir. John Guillermin)

Okay, if we're going to be technical it's not nail varnish in the nail-varnish bottle but red ink, which (Agatha Christie Spoiler Alert!) one of the murderers splashes all over his leg so that everyone will mistake it for blood and thus imagine him incapable of running all over the cruise ship, killing people. But, quite frankly, the ink's such a garish un-blood-like crimson that it might just as well have been varnish. Hercule Poirot (Peter Ustinov) isn't fooled, though. (Well, actually he is – failing to identify the murderers until they've shot or stabbed their way through half the cast, by which time the suspects have been substantially whittled down.) *'Quelle tragédie!'* he sighs.

8. *Velvet Goldmine* (GB/US 1998, dir. Todd Haynes)

Pierce Brosnan paints his toenails purple in *The Matador*, and Mel Gibson shows off flawless red-lacquered fingernails in *What Women Want*, but the clear winner in the guys-with-varnished-nails stakes is Ewan McGregor, who as an Iggy Popalike called Curt Wild flaunts glam-rock black lacquer. McGregor may not have the macho pedigree of James Bond or Mad Max, but he does take his trousers down and rub oil all over his naked torso, which in my book gives him an edge. This man is fearless.

7. *Lolita* (US/GB 1962, dir. Stanley Kubrick)

When a chap starts painting his loved one's toenails, you know he's been well and truly unmanned. While James Mason is putting the pedicure into paedophile by painstakingly applying varnish to Sue Lyon's tootsies (he even inserts little tufts of cotton-wool between the toes, to keep them apart) he's also whingeing, 'Why were you so late coming home from school yesterday afternoon?' like a jealous housewife. Great scene, but Kubrick undoubtedly stole the idea from Fritz Lang's *Scarlet Street*, where you know there's no longer any hope for Edward G. Robinson as soon he's shown applying lacquer to Joan Bennett's toenails.

6. *Dressed to Kill* (US 1980, dir. Brian De Palma)

Nancy Allen discovers a blood-covered Angie Dickinson in the elevator, and what does she do? She raises her hands and shows off her manicure in slo-mo! Lovely shape, perfect Bordeaux-coloured varnish. Brian De Palma is another director whose films are packed with good fingernails; you've never seen such beautifully manicured schoolgirls as the ones in *Carrie* and *The Fury*. Nancy Allen invariably has nice nails, as well, whether she's discovering blood-splattered bodies or dumping buckets of pig's blood all over *Carrie* or, even more bizarrely, when she's supposed to be a tough Detroit cop in Paul Verhoeven's *Robocop*.

5. *Daughters of Darkness* / *Les Lèvres Rouges* (Belgium/France/West Germany/Italy 1971, dir. Harry Kümel)

The best Belgo-Franco-German vampire movie ever made features an eclectic cast comprising a German porn star, a famous Dutch film-maker, a future regular on *Cagney & Lacey*, Miss Province de Québec 1967 and, most gloriously, art-house diva Delphine Seyrig, who plays an impeccably coiffed 300-year-old lesbian vampire with designs on a honeymoon couple in an off-season Ostend hotel. She also has long red fingernails, which can be seen to advantage when she pointedly doesn't drink her mint-green cocktail (let's face it, it's not her tipple of choice) and gazes into her compact mirror to touch up her already perfect red lipstick. But of course, since she's a vampire, there's no reflection of her face – only of those long red fingernails as they flitter girlishly in the void. Sublime.

4. *Cabaret* (US 1972, dir. Bob Fosse)

'Divine decadence!' says Liza Minnelli, trying to shock Michael York by waggling her fake-looking long green nails at him as he lights her cigarette. It's her favourite trick – she does it again for the ambassador from Washington, and yet again when introduced to Marisa Berenson. Unfortunately for Liza, this is Berlin in the Weimar Republic, and fingernails, however green, fade into insignificance by comparison to what's really going down outside the Kit-Kat Club. Anyway, I considered Minnelli so uncool that after seeing this movie I immediately switched my Biba nail-colour of choice from 'Matisse Green' to 'Royal Blue'.

3. *Pulp Fiction* (US 1994, dir. Quentin Tarantino)

Pray silence. It's one of the most significant moments in the filmed history of nail varnish. Thirty minutes in, Uma Thurman (invariably utter crap in any movie not directed by Tarantino) emerges as Mia Wallace, in flared black slacks and crisp white shirt, her nails lacquered in Chanel's latest – a deep, dark, rich red colour called 'Vamp', which would shortly be marketed in Europe as 'Rouge Noir'. Even though the packaging was never shown, it proved to be one of the most brilliant examples of product placement ever. Women immediately started clamouring for it. And so a style classic was born.

2. *The Tales of Hoffmann* (GB 1951, dirs. Michael Powell & Emeric Pressburger)

If only they'd made more films in colour, Powell and Pressburger might well have revealed themselves as nail fetishists of the first order. Take a look at the six-armed Silver Maid's ice-blue fingernails, all thirty of them, in *The Thief of Bagdad*. But the guys outdid themselves in the Venice segment of the seriously weird opera-cum-ballet *The Tales of Hoffmann*. Femme fatale Ludmilla Tchérina lures Hoffmann into the clutches of her diabolical pimp (Robert Helpmann, aka *Chitty Chitty Bang Bang*'s Child Catcher) in return for a glittery necklace. Then, to the strains of Offenbach's famous *Barcarolle*, she steps out over a sea of dead men's souls, bare feet decked in jewels, toenails gleaming in scarlet and gold.

1. *Showgirls* (US 1995, dir. Paul Verhoeven)

Verhoeven is fingernail-crazy, though when I once put it to him in an interview he denied it. But witnesses for the prosecution include *The Fourth Man* (femme fatale Renée Soutendijk swapping green and red nail varnish almost as often as she changes husbands), *Robocop* (Nancy Allen again!) and *Total Recall* (the Rekall Inc receptionist changing nail colour with the aid of a sci-fi magic wand). Above all, though, take a look at *Showgirls*, the *Citizen Kane* of fingernail movies. Not only does Elizabeth Berkley decorate her ridiculously long nails in a pink and purple harlequin pattern with silver spangles, but much of the film's dialogue is fingernail-related. As in, 'You can show off your nails', 'Your friend has nice nails' and 'Maybe I'll help you with yours sometime . . .' Here we can see the politics of nails played out for all to see on the Las Vegas stage: manicurists, however creative, are always subservient, and every showgirl secretly yearns to scratch the others' eyes out. As if that's not enough, the film also exploits the power of fingernails in displays of choreography so mind-bendingly awful that one can't resist trying to re-create them in front of the bathroom mirror. Clutch that brow as though you've got a throbbing headache! Spread those fingernails in front of your face! And *snarl*!

More Syrup, Sir?

The Ten Worst Wigs an Actor Dared to Wear

PAUL DALE

Part of the magic of movies resides in the mysterious brilliance of the hair and make-up folk who toil endlessly behind the scenes.

But sometimes they get it wrong: they come in with a bad hang-over and their glue-gun isn't working so they grab a possum and stick it on the head of the nearest overpaid star. The result may be cheered or derided, but never forgotten. Only about three peo-ple I know have ever seen *Battlefield Earth* but everyone knows what John Travolta's hairdo is like in that film. Here are ten of the worst head-ferrets, toupees, syrups or bad hairpieces ever commit-ted to celluloid.

10. Isabella Rossellini as Dorothy Vallens in *Blue Velvet* (US 1986, dir. David Lynch)

All the wigs in this list are bad, strange or at best peculiar, but not many are clearly identified as wigs within the films themselves. For a female character the donning or removal of a wig can be an affirmation both of weirdness and of sexual ambiguity, a trick pulled off recently by Natalie Portman in the film of Patrick Marber's *Closer*. Way back in 1986 the mighty Lynch was pulling tricks with wigs in *Blue Velvet*. We see the thatch come off Dorothy Vallens's head only once, shortly after budding pervert Jeffrey Beaumont (Kyle MacLachlan) breaks into her house and hides in her cupboard. As he squints through a crack we too see Dorothy enter the room, strip to her panties and bra and remove her long lustrous curls to reveal a dark gamine bob beneath. She then walks to the bathroom, before re-emerging with the wig intact again. The brief disappearing act is so bizarre, memorable, and incongruous with what follows that it deserves to edge on to this list – for, to misquote Godard, 'Cinema is the momentary mane that is snatched from eternity.'

9. Richard Burton (*Alexander the Great*, US 1956, dir. Robert Rossen) and Colin Farrell (*Alexander*, Germany/France/GB/ Netherlands/ Italy 2004, dir. Oliver Stone)

A double-header, this, simply because it is more to do with the character these two fine actors portray than their reputations for stick-on coiffures. Alexander the Great's story has wrong-footed film-makers repeatedly – he was too enigmatic and megalomaniacal a character to pin down. So both Rossen and Stone decided it would be a good idea to stick their lead actors in wigs to convey these complexities of Alexander's many excesses. Burton's is probably the worst of the two: bright blond and perched above his dark and still handsome Welsh features. Farrell's bouncy fair bouffant is little better. Alexander is sometimes identified in Persian and Arabic sources as the Two-Horned One, but this pair of mullets need some serious brocade work.

8. Tina Turner in her final reincarnation in *Tina: What's Love Got to Do With It?* (US 1993, dir. Brian Gibson)

Angela Bassett is a terrific and much-underused actress who may have peaked too early. The role of Anna Mae Bullock, later to transform herself into the mighty Tina Turner, was a gift for any young black actress. But for Bassett in 1993, when the lead roles she so richly deserved had eluded her for almost a decade, it was divine intervention. The film is a major feat of wardrobe, hair and make-up; Bassett does not so much look like Turner as inhabit her abused, ultimate-survivor frame in nearly every scene of the film. For the most part it all passes with the gusto of high melodrama as Bassett's hair is expertly teased and pieced by legendary stylist Carolyne Ferguson (*Dangerous Minds*, *Say Anything*). And then – horror of horrors – British director Gibson decides to allow the real Turner on to the stage and into the final section of the film. Not only is all credibility thrown out the window, but no one seems to be in charge of Turner's humungous spiky hairpiece. Talk about good work going down the drain.

7. John Wayne in *North to Alaska* (US 1960, dir. Henry Hathaway)

By the age of forty-one Wayne had lost most of that fine bush of hair that made him stand out in *The Big Trail* and *Stagecoach*. Along with his heavy drinking, smoking and fighting lifestyle, Wayne was typically macho about his loss of hair: he deigned that in every film from *Wake of the Red Witch* (1948) onwards he would wear a toupee. Sometimes this was one of the ones he wore every day, sometimes it was one the studio provided. Generally it worked pretty well: Wayne's preferred genres tended to demand the wearing of hats, and lots of them. The only drawback was that in fight sequences the old syrup wasn't always as sticky as it should be, and in many scenes you can see it lift off Wayne's head. The best example of this is when the Duke went north in Henry Hathaway's enjoyably throwaway comedy western *North to Alaska*. In the scene where Ernie Kovacs's con-man gets into a fight with Wayne's drunken gold-digger, the faithful toupee flies across the room after a single sucker punch from Kovacs.

6. Barbara Stanwyck in *Double Indemnity* (US 1944, dir. Billy Wilder)

Great movie, shame about the wig. Wilder's brilliant noir in which smooth-talking insurance salesman Walter Neff (Fred MacMurray) allows himself to be talked into the biggest insurance scam of them all by attractively unhappy housewife Phyllis Dietrichson is a masterwork in every respect – apart from the sunset syrup on Stanwyck's head. The wig was the idea of Wilder, who only realized how bad it looked a month in to shooting. By then unfortunately it was too late to re-shoot the earlier scenes. In later years Wilder attempted to rewrite history by claiming that the wig's ill appearance was intentional.

5. Joe Pesci as Jimmy Alto in *Jimmy Hollywood* (US 1994, dir. Barry Levinson)

Pesci is a walking advert for bad wigs – just go and re-watch *GoodFellas*, *Casino*, *JFK* or *My Cousin Vinny* and look for the join. The very worst of all, however, has to be in Levinson's likeable crime caper *Jimmy Hollywood*. Pesci plays a wannabe actor who suddenly lands the role of a lifetime, that of a vigilante crime-fighter who becomes a national hero (which in itself causes hapless Jimmy and his uptight girlfriend other problems). Pesci's blond middle-parted barnet here has got to be one of the worst ever to be worn by a man who had just turned fifty.

4. John Travolta in *Battlefield Earth* (US 2000, dir. Roger Christian)

You can lose hours if not days on the Internet trying to work out whether John Travolta actually still has his own hair or whether he has a weave or as the experts like to call it a 'hair system' (basically an expensive high-maintenance scalp mesh). Either way Travolta certainly seems to like his wigs: he's been known to sport a crew-cut one day and then appear at an awards ceremony with pompadour skunk on his head the next. Anyway it is not our duty to delve into such inanities, we have our own to de-louse. Travolta's crowning glory has to be the pantomime get-up he wore in his adaptation (as producer) of the L. Ron Hubbard book *Battlefield Earth*. As allegedly magnetic and powerful alien conquistador leader Ter, Travolta sports a bizarre array of beehive pieces and dreadlocks; it's so out there it's almost in. Not unlike Scientology itself.

3. Bruce Willis in *The Jackal* (US 1997, dir. Michael Caton-Jones)

Willis, like Pesci, is a gift to comedy wig-makers the world over. The man is clearly a good deal more self-aware than most of his other balding contemporaries, comfortable with a shaved head, and his wigs generally tend to be fairly low-key and in line with what used to be his true hair colour. But in this appalling remake of *The Day of the Jackal* Willis went a bit off-radar with a series of really bad, really bonkers syrups. Okay, so he was playing a hit man on the run, but surely terrorists aren't meant to draw attention to themselves, much less ridicule?

2. Kevin Spacey in *Beyond the Sea* (Germany/GB/US 2005, dir. Kevin Spacey)

And the best performance as one balding man by another balding man is by Spacey in his pet project musical biopic of the mighty big-band, rock, folk, jazz and pop star Bobby Darin. Having acquired the film rights to Darin's remarkable life story (sickly gifted child outlives predicted lifespan, becomes a star and then a sixties protest singer before staging a comeback but still dies at thirty-seven years old) Spacey thought he may be too old to play the role but did it anyway (hell, they had hair loss in common). The wigs used here are ridiculous but – and this separates this entry from all the others here – they are supposed to look ridiculous. Wig technology in the 1940s and 1950s was crude at best, so Darin, frightened of losing his younger fans, had loads made to the highest specifications of the time. Thus Spacey makes the wigs stars in their own right. They sit alone on the head mannequins waiting their moment to perform their cheesy cover-up duties. Even when hippy radical Darin discards them in favour of a more natural appearance, they wait for Darin to reclaim them for the final big comeback show. This is a case of 'the wig stays in the picture'.

1. Sir Ian McKellen as John Profumo in *Scandal* (GB 1989, dir. Michael Caton-Jones)

From Middle Earth to Planet Earth there is no one in the thespian community who wears a syrup worse than that most beloved of gay British thespians, Sir Ian. The number one spot on this list has to go to the one he sports as the famously disgraced politician Profumo – a wig of such diametric weirdness and oriental affliction that it not only looks nothing like Profumo's own hairline, it looks unlike any other screen wig ever. Chief hair stylist Meinir Jones-Lewis and hair stylist Liz Michie deserve to be named and shamed for it. The wig is so distracting, in fact, that every time I have watched this film I completely forget about the plot (I know what happens anyway) and just wait for another glimpse of that flyblown dead red squirrel sitting atop the dirty old Tory. McKellen's laughable mop in *The Lord of the Rings* trilogy seems positively conservative by comparison.

The Ten Baddest Hair Days in Film

ANDREW O'HAGAN

I know the best book ever written and it's called *Crowning Glory: Reflections of Hollywood's Greatest Confidant* by Sydney Guilaroff,

the king of the movie hairdo. And Guilaroff didn't just do hair, he
created hairstyles, pleasing and primping everyone from Jean
Harlow to Faye Dunaway. But the sad thing about the movies is
that Guilaroff sometimes took a holiday, and the history of cinema
is also resplendent with barnets that seem destined to keep us
laughing for as long as we have breath. The best bad hair days usually involve an attempt to be either historically accurate or aggres-
sively hip, but, either way, the results are often such that the
actors' speeches could barely be heard for the screeches of the
audience. It has to be said that some decades – especially the 1950s
– witnessed a shocking dearth of bad hair days, but the 1970s and
1980s more than make up for it, allowing a fierce plenitude of horrible hair on to the screen, more indeed than might be thought
healthy. Anyway, with a song in my heart, I offer you my pick of
the worst ten ever. True actors, as Stanislavsky might have said,
don't wear wigs: they suffer through the night for their art, and the
following screen outings prove that genius will always and forever
be ready to make concessions to the completely ridiculous.

10. Moe Howard in *Disorder in the Court* (US 1936, dir. Jack
White)

Moe was the chief knucklehead in The Three Stooges, and all the
children I knew lived in dread of ending up with his terrible bowl-
job for a haircut. History records that Moe actually invented the
haircut for himself to escape his mother's sissy-making way with
the curlers, but there can be no excuses: Moe's hair is enough to
make Meryl Streep's various abominations look positively sizzling,
and I defy anybody under eighteen to see this movie without crying out in sympathy.

9. Carrie Fisher in *Star Wars* (US 1977, dir. George Lucas)

As the flowing Princess Leia Organa, Carrie Fisher was the throb
of every male teenager's heart, but even the truly adoring could not
ignore those Danishes strapped to the side of her head. One might
have imagined her ears were weirdly coiled like a pair of
Cumberland sausages, and that she could hear cool stuff across the

other side of the universe, but in fact the whole hair fiasco was just the result of some over-zealous mental meanderings on the part of George Lucas. It is something of a tribute to the scale of Ms Fisher's charms that her fans were willing to put aside her hideous locks, and see her as the perfect, if damaged, modern woman.

8. Louis Calhern in *Julius Caesar* (US 1953, Joseph L. Mankiewicz)

Roland Barthes once got very excited about the hairdos in this starry Joseph Mankiewicz production of 1953. Louis Calhern is a regally hook-nosed Caesar, but the barnet never entirely convinces, despite its glorious swept-forward grandeur. It looks, in fact, too much like a Romanesque version of the common or garden comb-over, pointing up the possible fact that JC's famous vanities, as understood by William Shakespeare, were added to by an actor too much afraid of incipient male pattern baldness.

7. Elsa Lanchester in *Bride of Frankenstein* (US 1935, dir. James Whale)

Long before Susan Sontag made the single streak fashionable, Charles Laughton's long-suffering English wife Elsa Lanchester was proving how to frighten the young team, making with the leaning tower of frizzy head-fibres and the crazy lightning forks of grey. Not that Boris Karloff's Monster sported such a good look, either, what with the shorty fringe thing, but at least he had his eyes half-shut and looked like he wasn't keen to catch himself in the mirror. The Bride, on the other hand, was wide-eyed all the way, looking as if the hairdo was her greatest asset. The film's narrative doesn't record where she got it from, though an over-resourced Universal Studios hairdressing department might have been a good place to start looking.

6. Paul Hogan in *Crocodile Dundee* (Australia 1986, dir. Peter Faiman)

Central problem at the heart of the movie: if Hogan's character is a crocodile-wrestling macho man, butch 'Strine *cojones* made flesh, then why does he clearly spend hours in the dunny dying his hair a wannabe-Marilyn shade of freshly hatched blond? Dude looks like a lady. Dude looks like a working girl, actually, never attaining the requisite shade of minxy platinum but settling instead for an unattractive cut-price pee-yellow. Team with overly tight jeans and the leather jerkin Hogan sports throughout to demonstrate his manliness, and you could be forgiven for thinking you've stumbled across a film about gargantuanly physically fearless she-males.

5. Warren Beatty in *Shampoo* (US 1975, dir. Hal Ashby)

Hey, studly guy! Hel-lo! A film that, inexplicably in retrospect, confirmed Beatty's status as the hottest guy on the planet. He appears – not inappropriately – to have a beaver glued on to his head, along with the mightiest sideburns this side of Nashville. A combination of the layered look and the flick, it was meant to drive the ladies crazy, which it did, so long as they yearned for a man who looked like a leather-bound version of Farrah Fawcett.

4. Barbra Streisand in *A Star is Born* (US 1976, dir. Frank Pierson)

The perm to end all perms. Like 200 poodles with heads full of curl-activator had been microwaved on High for ten minutes, until their corporeal bodies disintegrated and all that was left was tight, tight coils – some brown, some ginger, some spookily golden. Or like some birds had made some nests and deposited them atop Streisand's head (insert your own beak joke). Unspeakable hair, really, possibly the worst ever. The film's poster, in which an equally hirsute Kris Kristofferson implausibly runs his hairy hands through Streisand's impenetrable thatch, can induce nausea at five million paces.

3. Tom Cruise in *Born on the Fourth of July* (US 1989, dir. Oliver Stone)

Cruise played Ron Kovic, who was paralysed in the Vietnam War and became a political activist. Pre-paralysis, the hair was the usual fine military crop. Post, it was off-the-scale hideous, though certainly authentically seventies. Cruise's moustachioed face was surrounded by a thin cloud of long brown fluff, baldy at the front and matted at the back, somewhat like a Village Person direly in need of a stylist.

2. Bette Davis in *The Private Lives of Elizabeth and Essex* (US 1939, dir. Michael Curtiz)

Davis shaved her hairline back by a couple of inches for period authenticity, causing her huge, alien-style forehead – framed by ginger tendrils – to glisten palely and distractingly throughout Michael Curtiz's period drama, also starring Errol Flynn, whose hair was okay but who was forced to wear girls' tights.

1. Meryl Streep in *A Cry in the Dark* (Australia/US 1989, dir. Fred Schepisi)

The dingo might (or might not) have eaten the baby, but it also clearly had a little nibble round the edges of Streep's abysmal hair-don't. Sporting a tilted black pudding-bowl, except worse, Streep played Lindy Chamberlain, whose daughter Azaria disappeared mysteriously in the Australian outback. And who could blame her? You might disappear mysteriously too, if your mum had such an obvious sprouting of scare-hair.

Veil, Visor, Disguiser

Ten Fascinating Face-Masks

RICHARD T. KELLY

The movies love masks, for umpteen excellent reasons. Acting as we know it was founded on them at some point in the Golden Age of Athens. Two and a half centuries later actors still seem to get a kick out of facialwear (as long as it can be easily slipped on and off, rather than applied in layers over five hideous hours in a make-up chair). Behind the mask, for actor as for character, one is truly free to be somebody other than oneself. There's also the theory in sociology, pertinent to both theatre and cinema (and freely mocked in entry number 10 below) that social life itself is but a stage on which all of us, at times, wear our faces as masks . . . But above all there are umpteen great movie stories deriving from the mystery of face-masks that offer a frozen vision of beauty, only to conceal a grisly truth on the part of the wearer. Masks – like clowns – are sometimes funny, but mainly creepy. For this Ten, with regret, one has to exclude the iconic black eye-masks of Zorro and the Lone Ranger. Only a full-face veil, visor or disguiser is fit to our purpose. Sorry, Tonto.

10. Stanley Ipkiss (Jim Carrey) in *The Mask* (US 1994, dir. Chuck Russell)

The stock format in comic-book superhero stories is that a shy, retiring type finds his way into a costume and mask and suddenly becomes mean, moody, magnificent. The edgy US comics house Dark Horse twisted this tradition in a series called *The Mask*, whereby an enigmatic wooden artefact of African origin unleashed the Mr Hyde in whosoever donned it. But the movie version became a vehicle for the comic energies of Jim Carrey, playing a sad-sack bank clerk who finds that this mask endows him with the chops to seduce Cameron Diaz. 'It's like it brings your innermost desires to life,' Ipkiss marvels in a sedate moment between his changes into a 'love-crazy wild man'. Carrey's CGI alter ego was like Cab Calloway crossed with a toothy green-skinned Joker in canary-yellow zoot-suit, his whirling, wolf-whistling shtick straight out of Tex Avery cartoons. The mask changed hands in the movie, transforming Carrey's yappy dog as well as the perfunctory gangster-villain. But these were distractions: the viewer always wanted more Carrey.

9. The supporting players in *Le Testament d'Orphée / Testament of Orpheus* (France 1958, dir. Jean Cocteau)

Cocteau had the gift of placing his spidery signature upon almost everything he touched, somehow taking creative ownership of it, even in the case of the most seemingly commonplace poetic symbols – rose, mirror, mask. There's a curious mask spinning about its axis in his early piece *Le Sang d'un Poète* (1930), and he put his lover Jean Marais behind a magnificent furry make-up so that he could play the Beast in *La Belle et la Bête* (1946). In his swansong *Le Testament d'Orphée*, very much a homemade labour of love, Cocteau himself wandered through a symbolic landscape of his own creations, most of them masked in one fabulous form or another, so setting a template for a host of future pop videos.

8. Mordred (Charley Boorman/Robert Addie) in *Excalibur* (US/GB 1981, dir. John Boorman)

Boorman might be thought to have a bit of a penchant for masks, and *Zardoz* (1974), his crazy Wicklow-set sci-fi dystopia, would bid fair for entry here were it not that – aside from the glaring heads worn by Sean Connery and his fellow loin-clothed 'Exterminators' – the movie is hard to take seriously. So to *Excalibur*, Boorman's emerald vision of Arthurian legend, and the gold visor of the baleful Mordred, lovechild of Helen Mirren's Morgana and Nicol Williamson's Merlin, conceived in deceit as a usurper of King Arthur (Nigel Terry). Supercilious and sinister, the mask is first glimpsed darting between trees, Mordred a child on horseback (played by Boorman's young son) but with an oddly evil laugh, childish yet lethal, a harbinger of doom.

7. Dr William Harford (Tom Cruise) and the cast of the 'orgy' sequence in *Eyes Wide Shut* (US/GB 1999, dir. Stanley Kubrick)

Kubrick, like Boorman, was probably a creepy-mask fan, on the evidence of *The Killing* (1955), *A Clockwork Orange* (1971) and *The Shining* (1980). *Eyes Wide Shut*, if a let-down for many among its first audiences, was at least an embarrassment of riches for mask connoisseurs, certainly from the moment Dr Harford crosses the threshold of a mansion where a cabal of New York's great and good enjoy masked, writhing sex sessions. We are probably to understand that Harford has also crossed into a land of dream (for this is a Kubrick picture best appreciated by Slovenian devotees of psychoanalysis). But for the viewer any frisson is dispelled by the aura of Black Mass, a high priest in crimson gown, droning Ligeti music, and all those masks – some Venetian and doll-like, others surrealistic (a bird's beak, a teardrop). It's not wildly appealing. But then this movie is on the side of monogamy, against temptation and weirdness, and a mask of macramé lace later appears on Harford's pillow as a warning to give the dark world a wide berth in future.

6. Erik, the Phantom (Lon Chaney) in *The Phantom of the Opera* (US 1925, dir. Rupert Julian)

The godfather of masked movie monsters, Chaney's Phantom sports a waxen mask with aplomb even as he conveys his beloved Christine down to the lower depths of his lair. What we're really waiting for, though, is Christine's part in one of the great, dread unmaskings in movie history. A bonus for mask fans is the Phantom's subsequent show-stopping appearance at a costume ball, dressed up as Death in red robes, his mask a skull, though hardly more skeletal than Chaney's legendarily ghastly make-up underneath.

5. Leopold Mozart (Roy Dotrice) and Anton Salieri (F. Murray Abraham) in *Amadeus* (US 1984, dir. Milos Forman)

The Mozart drawn by Forman from Peter Shaffer's 1979 play, acted by Tom Hulce like shaken pop in a bottle, is perhaps a bit too much the giggling jackanapes. But the fun has to stop at some point, and even before his jealous rival Salieri can really get to work Mozart suffers the sting of conscience. At a bacchanalian costume party his visiting father Leopold, disapproving of him entirely, presents him with the grinning side of a tragic/comedic mask, but when he reveals his bare face it is dark as thunder. Mozart's guilt over Leopold's subsequent demise is seen to inspire the black-armoured ghost of Don Giovanni. Salieri, in a satanic stroke of ingenuity, then adopts the frozen black frown of the mask's flipside in order to harass Mozart yet further toward his grave.

4. 'Mother' (Nobuko Otowa) in *Onibaba / The Hole* (Japan 1964, Kaneto Shindo)

Japanese ghost stories returned to Western screens with a vengeance in the 1990s, rather recalling an analogous vogue in the

1960s for eerie pictures out of Japan, such as Teshigahara's *Woman of the Dunes* and Shindo's *Onibaba* ('Demon-Hag'), one of those hellish movies that reminds us we're all headed for a hole in the ground, albeit not necessarily one hemmed by tall swaying susuki grass. In feudal times an earthy young woman and her fierce mother-in-law make forays from their rural hut to prey on passing samurai, dispatching them into aforementioned hole and trading their armour for food. Then the louche Hachi (Kei Sato) enters the picture to report the death of the husband-and-son for whom the women have waited. He and the widow soon decide to comfort one another, and Mother, fearing abandonment, must break the erotic current. She happily alights upon a demonic horned mask that helps her to upset and deter her daughter-in-law's nightly excursions through the long grass; but then fails to heed the old saw that a mask may sometimes grow to fit a face.

3. Michael Myers (Nick Castle) in *Halloween* (US 1978, dir. John Carpenter)

'Because he was masked, you could project anything you wanted to on him.' Thus John Carpenter, musing on the appeal of his implacable boiler-suited boogeyman, whose trick of returning to life despite the extinguishing efforts of Jamie Lee Curtis and Donald Pleasence became, alas, the seed of a zillion dull sequels. Originally it was going to be a clown mask: proof that it's always worth thinking twice about these things. Designer Tommy Lee Wallace then called by Burt Wheeler's Magic Shop on Hollywood Boulevard, bought a William Shatner 'Captain Kirk' mask for $1.98, gouged the eye holes a little wider, spray-painted the plastic bluish white, and so unlocked a suppressed menace that Shatner-phobes had been sensing for years.

2. Darth Vader (David Prowse/James Earl Jones) in the *Star Wars* movies

Is it a mask or a helmet? Well, both, since the insect-armoured Lord Vader flies into battle at the head of imperial forces, but also takes care that his true visage is never beheld, something we grasp in *Episode V* when an underling intrudes upon Vader's toilette and so glimpses an appalling vista of scarred scalp. Vader's mask loomed over the artwork of all the *Star Wars* lobby posters, but it was shot with maximum gleam and menace in Irvin Kershner's *Episode V*. Clearly it concealed a horror. Others projected horror on to it, Luke Skywalker presciently dreaming of his own face there. In *Episode VI* Vader's death scene finally saw the mask come off to reveal . . . vintage English thespian Sebastian Shaw. (Critic Danny Peary later asked if he was alone in having expected to see James Earl Jones.) When Lucas undertook his prequel trilogy in the late 1990s the mystery of how Anakin Skywalker came to be imprisoned behind that mask was reopened; and in casting the vapid Hayden Christiansen, Lucas instantly voided said question of interest.

1. Christiane Génessier (Edith Scob) in *Les yeux sans visage* / *Eyes Without A Face* (France 1959, dir. Georges Franju)

'My face frightens me; my mask terrifies me even more.' The evil fate of the Phantom of the Opera may inspire pity, but how can it compare with that of a mere slip of a girl, awfully disfigured by her own father, somehow retaining her innocence while confined to a chateau that crawls with quiet lunacy? Christiane's obsessive doctor-daddy (Pierre Brasseur), cause of the car crash that left her face 'an open wound', tasks his nurse (Alida Valli) to kidnap collegiate females as grist for radical face transplants that never quite 'take'. (At dinner after one such doomed effort Génessier bids his daughter smile, but 'pas trop'.) Scob is a forlorn doll as she wanders the chateau's corridors in her white mask and raincoat with high collar and short sleeves. Denied human intimacy, she has an eerie communion with the ravening Great Danes her father keeps in the basement; they will be the agents of her revenge. Would the world remember Franju were it not for this grisly and lyrical work of horror? He co-founded the Cinémathèque Française and directed the grim slaughterhouse documentary *Le Sang des Bêtes* (1949), but had a love of fantasy (see also *Judex*, 1963) that achieved its full dark bloom in the form of Christiane's waxen mask.

7

Careers You Might Consider

Obsessive Professions and Callings

A Key Flaw in the Design

Ten Brooding Architects

DEMETRIOS MATHEOU AND RICHARD T. KELLY

Architects get a bum rap in the movies. There are good cops and bad cops, honourable lawyers as well as venal ones, a campaigning journalist for every hack; but when a director needs an anti-hero – someone self-absorbed and obsessive, a man insanely passionate about his work while his private life goes to pot – then architecture is one of the first jobs pencilled in. Why should one of the noblest of professions be so poorly regarded? Perhaps it's because, while we all live in buildings, we have next to no idea how they are created; and we have an image of architects in real life as inaccessible, a little aloof, living in their perfectly designed worlds while looking down on the rest of us for not being able to comprehend (or afford) the same. Basically, we're just jealous. And on our behalf, film directors exact revenge, portraying architects as flawed individuals whose personalities, if not their buildings, need to go back to the drawing board. (DM)

10. David Murphy (Woody Harrelson) in *Indecent Proposal* (US 1993, dir. Adrian Lyne)

The lengths to which an architect may go to secure his dream house are tested by this young, idealistic, rather goofy character who understands bricks and mortar infinitely better than he does people. The beachside home David has designed for himself and wife, Diana (Demi Moore), is only half-built when a recession strikes. The couple go to Vegas in a bid to win a reprieve at the tables, but are offered a more bankable option from smug billionaire John Gage (Robert Redford): one night with Diana, for a million bucks. Hell, it's only sex, they say. Silly. Gage wins much more than a night. David loses his home anyway and spends the whole million on a hippopotamus. (DM)

Manicure Madness – Ten Shining Examples of Notable Nail
Varnish, p 136

9. Nick Kaminsky (Kevin Anderson) in *Liebestraum* (US 1991, dir. Mike Figgis)

Professor Kaminsky is a scholar of architecture rather than a practitioner, but he can obsess over fine details with the best of them. He has returned to Elderstown, Illinois, to attend the bedside of his delirious, cancer-stricken adoptive mother (Kim Novak). A caring sort then, surely? Then he runs into Paul (Bill Pullman), a college pal whose construction company is now tearing down a glorious old cast-iron department store: the scene thirty years previously of a notorious infidelity-related murder. Nick's roving eye is drawn to the building and its history, but most arrestingly to Paul's very alluring wife Jane (Pamela Gidley). He becomes a slave to his passions, and Figgis stealthily gives us to understand that even orphans may be doomed to unwittingly repeat their family history. (RTK)

8. Alex Wyler (Keanu Reeves) in *The Lake House* (US 2006, dir. Alejandro Agresti)

It's difficult to say what is more unbelievable about this movie: the time-travelling love story, in which an architect and a doctor commune over space and time via a magic mailbox, or said designer's horrid taste in buildings. It's not that Alex Wyler is having to make a buck building suburban condos – most architects are forced to slum it at some point – but that he is in thrall to his acclaimed dad's eponymous lakeside home. This is designed as a glass and steel pavilion on stilts, with no utilities, no rooms, no functional parts of any kind. Plumbing? Privacy? Forget it. But it does have a large tree growing through the middle. Thus Alex lives in a giant exhibition case, and wonders why he's losing his mind. (DM)

7. Louis Kahn in *My Architect* (US 2003, dir. Nathaniel Kahn)

Louis Kahn was one of the greatest architects of the twentieth century. As a husband, lover, and father, he left a lot to be desired. In fact, the designer of such inspiring buildings as the Salk

Institute and Kimbell Art Museum is the archetypal architect: he didn't make his breakthrough until he was fifty (unlike film stars, architects are expected to 'blossom' late), he was uncompromising and difficult to work with; he sought truth and clarity in his work, but settled for secrets and lies at home – three homes, actually, one with his wife of many years, two with long-term lovers. Kahn was fond of saying: 'I asked the brick, "What do you like, brick?" And brick said, "I like an arch."' He clearly had a better relationship with his materials than with his illegitimate son, Nathanial, whose investigation – of a man he barely knew – is the substance of this fine documentary. (DM)

6. Hjalmar Poelzig (Boris Karloff) in *The Black Cat* (US 1934, dir. Edgar G. Ulmer)

When we first see Poelzig in silhouette he looks like some lofty and angular art deco construction of his own design. Saturnine in appearance, he's totally at home amid the severe modernism of his steel-and-glass Hungarian mansion, a prime piece of what Charles Jencks would call 'the architecture of control'. As the visiting Dr Vitus Verdegast (Bela Lugosi) makes us aware, Poelzig's place is erected over the remains of Fort Marmorus, where Poelzig held a military command in the Great War before betraying ten thousand men, Verdegast among them, to the Russians. For this alone we appreciate why Verdegast has an axe to grind – and this before he learns that downstairs Poelzig is keeping his daughter imprisoned and his wife's corpse in a glass case. One of Ulmer's pricier productions, this was a remarkably dark and crazed entry in the Universal horror cycle of the 1930s. (RTK)

5. Stourley Kracklite (Brian Dennehy) in *The Belly of an Architect* (GB 1987, dir. Peter Greenaway)

Kracklite is an American architect visiting Rome and, in an ideal locale, becomes the leading actor of his own hubristic tragedy. He's in town to oversee an exhibition of the French visionary Etienne-Louis Boullée; a powerhouse who, like himself, had trouble finishing projects. But Kracklite's mind is distracted by the pains in his gut, by his wife's adultery, and by the machinations of his rival Italian architects. If he spent less time at the photocopier, comparing his stomach to that of the Emperor Augustus, he might be able to sort himself out. But, as his doctor suggests, Kracklite is suffering from too much gas and too much egotism. Many would argue that both characteristics are merely part of the job description. (DM)

4. Mark Wallace (Albert Finney) in *Two for the Road* (US 1967, dir. Stanley Donen)

'When we married, you were a disorganized, egotistical failure,' Joanna (Audrey Hepburn) tells him. 'Now you're a disorganized, egotistical success.' Indeed Mark Wallace is not backward in coming forward, always ready for a verbal altercation, even with the employer (Claude Dauphin) to whom he owes his career. 'But that makes nonsense of the whole spacial concept – *spay-shul con-sept* – it messes up the whole lousy design!' As Frederic Raphael's sophisticated script moves around in time we witness Mark's loss of idealism and its part in the souring of his marriage: the real subject of the film, and the reason for its cult following, who see it as telling many a truth in that department. Indeed Finney and Hepburn bicker brilliantly, though her fanbase are thought to like the film less, finding Finney somewhat coarse and unsympathetic next to their heroine. Michael Caine nearly played the role. But Finney feels very true as the sort of arty Salford lad whom the 1960s permitted to make it big in St Tropez. (RTK)

3. Jim (Cary Grant) and Muriel Blandings (Myrna Loy) in *Mr Blandings Builds His Dream House* (US 1948, dir. H.C. Potter)

Jim Blandings and his wife, Muriel, are the sort of amateur architects who grace today's TV architecture programmes – namely, punters who think they can do better themselves. The Blandings blindly buy a Connecticut pile, only to be advised to knock it down and start over; after which their nominal architect is shunted aside at his own drawing board as the pair get to work on their Grand Design. 'By extending the breakfast room you eliminate the possibility of any stairs going up to the second floor,' he humbly suggests. That their builder's name is John W. Retch is a further sign of the hilarious tribulations to come. (DM)

2. John Baxter (Donald Sutherland) in *Don't Look Now* (GB/Italy 1973, dir. Nicolas Roeg)

Sutherland has often looked donnish or bohemian, disturbed or a little dangerous – sometimes all of these simultaneously. He was fine casting as the architect married to Julie Christie, padding around a big family home in rainy Hertfordshire, his library stocked with such titles as *Beyond the Fragile Geometry of Space*. We find him bent over a light-box, mulling over a church restoration, when his head rises slowly. 'What's the matter?' asks Christie. 'Nothing.' But he is already moving, too late to save his daughter, who drowns in the garden pond. Grief carries him and Christie to misty, wintry Venice, where he has committed to work on that sixteenth-century church. She becomes susceptible to a milky-eyed Scottish lady who claims that their lost child wishes contact with them, and that John is in personal danger. John thinks himself too clear-eyed for such nonsense. Why does he dismiss those precognitive powers, in which we know he has a share himself? Possibly because that share is only and ever too partial to prevent dreadful things from happening. (RTK)

1. Howard Roark (Gary Cooper) in *The Fountainhead* (US 1949, dir. King Vidor)

In the real world Howard Roark would be voted the architect's architect; if there was a secret ballot. The hero of Ayn Rand's reactionary novel is a smug, self-righteous egoist, a man who cares less about his clients, or society, than he does his precious integrity. But he's also a genius, who's willing to suffer for his art. 'There's no place for originality in architecture,' Roark's defeated mentor tells him, priming the over-the-top melodrama. 'Do you want to stand alone against the *whole world*?' Tall, silent, strong Cooper would rather drill at the quarry than compromise his designs with a single classical curlicue, until his visionary work (neatly filched by the film-makers from the styles of Frank Lloyd Wright and Mies van der Rohe) slowly wins favour. And when one project is altered against his wishes – hell, he'll just blow it up. Roark's passion isn't confined to glass and steel. 'I wish I had never seen your . . . building,' whines barking-mad Patricia Neal on eyeing his skyscraper. (DM)

Playing God? Somebody Has To!

Ten Mad Movie Scientists

JONATHAN CARTER

Since the beginning of cinema, scientists have been depicted as mad outsiders possessed by a demiurge. From J. Searle Dawley's silent stab at Frankenstein in 1910 to Dr Evil in *Austin Powers* they've been crazed blasphemers throwing back their heads and laughing carelessly at the cosmos. Which is exactly how we like it: megalomaniac loners dealing with public anxieties from a safe distance. Poison gas and death rays in the 1920s, the human body in the 1930s (the golden age for mad movie scientists), nuclear physics in the 1950s, the end of the world in the 1960s. Nowadays, these demented figures are tailing off as a threatening presence, turning into hopeless pantomime villains. After all, a lot of what once seemed mad science has come to pass; with the likes of cloning, genetic engineering, nanotechnology and robotics an everyday reality, maybe we don't need them any more.

So let's celebrate these wild-eyed, railing maniacs who are mad, mad, *mad* for all to see. Evil geniuses ranting in their labs filled with unreliable electrical equipment and a massive switch which seems to turn everything off at once. Madmen who never heed the warnings of more sensible types, letting their egotistical mission override all religious and/or ethical considerations. Brave souls who persevere despite repeated failure, letting nothing and no one get in their way. Nothing, do you hear? *Nothing*, I tell you!

10. Dr Michael Hfuhruhurr (Steve Martin) in *The Man With Two Brains* (US 1983, dir. Carl Reiner)

'Ladies and gentlemen, I can envision a day when the brains of brilliant men can be kept alive in the bodies of dumb people.'

Brain surgery is rarely a laughing matter, but here Steve Martin proves otherwise. Dr Hfuhruhurr, famed for using the 'screwtop method' during transplants, is climbing the walls with frustration, trapped in a sexless marriage to ruthless vamp Kathleen Turner. That is until he takes a trip to Vienna, where he falls head over heels with Anne Uumellmahaye, a brain (voiced by Sissy Spacek) kept in a jar in a colleague's lab. It's love at first sight, especially when he takes her on romantic boat trips and puts big plastic lips on her shiny glass face. Mad? Definitely.

9. Duran Duran (Milo O'Shea) in *Barbarella* (France/Italy 1968, dir. Roger Vadim)

'I find horrible the idea that one could do to me, that which I do to others.'

He may have fled to the Tau Ceti star system, but the baby-faced Duran, evil inventor of the deadly positronic ray which destroys planets by 'placing them into the fourth dimension', is still a threat to forty-first-century Earth. At least enough to have director Vadim's wife, Jane Fonda, on his tail. Despite the ludicrously camp setting, O'Shea is genuinely creepy as the leering inventor, particularly when he's trying to pleasure Fonda to death with his 'Excessive Organ', playing 'Sonata for Executioner and Various Young Women'.

8. Seth Brundle (Jeff Goldblum) in *The Fly* (US 1986, dir. David Cronenberg)

'You have to leave now, and never come back here.'

Never mind driving under the influence, geeky scientist Seth Brundle makes the fatal drunken mistake of personally testing one of his teleportation pods without checking the booth for houseflies. And it's bad news when the fly's genes start taking over. 'Am I becoming a hundred-and-eighty-five-pound fly? No, I'm becoming something that never existed before. I'm becoming . . . Brundlefly!'

Cronenberg's meditation on mortality doesn't shy away from gore – a sequence where Brundle sends a cat and a baboon through the telepods, then beats the resulting mutation to death was cut – but, ultimately, it's Goldblum's career-best performance that packs the punch.

7. Dr Strangelove (Peter Sellers) in *Dr Strangelove, Or: How I Learned to Stop Worrying and Love the Bomb* (GB 1964 ,dir. Stanley Kubrick)

'The Doomsday Machine is terrifying and simple to understand.'

Sellers's extraordinary portrayal of the wheelchair-bound ex-Nazi, creator of the apocalyptic Doomsday Machine, is one of the most memorable screen performances ever. Sellers based his mangled accent on the legendary German-born New York crime photographer 'Weegee' Fellig, who was the film's stills photographer. But it's the shtick with his 'alien hand' – a reference to Rotwang's gloved hand in Lang's *Metropolis* (see below) – that everyone remembers. This was later identified as a genuine neurological affliction (agonistic apraxia) by researchers at the University of Aberdeen, who also named it Dr Strangelove syndrome.

6. Paul Lavond (Lionel Barrymore) in *The Devil-Doll* (US 1936, dir. Tod Browning)

'You think I'm mad . . . The world would too, if they knew what I was going to do.'

Crazy even by 1930s standards, beleaguered *Freaks* director Tod Browning's penultimate film was, not surprisingly, mangled by the censors. It sees Lionel Barrymore as ex-con Paul Lavond, wrongly imprisoned for fraud, miraculously escaping from Devil's Island, stealing another scientist's diabolical discoveries and planning his revenge on those who framed him. So what does he do? He disguises himself as an elderly doll-maker called Madame Mandelip, opens a shop in Paris, drugs people, then shrinks them down to doll-size and brainwashes them into stabbing the guilty parties. Well, of course.

5. Dr Jekyll (Fredric March) in *Dr Jekyll and Mr Hyde* (US 1931, dir. Rouben Mamoulian)

'Oh, God. This I did not intend. I saw a light but did not know where it was headed.'

This thoroughly Freudian version of Stevenson's novella sees Hyde as an animalistic free spirit, hysterically chanting 'I'm free! Free!' and becoming evermore lust-ridden with every transformation. At one time the film was believed to be 'lost', with fingers pointing at the distributors of the inferior 1941 version, starring Spencer Tracy. Although censored when the Hays Code came into force in 1934, it still dared to go where the later film feared to tread. As did Fredric March – who won an Oscar for his efforts – furrowing his brow as gentleman Jekyll, then falling to his knees in theatrical anguish as Hyde.

4. Dr Griffin (Claude Rains) in *The Invisible Man* (US 1933, dir. James Whale)

'The fools wouldn't let me work in peace. I had to teach them a lesson.'

A stranger, looking like the Mummy in shades, stumbles through a snowstorm into a country inn. The bar goes quiet. There's a pause. The landlady eyes him suspiciously. 'I've had an accident,' he explains. Say hello to Dr Jack Griffin, a reasonably sane scientist who discovers an invisibility serum then loses his mind when he does what all great mad movie boffins do – experiment on themselves. From here on in it's downhill: 'An invisible man can rule the world. No one will see him come, no one will see him go . . . We'll start with a few murders. Big men, little men – just to show we make no distinction.' Just a voice and some landmark SFX until the very last scene; it's a brilliant debut from Claude Rains.

3. Rotwang (Rudolf Klein-Rogge) in *Metropolis* (Germany 1927, dir. Fritz Lang)

Lang's silent masterpiece took two years to shoot, featured 37,000 extras and cost the modern-day equivalent of 23 million dollars; by far the most expensive European movie of its time. It was worth it, though, because what H.G. Wells called 'quite the silliest film' gave us the blueprint for the mad movie scientist – the wild-eyed, wire-haired Rotwang. Even his laboratory with its towering Tesla coils and banks of switches became the universal gothic lab prototype. Rotwang (Rudolf Klein-Rogge) creates a robot as a replacement for his ex-wife, who left him for the mayor of the city, using it to exact revenge on pretty well everyone. Ironic, seeing as Klein-Rogge's own wife had left him for Fritz Lang six years before.

2. Dr Moreau (Charles Laughton) in *Island of Lost Souls* (US 1933, dir. Erle C. Kenton)

'Do you know what it means to feel like God?'

Pipped to the winning post only by Frankenstein himself, Charles Laughton's first starring role in Hollywood is one of cinema's grisliest creations. Not surprising, seeing as Laughton always claimed that he based insane vivisectionist Dr Moreau's suave, goateed appearance on his dentist. The film was banned in England and parts of the United States for being 'against nature', not to mention the hideous half-man, half-animal creations that roam Moreau's island when not being tortured in the House of Pain. After finishing the film, Laughton claimed he would never visit a zoo again in his life.

1. Dr Henry Frankenstein (Colin Clive) in *Frankenstein* (US 1931, dir. James Whale)

'Crazy, am I? We'll see whether I'm crazy or not.'

Without doubt the maddest of them all. Bela Lugosi was originally offered the role, but few things say 'mad scientist' more effectively than a posh, hysterical Englishman. So who better than Colin

Clive, son of a British colonel and descendant of Clive of India, earmarked for the army until a nasty riding accident ended his ambitions. After sparking the Monster (Boris Karloff) into life in his laboratory – re-used forty-three years later in Mel Brooks's comedy *Young Frankenstein* – the mad doctor shrieks, 'Now I know what it's like to be God!' This now famous line was removed for a while in the late 1930s for being blasphemous, and replaced by a clap of thunder. It was to be Clive's greatest moment: he died of alcoholism six years after making the film, at the age of thirty-seven.

Worried Fingers

Ten Angst-Ridden Piano-Playing Protagonists

ANDREW BENBOW

No other instrument accompanies film quite like the piano. From the early days of the film-house pianist lulling chain-smoking punters into the dream-world of the 'silent' screen, to the modern scores of Michael Nyman or Randy Newman – the movie and the piano appear to live together in perfect harmony.

So it makes perfect sense that many films, across many genres, feature piano-playing protagonists – from the obvious biopics of classical or modern musicians, through to musicals, rom-coms, noir and *nouvelle vague* thrillers, ghost stories, even feminist period pieces. But the lot of the pianist in these films is seldom a happy one, their lives usually burdened by past failings, unfulfilled dreams, or awkward family ties. At least for the actor in search of an Oscar there is the consolation that playing an afflicted pianist is as good for one's odds as suffering a debilitating screen illness. So here are ten gifted pianists who can't help but play their roles, as well as their instruments, with a furrowed brow.

10. Charlie Kohler (Charles Aznavour) in *Tirez sur le Pianiste* / *Shoot the Piano Player* (France 1960, dir. François Truffaut)

In Truffaut's new wave/noir classic Charlie plays piano in a dive and falls for Lena, a waitress at the bar. But, as often turns out to be the case with piano men in the movies, Charlie has a previous life as a classical pianist, and a set of family problems: he used to be Eduoard Saroyan, a brilliant talent whose wife, Therese (a former waitress – nice theme running there), killed herself. We discover this as Charlie, despite trying to hide behind the upturned collar of his timeless mac, slips into a seedy crime underworld in an effort to save his kidnapped brother.

9. Erika Kohurt (Isabelle Huppert) in *La Pianiste* / *The Piano Teacher* (Austria/France 2001, dir. Michael Haneke)

No one takes angst quite to the same depths as the Austrians. As the sexually disturbed Erika in Nobel Prize winner Efriede Jelinek's semi-autobiographical adaptation of her own novel, Huppert plays the piano for real. It's possible that her hand-double was saved for performing all of the scratching, beating, and slicing served up in this tense tale of sexual hyper-frustration and an overbearing mother. In some ways Erika mirrors the directionless frustration of Jack Nicholson's Bobby Dupea (see *Five Easy Pieces* below). Both are given to long looks in the mirror; but while Bobby is clearly scrutinizing his reflection therein, Erika seems to be readying herself to smash the glass into shards for the purpose of some release through sexual self-mutilation. The result was too gross for the Oscars but Huppert picked up Best Actress at Cannes.

8. George Faure (Gérard Depardieu) in *Green Card* (US 1990, dir. Peter Weir)

There was a moment *c.* the late 1980s when forgetful, insensitive, chain-smoking, meat-eating, vegetarian-hating, French slobs were more fashionable in New York than at present. Thus Depardieu's first Hollywood lead, as a pianist entering into a marriage of convenience with Andie MacDowell's Brontë Parrish – he needs a green card, she wants a greenhouse. When it transpires that they are about to be investigated by US Immigration George has to move in and convince Brontë that he is actually *trés* sensitive, can play piano, and will be able to remember the brand of face cream she uses. Whilst failing at least one of these, he does come up trumps at a dinner party when his sensitive and touching recital manages to win a donation of trees to Brontë's beloved urban project 'The Green Guerrillas'. It is the playing, however, of an earlier piece – intense, animalistic, and 'free' – that suggests the dark, injured background of Georges's upbringing on the street. All that Gallic passion produces a sweat within about thirty seconds of ivory pounding.

7. Wladyslaw Szpilman (Adrien Brody) in *The Pianist* (France 2002, dir. Roman Polanski)

Brody is perfectly cast in this true-life story of a Polish-Jewish concert pianist's nightmarish journey into the underworld of Nazi Occupation. From the opening scene of his radio performance being shattered by the shells of the advancing Germans, through to his having to play an imaginary piano while he escapes transportation and death, through the Warsaw Ghetto Uprising and a period in hiding before he finds refuge in an abandoned house with a real piano and the patronage of a sympathetic German officer, Brody manages to play the illness and fear and the exhausted look of someone who is determined that there is no way that this Oscar-winning performance will end up on the cutting-room floor.

6. David Helfgott (Noah Taylor, Geoffrey Rush) in *Shine* (Australia 1996, dir. Scott Hicks)

Helfgott is a child prodigy who dedicates himself to becoming a great concert pianist, and manages to get into the Royal College of Music. But student life and his sense of dedication become too much. Despite realizing that it is 'a mountain, the hardest piece you could everest play', he chooses Rachmaninov's *Piano Concerto No. 3* for his Concerto Medal final performance piece. The 'Rach 3' becomes his bête noir, a pantomime villain so evil that, if it were a character, it would have to be played by Vincent Price. He is already mentally frail and reduced to wearing his underpants around the college halls, but a worse fate awaits him as he is essentially hunted down by this evil piece of music. During the exam, nearing the peak of the 'Rach 3', both Taylor and the camera shudder, and he falls, as if slain, from the keyboard. Helfgott suffers a breakdown so severe that Taylor undergoes a metamorphosis, turning into the Oscar-winning Geoffrey Rush.

5. Winslow Leach (William Finley) in *Phantom of the Paradise* (US 1974, dir. Brian De Palma)

De Palma's cult musical horror comedy does for Faust and *The Phantom of the Opera* what *The Rocky Horror Picture Show* did for Dracula and Frankenstein. When evil music impresario Swan (Paul Williams) steals a pop concerto (based on Faust) from nerdy, intense young musician Winslow Leach (William Finley), the stage is set for the geek-pianist's revenge – but only after a facially disfiguring accident involving a record press, whereupon Winslow returns as 'The Phantom' to haunt Swan's newly opened concert hall, 'The Paradise'. The genius of this movie (beside William's Oscar-nominated score) is the fact that, although his awful injuries are all to the head, the Phantom still insists on playing the piano wearing super-stylish black leather gloves.

4. Thomas Seyr (Romain Duris) in *The Beat that My Heart Skipped / De battre mon coeur s'est arrêté* (France 2005, dir. Jacques Audiard)

In this stylish French remake of James Tobak's *Fingers* (1978), Duris assumes a mantle formerly inhabited by Harvey Keitel. When younger, Thomas showed the potential to follow in his mother's footsteps as a gifted concert pianist, but since his parents' divorce he has discovered that he has a talent for violence and extortion as would be required to succeed in his father's occupation of property shark. But the past comes calling with an opportunity for Tom to audition for an agent and prove to himself that he can still cut it as a pianist. He undergoes a rehearsal-training scheme, which would make even Rocky proud, taking further lessons from a young gifted Chinese immigrant. But when the audition arrives Tom bottles it and freezes: he is far too smart, and realizes that his piano tutor has the real gift. His own talent resides in extracting money and revenge while looking drop-dead cool with his clenched jaw, loosened tie and more than a splash of blood on the white sleeves of his unbuttoned shirt.

3. Holly Hunter as Ada Stewart in *The Piano* (Australia/France 1993, dir. Jane Campion)

When you have just travelled across the world from Scotland and landed on a beach, along with your piano, and daughter, in 1850s New Zealand, you know that things are not looking good when your new husband greets you with the words, 'You're small. I never thought you'd be small.' When your prized piano – essentially your voicebox, since you don't speak – is then sold in a land bargain to an uncouth settler called George Baines, things have gone from worse to Mills and Boon tragic. When the only option to get back the piano is to give lessons to Baines (Harvey Keitel), Ada must apply herself, but Baines is interested in fingering more than her keyboard, and there are other lessons to be learned. At this point, if she weren't already mute, she would certainly be dumbstruck.

2. Jack Nicholson as Robert Eroica ('Bobby') Dupea in *Five Easy Pieces* (US 1970, dir. Bob Rafelson)

The movie that sets out to prove that classical music is more depressing than country 'n' western. Nicholson is the estranged son of a musically gifted but domestically intolerable upper-middle-class family. He tries to bury his talent and upbringing by working in the oil fields, sleeping around, getting drunk and scratching Tammy Wynette records on his partner's record player. Sometimes his slip shows: caught in slow-moving traffic on the freeway one day, he spies an upright on the back of a flatbed truck, and gives a short recital. On learning that Rayette, his hopelessly hopeful country-singing waitress girlfriend, may be pregnant, Bobby finds himself drawn to revisit the stilted atmosphere of the family home, where his father is mutely ailing after a stroke. There Bobby finds he can still 'fake a little Chopin' on a baby grand and so bed his brother's protégé Catherine; but she's otherwise unimpressed by his hatred for himself and for others. Bobby's aimless disillusionment was a plangent thing to American audiences in 1970, and it earned Nicholson his second Oscar nomination.

1. John Russell (George C. Scott) in *The Changeling* (Canada 1980, dir. Peter Medak)

Scott is a distinguished composer struggling to come to terms with having witnessed the horrific demise of his wife and child in a road accident. In an effort to give his life and work a new start he moves to a beautiful mansion in Seattle. Strangely, it has sat unoccupied for twelve years. Russell's efforts to write are disturbed by repeated banging on the pipes, and the inconvenient running of baths by some other hand. Despite these problems Russell is still able to compose a beautiful lullaby – only to discover that the piece is exactly the same as the haunting melody he finds played by a turn-of-the-century music box, lost for years in a hidden attic.

Scott proves a master of playing the piano with his face. In separate shots of hands on the keyboard and close-ups of the actor, we see a beautifully worried expression: is it the look of an actor trying to imitate his hand-double, the look of a composer trying to decide where the strings should come in, or the look of a tenant mulling over whether he needs to call a plumber or an exorcist? To attend to these questions without issuing a spoiler, I can only suggest you schedule a viewing of this unsung masterpiece.

Gentlemen of the Press

Ten Headlining Journalists in Film

DEMETRIOS MATHEOU

Years before I put my feet up and became a film critic, I was a reporter, a newspaperman. And in my time on the news beat I found that every cliché about journalism is true, from the monotony of

local council meetings and church fetes, to the adrenalin rush –
like no other – of covering murder trials, riots and wars. I also
realized that only the worst journalists are cynical, the best combining a necessary scepticism with finely tuned antennae for a
genuinely good story. The memorable films about journalism
don't necessarily feature the most admirable journalists: for every
inspirational figure, there is one whose idealism has turned to
scorn; for every bona fide reporter, a hack. I've chosen films that
cover that spectrum; what they have in common is a certain
fidelity to the process of reporting and, appropriately for their
scribing subjects, some of the most dazzling dialogue in the
movies.

10. Chuck Tatum (Kirk Douglas) in *Ace in the Hole* (US 1951,
dir. Billy Wilder)

Tatum is the best or the worst journalist ever seen on film, depending on whether you think the best, or the worst, of the profession.
It's a credit to Billy Wilder, his co-writers and snarling star Douglas
that their diabolical creation can sit happily at either end of the
scale. Tatum is the epitome of the gutter press, cynical, cut-throat
and sensationalist, who will do anything to get a story. 'I can handle big news and little news and, if there's no news, I will go out
and bite a dog,' he tells the editor of backwater paper the
Albuquerque Sun Bulletin. On sniffing the story that will return him
to the big time, he surpasses himself. A man is trapped down a
mine: Tatum stalls the rescue while he milks the impact of his
'human interest' exclusive. 'I've met a lot of hard-boiled eggs,' says
an equally ghastly accomplice. 'But you – you're twenty minutes.'

9. Marcello Rubini (Marcello Mastroianni) in *La Dolce Vita*
(Italy/France 1960, dir. Federico Fellini)

It's an old adage that journalists are frustrated authors; another
that, by extension, a fair number are gripped by self-loathing. No
one better illustrates the condition than dissolute hack Marcello,
purveyor of society sleaze in Fellini's bitter-sweet paean to sixties
Rome. Accompanied by his photographer pal Paparazzo – whose

name now coins the breed of hyena-like celebrity snapper –
Marcello stalks the film stars and aristocrats of the city's café society, for scraps of celebrity tittle-tattle. And when not trying to
seduce the people he's ostensibly writing about (notably a spectacular Anita Ekberg in the Trevi Fountain) the pathetic
Marcello bemoans the loss of his literary ambition. It's hard to
care, so well does Mastroianni nail his character's self-serving
charm and moral indolence.

8. Charles Foster Kane (Orson Welles) in *Citizen Kane* (US 1941, dir. Orson Welles)

Knowing as we do that *Citizen Kane* was based, in part, on the life
of the yellow press baron William Randolph Hearst, it's easy to
overlook the initial, idealistic appeal of Welles's eponymous hero.
At the outset of his editing career Charley Kane has the naive
enthusiasm of a student journalist, with his Declaration of
Principles, his desire to be a 'fighting and tireless champion' for
his readers, his constantly remaking of the front page. Kane, of
course, has the money to back those principles, and if he were to
remain an editor he might keep them; sadly, he is also a tycoon
with political ambitions. As writer, director and actor, Welles
brilliantly condenses the slow erosion of journalistic integrity into
one scene – the famous breakfast exchange with his first wife.
'Really, Charles,' she says, 'people will think . . .' At which he
interjects, 'What I tell them to think.'

7. Richard Boyle (James Woods) in *Salvador* (US 1986, dir. Oliver Stone)

'How about freezing my fucking nuts off for you guys in the
Khyber Pass? I was stapled under the toilet for that one.' Thus
maverick photojournalist Richard Boyle pitches for a 'string' to
cover the brutal dictatorship in El Salvador at the end of the seventies. He fails to get the gig, but drives down to Central America
anyway, with hapless chum Dr Rock (James Belushi) in tow, and
pretty soon they're in the thick of civil war. Oliver Stone wrote
his script with the real Boyle, who is portrayed by James Woods as

a classic gonzo journalist, confronting the news subjectively, in extremis, out of control: with Dr Rock the drug-addled attorney to Boyle's Hunter S. Thompson, the intoxicated pair tiptoeing between the death squads and the guerrillas. When the shit hits the fan, though, the newsman's instinct takes over: the silent cry of triumph shared by Boyle and fellow photographer John Cassady (John Savage) as the FMLN horsemen ride into town is a moment of stunning fidelity to journalistic desire.

6. J.J. Hunsecker (Burt Lancaster) in *Sweet Smell of Success* (US 1957, dir. Alexander Mackendrick)

Based on infamous New York gossip columnist Walter Winchell, Hunsecker is one of the creepiest villains in the movies: a psychopath with a pen and the city in his thrall. Through his column 'The Eyes of Broadway', the ruthless J.J. can make or break a career – and the power leaves him with nothing but disdain for all around him. When he says 'I love this dirty town', it's only because he owns it. He also owns fawning publicist Sidney Falco (Tony Curtis), who would sell his soul for just a few of J.J.'s column inches. Alexander Mackendrick's presentation of their unsavoury association as a film noir is spot on, since this is a world ruled by cynicism. The leads bring the very real interdependence of hack and publicist vividly to life, with Lancaster offering the worst possible advertisement for the Fourth Estate.

5. Nick Mullen (Gabriel Byrne) in *Defence of the Realm* (GB 1985, dir. David Drury)

One of the most authentic depictions of the journalistic milieu, this is set in London's Fleet Street when it was still the hub of the British newspaper world. The thriller plot – a British government's cover-up of a nuclear accident – may be a fiction, but it's played like a journalistic procedural, with Nick Mullen going about his business in a way all too familiar to real reporters: 'doorstepping', phoning in copy, poring over cuttings, fighting for his story with the editors – all for the triumphant celebration of the scoop down the pub. The best moment is when he pretends to be a sympathetic copper to get a disgraced MP's wife to open up. As one colleague acidulously laments, 'There are no secrets from the street of shame, dear boy.'

4. Guy Hamilton (Mel Gibson) in *The Year of Living Dangerously* (Australia 1982, dir. Peter Weir)

Set in Indonesia during the months leading up to the fall of the Sukarno government, this offers a potent evocation of the life of the foreign correspondent – in this case, one on his first assignment overseas. Australian radio reporter Hamilton has to learn the ropes fast, in a totally unfamiliar environment, with no help from the complacent, jaded press corps, who see him first as someone to laugh at, then – as he starts to file stories of note – as a threat. But even good journalists can't do it alone, and Guy's saviour comes in the dwarfish form of Billy Kwan (Linda Hunt), a half-Indonesian, half-Australian photojournalist who knows the culture and has the contacts. Gibson's Guy is at the most romantic end of the screen reporter spectrum – a chain-smoking, excitable young stud who gets the girl (Sigourney Weaver) as well as the story. Even the sweat that pours from his back has the allure of a scoop waiting to happen.

3. Edward R. Morrow (David Strathairn) in *Good Night, and Good Luck* (US/France/GB/Japan 2005, dir. George Clooney)

Morrow was a journalist cast from the original mould: making his name with his first-hand radio reports of the London Blitz, before setting the standard for broadcast journalism back home in the US in the fifties. In his second film as director, George Clooney charts the famous confrontation between Morrow and the anti-communist, witch-hunting Senator Joseph McCarthy. Playing like a good news story – succinct, with a tight, no-nonsense structure – the film follows the newsman (David Strathairn) and his CBS producer Fred Friendly (Clooney) as they 'take a little poke with a stick, see what happens'. While Clooney captures the camaraderie of crusading journalists, it would be nice to think that Strathairn's riveting

display of chain-smoking charisma and melancholic resolve
has inspired a new generation.

2. Walter Burns (Cary Grant) and Hildy Johnson (Rosalind
Russell) in *His Girl Friday* (US 1940, dir. Howard Hawks)

'You're a great newspapermaaan' proclaims Chicago editor Burns
to his ace reporter. No matter that she's a woman, for in the for-
ties this is a man's world; Hildy just happens to be better than all
of them – sharp, wily and fast, but with a compassion her fellow
reporters lack. 'Gentlemen of the press' she mutters, as the cynical courthouse hacks play cards and ignore a girl's plea for a con-
demned man's life. Hawks's great screwball comedy smacks of
verisimilitude, from the terrific pan of the empty press room –
phones ringing, ashtrays smoking, waiting for the newshounds to
return with their story – to the symbiotic relationship of the brash
editor and his top gun, played at breakneck speed by Grant and
Russell. While Russell wins the 'Best Hat' stakes, Grant shades
the best lines: 'I want you to tear out the front page. Never mind
the European war, we've got something a lot bigger than that . . .
No, no, leave the rooster story alone. That's human interest.'

1. Bob Woodward (Robert Redford) and Carl Bernstein (Dustin
Hoffman) in *All the President's Men* (US 1976, dir. Alan J.
Pakula)

The canny liberal Redford picked up on the *Washington Post*'s
investigation of Watergate in its early stages, and pursued
Woodward and Bernstein with his desire to make a movie while
the reporters themselves were still in hot pursuit of the White
House. Everyone got what they wanted, and the result is the
greatest depiction of investigative reporting in action. 'Howard,
they're hungry. Remember when you were hungry?' says the boys'
city editor to a colleague. 'Woodstein', as they become known in
the *Post* newsroom, have a pure desire for the story that transcends ambition and righteousness; and as the pair enters the
shadowy world of undisclosed sources and 'non-denial denials',
Redford and Hoffman play their obsession to perfection. Director

Pakula and scriptwriter William Goldman bravely make the nuts and bolts of the trade – endless interviews, note-taking and typing – the dramatic impulse of the film. This is investigative reporting as it really is: less inspiration than legwork; albeit with a little help from Deep Throat, Woodward's secret source in the car park and every reporter's wet dream. 'Follow the money . . . Just follow the money.'

More Syrup, Sir?: The Ten Worst Wigs an Actor Dared to Wear, p 140

8

Nearly Human

Animal, Mineral and Ethereal Icons of the Movies

PAUL DALE AND RICHARD T. KELLY: All God's Creatures Got a Place in the Movies – Ten Great Performances by Animals

MATT THORNE: Domo Arigato, Mr Roboto – Ten Dodgy Robots

RICHARD T. KELLY: Heaven Must Be Missing an Angel – Ten Otherworldly Girls

All God's Creatures Got a Place in the Movies

Ten Great Performances by Animals

BY PAUL DALE AND RICHARD T. KELLY

'If you pick up a starving dog and make him prosperous, he will not bite you. This is the principal difference between a dog and a man.' So noted Mark Twain in the days before the rise of Hollywood and world cinema. As usual Twain was both ahead of his time and wiser than those who were to follow. Certain animal stars were much indulged in the early decades of cinema (Trigger, Rin Tin Tin) but for the most part animals were dumb, malleable commodities who accepted the iniquities that wranglers and handlers hoisted upon them, despite the fact that these furry performers often got more fan-mail than their spoiled, ungrateful human counterparts (Rin Tin Tin received 30,000 letters a week in the 1920s). But as with humans, there are some animals who are just better performers than others: they take the ham out and put the method in. Here, then, are ten real troopers from the animal kingdom. (PD)

10. 'Tai' as Vera the elephant in *Larger Than Life* (US 1996, dir. Howard Franklin)

Tai had a bad experience in the title-role of *Operation Dumbo Drop* (1995), resolving thereafter to avoid painful studio comedies about Vietnam and to work only with hip ironists like Bill Murray. Well, you'd like to think . . . Here Murray is a painfully insincere 'motivational speaker' whose life takes a deserved turn for the worse when he learns that his late father was a circus clown, his patrimony a supposedly trained elephant called Vera. Murray's mission becomes to get Vera across the USA to California, there to choose between selling her to a circus or donating her to environmental activist Janeane Garofalo. You can surely imagine how the stoically wrinkly Vera works magic on Murray's heart en route. The crux comes when, trekking through a New Mexico desert rainstorm, man and pachyderm stumble upon some villagers struggling to keep their adobe church from collapsing into the mud. The manner in which Vera puts her back and trunk into the effort brings a tear to Murray's eye. 'They say an elephant never forgets,' he observes later. 'But what they don't tell you is, you never forget an elephant.' (RTK)

9. 'Keiko' as Willy the whale in *Free Willy* (US 1993, dir. Simon Wincer) et al.

Three-ton orca whale Keiko had quite a life before he was propelled to fame in a lucrative family film franchise. Captured off the coast of Iceland in 1979 he endured the indignities of exhibition first in an Icelandic aquarium, then in Ontario's 'Marineland' and a Mexico City amusement park. By the time of his big break he was in poor health: lesions that had begun to develop in Canada were exacerbated by poor conditions in Mexico. Not that you would know from his performance in *Free Willy*, wherein he leaps, bounds, and yelps like a pro. Manipulation and special effects aside, there can be little doubt that Keiko was milking it for all he could. It took two more sequels, donations from the studio and fans, the formation of a Free Willy Keiko Foundation and some careful preparation before the beloved mammal was returned to the wild in 2002. Keiko died off the coast of Norway in December 2003, aged twenty-seven, some way short of the average orca lifespan. Stardom had exacted its toll. (PD)

8. Betty the pig in *A Private Function* (GB 1984, dir. Malcolm Mowbray)

As Denholm Elliott's snobby Dr Swaby points out to Michael Palin's weak-willed chiropodist Gilbert Chilvers, 'You've got something we want, something that belongs to us, something with four legs and a curly tail . . .' That something is Betty, an illegally raised porcine beauty who, in still-rationed post-Second World War Northern England, has been kidnapped by Chilvers in an attempt to impress his bullying wife Joyce (Maggie Smith). Betty appears only in the few scenes, behaving much as would any pig being kept in the kitchen of a 1940s tenement. The thing is –

she's unbearably cute, and it is her personality that wins over both Gilbert and Henry Allardyce the accountant (Richard Griffiths) in the heartfelt final scene. Betty ties and clinches both the intricacies and hypocrisies evident throughout Alan Bennett's bittersweet screenplay. (PD)

7. Widow Runk's cow in *L'Albero degli Zoccoli / The Tree of Wooden Clogs* (Italy 1978, dir. Ermanno Olmi)

Depending on your sensibility – whether you care more for the pain of animals or the painstaking intent of auteur directors – you may come away from Olmi's film (winner of the top prize at Cannes) thinking about the pig that is slaughtered at length, the horse soundly beaten – or the cow saved by a slug of holy water. Amid varied vignettes and threads about tenant farmers in the Bergamo region in 1898, we meet Widow Runk (Teresa Brescianini), struggling mother of six. The orphanage doesn't have room for them, but this family resolves to work together anyway. They cannot, however, afford to lose their sickening cow, but the vet says the animal is dying, should be slaughtered. So Widow Runk fills a bottle in a stream, walks to the chapel and begs for a holy blessing. Praying all the while she returns and feeds the water to the cow, who struggles back to her feet in due course. It's a miraculous touch from a very pro-Catholic director in a film where injustice is otherwise conspicuous. As for the cow's performance? It's perfectly fine, certainly no more or less modulated than anyone else in the amateur cast. (RTK)

6. 'Cheeta' as Cheeta the chimpanzee in *Tarzan the Ape Man* (US 1932, dir. W.S. Van Dyke) et al.

Would you believe that Cheeta, star of twelve Tarzan films, is still alive (or was at time of writing) and living in a primate retirement home in Palm Springs? This hairy, four-foot, 150-pound sidekick often had more charm, wit and timing than his human co-stars. He was discovered by animal trainer Tony Gentry during a scout of Africa in the 1930s, and Gentry realized he had a star on his hands when Cheeta's diary became more busy than his own.

Having retired from films in 1967 (his final appearance in Richard Fleischer's *Dr Doolittle*) Cheeta continued to live with Gentry and his family. It was Gentry's intention that following his own death Cheeta too should be 'put to sleep' lest he suffer at the hands of others who cared for him less. But Gentry's nephew Dan Westfall took Cheeta in when his uncle died. Today, Westfall's Cheeta Primate Foundation is home to Cheeta and many other retired chimps, orangutans, and unwanted or abused showbiz primates. Cheeta has lately turned seventy-five, and the question of his continued existence and relevance to the world was lately a subplot in Darren Aronofsky's *The Fountain* (PD).

5. 'Pal' as Lassie the dog in *Lassie Come Home* (US 1943, dir. Fred M. Wilcox) et al.

Pal was the first to play Eric Knight's fictional 'rough collie' on screen in this cherished saga of courage and loyalty. Like the many Lassies that were to follow, Pal was a male playing female, but he made an immediate hit. Trained by actor and animal wrangler Rudd Weatherwax, Pal became a movie star by default. MGM had decided to use a show collie trained by Frank Inn, but when it came time to shoot the movie's crucial flood scene (utilizing the flash flooding of the Sacramento River in California) Inn's collie seemed unable to execute the complicated stunts. So MGM hired Pal as a stand-in for the scene, and the rest is history. Or, as MGM head Louis B. Meyer allegedly put it, 'Pal entered the water, but Lassie came out.' Pal went on to make another six Lassie films before his death in 1958, so versatile that in some of them he played Lassie's son or father. (PD)

4. Cass Ole, Fae-Jur, Star, Junior, Olympic and Rex as 'The Black', the horse in *The Black Stallion* (US 1979, dir. Carroll Ballard)

Ballard is one of several directors on this list with a special interest in – and aptitude for – this kind of work. His entrancing adaptation of Walter Farley's novel – produced by Francis Coppola, critically lionized by Pauline Kael – is deservedly one of the most adored of all children's movies, a work that suggests the force of myth to young minds in a form far more plangent than Harry Potter. A young boy (Kelly Reno) survives the wreck of a passenger boat only to be stranded on an island with an Arabian black stallion whom he admired while aboard. Stealthily, wordlessly, he builds a rapport with the magnificent creature after it rears out of nowhere to save him from a memorably sinister cobra. By the end of the picture boy and horse are an unbeatable racing team, trained by Mickey Rooney. Former show horse and champion racer Cass Ole took most of the kudos, though his white markings had to be dyed, and several other horses performed the fighting and running stunts. (RTK)

3. Tao the cat in *The Incredible Journey* (US 1963, dir. Fletcher Markle)

It's a tough call choosing between Luath the retriever, Bodger the bull terrier and Tao the Siamese cat in Markle's wonderful, evergreen Canadian family film. Certainly they all make the human actors look like the third-rate jobbers they were. But it's Tao who inches it. Based on Sheila Burnford's popular novel about three pets who have to find their way home when their owners mislay them on holiday, *The Incredible Journey* features many great action sequences, but Tao enjoys the best of them, particularly in the now near-iconic scene where he gets into a spitting match with a lynx on a branch. Within the space of a few years Tao had more rivals than you could dangle a ball of string in front of – generic rubbish like *The Three Lives of Thomasina* (1964) and *That Darn Cat!* (1965). But accept no imitations, Tao was the original and the best. (PD)

2. Kumal and Sangha as the tigers in *Two Brothers / Deux Frères* (France/GB 2004, dir. Jean-Jacques Annaud)

Arnaud knows a lot about animals, and he certainly knows how to get good performances out of them. Best known for *The Bear* (1988), Arnaud is now synonymous with animal-orientated live-action family films, despite a few human-centred epic misfires along the way (*The Lover*, *Seven Years in Tibet*, *Enemy at the*

Gates). *Two Brothers* is the story of a pair of tigers born in the 1920s and raised peacefully by their parents in the overgrown remains of a Buddhist temple in the Indochine jungle. But the cubs are separated from their parents and then each other after an archaeological looting party enters their vicinity. Even if you allow for the manipulations of a huge visual effects team, the performances by both cub and adult tigers in this film are unsurpassable. It wouldn't work if the audience couldn't tell the difference between the two leads (with the exception of Guy Pearce's sulky explorer, the human characters are nearly negligible), because one of the tigers is as shy as the other is bold. The fact that from the off the audience is never in any doubt as to who is who is of great credit to all concerned, particularly in the final showdown between the two estranged siblings. (PD)

1. Balthazar the donkey in *Au Hasard, Balthazar* (France 1966, dir. Robert Bresson)

One could populate this list almost entirely with Bresson – the fraught horses of *Lancelot du Lac* (1974), the mournful orphaned dog in *L'Argent* (1983). In interviews this inimitable French master continually hymned what he saw as the 'exquisite sensitivity' of certain animals. Re-reading Dostoyevsky's *The Idiot* he was captivated by the passage wherein Myshkin senses some profound communication in the braying of a donkey. 'Absolutely admirable', Bresson declared, 'to have an idiot informed by an animal, to have him see life through an animal, who passes for an idiot but is of an intelligence.' The donkey lead in Bresson's rural parable *Au Hasard, Balthazar* is, over the course of a thankless life, made to endure all that men and women may inflict on those whom they consider their inferiors. The stroke of Bresson's genius is that we see the stages of Balthazar's life as hardly so different from our own; certainly not from those of his intermittent owner, the ill-used Marie (Anne Wiazemsky). Bertolt Brecht is said to have kept a small toy donkey on his work-desk, around its neck a hand-lettered sign saying, 'I too must understand.' One fondly imagines that he too would have seen his own reflection in Balthazar. (RTK)

Domo Arigato, Mr Roboto
Ten Dodgy Robots

BY MATT THORNE

Every now and again, on a slow news-day, you will read an article about how scientists and legal experts are busily working out 'rights for robots' considerations to cover the future time when automatons become sentient. But when this day finally dawns it's likely that our biggest problem will be explaining how badly we've represented them in the movies. Decide for yourself whether the recent Michael Bay version of *Transformers* has made amends . . . In the meantime, here are some of my favourite dodgy robot/android films, all of which will no doubt be used in some future robo-court as grounds for our extermination.

10. Ulysses (John Malkovich) in *Making Mr Right* (US 1987, dir. Susan Seidelman)

Relations between the sexes must have hit bottom in this year if women were lusting after an android played by John Malkovich. Seidelman's follow-up to *Desperately Seeking Susan* is really a moan about emotionally distant commitment-phobes, as Malkovich plays both Dr Jeff Peters, a scientist who lacks the ability to love and Ulysses, an android he has made in his own image. Malkovich, in fairness, was about to become an improbable sex symbol due to *Dangerous Liaisons*, but the main reason for watching this picture is the female lead performance by occasional actress and Bongwater vocalist Ann Magnuson – something of a magnet for cult projects, from *The Hunger* to the extraordinary Mariah Carey vehicle *Glitter* – and, to this writer's mind, a far more appealing fantasy partner than Mr Malkovich.

9. Various in *Screamers* (Canada/US/Japan 1995, dir. Christian Duguay)

The writings of Philip K. Dick have inspired some of the best science-fiction films ever made, most eminently *Bladerunner*. *Screamers* isn't in that first rank, but is a great guilty pleasure in the manner of the giant worm movie *Tremors* or John Carpenter's *In the Mouth of Madness*. The dodgy robots here are 'Screamers', who come in both child- and adult-sized forms, have saw-teeth mouths, and are capable of emitting ear-piercing shrieks. Be warned, *Screamers* is perhaps the most frightening film on this list, and among the most imaginative, despite (or because of) a smaller budget than most. Peter Weller, the *Robocop* star also accustomed to working with Antonioni and Cronenberg, treats the potentially risible material with absolute seriousness, and the rest of the cast follow suit.

8. Teddy (voiced by Jack Angel) in *A.I.: Artificial Intelligence* (US 2001, dir. Steven Spielberg)

As with George Lucas's *Star Wars: Episode 1 – The Phantom Menace* (1999), this was a film that so incensed audience members that one of them went so far as to produce their own alternative edit. It's the end section that upsets most people, since it takes place thousands of years after the rest of the film, severing the essential emotional link with the present that makes the rest of the film so brilliantly punishing. As for the dodgy robot, take your pick; but the animatronic 'Teddy', a walking, talking toy bear the wrong side of cute, is only marginally less creepy than Haley Joel Osmond (who, when sitting in his creepy child's tuxedo at the Oscars, always reminds me of a miniaturized Stan Laurel).

7. Various in *I, Robot* (US/Germany 2004, dir. Alex Proyas)

The first of two Isaac Asimov adaptations here, everything about this film is first-rate . . . aside from the robots, obsequious butler-types seemingly modelled on Sir John Gielgud. As with many adaptations of authors from the golden age of sci-fi, this offers a supposed future that already feels dated, but features one of Will Smith's finest performances and addresses the (seemingly burning) topic of 'robot rights' in a way that manages to make it feel like a genuinely compelling public matter. It lacks the gothic edge of director Proyas's finest work (*The Crow, Dark City*), but seems likely to make repeat appearances on Robot TV in the twenty-second century.

6. Number 5 (voiced by Tim Blaney) in *Short Circuit* (US 1986, dir. John Badham) and *Short Circuit 2* (US 1988, dir. Kenneth Johnson)

In Noah Baumbach's deliberately excruciating nostalgia-fest *The Squid and the Whale*, the protagonist's pretentious author-father (Jeff Daniels) hijacks his son's trip with his girlfriend to see *Short Circuit*, making them watch *Blue Velvet* instead. Of course the scene is supposed to reveal the father as overbearing, but really the kids had a lucky escape from the adventures of one of celluloid's least compelling robots, Number 5 – a face-on-wheels about as likeable as Dusty Bin from the unlamented Saturday night game-show *3-2-1*. I include both it and its follow-up here as examples of how 1980s directors could make family fodder out of almost anything. Astonishingly for a man who made four *Police Academy* films, Steve Guttenberg bailed on the sequel.

5. Samantha Pringle (Kristy Swanson) in *Deadly Friend* (US 1986, dir. Wes Craven)

Craven fans value his bad films (*Shocker, Swamp Thing, The People Under the Stairs*) almost as highly as his good ones (*Last House on the Left, Nightmare on Elm Street*, the *Scream* trilogy), and this mid-1980s adaptation of Diana Henstell's part-genius/part-schlock novel is his finest guilty pleasure. Matthew Laborteaux is a geeky computer whizkid with a robot pal named BB and a sly crush on the sexy girl next door (Swanson, pre-Buffy). When BB gets trashed and Swanson is killed by her alcoholic father, Laborteaux turns Frankenstein and re-animates his beloved in robot form. Cue lots of Swanson walking around with her hands ridiculously stiffened to look like robot clamps.

4. Lieutenant Ilia (Persis Khambatta) in *Star Trek: The Motion Picture* (US 1979, dir. Robert Wise)

In space, no one can hear you shear. Science-fiction fans do appear to have a thing for bald women. Whether it's Sigourney Weaver in *Alien3*, Natalie Portman in *V For Vendetta*, the cast of *THX 1138*, or Samantha Morton in *Minority Report*, the future often seems to involve sexy women with shaved heads. But perhaps the best of this bunch is the robot replacement for Deltan navigator Lieutenant Ilia in the first *Star Trek* feature film. A former Miss India, Persis Khambatta died of a heart attack in 1998. She was honoured with the 2003 award for Bald Woman of the Year from the Bald R Us society and website, a mere twenty-four years after her fleeting entry into *Trek* lore.

3. The eponymous robot (Pamela Gidley) in *Cherry 2000* (US 1987, dir. Steve De Jarnatt)

Released the same year as *Making Mr Right*, this is the male version of the same fantasy. Although ostensibly a sci-fi film, its first ten minutes encapsulate the 1980s better than any other release of that decade. In the middle of a blue-and-red neon bachelor-flat paradise, future TV journeyman David Andrews enjoys a date with his robot partner, the Cherry 2000 (Gidley, later to play fantasy-women for Mike Figgis – in *Liebestraum* – and David Lynch – as Teresa Banks in *Twin Peaks: Fire Walk With Me*). Midway through their lovemaking she malfunctions, so sending him on a *Mad Max*-style adventure (accompanied by a young Melanie Griffith) to find a duplicate. Unfortunately, along the way he decides that flesh-and-blood is better than his robot-lover, so turning the picture into a far more conventional piece than the perverse masterpiece it initially appeared.

2. Val (Andy Kaufman) and Aqua (Bernadette Peters) in *Heartbeeps* (US 1981, dir. Allan Arkush)

Do you remember 1999, the year of Andy Kaufman? When Jim Carrey starred in *Man on the Moon*, the Milos Forman biopic of the late comedian's crazed existence, every part of Kaufman's career was immediately celebrated. Apart from this film. One of his few celluloid appearances, *Heartbeeps* features Kaufman drawing upon the more moronic side of his persona to play a robot short of a few circuit boards, who dreams of running away from household servitude and starting a family. With a dynamite supporting cast (including Peters as Val's girlfriend, and Randy Quaid as an even stupider robot pal), *Heartbeeps* actually holds up as an entertaining family film. But only for the very young . . .

1. Andrew Martin (Robin Williams) in *Bicentennial Man* (US 1999, dir. Chris Columbus)

Someone once told me that the quickest way to befriend Chris Columbus is to tell him you enjoyed this critical disaster. I have a genuine soft spot for it, although it's one of those films that seem unlikely to be fully understood for at least another thousand years. Another Asimov adaptation, it asks of an audience the same as Spielberg's *A.I.*, namely to be moved by a situation impossibly far-removed from the human condition: when we mortals have a life expectancy of approximately eighty years, why should we care about a two-hundred-year-old robot who wishes to become human? Especially when that robot is played by Robin Williams?

Heaven Must Be Missing an Angel

Ten Otherworldly Girls

BY RICHARD T. KELLY

'There ought to be something eternal about a woman,' muses old Cecil Kellaway in *Portrait of Jennie* (1948) – an elegant fancy, albeit one that sets the bar rather high for womankind. Nevertheless the movies have offered any number of supernatural romances in which svelte, enigmatic females turn out to be immortal or literally ethereal. A darker alternative is offered by certain horror/fantasy films wherein a woman can appear in superficially pleasing form yet be nothing but a wraith or a devil, veiling a threat or playing some wicked game. The allure is quite obvious, for there can be something terribly appealing about someone who's a bit different, a bit special – and then something terribly unappealing too. You could get a nasty nip.

This is a list of assorted girls who are not what they seem – or exactly what we might fear. They are either dead but have risen, or have trespassed into this world from some Other Side, or they are emissaries of the Evil One Himself. I wish I could have included the young Jessica Lange as Roy Scheider's soul-taker in Fosse's *All That Jazz*, or Veronica Lake in René Clair's *I Married a Witch* (the obvious riposte being 'Well, you would, wouldn't you? Since she looks like that?'). And had the rules allowed for TV work I would have thrown in Sheryl Lee from *Twin Peaks* as the ghastly shrieking double of Laura Palmer who menaces Agent Cooper in the Black Lodge.

10. Eva Galli/Alma Mobley (Alice Krige) in *Ghost Story* (US 1981, dir. John Irvin)

South African-born Krige went on to confirm that her glacial, well-bred looks were not quite of this earth by subsequent turns as a cat-beast in Stephen King's *Sleepwalkers* and as an alien queen in one of the many *Star Trek* spin-offs. But her finest hour is perhaps her debut, as a lady who quite rightly returns from the grave to plague a quartet of codgers who call themselves The Chowder Club. These old boys (including Fred Astaire and Douglas Fairbanks Jr.) share an awful secret from their salad days, when they caused the death of a girl on whom they were all sweet. One by one they start to drop, as flies to wanton girls, and it becomes clear they are being taught a hell of a lesson. As youthful Alma and frightful Eva, Krige is so wispily lovely that one learns to dread her reversions to rotted-corpse form nearly as much as do her victims.

9. Sadako (Rie Inou) in *Ringu / The Ring* (Japan 1998, dir. Hideo Nakata)

The Asian horror sensation of the late nineties was founded on a splendidly simple urban-myth premise – a chain videotape that promises doom to any viewer. As journalist Nanako Matsushima stumbles into the web and tries to unmesh herself by solving the mystery, Nakata keeps the tale very cool and understated, probably because in the monster stakes he has an ace in the hole – or the well, if you like. White-robed, her sheet-black hair hiding all but one fishy eye, the wraith Sadako is like a Goth legend in the making. Her jerky, shuffly, supremely creepy walk was made by simply reversing film of actress Rie Inou stepping backward: economical movie magic, worthy of Cocteau or Murnau.

8. Selina Kyle/Catwoman (Michelle Pfeiffer) in *Batman Returns* (US 1992, dir. Tim Burton)

Well, she's dead, isn't she? No mortal survives being thrown from a high-rise window by Christopher Walken. Nine lives or not, Selina looks distinctly bloodless in the following scene as she returns to her spinster flat, decides she is through with all the indignities visited on her, and furiously stitches a costume out of a patent leather raincoat, so transforming herself into one more on the chorus-line of Tim Burton's fetishistic dream-girls.

7. The Girl Angel/Satan (Juliette Caton) in *The Last Temptation of Christ* (US/Canada 1988, dir. Martin Scorsese)

Scorsese was the first director to really nail Jesus up on to that Golgothan cross. An anguished performance by Willem Dafoe, forsaken on all sides, helps to evoke the stony, bloody desolation. Then abruptly the Nazarene finds the noise gone mute all around, and his gaze falls on a perfect little blonde girl who beckons him down. Calling herself his 'guardian angel', she has golden curls, a full mouth and a Roman nose. She offers him the life of a normal man, assures him he has already suffered quite sufficiently for his Father's purpose. She sits serenely outside as Jesus and Mary Magdalene make love, then blesses their marriage, and consoles him when Mary dies in childbirth. She watches over his patriarchal old age, and steers him away from that troublemaker Paul (Harry Dean Stanton). It's only when Jesus is visited on his deathbed by a bitterly anguished Judas (Harvey Keitel) that this 'angel' is called by her true name: for the last temptation is domesticity, and in short order Jesus is renouncing Satan and begging to be set back upon the upright.

6. The Devil (Silvia Piñal) in *Simón del Desierto* / *Simon of the Desert* (Mexico 1965, dir. Luis Buñuel)

The great Buñuel (who famously thanked God he was an atheist) likely had a soft spot for the Devil, or at least would have chosen His party if it came to it. In the early sixties the Mexican singer/actress Silvia Piñal was to Buñuel what Monica Vitti was for Antonioni (on screen, that is), and in the maestro's half-length skit inspired by fourth-century anchorite Simeon Stylites, she is the sulphurous female who appears in the form of a naughty schoolgirl and a bearded goatherd, trying to lure Simon from his self-mortifying spot atop a high column. It would be a fine thing if Lucifer looked and sounded like Silvia Piñal . . .

5. Regan McNeil/Pazuzu (Linda Blair) in *The Exorcist* (US 1973, dir. William Friedkin)

. . . Then again, one may prefer to imagine the Devil as a vile goblin who masturbates with a crucifix, knows all your dirty secrets, vomits forth obscene insults like bile, and also vomits forth a good deal of bile. Blatty's sensational novel, a hot read for adults and school-kids alike in the early 1970s, was realized with stupendous boldness by Friedkin. There's a certain pathos in the sufferings of thirteen-year-old Blair, her apple-cheeks gradually caked in Dick Smith's ghastly make-up, her notorious utterings ('Lick me!' et cetera) dubbed in by gravelly Mercedes McCambridge. The whole package, though, is an undeniable winner, such stuff as nightmares are made of.

4. Lilith Arthur (Jean Seberg) in *Lilith* (US 1963, dir. Robert Rossen)

'The mad ones spin out fantastic, asymmetrical and rather nightmarish designs.' Asylum director Dr Lavrier is describing the webs of schizophrenic spiders. Or is he? Vincent Bruce (a young Warren Beatty) takes a job at Lavrier's institution in the hope he may be 'of direct help' to its inmates. Fairest of them all is Lilith, who draws, spins, and plays the flute 'quite magically'. She speaks casually of having been taught by her 'people', as if they were gods. There is 'rapture' about her, all agree. Is it just the power of beauty, wed to insanity? She certainly keeps the milquetoast Steven (Peter Fonda) rapt in admiration. Beatty seems wise to her wiles, and yet still he is lured over the threshold into her magical little world, whereupon Lilith becomes a maddening tease and a worrying taunt, wont to speak of herself in the third person ('She wants to leave the mark of her desire on every living creature in the world'). The Lilith of mythology was a Babylonian seductress and child-catcher, also the insubordinate first wife of Adam, expelled from the canonical Bible. Jean Seberg's Lilith is a nymphomaniac, with an unhealthy way of addressing pre-pubescent boys. At base, though, she's just insane, right? The viewer may feel otherwise, but for sure there is no better film about lovesickness (or sick love) than this.

3. Jennie Appleton (Jennifer Jones) in *Portrait of Jennie* (US 1948, dir. William Dieterle)

The cult of Jennie is founded on two exceptional film-historical factors: it was a pricey super-production from the obsessive mind of David O. Selznick, devised for his wife Jennifer Jones; and it is one of the few Hollywood studio products that had Buñuel in rhapsodies ('a mysterious, poetical and largely misunderstood work'). Joseph Cotten plays a penniless, disconsolate painter who encounters a strangely fervent little girl in Central Park. She dresses and talks as though from a bygone era, and sings an odd unsettling song ('Where I come from, no one knows / And where I'm going, everyone goes'). Thereafter he continues to run into Jennie or, rather, she is continually running towards him from out of the gloom (always shot in low angle, a hazy sun or glowing moon behind her). And she's a little older each time. Cotten's painting, meanwhile, is marked by a new passion. He realizes the strangeness of what he's doing –

Veil, Visor, Disguiser: Ten Fascinating Face-Masks, p 149

some basic detective work confirms to him that he's in love
with a dead girl – yet gives himself up to it, not least because
of the powerful nothings she whispers into his ear ('Of all the
people who lived from world's end to world's end, there is just
one you must love, and you must seek until you find him').

2. Lady Wakasa (Machiko Kyo) in *Ugetsu Monogatari* (Japan
1953, dir. Kenji Mizoguchi)

The eyebrows have it – painted as perfect smudges on the
alabaster forehead of the exquisite Wakasa. Her bearing and
regard for fine handicrafts are sufficient to lure the money-mad
potter Genjurô (Masayuki Mori) back to her castle, Kutsuki
Manor, a candlelit place of curtains and Shoji screens. The mood
is so heady that Genjurô is hardly fazed by the maid's assertion
that he and her mistress must marry: he has lived in a kind of fog
ever since departing from his home and family seven years previous. By some speeding grace (that of Mizoguchi's camera) he and
the Lady are soon picnicking amid wild reeds: 'I never knew such
pleasures existed,' he cries. It is only when he boasts of his new
address while bartering with a priest that he is told what we have
guessed: 'Lady Wakasa is a spirit from the dead.' When next she
reaches to touch him she recoils like a scalded cat ('He has something on his skin!'), for the priest has marked Genjurô with protective Sanskrit symbols of prayer. She retreats from him, into
enveloping and terminal shadow. Freed of the fog Genjurô returns
to our world, wherein he can see Kutsuki Manor for the ruin it
truly is – though his meetings with the dead are not yet conclud-
ed in this Mizoguchi masterpiece.

1. The Princess/Death (Maria Casarès) in *Orphée* (France 1950,
dir. Jean Cocteau)

When first we and Orphée (Jean Marais) see her in daylight at a
literary cafe, testy patron to the loutish young poet Cegeste, she
looks a tad mannish – black dress and bolero, gloves and pearls,
hair scraped back, a hard smoker. After she's swept away in her
black sedan with leather-clad outriders, we realize she needs the

night and a key light on her face to flourish. After dark we start to notice her figure, the gloss of her hair, the grain of her voice, her ability to raise the dead and walk through a mirror as though it were water. 'Did you expect a shroud and scythe? If I appeared to mortals in the guise they expect it would make our task more difficult . . .' Despite her powers, she is compelled to face an underworld tribunal on account of her feelings for Orphée. ('I have no right to love. Yet I do.') There are, of course, heavy gay undertones here, commingled with the imagery of the Resistance. But on the surface Casarès is totally marvellous, radiantly dark. Born in Galicia, her family exiled by the Civil War, she trained at the Paris Conservatoire and entered movies formidably with Carné's *Les Enfants du Paradis* and Bresson's *Les Dames du Bois de Boulogne*. She was also for several years the lover of Albert Camus, who clearly knew even more than he's credited for.

9

Cruel and Unusual

Quirks, Landmarks and Innovations in Screen Violence

ANNE BILLSON: Capital Offences – Ten Places You Wouldn't Expect to Find a Severed Head

JAMES MOTTRAM: Sleeping With the Fishes – The Top Ten Most Violent Gangster Deaths

JAMES LITTLE, GORDON SPIERS, JAMES SPIERS AND RICHARD T. KELLY: It's Raining Bullets – Ten Gratuitous Machine-Gun Frenzies

KIERON CORLESS: You and Whose Army? The Ten Toughest Gangs in Movies

ANNE BILLSON: Digital Nightmares – Ten Wince-Making Instances of Finger/Toe Abuse

RICHARD T. KELLY: Rope, Dagger, Revolver? Too Easy – Ten Improvised/Unlikely Weapons

Capital Offences

Ten Places You Wouldn't Expect to Find a Severed Head

ANNE BILLSON

Salome and John the Baptist, Perseus and Medusa, Isabella and her Pot of Basil . . . Severed heads have always been with us in classical art, literature and opera, but for a long time the cinema fought shy of depicting the ultimate bodily violation – Nazimova's *Salome* didn't even show the post-decapitation Baptist, though unattached heads could occasionally be glimpsed in early versions of *Dante's Inferno* or *Ben-Hur*. But those were the decadent days of the uninhibited silent epic. Hollywood quickly pulled itself together and kept its heads firmly glued to its actors' necks. When I was growing up, the idea that I might go to the cinema and see a severed head was unthinkable.

And then, in the early 1970s, one of the last great taboos – the unspoken rule that explicit beheadings were off limits – began to crumble. At first it was a slow trickle – a head continued to count even after it had been chopped off in Herzog's *Aguirre: Wrath of God*, while David Warner's close encounter with a sheet of glass in *The Omen* was the first graphic decapitation I'd seen in a major Hollywood release. I was suitably shocked. But thrilled. And only a little disappointed that one of the most notorious severed heads of the 1970s, in *The Godfather*, was not that of a human but a horse.

From then on, decapitated heads started popping up all over the place: in fridges (*Macabre*, *Friday the 13th Part 2*), toilets (*The House on Sorority Row*, *Curtains*), even in children's films (*Return to Oz*). In 1999, Tim Burton indulged his mile-wide macabre streak by depicting no fewer than seventeen decapitations in *Sleepy Hollow* (eighteen if you count a witch sawing the head off a bat), while in the same year the blockbuster flop *Wild Wild West* not only opened with a pre-credits decapitation, but later brought back the severed head in question for use as a slide projector. Relaxed censorship, improved special effects and increasing gore tolerance of film-makers and their audiences have nowadays made severed heads almost commonplace. Let's face it, they don't carry the frisson that they used to.

TEN BAD DATES WITH DE NIRO

But we will not detain ourselves with horror specialists such as Dario Argento or George Romero or Sam Raimi, or in films detailing the exploits of serial-killers such as Freddy Krueger or Jason Voorhees or Michael Myers. After all, you'd be entitled to be disappointed if these guys didn't rip a few heads off every once in a while. What we're concerned with here are the severed heads that are all the more shocking for turning up where they're least expected . . .

10. In a fish-tank: *The Silent Partner* (Canada 1978, dir. Daryl Duke)

It's not so much the severed head per se that's shocking in this underrated thriller (with a smart screenplay by Curtis Hanson). The head-in-the-tank is a popular slasher convention that also crops up in, for example, *He Knows You're Alone* and *Eyes of a Stranger*. It's the identity of the actor playing the psychopath who leaves it there that will make your jaw drop. Even by today's standards, this is an extraordinarily vicious sadist, as mild-mannered bank clerk Elliott Gould finds out to his cost. Put it this way: *The Sound of Music* will never seem the same again.

9. In a box delivered by an express parcel service: *Se7en* (US 1995, dir. David Fincher)

'What's in the box? What's in the fucking *bohhhx*?' whines Brad Pitt. One of the best touches in this twisted serial-killer thriller is the way that Fincher doesn't actually show the severed head so much as suggest it, which, after a filmful of in-your-face atrocity, only makes it all the more disturbing. But canny, because however realistic the severed head might have been, I for one would have been unable to suppress a chuckle as it was revealed. For more head-in-box fun, see the Coen brothers' *Barton Fink*.

8. Scuttling across the floor: *The Thing* (US 1982, dir. John Carpenter)

Admittedly, it's not so surprising to find a severed head in a science-fiction movie directed by John Carpenter. But in terms of ickily baroque special effects, this one takes the biscuit: the head drags itself free from the neck, hauls itself across the floor by wrapping its tongue around a chair-leg and then, as a *pièce de résistance*, sprouts spider-legs and scuttles towards the door. Palmer the pothead, happening to glance in that direction, expresses what we've all been thinking: 'You gotta be fucking kidding.'

7. In Piccadilly Circus: *An American Werewolf in London* (GB 1981, dir. John Landis)

If you were ever in any doubt that Landis's horror-comedy is as much horror as it is comedy, the climax will set you straight, with a vengeance. The werewolf bursts out of a Piccadilly Circus porn cinema, bites the head off a policeman and proceeds to cause non-comic multi-vehicle carnage in the heart of London. The head, meanwhile, bounces off the bonnet of a car.

6. In bed with Joan Hickson: *Theatre of Blood* (GB 1973, dir. Douglas Hickox)

TV's future Miss Marple doesn't even wake up while her husband (played by Arthur Lowe from *Dad's Army*, no less) gets his head sawn off by villain Vincent Price, dressed as a surgeon and paying hammy homage to the decapitation of Cloten in Shakespeare's *Cymbeline*. Lowe's head later turns up jammed on to a bottle of milk on hero Ian Hendry's doorstep – another place you wouldn't expect to find it – though we never do find out how it got there, a cloudy plot point I fretted over endlessly when the film came out.

5. On a dog's body: *Mars Attacks!* (US 1996, dir. Tim Burton)

Heads are forever ending up on other people's shoulders: consider *The Thing with Two Heads*, *The Incredible Two-Headed Transplant*, *Flesh for Frankenstein* (in 3-D!) and so on. But in *Mars Attacks!* it's Sarah Jessica Parker's head! On a chihuahua's body! This is maybe not as horrible as the homeless guy who ends up merged with his dog in the 1978 remake of *Invasion of the Body Snatchers*, but it's just as grotesque, and a lot funnier. Oddly enough, no one ever queries the discrepancy in scale. But since the Martians use a shrinking ray on Rod Steiger, getting SJP's head similarly reduced can't have posed much of a problem.

4. In someone's lap: *Re-animator* (US 1985, dir. Stuart Gordon)

There are more severed heads in crotches than you might think: Frederic Forrest dumped on to Martin Sheen's by Brando in *Apocalypse Now*, for example, or Vincent Perez in Isabelle Adjani's during *La Reine Margot*. But it's the overtly sexual ones we're talking about here: the French slasher movie *Haute Tension* (aka *Switchblade Romance*) spins a nasty visual gag out of it, but the classic example, the one that goes all the way and then some, is *Re-animator*. Poor Barbara Crampton is strapped naked to an operating table and the severed head of Dr Hill (David Gale) puts its tongue in her ear, slobbers over her breasts and is just preparing to give head, literally, before it's rudely interrupted. If you've only ever watched the British version, by the way, you won't have seen any of this because it was cut by the BBFC.

3. In a film starring Shirley MacLaine: *The Possession of Joel Delaney* (US 1971, dir. Waris Hussein)

Yes, it's true. Miss Kook plays a wealthy New Yorker whose brother is possessed by the spirit of a Puerto Rican serial-killer with a penchant for decapitation in this psycho-thriller with an unpleasant children-in-jeopardy ending. Psycho-bro chops his girlfriend's head off and leaves it hanging by the hair from a large houseplant, but the best bit is when Shirl flees to her isolated beach house (as you do) whereupon she finds her best friend's severed head sitting on top of her fridge.

2. In a film by Eric Rohmer: *L'Anglaise et le duc / The Lady and the Duke* (France/Germany 2001, dir. Eric Rohmer)

Of all the film directors in the world, Rohmer – auteur of tasteful films full of droopy young French people who talk a lot – is probably the last in whose *oeuvre* you would expect to find a severed head. And yet here it is, on a pike. Admittedly the entire film is something of a change of pace for the veteran film-maker; a heavily stylized period piece set during the French Revolution and, by Rohmer standards, action-packed. The head is that of that well-known victim of the Revolution – the Princess de Lamballe, who was butchered by a mob and whose pubic hair was rumoured to have been worn afterwards by one of her murderers, as a moustache. Needless to say, Rohmer hasn't included this last detail in the film. There are limits.

1. In the title: *Bring Me the Head of Alfredo Garcia* (US/Mexico 1974, dir. Sam Peckinpah)

And not just in the title, but also in the passenger seat of a car, in a picnic hamper belonging to Warren Oates's girlfriend, cooling off under a motel shower. Seldom has a severed head played such a central role in a movie, and yet we never see the face: just a coil of hair poking out of a dirty cheesecloth bag surrounded by flies. If, as is often proposed, the severed head is a castration symbol, then maybe one could look on Peckinpah's Gothic Mex-western as a gesture of atonement for the shoddy treatment meted out to the female characters in his films. On the other hand, *Bring Me the Head* features one of the director's strongest, most sympathetic females, even if she is a prostitute with a typically Peckinpah ambiguous attitude towards rape. (Hey, it's not as bad as all that – in fact, some girls even like it.) It all ends in tears, of course, and Oates saying to the bad guy, 'Sixteen people are dead because of you, and one was a damn good friend of mine.'

Sleeping With the Fishes

The Top Ten Most Violent Gangster Deaths

JAMES MOTTRAM

That most perennial of genres, the gangster movie, has never had a problem in finding sickening ways for its characters to exit

stage-left. The fates of the following celluloid mobsters all serve
to prove the old adage that those who live by the sword also die by
the sword – or the axe, or the chainsaw, or the broken bottle if you
prefer. Of those who fill out this ten, some are central characters,
others mere bit players, but all have two things in common: they
are career criminals, and they come to appropriately nasty ends.
Ironically, all are sent to their makers thanks either to rival gangsters or to one of their own – an indication of the primitive brand
of 'justice' that rules the underworld.

10. Tom Powers (James Cagney) in *The Public Enemy* (US 1931,
dir. William A. Wellman, scr. Harvey Thew, from the story *Beer
and Blood* by Kubec Glasmon and John Bright)

An unforgettable demise for one of the most famous gangsters in
movie history, it's also one of the most apt. Tied up inside a blan-
ket that covers him from the neck down (so that only his bandaged and bloodied head can be seen), Powers is left on the
doorstep of his family home looking like an Egyptian mummy. As
the corpse falls timber-like into the hallway, this horrific fate
seems designed to remind us of Powers's unbridled love for his
mother. But as the film's end-caption notes – in deference to the
strict censorship laws of the Hays Code – 'The end of Tom Powers
is the end of every hoodlum.'

9. Al Capone (Rod Steiger) in *Al Capone* (US 1959, dir.
Richard Wilson, scr. Marvin Wald & Henry F. Greenberg)

Wilson's B-movie biopic might take a few liberties with the
truth – in reality the infamous Chicago mobster died the day
after he contracted pneumonia – but there's no doubting the
power of the conclusion to this story of the real-life 'Scarface'
as it escalates to an hysterical peak. Incarcerated, Capone is
beaten to death with bricks by fellow inmates as he defiantly
screams, 'I'm Al Capone!' But this is really the only way out for
Steiger's testosterone-fuelled turn, one that eclipses other
screen impersonations of Capone by the likes of Ben Gazzara
and Jason Robards.

8. Albert Spica (Michael Gambon) in *The Cook, the Thief, His Wife & Her Lover* (GB 1989, dir./scr. Peter Greenaway)

More a Jacobean revenge-drama than a gangster picture, Greenaway's film nevertheless has, at its centre, a despicable London crime-lord who holds court every night in a plush restaurant. Although he's eventually slain by a mere bullet to the head, fired by his wife after she discovers he's had her lover murdered, it's what precedes it that makes his demise so hard to swallow. Presented with the roasted body of the lover, he is forced, at gunpoint, to eat some human flesh. 'Try the cock,' she urges. He does so, then vomits, unsurprisingly. 'Cannibal,' she says, pulling the trigger.

7. Bonnie Parker and Clyde Barrow (Faye Dunaway and Warren Beatty) in *Bonnie and Clyde* (US 1967, dir. Arthur Penn, scr. David Newman & Robert Benton)

A watershed moment for the gangster film. Director Penn elevated America's most famous bank-robbing couple to near-mythic status with this brutal but beautiful climactic demise. With Bonnie seated in their stationary car and Clyde just beside it, the duo's bodies are torn apart in slow motion as law enforcers hiding in the undergrowth open fire in a cold-blooded attack. The tender expression on Bonnie's face as she gazes at Clyde in the moment they realize they've been ambushed was what inspired critic David Thomson's notion that this is 'the crucial American film about love and death' – or *liebestod*, as the Germans call it.

6. Jeff Hughes (Derek Thompson) in *The Long Good Friday* (GB 1980, dir. John MacKenzie, scr. Barrie Keeffe)

'You ever worry about your liver?' asks London kingpin Harold Shand as his right-hand man Jeff takes another slug of Scotch. But it's not the booze that does for Jeff, rather the bottle, as moments later he is smashed over the head then repeatedly jabbed in the neck with the broken glass by his enraged employer. As a gush of blood spurts from a severed artery in Jeff's neck, hissing like a hosepipe, the result is so shocking that even Shand is taken aback. Like a father might hold a son, he cradles Jeff while the ill-served sidekick gulps for his last breath.

5. Santino 'Sonny' Corleone (James Caan) in *The Godfather* (US 1971, dir. Francis Ford Coppola, scr. Coppola & Mario Puzo, from his novel)

Like a soldier dying in combat, a gangster going down in a hail of bullets can be seen as a badge of honour, at least in movie lore. Yet there's nothing glorious about the death of Sonny Corleone. Trapped at a tollbooth, a group of fedora-wearing hoods opening fire on his car with tommy-guns, Santino staggers out on to the tarmac and screams in agony as his body is pumped full of lead. Shot in just a single take via multiple cameras, with Caan wearing a record 147 explosive 'squibs' on his body, this scene marks a suitably violent end to a volatile life, albeit a not hugely atypical one in the bloody annals of the Corleone clan.

4. Nicky Santoro (Joe Pesci) in *Casino* (US 1995, dir. Martin Scorsese, scr. Scorsese & Nicholas Pileggi)

Let's face it: being beaten repeatedly by baseball bats before being tossed into a shallow grave in the Nevada desert is the least Santoro deserved. Even though he then suffers the further indignity of being buried alive in his pants, this latter-day Las Vegas cowboy has just spent three hours of screen time disposing of his foes in the nastiest of ways – stabbing one in the neck with a pen, crushing another's skull in a vice . . . Yet if anything makes this murder most foul, it's that Santoro is made aware of his fate moments before, as he watches his innocent brother Dominic go the same way.

3. Angel Fernandez (Pepe Serna) in *Scarface* (US 1983, dir. Brian De Palma, scr. Oliver Stone)

Resubmitted to the US censorship board several times in an effort to soften its original X-certification, De Palma's remake of Howard

Hawks's 1932 classic not unsurprisingly garnered a reputation for excessive violence. Prominent among the evidence for same is the scene in which Cuban émigré Tony Montana, held at gunpoint in a Miami motel bathroom, is forced to watch as a chainsaw cuts into his young associate's arm. Ironically, De Palma – by his usual standards, at least – is a model of restraint here. Showing just a tight close-up of Angel's terrified eyes as blood begins to splatter over his face, the manipulative director forces us to use our own imaginations as to what's going on beyond the frame's edge.

2. Lennie Taylor (Jamie Foreman) in *Gangster No. 1* (GB/Germany/Ireland 2000, dir. Paul McGuigan, scr. Johnny Ferguson)

With the unnamed chief criminal played with callous detachment by Paul Bettany, his dismembering of a rival London gangster is one of the most chilling scenes in film history – not least because it's all done to the sound of housewives' favourite Anthony Newley singing 'Why?' Incapacitating Taylor with a bullet in the leg in his own front room, Bettany's character prepares for his slaughter with almost ritualistic precision, carefully stripping to his underwear before taking an axe to the hapless victim. All of this is shot from the victim's POV, with repeated fades to black as Taylor drifts in and out of consciousness while his killer is progressively covered in more and more blood . . .

1. Billy Batts (Frank Vincent) in *GoodFellas* (US 1990, dir. Martin Scorsese, scr. Scorsese & Nicholas Pileggi from his book *Wise Guy*)

'You got outta line,' intones Ray Liotta's apprentice gangster Henry Hill, 'you got whacked.' A pity this wisdom was forgotten by the bouffant-haired 'made man' Billy Batts – beaten, knifed and shot four times, and all for ribbing the explosive Tommy DeVito (Joe Pesci) about his former occupation as a shoe-shine boy. This is the murder on which Scorsese's film hinges, and we're given a taste of it in the brutal prelude as we see Batts's convulsing body carved up in the boot of Hill's car, before Scorsese takes us to the actual scene of the crime much later. Stomped into the floor of a barroom to the strains of Donovan's 'Atlantis' (Robert De Niro's Jimmy Conway showing particular relish for the task), old Batts learns too late to watch his mouth around 'Spit-Shine Tommy'.

It's Raining Bullets

Ten Gratuitous Machine-Gun Frenzies

JAMES LITTLE, GORDON SPIERS, JAMES SPIERS AND RICHARD T. KELLY

'Guns, guns, guns!' So cries the villain of Paul Verhoeven's *Robocop* (1987) at a fraught moment when everyone in the room has pulled out a piece. Since the 1980s in particular, movies have got very jocular about big displays of automatic weapons. John McTiernan, director of *Predator* and *Die Hard* (who might be held partly accountable for the craze) has mused about the 'almost pornographic' fascination of male audiences for moving pictures of heavy guns blazing. He can say what he likes.

The choices below are based on novelty and, to some extent, quality. The so-called 'mini-gun' is a popular contender, though this whopping weapon was designed to be mounted in helicopters, requires a hundred-pound-worth of batteries alone, and is capable of burying a man in shell cases. James Cameron's *Terminator 2* (1991) has a very long mini-gun sequence, though it's inherently flawed by Schwarzenegger's pledge not to 'hurd anyone'. The slo-mo, showering-in-spent-cartridges-POV mini-gun scene from *The Matrix* would merit a mention were it not for Keanu Reeves. Science-fiction gunplay is probably a cheat, so no room for the remote sentries in Cameron's *Aliens* (1986) or the lethal prototype who deals out boardroom 'rough justice' to a hapless volunteer in *Robocop*. A rued absentee is Albert Finney with the tommy-gun in the Coen brothers' *Miller's Crossing* (1990), a better film than some of those below. There's even a case for Stallone's protest in *Rambo* (1985), aiming his M60 upward and firing needlessly while deliver-

ing the immortal line 'Aaarrrggghhh!' But one must draw the line somewhere. We begin instead with a different attempt to re-run the Vietnam War.

10. *The Green Berets* (US 1968, dir. John Wayne & Ray Kellogg)

Wayne, bogeyman of the anti-war left, sealed his infamy on that score in the year of the Tet Offensive by directing and starring in a movie whose very existence serves as its own punishment. It remains noteworthy for armament buffs, owing to the fiery sequence where a US AC-47 gunship ('Puff the Magic Dragon') uses its three 7.62mm mini-guns to rain metal down on unsuspecting Viet Cong who believe (mistakenly) that they have just captured a US firebase.

9. *Four Brothers* (US 2005, dir. John Singleton)

This terrible picture (starring recently Oscar-nominated 'Marky' Mark Wahlberg) tries to bank on an appeal to fourteen-year-olds everywhere by exhibiting an almost A-Team-like abandon with machine-gun play, not least in the scene where the hero's home is shot to pieces by a couple of gangstas, culminating in the precision-cutting of a hole through a brick wall behind which one of the good guys is hiding.

8. *Escape from New York* (US 1981, dir. John Carpenter)

Talk of precision-cutting calls to mind the quite splendid Mac-10 Ingram that 'Snake' Plissken (Kurt Russell) uses to carve a hole in an apartment wall. The effect might have been stronger had Russell not then immediately jumped through said wall, so proving it to be constructed from polystyrene and saliva, and leaving the impression that had he more time he could have been just as effective gently pushing his finger through it at various intervals. No arguing, though, with the Duke's (Isaac Hayes) precision shooting of the same weapon – single shots followed by lovingly blowing the cordite smoke from the weapon's breech – at Donald Pleasence's trembling US President.

7. *Waterworld* (US 1995, dir. Kevin Reynolds)

In a film generally rated as less than the sum of its good parts, chief among the latter is the appearance of quad-mount 'Ma Deuces' (M2 heavy machine guns, aka Browning .50 calibre) in a fiery action sequence that ends in the destruction of Dennis Hopper's boat and his left eye. Hopper's 'Smokers' are attacking the atoll dwellers' base, and porcine gunner Chuck, his tongue protruding from his mouth, is doing a good job of riddling the fortified atoll from a seated position when the Mariner (Kevin Costner) snares this gun-boat with a harpoon and draws its arc of fire inexorably toward the vessel where Hopper is enthroned.

6. *Full Metal Jacket* (GB 1987, dir. Stanley Kubrick)

The star of Kubrick's picture, it's generally agreed, was J. Lee Ermey as Gunnery Sergeant Hartman, and yet Ermey was only drafted late to the role as a replacement for another ex-serviceman, Tim Colceri. Colceri's consolation was a cameo as a marine manning the starboard gun on a helicopter carrying Joker and Rafterman to a designated drop in Phu Bai. Colceri sprays fire at fleeing farmers while grunting with concerted pleasure ('Get some! Get some!'). In a short break from strafing, the gunner explains the rationale behind his seemingly indiscriminate trigger-finger: 'Anyone who runs is a VC. Anyone who stands still is a well-disciplined VC.'

5. *Scarface* (US 1983, dir. Brian De Palma)

This earns its place owing to the efforts of Tony Montana (Al Pacino) and his 'leetle fren', the M203, a standard M16 assault rifle with a single-shot 44mm grenade launcher attached to the barrel. Armed thus, Montana makes his fundamentally flawed last stand against waves of gunmen, hired by drugs kingpin Sosa, who have invaded his tacky palace. Holding the high ground of the upstairs balcony, and seemingly impervious to certain bullets (having snorted up a hillock of cocaine), Tony lasts surprisingly long under a blizzard of fire and even tastes a moment of euphoria after successfully testing the gun's grenade facility.

4. *The Outlaw Josey Wales* (US 1976, dir. Clint Eastwood)

Eastwood the director here offers a perfect muzzle-eye-view of an old hand-cranked Gatling gun in action, while Eastwood the actor extracts some payback on behalf of fallen comrades betrayed by their leader Fletcher (John Vernon), in cahoots with a crooked senator. Even Vernon, having previously watched his men unexpectedly mown down by the same Gatling, has protested vainly to the senator. 'They were decently treated,' snarls the crook. 'They were decently fed, and then they were decently shot.' He doesn't know what's about to spray him.

3. *Heat* (US 1995, dir. Michael Mann)

Mann is a meticulous film-maker and one could argue that *Heat*'s celebrated bank-heist scene is a *vérité* depiction of how a serious armed incident between tactically adept cops and robbers might play out in downtown LA. One could also say it's just Mann and a load of movie armourers having a magical day at work, firing big guns and savouring the amazing echoes you get off the streets and tall buildings. Robert De Niro's gang pack 'Shorty' M16 short-barrelled carbines. The law respond with Remington and Mossberg shotguns. The chief face-off is between detective Al Pacino (a chic Swedish Army FNC rifle) and thief Tom Sizemore (an Israeli upgrade of the AK47). Yes, Mann loves his guns, as made clear in his *Miami Vice* (2006) wherein he stages another lengthy gratuitous shoot-out, over an ambushed drug deal, the star of the scene being the Barratt light .50: body armour is worthless, even at two miles, against that beast.

2. *Predator* (US 1987, dir. John McTiernan)

In search of distinctive weaponry for his sci-fi jungle adventure McTiernan duly paid a call upon the armourer and there fell in love with a mini-gun he would fondly nickname 'Painless'. This hefty item is lugged about by Jesse Ventura in the early reels, but when Ventura is felled by the invisible alien enemy then Bill Duke takes up the big gun, plants his feet squarely and opens fire – levelling an acre of jungle, with enthusiastic back-up from

Schwarzenegger and friends. (Duke will later claim to have 'capped off two hundred rounds'. Who is he fooling? Known as 'The Money Eater', the mini-gun fires three thousand rounds a minute, and Duke fires for at least a minute of screentime.) McTiernan, who has done some hard thinking on this topic, saw the sequence as essentially comic, because the invisible enemy escapes almost clean. ('Not a thing. Not a fucking trace. No blood, no bodies. We hit *nothing*.')

1. *The Wild Bunch* (US 1969, dir. Sam Peckinpah)

The Mexican stand-off of all Mexican stand-offs, or 'The Battle of Bloody Porch' as it was cheerily known to Peckinpah's crew. The ageing Bunch, wanting one final score, have wound up ripped off by Mapache in a weapons-for-money deal, their comrade Angel kidnapped and seemingly doomed. Backing off is no longer an option. Thus they load up with all the shooters they can carry and take a long walk into the heart of Mapache's Aqua Verde camp. Their request for Angel's release only prompts the drunken Mapache to slit his throat, for which offence Pike (William Holden) and Dutch (Ernest Borgnine) gun him down. After a tense moment, all unsure of what to do, the Bunch *smile* at each other. The ensuing battle becomes about control of the M1917 A1 Browning machine gun on the veranda, and the Bunch take turns at it, most eminently Holden ('Give 'em hell, Pike!' cries Borgnine). It's absolute bloody mayhem, but finally numbers tell against the Bunch. Holden, already shot by a whore, is finished off by a child. Dutch is gunned down rushing to his side. But by god it was worth it.

You and Whose Army?

The Ten Toughest Gangs in Movies

KIERON CORLESS

It's easy to understand the attraction of the gang for film-makers. A gang is an alternative family and as such, it will always generate intense emotions brought about by the interactions of a close-knit group. But the gang will also provide a readymade dramatic template, based around loyalty, peer pressure, rivalry, internal politics, moral choices, rites of passage, tribalism, a perceived enemy to define yourself against and fight with, proximity to violence and death; and of course the charismatic leader. The more philosophically inclined gang films can engage in and prompt speculation about the nature of good and evil. Layer on top of those structural elements an abundance of more historically specific themes to do with style, rituals, youth- and sub-cultures, and you've got yourself a winner. None of us is immune to the attractions of the gang: the very idea mobilizes nostalgia, but also primal fears around status, belonging or not belonging, inclusion and exclusion, the political power of the collective. And of course every decent gang film provides an opportunity to depict a specific milieu, which has brought the gang into being. I've left out westerns, kung fu, gangster and other specific genre films, and focused predominantly on what you might call street gangs.

10. *Small Faces* (GB 1996, dir. Gillies MacKinnon)

Set in Glasgow in 1968, this underrated film tells of three brothers growing up with their widowed mother in a tough working-class neighbourhood. The eldest brother is a member of the local gang the Glen, the middle brother is trying to avoid gang life by pursuing an artistic vocation, but the film is told from the point of view of the youngest brother Lex, who must make a choice between the two poles they represent. Much more low-key than *Trainspotting* but all the better for it, MacKinnon shows us razor fights and beatings, and manages to create a credible atmosphere of encroaching dread.

9. *Assault on Precinct 13* (US 1976, dir. John Carpenter)

One of cult director John Carpenter's best films, this tells of an LA street gang with the evocative name Street Thunder laying siege to a police station in revenge for the murder of several of their members. Cross-hatching *Rio Bravo* with *Night of the Living Dead*,

Carpenter's blank-faced, depersonalized gang members seem completely indifferent to either their own or anyone else's death, shooting an innocent young girl before relentlessly launching themselves in pestilential waves at their designated target. It's a lean, nightmarish paranoid thriller, but through an astute mix of characters it also gauges shifting racial and sexual politics in America at the time.

8. *Brighton Rock* (GB 1947, dir. John Boulting)

Some of the darkness of Graham Greene's masterful, morbid tale of a Brighton gang running a racket at their local racecourse was lost in transit to the screen, but the film still brilliantly captures the squalid, sinister underside of seaside gaiety and a moral vacuum in England between the wars. Like all the great gang films, it gets two things absolutely right – a milieu so vividly evoked you can practically taste the salt air; and an unforgettable protagonist, in this case the irredeemable Pinky Brown. Ruthless, amoral, as cold as the pebbles on Brighton beach, it's still hard to believe he was played by genial old luvvie Dickie Attenborough.

7. *The Wanderers* (US 1979, dir. Philip Kaufman)

Kaufman's 1979 take on New York's 1963 gangland culture adopts a generally affectionate tone and the Wanderers themselves feel fairly benign. Elsewhere though, there are strange irruptions. Take rival gang the Fordham Baldies, for example; shavenheaded monsters primed for terror and violence who seem utterly surreal in this historical context – the fat ones in particular would be better suited to football terrace warfare in *The Firm* (below). Best of all, though, are the phantasmagoric Ducky Boys, who suddenly materialize in darkened tunnels wreathed in fog and armed with baseball bats. It's as if they've just arrived from the set of a zombie film, or *Assault on Precinct 13*, primed to destroy anything in their path.

6. *A Clockwork Orange* (GB 1971, dir. Stanley Kubrick)

In his customary invested manner Kubrick lifted the portrayal of gang culture on screen to a new level. For a start the rituals of gang life here have evolved into a completely separate language, Burgess's Nadsat. Then there's the fantastical Droog look – black bowler hat, white clothes, eye make-up – which so captured the imaginations of British youth that groups of similarly attired young men started appearing in such unlikely places as Sunderland. And Malcolm McDowell's voice-over puts us right inside the protagonist Alex's head as he cheerfully propounds his philosophy of rape, pillage and ultraviolence, leaving the viewer no escape route from the escalating madness.

5. *Los Olvidados / The Forgotten Ones* (Mexico 1950, dir. Luis Buñuel)

A masterpiece, the street gang film against which all others must be judged, and one that points the way directly to *City of God*. Not long arrived in Mexico in exile from Franco's Spain, Buñuel's portrait of Mexico City's slum kids revived his international reputation but didn't exactly endear him to the Mexican establishment. The gang mentality here is a product of a cruelly deprived environment where the struggle to survive inevitably entails banding together to prey on those weaker than you. It's still shocking in its complete refusal of easy sentimentality or hope or redemption. The casting is incredible; you rarely see these kinds of faces – coarsened, defiant, streetwise – even in today's low-budget cinema, let alone in 1950.

4. *Cidade de Deus / City of God* (Brazil/Germany/France 2002, dir. Fernando Meirelles & Kátia Lund)

The title refers to a Rio housing project, tracked from its inception as a sixties dumping-ground to its eighties incarnation as a boiling inferno of ferocious slum-gang warfare, much of it perpetrated by cackling children armed to the teeth with guns – the casting of non-professional street kids in virtually every role further elides the usually comforting distance between filmed fiction and appalling reality. Although much criticized, the stylistic ferment seems perfectly adapted to the rampant, amoral mayhem that produces an unforgettable character such as child-killer L'il Zé. Arguably this film represents the absolute degree zero of gang culture violence in cinema; it's hard to think of another film in which death is visited so casually and so shockingly. We've come a long way from *West Side Story*.

3. *The Firm* (GB 1989, dir. Alan Clarke)

Alan Clarke's hard-hitting exposé of Britain's 1980s football thug mentality locates its boisterous, lairy crew – headed by a rivetingly wired and fired-up Gary Oldman – not amongst the ranks of the then-countless unemployed, but in the comfortable Thatcherite suburban heartlands of the south-east. Clarke keeps the violence to a minimum in order to maximize its impact, and the viewer's shock at the relish with which it's inflicted. Nevertheless, despite the brio in the performances, the suspicion lingers that this bunch are not quite fat, ugly and thick enough to truly convince as the hooligan wing of England's 'support'.

2. *Heathers* (US 1989, dir. Michael Lehman)

If you can look past the terrible late 1980s hair and wardrobe, this glittering black comedy demonstrates it's not just boys (or men) who enjoy a spot of tribal bonding and lording it over lesser mortals. We are at an Ohio high school where three hard-boiled, unscrupulous girls, all called Heather ('Monday morning, you're history') and a fourth, more diffident, named Veronica (Winona Ryder) rule the roost. Unlike the often physical reigns of terror perpetrated by their male counterparts in the conventional gang picture, the Heathers resort to a much subtler but equally effective psychic variant, carrying all before them until nemesis, in the fetching form of Christian Slater, finally comes knocking.

1. *Romper Stomper* (Australia 1992, dir. Geoffrey Wright)

'We came to wreck everything' boasts one of Russell Crowe's cropheaded associates in the study of Melbourne neo-Nazi skinheads that launched Crowe toward stardom; and sure enough, that's exactly what they go on to do, including, ultimately, themselves. Crowe is mightily convincing, a dangerous tunnel visionary dishing out beatings to local Vietnamese victims with cool, malevolent relish. He and his gang attained such a level of immersive realism that the Melbourne police came close to arresting the actors during the shoot. That said, the notion that Crowe offered the last word in psychotic Aussie hard men was swiftly dispelled when *Chopper* arrived on the scene in 2000; as portrayed by the magnificent Eric Bana, this was a man so brutally hard and diabolically scary he didn't even need a gang to back him up.

Digital Nightmares
Ten Wince-Making Instances of Finger/Toe Abuse

ANNE BILLSON

What is it about fingers and toes that bring out the sadist in filmmakers? Heads, arms, legs and ears all suffer their share of mistreatment in the movies, but once you start noticing digit abuse, you can barely sit down in a cinema seat without being confronted by some fresh horrible instance of finger or toe torture. Ever since 1935, when slivers of flaming bamboo were driven beneath Gary Cooper's fingernails in *The Lives of a Bengal Lancer*, our smallest appendages have been at the receiving end of ill treatment, regularly getting broken or severed or sliced and diced – not just in horror movies such as *Hostel*, where you more or less expect it, but in graphic novel adaptations (*Sin City*), period dramas (*Ride with the Devil*) action adventures (*Vertical Limit*, which rings the changes with a spot of frostbite and dislocation), buddy movies (*Kiss Kiss Bang Bang*), cop movies (*Sharky's Machine*), fantasies (*The Prestige*), even musicals (*The Little Shop of Horrors*). It's not hard to think of examples; the hard part is picking just ten.

Maybe it's because fingers and toes are phallic symbols. (Phalange, phallus – hey, they even sound similar, so little wonder some people get confused.) Male screenwriters can't think of anything more frightful than violence being inflicted on their pri-

vate parts, and since they can't show that on screen, they reach
for the symbol instead. Or maybe it's because all manner of ghast-
liness can be visited on a protagonist's fingers or toes without risk
to his or her life. Or maybe it's simply because, while not everyone in the audience has personal experience of being strung
upside-down and flayed alive, everyone can relate to a cut finger,
a stubbed toe, an icky toenail. Take John Carpenter's *The Thing*,
in which aliens are erupting left, right and centre in a barrage of
extraordinary special effects. It's when Kurt Russell decides to
give everyone a blood test, and they start slicing their thumbs
with a scalpel, that you can *really* sense the audience wincing.

10. *The Piano* (Australia/France 1993, dir. Jane Campion)

Sam Neill axes off one of Holly Hunter's fingers in this arty-farty
Franco-Kiwi chick-flick with added crinolines and (courtesy of
Oscar-winning Anna Paquin – what was the Academy *thinking*?)
one of the most annoying child performances known to man.
Would that Neill had done it sooner so we wouldn't have had to
listen to any more of Michael Nyman's tedious tinkle-tinkle-
plunk score. But does losing a finger stop her piano playing? Does
it heck – she simply straps on a metal prosthetic, which changes
the score to tinkle-tinkle-plunk-zing. Still, it's not every day you
get such uncompromising digit abuse in a chick-flick.

9. *The Big Lebowski* (US 1998, dir. Joel Coen)

Trophy porn-star wife Tara Reid paints her toenails green, so it
was a toss-up as to whether the Coen brothers' slacker variation
on *The Big Sleep* should be included here or in my earlier Nail
Varnish selection . . . But when smarmy factotum Philip Seymour
Hoffman hands Jeff Bridges an envelope containing a severed toe
(with green-painted nail) wrapped in cotton wool, and millionaire David Huddleston exclaims 'By God, sir, I will not abide
another toe!' we tip over into unambiguous digit abuse territory.
And when later we get a close-up of a German nihilist's foot
wrapped in a bandage stained with blood where the little toe
should be, it seals the deal.

All God's Creatures Got a Place in the Movies – Ten Great Performances by Animals, p 183

8. *Taxi Driver* (US 1976, dir. Martin Scorsese)

When I first saw *Taxi Driver*, in the Leicester Square Theatre way back in 1976, I'd never heard of Martin Scorsese and, *pace* Peckinpah, I had yet to become blasé at the sight of blood not just pouring but actually *spurting* out of gunshot wounds. It wasn't as though I were expecting *Carry on Cabbie*, but even so, I was caught off guard by the bloodbath at the end, and when De Niro shoots the fingers off a man's hand, I began to feel queasy. Then Harvey Keitel turns up and shoots De Niro in the neck, which begins to pump out blood, and then De Niro shoots Harvey several times and gets shot again by another man, whom he then shoots several times, and then he bashes and stabs and shoots the fingerless guy, and then tries to shoot himself, but he's all out of bullets and when the cops arrive there's blood dripping off his finger as he points it at his head and makes 'pow! pow!' shooting noises. Which is when I had to put my head between my knees to stop myself fainting. This has happened to me only twice in a lifetime of movie-going, and I've been wary of Scorsese ever since.

7. *Mad Max 2* (Australia 1981, dir. George Miller)

Miller's post-apocalyptic version of *Wacky Races*, featuring warrior tribes dressed in leather S&M gear, shows a winning hand of mythological archetypes. The Feral Kid has a razor-sharp boomerang. We know it's razor-sharp because it has already sliced deep into the forehead of a pretty young catamite. The catamite's psychopathic owner, a human-attack dog called Wez, is so enraged he hurls the boomerang back at the Feral Kid, but of course the Kid ducks and it comes swooping back towards the bad guys. The Toadie sticks up his hand, back-pedalling furiously like a cricket fielder, and shouts, 'I've got it! I've got it!' And zip! His fingers go flying. Cue all-round hilarity.

6. *The Lord of the Rings: The Return of the King* (US 2003, dir. Peter Jackson)

It took place at the climax of an epic trilogy. It was essential to the plot. It was one of the most significant examples of digit abuse in the first half of the first decade of the twenty-first century, and yet no one *saw* it, because the victim was invisible. Gollum bites off Frodo's index finger, and with it the One Ring, before toppling backwards into the molten fires of Mount Doom, where both he and the much-sought-after bling are destroyed. And the now-visible Frodo is left with a stump. But if you think that's the end of Peter Jackson's stonking great adaptation of Tolkein's pointy-eared saga, you can think again, because there are still forty minutes to go. And the questions remain. If Gandalf can send eagles to pick up Frodo and Sam at the end, how come they didn't use Eagle-Air to fly straight to Mount Doom in the first place?

5. *Blade Runner* (US 1982, dir. Ridley Scott)

There's only one rogue replicant left for Harrison Ford to track down and 'retire'. But barrel-chested Rutger Hauer turns the tables, and the hunter ends up being hunted, pursued through the upper floors of a delapidated LA tower block. We've already seen Hauer crushing a man's head with his bare hands, but he obviously can't do that to the film's star. So he punches through a wall, grabs Harrison's gun hand, brings it back to his side of the wall and snaps two of his fingers like twigs, saying, 'This is for Zhora. *This* is for Pris.' And, scary though he is, it's hard not to see it from his side.

4. *Repulsion* (GB 1965, dir. Roman Polanski)

Next time you go for a manicure in a London beauty parlour, make sure it's not nutty Catherine Deneuve holding the nail clippers. A manicurist once accidentally cut too deep into my cuticle, so I can attest to the accuracy of the amount of dripping blood that ensues when our girl sinks into one of her reveries while in possession of a sharp-bladed instrument. The victim gets off lightly, of course, compared with the guys that come round to Deneuve's South Kensington flat later on.

3. *The Fly* (US 1986, dir. David Cronenberg)

Most digit abuse in the movies involves slicing or severing, and is visited on the victim by an outside party. The advanced digit abuse that occurs after Jeff Goldblum gets fused with a fly is self-inflicted, and will strike a chord with anyone who has ever squeezed a blackhead or picked at a scab. Goldblum stands in front of the bathroom cabinet and fiddles with his fingernail, which squirts pus all over the mirror. He continues to fiddle, and ends up *lifting the fingernail clean off the nailbed*. For an artfilm version of the same process, see Lodge Kerrigan's *Clean, Shaven*.

2. *The Hitcher* (US 1986, dir. Robert Harmon)

Rutger Hauer has the questionable distinction of being responsible for not just one but two Top Ten instances of digit-related unpleasantness, the second of them in this feverish psycho-chiller that's prevented from attaining classic status only by C. Thomas Howell's tragic 1980s haircut. After escaping from Hauer's clutches, the exhausted Howell stops at a roadside diner, where waitress Jennifer Jason Leigh (and we won't even *talk* about what's going to happen to her later on in the movie) serves him a burger and French fries. Howell, whose mind is on other things, like the truckfuls of people the hitcher has already slaughtered, absent-mindedly picks at his chips. Except the last one he picks up and moves towards his mouth isn't a chip at all, it's a . . . *severed finger*. Ewww.

1. *The Yakuza* (US 1975, dir. Sydney Pollack)

Trust the Japanese to turn digit abuse into a philosophy. *Yubitsume* is the yakuza gangster ritual of severing the last joint of the little finger, wrapping it in cloth and offering it to one's boss as a gesture of repentance. But since life is too short to catalogue all the severed pinkies amid all the sliced body parts flying around in the movies of Japanese directors such as Takashi Miike, Takeshi Kitano or Kinji Fukasaku, I'm wimping out and offering a Hollywood version in lieu. This is not to be sneezed at by Japanophiles, however, for the screenplay is by Paul Schrader, with contributions from Robert Towne, and treats Japanese culture with appropriate respect, while the strong cast is topped by the dream team of Robert Mitchum, at his world-weariest, and Ken Takakura, veteran of many an authentic Japanese yakuza movie. Both actors cut fingers off, though not in the same scene. Fifteen years later, the Hollywood movie *Black Rain*, in which Takakura co-starred, also featured finger-chopping, though Michael Douglas contrived to emerge with digits intact.

Rope, Dagger, Revolver? Too Easy

Ten Improvised/Unlikely Weapons

RICHARD T. KELLY

It's a grisly thing on the face of it but, novelty being the commodity it is, significant energies in the conceiving of movies are channelled into finding unlikely ways to kill, maim, stun or otherwise grievously injure people. In the thriller genre a hastily wielded implement often provides a way out of a dead-end plot. Hitchcock excelled at the game: you may also recall the celebrated episode of his weekly TV series wherein a woman used a frozen leg of lamb to fatally clout her husband, then cooked and served it to hungrily oblivious detectives. In horror movies the improvised weapon is increasingly a cause for crude gross-out chuckles: this list excludes the imaginative efforts of Sam Raimi's *Evil Dead 2*, but also the entire *Friday the 13th* school of pointed objects used to impale copulating kids. Whatever the Freudian connotations, sometimes a knife is just a knife, as a cigar may just be a cigar. Then again, sometimes not.

10. Margot Mary Wendice (Grace Kelly), with the scissors, in *Dial M for Murder* (US 1954, dir. Alfred Hitchcock)

Hard-up tennis pro Ray Milland's lunatic decision to bump off wife Grace Kelly via a blackmailed assassin fails even as the killer has his hands round her throat; for *her* hands are free to locate a pair of scissors and lodge them in his back. His stumble and fall then serves to jam the blades in up to the hilt. Ouch. In his marvellous book *Hitchcock*, François Truffaut describes a Hitch tribute at New York's Lincoln Center in April 1974, a screening of a hundred clips expertly edited into thematic groups – cameos, chases, bad guys, murders. At the end of the evening Hitchcock rose merely to say, 'As you have seen on the screen, scissors are the best way.' But not quite, Alfred.

9. Shaun (Simon Pegg) with the cricket bat, in *Shaun of the Dead* (GB 2004, dir. Edgar Wright)

This affable, mildly gruesome couch-potato comedy is the second retread of George Romero's *Dawn of the Dead* (1978) to feature in this list-book, while the original has yet to figure. Shame – perhaps there ought to have been a list of Best Shopping Malls. Playing a slacker who rises to a crisis, Simon Pegg takes hold of a stout-hewn willow, gingerly at first then with mounting relish, until the moment when – effecting the rescue of his (ex-)girlfriend from a North London housing estate beset by zombies – he starts issuing stitches left, right, and centre.

8. Frank Jacson (Alain Delon) with the ice-axe in *The Assassination of Trotsky* (France/Italy/GB 1972, dir. Joseph Losey)

Suffice it to say this was entirely the wrong film for hardly reformed Stalinist Losey to have made, and he made it in the wrong way too. Its interest lies beyond Losey's antipathy to the great man, in Burton's none-too-energetic efforts to portray him, and finally in the long-handled ice-axe (not a pick, as per legend and the Stranglers' 'No More Heroes') that Delon finally and shamefully cracks down upon the Prophet's cranium.

7. Wendy Torrance (Shelley Duvall), with the baseball bat, in *The Shining* (GB/US 1980, dir. Stanley Kubrick)

One's home and person are never undefended if there's a hardy slugger at hand. Shelley Duvall has great cause to clutch the bat to her chest during the five-minute scene wherein her mad-as-a-snake husband menaces her across the lobby and up the main stairway of the Overlook Hotel. But old Jack should really have kept his mind on the stated intention (to bash Wendy's brains in) rather than spooking her at length with big-bad-wolf voices. Because he first takes one blow to the hand, then a proper crack to the head that sends him back to the foot of the stairs. It's only a shame that he gets a second chance, with a sharper implement.

6. Mélanie (Déborah François), with the cello spike, in *La Tourneuse de pages / The Page Turner* (France 2006, dir. Denis Dercourt)

A mere girl, she fails her piano conservatory audition just because she is selfishly distracted by one judge, leading concert pianist Ariane (Catherine Frot). She gives up, but she doesn't forgive. Ten years later Mélanie is an intern at a Paris law firm whose chief partner is Ariane's husband. She inveigles her way into the family's affairs, first as an au pair, then as Ariane's performance page-turner. Ariane, much the worse for her, doesn't remember Mélanie. And Mélanie masks her intentions well, though her steely will is made clear when a smarmy cellist friend of the house decides to help himself to her breasts from behind, having foolishly given her his cello to hold. Though the letch eminently deserves it, the spike's inching descent toward his foot is a tough thing to watch.

5. Tom Ripley (Alain Delon) with the Buddha paperweight in *Purple Noon / Plein Soleil* (France/ Italy 1960, dir. René Clément)

The deadly decisiveness of Patricia Highsmith's ambitious psychopath Ripley is an enthralling thing to read, though it, too, can often be watched only from between one's fingers in the various film versions. In the pursuit and maintenance of the high life to which he reckons himself entitled, Ripley thinks nothing of picking things up and doing people in – oars, ashtrays, whatever is near to hand when the trouble starts. Clément's filming of *The Talented Mr Ripley* is far less swanky than Anthony Minghella's Hollywood version, in which no one could better merit a fatal head trauma than the nosy Philip Seymour Hoffman. But I find I prefer the equivalent scene in Clément. Ripley has been many actors, but Delon is Delon.

4. Robert E. Lee Clayton (Marlon Brando), with the bound spikes, in *The Missouri Breaks* (US 1976, dir. Arthur Penn)

With his foppish garb and Irish brogue and pettish conversations with his horse, Brando's performance as hired regulator Clayton is such a splendid hoot that you rather regret to see him finally get to the business of hunting down and killing Jack Nicholson's gang of horse thieves, on behalf of rancher John McLiam. But the cold kills are fairly impressive too, not least the one in which he employs a sort of improvised ninja throwing star made from two bound spikes. 'I always wondered why in the history of lethal weapons no one invented that particular one,' Brando told *Time* reporter Leo Janos. 'It appealed to me because I used to be very expert at knife throwing.' And it's poor Harry Dean Stanton who gets on the end of Clayton's best shot, the spike piercing his face and fixing him to a tree-trunk.

3. Debbie Marsh (Gloria Grahame), with the pot of hot coffee, in *The Big Heat* (US 1953, dir. Fritz Lang)

Dreadful things happen to women in Lang's black study of the efforts of righteous but wrong-headed Detective Bannion (Glenn Ford) to take down crime boss Mike Lagana (Alexander Scourby) and his right-hand man Vince Stone (Lee Marvin). Bannion's wife has been killed by a Lagana car bomb, but, even so, he ought to examine his principles. Stone's girl Debby seems made of impervious material, and she resists Bannion's efforts to make use of her, but just by going to his hotel room she earns a pot of boiling coffee in the face from the awful Vince. It's not shown, and thank god for that. Debby escapes the hospital, her face bandaged, and seeks Bannion's protection. But he more or less induces her to become a murderous tool of his crusade. With that Rubicon crossed, it's but a matter of time before Debby contrives to be in the same room as Vince and another scalding pot of coffee, this time conveniently within her own reach.

2. Trainee 4737 Carlin (Ray Winstone), with the snooker balls in a sock, in *Scum* (GB 1979, dir. Alan Clarke)

'I hate fights in films where they're hitting each other all day,' Ray Winstone once told me. 'That's just not the way it is.' He might know. In Clarke's harsh drama of borstal boys there's a crucial moment dearly beloved of all aspiring juvenile delinquents, as Carlin picks his moment to usurp 'Pongo' Banks, hitherto top dog in the facility. It's all one long handheld shot, beginning on a slow evening during recreation hour. Winstone tells it best: 'It starts with me walking down the stairs, follows me into the snooker room, I put the snooker balls in a sock. There was a geezer lying on the floor, under the frame-line, and we swapped the balls. Phil Daniels turns to me and I smash him in the head.' With the watchdog thus disabled, Carlin proceeds to the upstairs bathroom and bashes Banks all over the shop, spitting out the new house rules: 'Right, Banks, you bastard – *I'm* the daddy now.' This scene alone may account for *Scum*'s exalted status as a true British cult movie.

1. Mark Lewis (Carl Boehm) with the tripod spike, in *Peeping Tom* (GB 1960, dir. Michael Powell)

Nearly fifty years after its infamous release *Peeping Tom* still serves a warning about cinema's share in the danger of liking to look too much – 'the morbid urge to gaze', or 'scoptophilia', as it is therein diagnosed. Film studio focus-puller and nudie photographer Mark is a pitiful monster in an upstairs room, hopelessly warped by having been his father's guinea pig in childhood. 'Is it safe to be alone with you, I wonder?' murmurs model Pamela Green. 'Might be more fun if it wasn't.' But she knows not what she says. The ill-fated Moira Shearer shares our first look at the cruel tripod spike that Mark stretches, straightens and directs at the throats of the girls he films and kills. Later on, the sweet girl downstairs (Anna Massey) gets to see the twist: a mirror Mark mounts on to the camera itself, so the victims observe their own death-throes. As the police finally close in, Mark bolts the ghastly apparatus to an upright, running toward the extended spike, and so it becomes a fitting suicide-machine.

10

Intermission

A Bite to Eat, and a Bag of Pick 'n' Mix

DEMETRIOS MATHEOU: Are You Gonna *Swallow* That? Ten Memorable Meals

KALEEM AFTAB: Back of the Net! – The Ten Best Goals Scored in Movies

KALEEM AFTAB: The Words of Prophets – Ten Great Uses of Graffiti

KEVIN MACDONALD: Ten Great Films One Could (Loosely) Call 'Political Thrillers'

Are You Gonna *Swallow* That?

Ten Memorable Meals

DEMETRIOS MATHEOU

Like no other art form, cinema is inextricably associated with food, at the most basic level. Anyone munching on popcorn would be drummed out of a theatre; we don't need a hotdog when standing in an art gallery, or a gallon of Coke when sitting in a musical recital. But at the movies, we watch, and we eat. Reflecting this instinct back at us are the films themselves, many of which utilize food and the act of eating as both dramatic device and source of entertainment. Some can be called 'foodie films' in their entirety; others use a sweet, sexy or vinegary vignette to highlight a character trait or a key moment in someone's fate. There are many memorable meals in the movies. While omitting the formal dinner, these choices cover the range of functions – to delight, amuse, titillate and appal – to which scenes of, let us say, more *casual* dining have been put.

10. *Oldboy* (Korea 2003, dir. Park Chan-wook)

Park Chan-wook has employed a whole arsenal of shock tactics in his films, but none so hard to watch – or, indeed, stomach – as the scene in which Oh Dae-Su buys his first meal after fifteen years of captivity on a diet of dumplings. Having insisted 'I want to eat a living thing', he is presented with a live octopus – and promptly devours it, first biting off the head, then stuffing the still-writhing tentacles into his mouth. Viewers could be excused for gagging, even if Oh Dae-Su does not. Actor Choi Min-sik, who doesn't like raw food, performed this scene for real, professing that he felt sorry for the octopus.

9. *Super Size Me* (US 2004, dir. Morgan Spurlock)

In order to highlight the detrimental effects of fast food, documentary-maker Spurlock turns the camera on himself as he embarks on

a one-month, McDonald's-only diet. For breakfast, lunch and supper, Spurlock can eat only what's available over Mickey D's coun-
ters; if he is offered a super size option, he must accept it. His first
tall order is a double quarter pounder with cheese meal, which he
elects to eat in his car. 'There it is: a little bit of heaven,' he sighs
excitedly. Five minutes later, he is beginning to feel as though on
a workout. Fifteen more, he is reporting 'the McTummy, the
McGurgles and the McGas' and, more worryingly, the
'McTwitches' in his arms. After a few more minutes, he lurches out
of the window and vomits it all up. This is just day two.

8. *Pulp Fiction* (US 1994, dir. Quentin Tarantino)

Vincent Vega (John Travolta) has already given us the low-down
on the *Royale with Cheese* and the Dutch penchant for mayon-
naise on their fries. But he then partakes of a genuinely heavenly
burger experience when he escorts boss's girl Mia (Uma
Thurman) to Jackrabbit Slims. This is yet another Tarantino
homage to cinema, but one with foodie trimmings. 'It's a wax
museum with a pulse,' says Vega, as he surveys the film and music
star lookalikes serving table. Buddy Holly (Steve Buscemi), serves
up Vega's Douglas Sirk Burger, 'bloody as hell', and Mia's
Martin/Lewis 5-dollar shake. They eat, they chain-smoke, they
flirt, either side of Mia going to the ladies' room to, ahem, powder her nose. 'I said *God-damn*.' And that's before they dance. The
perfect date.

7. *The Fly* (US 1986, dir. David Cronenberg)

Bug-eyed Jeff Goldblum in the role he was born to play:
'Brundlefly', the unintended fusion of man and insect. This being
a Cronenberg movie, there's a sort of social anthropology applied
to Brundle as his mutation takes hold and his flesh and behaviour
are steadily corrupted. Among the first things to go are his table
manners: fly-like, he has to vomit corrosive enzyme on to his food
to liquidize it, before sucking it back up. His lover, Geena Davis,
gets to watch this process without prior warning. 'Oh . . . that's
disgusting,' he admits, seconds before his ear falls off.

6. *The Cook, the Thief, his Wife & her Lover* (GB 1989, dir. Peter Greenaway)

Peter Greenway enjoys his structural and thematic devices, so it was only a matter of time before he presented a film as a series of mealtimes; in particular, of menus. The *pièce de résistance* of this baroque diversion – and final, one-course presentation at La Hollandaise, culinary front for the crass gangster Albert Spica (Michael Gambon) – is mooted by Albert's disaffected wife Georgie (Helen Mirren). Her lover Michael has just been murdered, by Albert, whom she wishes to choke, literally, on his bad deed. 'Cook Michael for me,' she begs the conspiratorial chef. 'This was his favourite restaurant.' When Michael is then served up, with broccoli and cauliflowers, Georgie forces her husband at gunpoint to eat up, urging him to try one particular delicacy: 'And you know where it's been.'

5. *Tampopo* (Japan 1985, dir. Juzo Itami)

Itami referred to his wondrous concoction as a '*ramen* western'. It is certainly the ultimate 'foodie film', a celebration of the Japanese noodle dish that makes you yearn for a meal yourself. While it centres on the education of a widow in the art of noodle cuisine, it is sprinkled with tangential tales, the best featuring the exploits of a dashing gangster and his moll, who lustily combine eating with sex. Highpoints include the exchange back-and-forth of a raw egg yolk, and the woman screaming with pleasure as a pair of live shrimp thrash about on her belly. My favourite, though, is an elderly gourmet's lesson in the art of *ramen* eating. 'It is most important to apologize to the pork', he suggests, placing it to the side of his plate, 'by saying: "see you soon".'

4. *Diner* (US 1982, dir. Barry Levinson)

Barry Levinson's paean to male bonding in Baltimore features many a plate of French fries in gravy, but also young Mickey Rourke's pecker in the popcorn. Come again? Boogie (Rourke), badly in debt, makes a rash bet with his pals that well-bred Carol

Heathrow (Colette Blonigan) will 'go for my pecker' on their first date. Since this is an outing to the cinema, it seems a tall order, but over the course of a dreadful B-movie Boogie, who is in charge of the popcorn, manoeuvres his hard-on through the slot in the bottom of the box. Once poor Carol – who has been on auto-pop-corn mode for the course of the movie – dips below a certain level, she gets a most peculiar handful.

3. *Tom Jones* (GB 1963, dir. Tony Richardson)

A timeless classic of eating-as-foreplay is the scene between Albert Finney's lusty adventurer Tom and Mrs Waters (Joyce Redman), a woman he has rescued on the road. The pair make their way to an inn, where they seduce each other over supper. Richardson's masterstroke is to cut between close-ups of each actor, so that Finney and Greenwood effectively act to, eat to, and seduce the camera – getting increasingly messy and frantic as they make their way through soup, lobster, chicken, oysters and pears. There is then a delirious switch to a two-shot for the final glass of wine, before the dash to the bedroom. So classy is the build-up that all Richardson now needs to do is turn out the light.

2. *Werner Herzog Eats His Shoe* (US 1980, dir. Les Blank)

'I'm quite convinced that cooking is the only alternative to film-making,' opines Herzog, the brilliant eccentric of German cinema, although dining at his house might not be advisable if this menu is anything to go by. Les Blank's short documentary follows Herzog as he honours a promise: namely, to eat his shoes upon the completion of novice Errol Morris's first film. He does exactly that, before an appreciative audience at Brooklyn's aptly named Lic Theatre; but not before first boiling the desert boots with garlic, onions, lashings of chilli sauce and, to soften the leather, duck fat. This is as much an inspirational gesture as a comic one, one that says much about the spirit of independent film-making; for Herzog is very proud of Morris and his documentary *Gates of Heaven*, which he has encouraged. 'Once in a while I think we should be foolish enough to do things like that,' he commends. 'More shoes, more boots, more garlic.'

1. *La Grande Bouffe* (France/Italy 1973, dir. Marco Ferreri)

'Eat. If you don't eat, you won't die.' Strange words from a master chef, you might think, but Ugo Tognazzi plays no ordinary cook, and *La Grande Bouffe* is no ordinary film. There are films about food and sex, films about sex and death, and then this: a film about food, sex and death. Ferreri's orgy of excess concerns four middle-aged men who hole up in a mansion with the purpose of eating themselves to death, on a menu of the highest quality. Tognazzi, Marcello Mastroianni, Michel Piccoli and Philippe Noiret are joined for their 'gastronomic seminar' by three prostitutes and a school teacher who, though seemingly innocent, has a more voracious appetite than any of them. Together they eat, and they fuck. Of many gross-out moments, including death by flatulence and a final feast on a bosom-shaped blancmange, Tognazzi's demise stands out: prostrate on the kitchen counter, spoon-fed by Noiret from a mountain of pâté, while masturbated by the teacher, his two dead comrades 'observing' from their standing positions in the refrigerator. He dies, of course, in ecstasy.

Back of the Net!
The Ten Best Goals Scored in Movies

KALEEM AFTAB

Truffaut once pondered, 'Is life as important as movies?' In a strange synchronicity Bill Shankly, legendary manager of Liverpool FC, claimed 'Some people believe football is a matter of life and death. I can assure you it is much, much more important than that.' Maybe because of their rival claims to profundity, football and cinema rarely make a great team. Admittedly, sport in general has been a struggle for movies to get right. (As Spike Lee puts it, 'Most sports films are horrible, because athletes, they are *real*. And the key to sports is that the games are so dramatic, and you can't re-create that.')

But for this list it's important to remember another well-worn football cliché: goals change matches. They are the spur to the contest, not its inevitable conclusion. And the most important goals aren't always the prettiest or most spectacular, nor are they usually scored in the dramatic dying seconds. It could also be said that goals change movies.

Unlike some highlights clip reel, this list takes into account the dramatic effect of goals in certain films: what the goals mean to the characters, and relatedly, whether something of the spirit of the beautiful game has been captured. The goals must also have been created especially for cinema: so, for instance, archive footage of the winner in the 1982 World Cup Final as replayed in countless Italian movies, or Archie Gemmill putting Scotland 3–1 up against Holland in *Trainspotting*, have been given the red card. But real fans are welcome to contest these selections in the pub long after the final whistle has sounded.

10. *Escape to Victory* (US 1981, dir. John Huston)

Michael Caine, captain and manager of a team of Allied POWs, is using chalk and blackboard to explain the tactics he wants his side to use in an upcoming game against the German national side. He advocates passing to wingers and tossing crosses into the box. Watching in bemusement, football legend Pelé gets off his bunkbed and takes the chalk from Caine. He then proceeds to mark out how he would take the ball from the edge of his own area, weave through the opposition ('like this, and this, and this' – it looks like a wave on a electro-cardiogram) before getting to the edge of the opponent's box. 'Then I shoot. Goal . . . Easy.'

9. *Trainspotting* (GB 1996, dir. Danny Boyle)

We enter *Trainspotting* by way of Ewan McGregor's famous voice-over exhortation to 'Choose life!' We also receive an introduction to his comrades on a five-a-side football pitch. From their OTT tackling it's clear that Begbie and Sickboy are not to be messed with. Then the camera turns towards Spud (Ewen Bremner) in goal, sporting a T-shirt with a Superman logo, seemingly petrified as the opposing team advance on goal. When a shot on goal comes in, Spud jumps spectacularly over the ball: a technique that all those who play Sunday football in the park will recognize ruefully.

8. *Bend it Like Beckham* (GB 2001, dir. Gurindha Chadha)

Visualization is a psychological technique on which sportsmen will sometimes draw at key moments in a game. Take Asian female footballer Jesminder (Parminder Nagra), who is persuaded to quit a family wedding in order to play in the cup final. She arrives with thirty minutes left and her team losing 1–0. With Jesminder on the pitch, her team equalizes. Then with moments left she is fouled on the edge of the box. As she dusts herself down, we hear Pavarotti singing 'Nessun Dorma' from *Turandot* (theme to the BBC's 1990 World Cup coverage) and our girl looks up to the goal: in slo-mo she sees the wall of opposing defenders comprised of those members of her family who don't want her to play football or date boys. Showing mental toughness, she pulls herself together and wields a sweet right foot.

7. *Ladybugs* (US 1992, dir. Sidney J. Furie)

America has never really 'got' football. They misapply the very name of the game to one in which the ball is mainly carried in hands, and refer instead to something called 'soccer'. So it's only fitting that the 'goal' scored in this American film isn't really a goal at all. It appears on this list because it manages to capture the ecstasy of scoring much better than most football movies. Rodney Dangerfield agrees to teach his company's girls' football team. His secret weapon is his fiancée's son. When the boy first comes to watch the girls play, the blonde striker kicks the ball toward him, and in the time it takes to arrive at his feet, a montage shows us that he's dreamed a life together with this girl, from first kiss to marriage. Ah, the magic of scoring . . .

6. *Das Wunder von Bern* / *The Miracle of Bern* (Germany 2003, dir. Sönke Wortmann)

'Football', Gary Lineker once observed, 'is a game with twenty-two players, a ball, and in the end Germany win.' The backdrop to *Miracle of Bern* is Germany's first World Cup triumph in 1954. Everyone who's ever played the game has fantasized about scoring the winning goal in a cup final. Observe a broken man called Richard (Peter Lohmeyer), who walks on to a dusty deserted field and, with a 'ball' made out of rubber bands, plays 'keepy-uppy' before flicking it up into the air and attempting an overhead kick. The ball actually comes off his shin and creeps into the net. Alas, not everyone is Pelé but the goal gives Richard the renewed will to enjoy life, having just spent eleven years as a POW in Russia.

5. *Siu lam juk kau / Shaolin Soccer* (Hong Kong/China 2001, dir. Stephen Chow)

It's the semi-final of the cup and, in facing a team of women with facial hair drawn on their faces, our Shaolin kung fu football team finally have a tough game in front of them. Now is the time for the goalkeeper, dressed in a yellow tracksuit straight out of Bruce Lee's wardrobe, to prove his worth. Teasing the opponents, he throws the ball out to the opposing team's striker and challenges them to score. After a series of gravity-defying saves he picks the ball up and throws it a hundred yards directly into the opposition net. Magic.

4. *Cidade de Deus / City of God* (Brazil 2002, dir. Fernando Meirelles)

Football and crime are often considered as the only two escape routes from the Brazilian *favelas*. In the opening sequence of *City of God* the suggestion is underscored as we watch a boy playing 'keepy-uppy' with his pal, counting 'Eleven, twelve, thirteen . . .' Told that a tanker full of gas is approaching, the boy boots the ball up in the air, pulls out his gun and shoots it like a clay pigeon. The camera stops as the shot hits the target, and in this moment it's clear that these two kids at least will be choosing the 'crime' route over the 'football'.

3. *Temporada de patos / Duck Season* (Mexico 2004, dir. Fernando Eimbcke)

Two boys, Flama and Moka, home alone for the day: they order a pizza, then strike a deal with the delivery guy that if they beat him in a game of football on their games console then they get their meal free. A glamour tie between Man United and Real Madrid ensues. The game ends 3–3 with the delivery guy's 'Ronaldo' scoring a spectacular hat-trick. So to extra time and a 'Golden Goal' period in which the first team to score wins. After a sequence of close shaves, a perfect shot from the kid seems destined for the top corner – when the TV breaks down, the picture lost. Was it a goal or not? A debate ensues, fit to rival that over Geoff Hurst's disputed third in the 1966 World Cup Final.

2. *Kes* (1969, dir. Ken Loach)

It's PE class, outdoor football on a cold muddy day, and our young hero Billy Casper isn't up for it. But games teacher Mr Sugden has donned a Man United strip and reckons he's Bobby Charlton. Thus the screen debut of Brian Glover, previously a wrestler and a schoolmaster before he turned to acting. Like a big fat bald kid Glover decides they're playing Manchester United versus Spurs in the Fifth Round of the FA Cup. At 1–0 down Glover lumbers into the box then dives like a swan. Abusing his joint role as referee he gives the penalty, which he will take himself, naturally. His effort is soft and saved, but he penalizes the keeper for infringement and rules that the kick must be retaken. This time he shoots and scores. 'And that, boys, is how to take a penalty.'

1. *Together* / *Tillsammans* (Sweden 2000, dir. Lukas Moodyson)

A film in which football is not mentioned once until the final scene is, perversely, the classic movie about the game. Set in a Swedish commune in the 1970s *Together* is about how a community spirit can be wrecked by the needs of the individual. But as old coaches know, there is no 'I' in 'team', and in the final scene old grudges are forsaken as the characters play a game of footie in the snow outside the commune. This is how football should be, a universal game. And every goal – nearly all of them scored from two yards out – heeds the sage maxim of West Brom and England legend Cyril Regis: 'All goals are good goals.'

The Words of Prophets
Ten Great Uses of Graffiti

KALEEM AFTAB

The famous newspaper adage has it that a picture is worth a thousand words. But what does that say for movies, with their twenty-four frames per second? That amounts to an awful lot of reading matter, and cinemas are not libraries – we go to watch, and received wisdom has it that movies are a visual medium, a form of pictorial storytelling, light on the word-count. Still, it can't be denied that a lot of great movie moments have been provided by words marked crudely on to bare surfaces. These days, graffiti is indelibly linked to the hip-hop style that cropped up on the streets and subways of New York City in the 1970s. It became a global craze, and spray-painting graffiti crews ran the risk of arrest for their amendments to public space. Hip-hop has spawned a genre of films in which graffiti is a sub-category, but this list takes a broader approach to the subject: one that, like film-makers the world over, recognizes graffiti as a form with a history: used by political activists to make statements, by street gangs to mark territory, by school-kids to express their displeasure at their teachers or their peers.

10. *Riso Amaro / Bitter Rice* (Italy 1948, dir. Giuseppe De Santis)

Vivo morendo in caserma non in tempo di guerra ma in tempo di vita
(I live dying in the barracks not during wartime but in the time for living)

Since we owe the word *graffiti* to the Romans, who thus described the inscriptions and figure-drawings made on the walls of ancient sepulchres or ruins, it only seems fair to start our rundown in Italy. It would need to be something special to divert attention from the fabulous Silvana Mangano in her pomp, but director De Santis achieves this feat by plastering graffiti on the wall when she first enters the squalid dormitory where the rice workers are housed.

These words manage to capture the spirit of the Italian neo-realist movement within a single sentence.

9. *Turk 182!* (US 1985, dir. Bob Clark)

One of the most popular types of graffito in the hip-hop mode is known as 'tagging', a 'tag' being an individual's graffiti signature. The tags left by Timothy Hutton in this picture from the director of *Porky's* are nothing spectacular in themselves. They draw their power from the movie's debt to Taki 183, who was heralded as the 'original' tag artist in a *New York Times* article of 21 July 1971. Taki's newfound media fame inspired a wave of competitive tagging, and for a while New York was as well known for its spray-painted streets as for its romantic skyscrapers.

8. *Fast Times at Ridgemont High* (US 1982, dir. Amy Heckerling)

Little Prick

One of the best places to find graffiti is in any school building. Whether it be the slamming of a teacher in a toilet cubicle, an expression of love on a textbook, or just an early show of prowess in graphic art, teenagers have always had a special affinity to graffiti. But the finest examples are usually in the form of a puerile attack, exactly like that scrawled on the car and school-locker belonging to Mike Damone (Robert Romanus) in *Fast Times*. When Mike fails to do his duty and pay half the cost of Jennifer Jason Leigh's abortion, her outraged friend Phoebe Cates screams that he is no better than a 'little prick'. She must have then invested in some paint and a good marker-pen, since the following scenes see 'Prick' or 'Little Prick' emblazoned on everything Mike owns. The truth hurts.

7. *La Haine* (France 1995, dir. Mathieu Kassovitz)

La monde est à vous/nous (The world is yours/ours)

There's a lot of great graffiti in *La Haine*, including the most irreverent piece of same in cinema history ('Your Mother Sucks Bears'). However the moment of sheer literary genius is when Hubert amends a poster for a mineral water company, simply by swapping an 'n' for a 'v'. What on the surface seems a comment upon the futility of the lives of these young outsiders is rather a brilliant homage to several films: Howard Hawks's *Scarface* (1932) and its Brian De Palma remake, of course, but also a poster that appears in *Little Caesar* (1930), a granddaddy among crime movies.

6. *Downtown 81 / Glenn O'Brien's New York Beat Movie* (US/Switzerland/Belgium 1981/2001, dir. Edo Bertoglio)

The moment when celluloid captured graffiti's ascent into an art commodity of value was almost lost when director Edo Bertoglio managed to lose his precious original footage. What was left was a unique film capturing a point in time, not so long ago, when New York's East Village resembled war-torn Beirut. The film stars Jean-Michel Basquiat as himself, endeavouring to barter a graffiti-style painting (of which we never get a good view) in order to pay his rent. To choose one example from the welter of authentic graffiti on display would be a pointless task: let the whole film stand.

5. *Monty Python's Life of Brian* (GB 1979, dir. Terry Jones)

Romanes Eunt Domus

A piece of graffiti so instructive it has found it has way on to the school curriculum, as Latin teachers fondly imagined a bit of John Cleese magic could enliven their deadly classes. Roman legionary Cleese happens upon aspiring revolutionary Brian (Graham Chapman) daubing on a public wall and, seemingly oblivious to the affront of the message itself, orders him not to use the present indicative to write 'Romans Go Home'. As a punishment for this poor grammar he makes Brian write out the correct form a hundred times, so covering several hundred square feet of brickwork.

4. *Rumblefish* (US 1983, dir. Francis Coppola)

The Motorcycle Boy Rules

Even before Mickey Rourke emerges from darkness on the seat of his bike to break up a street-fight of the type he had forbidden in his absence, we know he's the king of the town. We know this from the moment straight after the credits when light flares on a street-sign sprayed with the legend 'The Motorcycle Boy Rules'. It's a motif glimpsed on several other occasions in this beautiful black-and-white teen movie, all serving to underscore the belief of Rourke's kid brother Rusty James (Matt Dillon) that the Motorcycle Boy is righteous in all respects. We see it too in a tunnel late on, the shadow of a rider streaking by as the mantle is passed from brother to brother.

3. *Do the Right Thing* (US 1989, dir. Spike Lee)

Tawana Told The Truth

Spike Lee hoped to second-guess what kind of graffiti would be written on Brooklyn walls by the time his volatile movie was released in the hot summer of 1989. His decision to implicitly side with black teenager Tawana Brawley in her claim that she was abducted and raped by New York policemen backfired when it was later proven that Tawana made it up. Still, 'Tawana Told The Truth' stands out in massive letters on a fresh-painted wall against which Mookie (Lee) and his sister Jade (Lee's real sister Joie) argue about inter-racial sex. The film presents a stiff critique of New York's police, its then-Mayor, and US society in general, but on this particular score Lee probably overplayed his hand.

2. *La Chinoise* (France 1967, dir. Jean-Luc Godard)

Il faut confronter les idées vagues avec des images claires (One must confront vague ideas with strong images)

It's difficult to choose a sole graffito from the Godard *oeuvre* when he could have filled out most of a Top Ten by himself: the former critic retained a healthy respect for the force of the written word on screen. *La Chinoise* indicated the start of his shift from giddy irreverent cinema to outright political cinema. On the wall of an apartment used by students who cherish and brandish the *Little Red Book* of Mao is this example written in block capitals, shrewdly anticipating the fervour of Paris in May 1968.

1. *Apocalypse Now* (1979, dir. Francis Ford Coppola)

Who would have thought Coppola would enjoy two entries on this list, not least when *Apocalypse Now* is renowned (among other reasons) for 'having no titles'? But viewers paying supremely close attention may notice that the movie does indeed have a title-card of sorts in the form of a graffito painted on the wall of Colonel Kurtz's jungle compound. It can be glimpsed at the top of the steps behind the natives when Captain Willard (Martin Sheen) is telling Chef (Frederic Forrest) to call in an air-strike if he hasn't returned in twenty-four hours. And, yes, it's inscribed in the very same style that became famous on the movie's poster art.

Ten Great Films One Could (Loosely) Call 'Political Thrillers'

KEVIN MACDONALD

Like any soup with only two ingredients, 'political thrillers' can often be bland and predictable to the taste. One could cite any number of films that are superficially set in the world of politics (usually the White House and its immediate environs), from *No Way Out* (1987) to *The Pelican Brief* (1993). But these need not detain us: they are all sugar-coating and no smelly fish-oil. No, the truly satisfying films of this genre need to have just the right amount of genre elements – narrative tension, a single mystery in need of a solution – but also contain sufficient political complexity to gratify our less basic instincts. They may well play on our endless fascination with conspiracy, with how the world is run – and by whom. But they will also encourage us to act more like investigators when we read our morning paper, to wonder about the 'story behind the story'. Such films make politics out to be a dangerous, sexy, endlessly intriguing world – which, of course, it is.

10. *The Parallax View* (US 1974, dir. Alan J. Pakula)

It's a political film only insofar as it's a paranoid film; and thus reflects the profound lack of ease in America after the disaster of the Vietnam War. The plot is preposterous – Warren Beatty's leftish journalist uncovers a sinister corporation specializing in assassinations – but the execution is breathtaking, right up to the dark twist-ending. Cinematographer Gordon Willis performs his unique magic with actors and architecture, making this one of the most graphically brilliant films there is. But the highlight for me is the short film that the Parallax corporation screens to prospective employees to elicit signs of psychological disturbance. A montage of evocative still images set to poundingly emotive music, it's a masterpiece of experimental film-making hidden away in this mainstream movie, and still gives me a chill every time I watch it.

9. *Silkwood* (US 1984, dir. Mike Nichols)

A picture for grown-ups: character-centred, based on a true story, slow, detailed, literate – and a tiny bit boring. But *Silkwood* is remarkable for being the only American political thriller I know that addresses the material basis of so much *real* conspiracy in American life – namely, the endless exploitation of the working class by corporate interests. Meryl Streep plays Karen Silkwood, a menial employee at a nuclear materials processing facility who tries to expose unsafe working practices, only to end up dead in mysterious circumstances. The end is beautifully and chillingly handled: all we see are headlights coming up behind Silkwood, her face turns around in the beam of light – and she is run off the road. We never know if this was a deliberate act, but we have to strongly suspect the hand of vested interests.

8. *Kongekabale / King's Game* (Denmark 2004, dir. Nikolaj Arcel)

Sweden's reputation as a cosy, reasonable place run by altruistic Volvo-drivers took a beating after the murder of Prime Minister Olaf Palme in 1986: an act that has spawned as many conspiracy theories as the 'grassy knoll' in Dallas, Texas. *King's Game* clearly grew out of that climate with its story of a naïve journalist out of his depth but on the trail of a big political scandal. It gets the symbiotic but putrid relationship between the politicians (their spin doctors in particular) and journalists absolutely right. And the slightly gormless, deeply manipulated journalist protagonist comes across as a fresh character.

7. All the President's Men (US 1976, dir. Alan J. Pakula)

Unlike Pakula's other entry in this list, this one is notable for its lack of sensationalism. The makers clearly felt it was enough to just present the facts and observe the protagonists (Hoffman and Redford, and neither were ever better) going about their work – work that would eventually unseat Richard Nixon and so become the benchmark of effective political journalism. We simply observe – through immensely long single takes – the two journalists going about the legwork: the numerous phone calls, the frantic jotting in pads, the fevered plock-plock-plock of old-fashioned typewriters. It's a film of texture, not plot – and again, Gordon Willis's lucid deep-focus photography is a marvel of its own.

6. The Constant Gardener (GB 2005, dir. Fernando Meirelles)

What I find so interesting about this film – apart from its swirling poetic cinematography – is that the thriller element is, to my mind, a complete muddle, and yet the film packs a big punch because its political component (the Third World guinea-pigging of drugs by pharmaceutical corporations) and the relationship at the film's core (between Ralph Fiennes and Rachel Weisz as his dead wife) manage to gel in a non-literal and emotionally satisfying way. We are actually left thinking about the lives lost – African and otherwise – rather than the stock 'faceless conglomerate'.

5. The Insider (US 1999, dir. Michael Mann)

In a rare stroke, Mann's film not only draws on a true story but also pinpoints a real-life industry, and skewers it royally. That the industry in question is tobacco rather than, say, arms (a staple of the genre) gives The Insider everyday relevance as well as real bite.

What's particularly impressive is the lack of sensationalism, given this is, after all, a big-budget star vehicle. There are no murders, no giant revelations: just a story about the disintegration of a man's life under pressure from a huge corporation, and the daily grind of bringing a court case (successfully) against them. Mann takes what could have been a BBC current affairs documentary and turns it into a full-blown piece of cinema. The crystal-sharp cinematography and gorgeous but naturalistic design – arising from a great choice of locations – also make *The Insider* one of the most visually influential films of the 1990s.

4. *The Dancer Upstairs* (Spain/US 2002, dir. John Malkovich)

Who would have thought that Malkovich would choose to make his directorial debut with a Latin American political thriller? It's a lovely film, with a masterful performance from Javier Bardem, but its ending is a letdown. It's clearly inspired both by *State of Siege* (1973), Costa-Gavras's film about a revolutionary group, and by the true story of the Peruvian Maoist terror group Sendero Luminoso ('Shining Path') and the eventual capture of its leader Abimael Guzmán. The film is strangely – but somehow appropriately – book-ended with a terrible off-mic recording of Nina Simone singing Sandy Denny's 'Who Knows Where the Time Goes?', somehow summing up the film's sense of romantic and political pessimism: it could as well be called 'Who Knows Where One's Ideals Go?'

3. *Mephisto* (Hungary 1981, dir. Itsván Szabó)

I qualify Szabó's film as political thriller – although it is light on the genre elements – because it's a re-telling of one of the *ur*-texts of the genre: Marlowe's *Dr Faustus*. The human desire for power and success at the expense of morality and decency is really the theme of all political thrillers (if not all politics). Like most of Szabó's films *Mephisto* is at once theatrical and brilliantly cinematic. This style I always assumed was a consequence of a low budget – but it allows us to concentrate all the more on the towering performance by Klaus Maria Brandauer, which so beautifully and terrifyingly delineates one man's fall from grace.

2. Z (Greece 1968, dir. Constantin Costa-Gavras)

Opening with a caption that reads 'Any similarities between this story and actual people and events is intentional', Z is a 'fictionalized' version of the events leading up to Greece's right-wing Coup of the Colonels in 1967. Costa-Gavras uses long lenses, hand-held cameras and unconventional staging to give (what was then) a boldly novel documentary feel to proceedings: lots of long, detailed political conversations conducted by men in dark glasses and brown suits. But it also operates as a mystery story: who killed the liberal politician, played by Yves Montand? This film more than any other provided the spur to the great American paranoid thrillers of the 1970s, although those films were largely lacking in real political substance. One can't mention Z without praising its extraordinary music: Mikis Theodorakis's drum-heavy, Greek-folk-tinged (and occasional rock-opera-like) score is a personal favourite of mine. It drives the film from start to finish with a sense of righteous anger.

Interestingly, I recently read how the reality of the coup was even more of a conspiracy than Costa-Gavras could have imagined: apparently the Colonels in question were all members of a secret CIA-backed anti-communist paramilitary organization (or 'stay-behind army').

Costa-Gavras, of course, went on to make an entire career out of political thrillers, two of which – State of Siege (1973) and Missing (1981) – would also be on this list were it not that I didn't want to repeat myself. Both combine genuine political discussion and insight with genre elements and devastating human drama. Missing is particularly notable because it was studio-funded, featured two iconic American stars (Sissy Spacek and Jack Lemmon), and yet managed to be a genuine and sophisticated critique of US foreign policy in Latin America.

1. La Battaglia di Algeri / The Battle of Algiers (Italy 1966, dir. Gillo Pontecorvo)

Alongside Z this is the film that invented the genre. Like Z it is a documentary-style fictionalized version of real events, here, in the

1954–1962 Algerian war of independence. But unlike Z there is no straightforward 'mystery' driving the plot, no central conspiracy. Instead, a series of interconnecting stories – drawn from both sides of the war – are pulled together into a narrative as tense as any thriller ever made. The sequence (cut to Morricone's insistent Algerian-influenced score) in which three Algerian women dress as Europeans complete with lipstick and handbags and leave the Kasbah to bomb French cafés is one of the most brilliant I have ever seen. But what I admire most about this film is its humanity. Nobody is damned – not even the French paratrooper who tortures his Algerian prisoners. He is presented as a man who is following the will of his political masters, and genuinely believes that he is preventing terrorist attacks on innocent civilians in the only way left open to him. It is no surprise that *The Battle of Algiers* was screened at the Pentagon in the early months of the current Iraq War as a primer in military strategy during an insurgency. Were they troubled by – or did they even notice – who actually emerged victorious in Algeria?

11

Planes, Trains and Automobiles

They're Called 'Motion Pictures'

RICHARD T. KELLY: Choosing at 35,000 Feet – Ten Great Passenger-Plane Moments

GRAHAM FULLER: Express Desires – Cinema's Obsessive Affair with Railways

JASON WOOD: The Code of the Road – Ten Great Road Movies

Choosing at 35,000 Feet

Ten Great Passenger-Plane Moments

RICHARD T. KELLY

Since the emotions most commonly associated with commercial air travel are excitement, clammy-handed fear or booze-induced rage, civil aviation does lend itself fairly well to the movies. Once upon a time it was even thought quite glamorous, but the age of mass transit and package holidays put paid to that fantasy, even as the risible 'mile high club' sequence in *Emmanuelle* (1974) was trying to prolong it. Instead the selections below tend towards white-knuckle rides rather than relaxing jaunts with free champagne and loads of extra leg-room. I have tried to go easy on crash scenes – just too awful – so no room for *Alive* (1993), though the upper end of the list features a couple of undeniable claims on that score.

10. Sean Penn air-bound in *It's All About Love* (Denmark 2003, dir. Thomas Vinterberg)

This dystopian romance is all about Clare Danes and Joaquin Phoenix as a world-famous ice dancer and her scholarly young husband fleeing a murder plot, recovering in the process their fine feelings for each other. They have a Greek chorus in Penn as Phoenix's older brother Marciello, calling up repeatedly from a cellphone while circling the earth onboard a plane. He's exuberant, having found a new cure for his fear of flying: 'They gave me an injection so I can *only* fly now . . .' But it's 2021, snow is falling all over the world, and his flight can't land. So in the quiet Marciello smokes and muses, allowing himself a few heightened thoughts that may strike a chord with gloomy frequent fliers out there: 'It's wrong, everybody is *away* from each other, occupied with their own shit, *forgetting* about each other . . .'

9. John Cusack calms Ione Skye in *Say Anything* (US 1989, dir. Cameron Crowe)

If only Penn could have had John Cusack to hold his hand. Some

movie moments are so simple and yet so original as to make you
think of them always in corresponding life-situations. At the end
of Crowe's very sweet and much-adored teen romance Cusack and
Ione Skye board a flight for Europe, but she's petrified. He sooth-
ingly assures her that the ascent is the only real hurdle, and as
soon as the seatbelt lights go *bing!* and off, their future will be
assured. I only saw this movie once, but I'm not sure I've got
through a single flight since without being reminded of it fondly
once our cruising altitude has been reached.

8. Edward Norton meets Brad Pitt in *Fight Club* (US/Germany
1999, dir. David Fincher)

One man's fear of flying is another's crushing boredom, relieved only
by such company as one may find in the next seat over. 'And this is
how I met Tyler Durden . . .' Business traveller Norton has been
regaling us flatly in voice-over, lamenting his air-conditioned nightmare of a life: too many planes, single-serve meals and toiletries, bullshit conversations. But he stretches credulity by claiming to long for
a mid-air collision (and Fincher doesn't stint from giving us a quick
CGI vision of the plane splitting apart). Relief, then, when Norton
(aisle seat) strikes it up after a fashion with Brad Pitt (window). They
carry identical briefcases, and something about Pitt's insouciance –
his career in soap, his contempt for the illusory 'security' procedure,
his tips for making household napalm – makes a strong impression on
young Norton, as though this were the man of his dreams.

7. Shirley Temple entertains passengers by singing 'On the Good
Ship Lollipop' in *Bright Eyes* (US 1934, dir. David Butler)

But then if you're so very bored, why not sample the in-flight
entertainment? Small children in mid-air are usually in need of
distraction; only six-year-old Shirley Temple ever took it on herself to relieve everybody else's tedium. Look at the little moppet
with the strawberry curls, entertaining all the grown-ups as she
troops and sings her way down the aisle! Those less charmed
might like to try to imagine the off-camera promptings. ('Make
your arms like a plane, Shirley! Rub your tummy! *Smile!*')

6. Charles Grodin fakes a panic attack in *Midnight Run* (US 1989, dir. Martin Brest)

Bounty hunter Jack Walsh (Robert De Niro) has just nabbed his man – embezzling Mafia accountant Jonathan Mardukas (Charles Grodin) – and they're newly boarded on a plane to LA that will carry Jack to his money and 'The Duke' to prison and likely execution. Having sprung for first class, De Niro is smacking his lips in anticipation of a surf 'n' turf dinner: whereupon Grodin pulls an aviophobic crisis of such seat-crawling proportions ('These things go *down*, these things go *down* – it's too *big*, it can't go *up*!') that the two are kicked off the plane: the first intimation that 'The Duke' has something more than just mumbled wiseacre remarks with which to resist Jack's plan for him.

5. 'Nightmare at 20,000 Feet' in *Twilight Zone: The Movie* (US 1982, dir. George Miller)

This portmanteau homage to the Rod Serling TV show proved a misfire, destined to be remembered mainly for the dreadful deaths on-set of actor Vic Morrow and two children. George Miller at least gave the movie some worth with a well-made retool of a famous episode in which William Shatner played a newly recovered mental patient who saw a weird furry critter out on the wing wrecking the engine, yet could convince nobody else of the danger. Miller's passenger is just an average Joe, but with a higher-than-average fear of flying: John Lithgow, expertly perspiring, chain-smoking and popping pills. The creature, though, is no longer furry or weird but scaly and downright malevolent.

4. Escaping Idi Amin in *The Last King of Scotland* (GB 2006, dir. Kevin Macdonald)

Many a drama and quite a few romances have ended on that rising sense of wind under the wings as a plane makes its take-off and climbs toward a new tomorrow. Has the sense of relief ever been stronger than in the case of Dr Nicholas Garrigan (James McAvoy) as he slumps into his seat and sees Entebbe Airport diminishing behind him in the dying moments of *The Last King of Scotland*? Moments earlier we were watching this former 'personal physician' to Idi Amin strung up by his nipples for treachery, while on the tarmac outside is an Air France flight from Tel Aviv hijacked by Palestinians. Amin's distracted need to grandstand on behalf of the terrorists offers Garrigan a window of escape, but only thanks to a nobly self-sacrificing colleague who helps him on to a non-Israeli planeload permitted to go free by the hijackers. It's more than Garrigan deserves. But for the prideful sin of believing his extraordinary job was a sign of extraordinary personal qualities, he has probably been punished enough.

3. The crash in *Foreign Correspondent* (US 1940, dir. Alfred Hitchcock)

'The most thrilling scene ever filmed' boasted the trailer, but not without call, given this was 1940. Onboard this plane, bound for the US on the day war has been declared, are newspaperman Joel McCrea and Laraine Day, daughter of Herbert Marshall, who heads up a British pacifist organization yet is himself a Nazi spy. But Marshall, near to being unmasked, is also on the plane. Then the Germans attack and the plane nose-dives toward the ocean. We watch from behind the pilots as the sea rises up to meet them – then, without a cut, crashes through the glass and into the cockpit. Want to know how it was done? Read *Hitchcock* by Truffaut: it's got a load of other great stuff in it too.

2. Warren Beatty and a bomb in *The Parallax View* (US 1974, dir. Alan J. Pakula)

Beatty's wary reporter Joe Frady has to live on strained nerves the further he goes into deep cover, pursuing the shadowy Parallax Corporation, whom he has come to suspect of the assassination of US Senator Carroll plus a string of potential witnesses. Frady passes the creepy induction test for new Parallax hires but on his way out of their building he spots a man (Bill McKinney) he suspects as the Carroll assassin, and tails him all the way to the airport. McKinney checks in with a suitcase for the hold, but doesn't board. Frady does, spies another US senator chatting away in first class, and so begins silently to question his previously dauntless pursuit of impulse. The movie has been enigmatic and elliptical to this point, but now we get good fraught extreme close-ups of Beatty. His first sortie is an etching with soap on the toilet mirror: THERE IS A BOMB ON THIS PLANE. But there's a guy waiting outside: no good. He has to find a way to raise the alarm undetected. Well, what would *you* do?

1. *United 93* (US 2006, dir./scr. Paul Greengrass)

For the foreseeable future this is the heavyweight champ of plane pictures, a riposte to the action genre and to conspiracy theorists, not to say an evocation of a vanished world. It was a film Universal weren't certain anybody wanted to see. (Someone you know probably said, 'But I know what happens . . .') Yet Paul Greengrass assembled an involving drama impeccably, with multi-focal care. He shows America going about its business (which is, after all, business) with laptops and cell-phones as on any other weary-eyed morning, unaware that jihadist rat-bags are about to take knives to the soft underbelly of American civil aviation. Once the attack has been launched, the mounting dread of the passengers is intense, but then Greengrass tries to imagine the moulding of a group spirit: 'We have to do it now, because we know what happens if we just sit here and do nothing.' Todd Beamer's world-famous exclamation 'Let's roll' hardly registers before the boldest passengers, American war heroes in polo-shirts and chinos, are summoning all their strength to smash into the cockpit. Even as the ground rises, the viewer still hopes it might end differently this time. Was this remotely how the real events played out? It is somewhat consoling to think so.

Express Desires

Cinema's Obsessive Affair with Railways

BY GRAHAM FULLER

Right on time, trains had arrived at the birth of the movies with the screening of the Lumière brothers' *L'Arrivée d'un train en Garé de la Ciotat* in 1895, followed by *The Great Train Robbery* in 1903. John Ford's *The Iron Horse* (1924) and Victor A. Turin's *Turksib* (1929) subsequently depicted railway construction as nation building. But it was Graham Greene's 1932 novel *Orient Express* – which became an undistinguished film two years later – that made implicit the spiritual connection between rail travellers and cinemagoers, all gazers at windows who project their own feelings on the scenes passing before them. Greene was prescient, because the train movie – enhanced by the shush of released steam afforded by sound – became one of the great staples of the 1930s. It's a fact reflected on this list, though I could find no room for Howard Hawks's *Twentieth Century*.

My choices smack as much of the trainspotter as the cineaste – so there are plenty of films here with belching, oil-black locomotives, but no *Pather Panchali*, *Tokyo Story*, *Closely Observed Trains*, *The American Friend*, *Days of Being Wild*, or *Café Lumière*, which all contain formidable train scenes. I've included films in which train travel is a metaphor for love and sex. I lament the absence of *Dumbo* – with its wheezing anthropomorphic circus train – and *The Triplets of Belleville*, in which the hero's dog is driven crazy by the city train that thunders past his lonely tenement each night.

10. *Zhou Yu's Train* (China 2002, dir. Sun Zhou)

In this underrated romantic tragedy Gong Li is at her most sensual and bitter as a North China ceramics artist who travels obsessively by rail to visit her shy poet boyfriend in rural Chongyang. On one journey, she deliberately smashes one of her vases to fend off the cocky veterinarian who's pursuing her. It's a metaphor for her soon-to-be shattered life. After the boyfriend leaves her, she sleeps with the vet, but ends up walking the tracks in search of the lake to which her lost love compared her in a poem. Like the railway pedestrians of *Housekeeping* and *The Station Agent*, she seeks spiritual solace in physical contact with the actual rails.

9. *Night Mail* (GB 1936, dir. Harry Watt & Basil Wright)

This 25-minute documentary was produced by John Grierson's GPO Film Unit to show British Post Office workers how the Euston-to-Edinburgh mail train operated. Benjamin Britten composed the music and W.H. Auden the celebrated poem, narrated by Grierson, that had to be adjusted to the cutting of the final passage. *Night Mail* has transcended its status as a masterpiece of industrial film-making: there is no greater advertisement for the mystique of pre-war locomotives, and one assumes that thousands of British schoolboys saw it and asked their dads for a Hornby train set. Unlikely analogues include Hitchcock's *The 39 Steps* – see below – and Powell and Pressburger's *I Know Where I'm Going!*, each of which depicts rather more fraught train journeys from London to Scotland. Better these than the touristy evocations of Scottish train travel in the *Harry Potter* films and *Charlotte Gray*.

8. *Europa / Zentropa* (Denmark 1991, dir. Lars von Trier)

Leo (Jean-Marc Barr), the hapless protagonist of Trier's thriller, is an idealistic, American-educated young German hired as a train conductor on the state-owned Zentropa railway company after the fall of the Third Reich: he works behind the locos and on the routes that carried the Jews to the camps, even as neo-Nazi terrorists plot the socialist system's demise. Audacious in its surreal use of back projections and outsized flashing neon, Von Trier's direction blends Wagnerian grandeur with Hollywood noirishness: the visual dialectic underscores the clash between American capitalism and German fascism. Leo's external reality is but a dream within a dream – the one he has been lured into by the unseen hypnotist (Max Von Sydow) whose voice-over narration accompanies the opening travelling shot of rails: 'You will now listen to my voice. My voice will help you and guide you still deeper into Europa . . .'

7. *Human Desire* (US 1954, dir. Fritz Lang)

With its lurch and sway, a train can throw people together for a second and for eternity. So it is with railroad engineer Jeff Warren (Glenn Ford) and unhappily married Vicki Buckley (Gloria Grahame) in Fritz Lang's thriller. As they are borne through the night somewhere in America, sultry Vicki claims she has a speck of dust in her eye – and Jeff, who's off-duty, rushes in where angels fear to tread. Just back from Korea, he looks like the kind of lethal hunk who can help her get rid of her brutal sot of a husband (Broderick Crawford). This adaptation of Zola's *La Bête Humaine* is seldom compared favourably to Renoir's 1938 film or to Lang's other noirs. Certainly, in terms of cinematic railwayana, it has nothing as remotely powerful as Renoir's opening sequence in which Jean Gabin's locomotive thunders into Le Havre. But Lang's fatalistic approach to the way lives intersect – denoted by criss-crossing tracks in the title sequence – and his story's Zola-ish sordidness exert their own fascination. Then there's Grahame's wonderfully vulgar Vicki – definitely a second-class passenger, definitely going all the way.

6. *The 39 Steps* (GB 1935, dir. Alfred Hitchcock)

Although Hitchcock used a continental train as the set for 1938's *The Lady Vanishes*, the few railway scenes in his great adaptation of John Buchan's best Richard Hannay novel are more impressive. I was introduced to it in a 1959 children's encyclopedia that reproduced stills from the film to demonstrate the brilliant sound editing: the first showed the screaming charwoman who has dis-covered the body of the stabbed female spy in Hannay's flat; the second showed the 'whistling' Flying Scotsman that's carrying Hannay (Robert Donat) to Scotland; seeing the juxtaposition of these shots 'live' completed my education. A children's encyclo-pedia couldn't contain, however, the shot of a salesman rummag-ing in his case of bras and corsets as Hannay dozes opposite him, or the desperate hero forcing himself on Madeleine Carroll's lady passenger. When she gives him away to the police, he climbs out of the compartment window and edges along to the next as the train crosses the Forth Bridge – to these eyes, there's nothing so thrilling in *Von Ryan's Express*, *The Train*, or *Runaway Train*.

5. *Oh, Mr Porter!* (GB 1937, dir. Marcel Varnel)

'Next train's gone!' ancient Harbottle (Moore Marriott) snaps at failed wheeltapper William Porter (Will Hay) as he arrives to take command of a godforsaken whistle stop in rural Ireland; similarly helpful is fat idler and fellow freeloader Albert (Graham Moffatt), who excels in puncturing his new boss's officiousness. Showing deep affection for its branch-line setting, Hay's funniest vehicle is driven by the priceless interaction between the three incompetents, though director Varnel made much of the physical comedy involving recalcitrant crossing gates, a windmill, and the nineteenth century engine *Gladstone*, in which the trio chases a gang of gunrunners to Belfast. The eeriest scenes meanwhile make clear the debt Frank Launder's story owed to *The Ghost Train*, a 1923 play (written by future *Dad's Army* co-star Arnold Ridley) that was itself filmed as an Arthur Askey vehicle in 1941. In *Good Morning Boys – Will Hay, Master of Comedy*, authors Ray Seaton and Roy Martin assert that Michael Redgrave paid homage to Hay in the scene in *The Lady Vanishes* wherein Michael Redgrave affects a pair of pince-nez.

4. *Shanghai Express* (US 1932, dir. Josef von Sternberg)

Of Sternberg's seven films with Marlene Dietrich, this is the one that most discreetly harnessed his exotic artifice to the mood of romantic fatalism. Plumed, furred, feathered and veiled, Dietrich's 'notorious white flower of China' encounters a former lover, British Army officer 'Doc' Harvey (Clive Brook), on a train travelling from Peking during a rebellion: Sternberg's use of locations and back projection behind the carriage windows made the journey seem authentic enough. As the warlord who leads the rebel band, Warner Oland plays the familiar Sternberg manqué, while Anna May Wong is the retired courtesan he rapes. Dietrich's amorous adventuress tells Doc, 'It took more than one man to change my name to Shanghai Lily', dons his cap, impudently flicks it up with a finger after they first kiss, and takes a midnight promenade in a black negligee. Yet this was her most convincing and moving portrayal of a woman in love in a Sternberg film: she trembles in the famous shot of her upraised face before the screen goes black prior to the train's arrival in Shanghai. (Michael Powell pulled the reverse trick in A *Canterbury Tale*, haloing Dennis Price's sergeant with white light as his train arrives in the cathedral city.)

3. *Color of a Brisk and Leaping Day* (US 1996, dir. Christopher Münch)

In 1945, John Lee (Peter Alexander), a middle-class Chinese-American train buff who wants to honour the 'coolies' who helped build the national rail network, persuades a tycoon to finance the dying Yosemite Valley Railroad for a year; while running it, he becomes involved with a Miwok Indian park ranger (Jeri Arredondo) and inspires the unrequited love of the taciturn engineer (Michael Stipe). The epiphany that begins Münch's sublime elegy could have been scripted by Wordsworth, art-directed by J.M.W. Turner in *Rain, Steam, Speed* mode, and photographed by Ansel Adams (the landscapes) and O. Winston Link (the locos). As a mountain cataract sends up a mist, Charles Ives's 'The Unanswered Question' wells up on the soundtrack and, down below, a steam locomotive pulls a train through a valley of pines. Münch's movie thus salutes Yosemite's natural splendour *and* the industrial progress that desecrated it. Though Yosemite conservationists (like Adams) won out, train lovers will feel the ecstasy.

2. *The General* (US 1927, dir. Buster Keaton)

'Railroads', Keaton told Kevin Brownlow, 'are a great prop. You can do some awful wild things with railroads.' His Civil War epic was based on the failed Andrews Raid of 1862. Union soldiers led by a civilian spy hijacked a locomotive named the *General* in Georgia with the intent of causing mayhem behind Rebel lines. Two Southern railroad men gave chase and the raiders were arrested after a sixty-mile chase; eight of them were hanged. Keaton plays a solo engineer who goes after the hijacked loco and is chased in turn after he retrieves it. The accident-prone production in Oregon, which required Keaton to perform some of his most dangerous stunts, culminated in the filming of a spectacular train crash – reportedly, the costliest shot in silent film history. Keaton's fascination with machinery and its dangers was never more beautifully expressed than in the scene in which his self-absorbed hero is oblivious to the motion of the connecting rod on which he is sitting. There is also the unparalleled shot in which he dislodges a sleeper from the track by bouncing another on to it from the cowcatcher.

1. *Shoah* (France 1985, dir. Claude Lanzmann)

Lanzmann's Holocaust documentary runs to nine and a half hours – the time it took for the rail transports to deliver Jews from Western Europe to the Polish extermination camps. Lanzmann places us on board locomotives as they thread their way through forests and fields. We spend time with a surviving engineer. We imagine the drunken crews on the footplates, the prison vans with their human freight dying of asphyxiation and dehydration, and the Polish peasants on the ground jeering at them. The sounds on the track – birdsong, the rattle and clank of wheels on rails, the whistles, the hisses of steam – are rendered ominous by their crisp recording. One set of tracks leads to the tower and arch at Auschwitz II-Birkenau – the loco bearing Lanzmann's camera moves inexorably toward it, but it seems beyond reason that it intends to go all the way there.

The Code of the Road
Ten Great Road Movies
JASON WOOD

Synonymous with American culture and self-image, the road movie remains one of the most enduring and adaptable of genres, capable of cross-breeding with horror, thriller, screwball comedy or buddy-pic. Invariably involving some form of personal quest, road movies rarely prove to be 'about' the destination so much as the process of arriving, and the unforeseen incidents that can usefully upset the itinerary. It is this tendency towards spontaneity – even impetuousness – that has most endeared the genre to me.

Of course, the romance with cars and roads – the dangers, delights and drudgeries of covering distance over tarmac – is not uniquely American: other national cinemas have offered their own takes, reflecting their own sensibilities and geographies. But whatever its nationality, the road movie has always championed the outsider, and served up fascinating metaphors for the journey we make through life. I hope the films listed below hint at some of its intrinsic characteristics whilst also reflecting its diversity, not to say its intoxicating combination of optimism and nihilism. You may now start your engines.

10. *Duel* (US 1971, dir. Steven Spielberg)

This synthesis of road movie with horror/monster-movie was Spielberg's first feature assignment. A travelling salesman (Dennis Weaver) and a mysterious truck that pursues him down a Southern California highway are the only story ingredients. But Spielberg, shooting on location in Soledad Canyon with a sparse budget and a tight schedule, planned and choreographed his operation precisely. The action set-pieces (of which *Duel* is really a 90-minute series, punctuated by Weaver's weary interior monologue) were storyboarded to the smallest detail with Spielberg filming in chronological sequence. He pitches the roar of the duelling engines at an uncomfortable volume, but the dogged driver of the truck is never seen – a device leading us to suspect this is a random act of psychological torture, so heightening Weaver's ordeal. *Duel* was first premiered on US television but proved so popular that a longer version (with added violence) duly emerged for theatrical release.

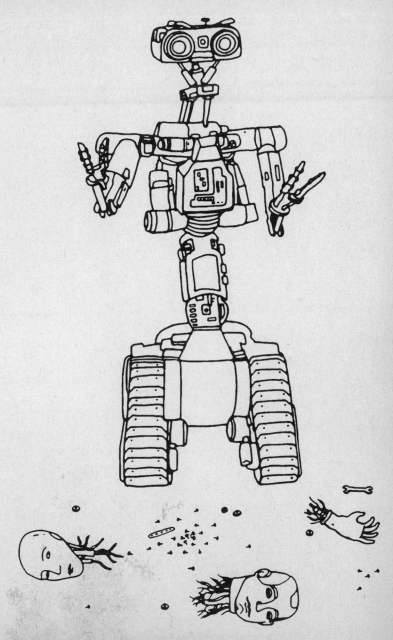

Domo Arigato, Mr Roboto: Ten Dodgy Robots, p 189

9. *Le Grand Voyage* (France/Morocco 2004, dir. Ismaël Ferroukhi)

A labour of love six years in the making, Ferroukhi's film was inspired by an epic journey undertaken by his father. Nicolas Cazalé plays French teenager Reda, whose dominating Moroccan Muslim father speaks only Arabic. The pair become uneasy travelling companions (a well-tried conceit, this) when Reda's father forces him to drive 3000 miles across Europe to Mecca in a battered old car so that he can undertake his final pilgrimage – or *hajj* – before he dies.

Ferroukhi drolly exploits the comic/dramatic potential to observe an intricate interplay between two people who set out with little understanding of each other, and yet inch toward mutual respect as the kilometres rack up. Setting some breathtaking scenery alongside mundane imagery of customs checkpoints and queues of stationary vehicles, *Le Grand Voyage* makes for a moving account of inter-generational relationships in a globalized world.

8. *Gallivant* (GB 1996, dir. Andrew Kötting)

In a singular example of what novelist Iain Sinclair calls 'psychogeography', artist/film-maker Kötting embarked on a coastal trip around Britain with his octogenarian grandmother Gladys and seven-year-old daughter Eden, who suffers from Joubert's syndrome, a communication restricting condition. This freeform camper-van travelogue, involving various encounters with the flotsam and jetsam of the British public, is at once larky and epic, an uplifting and strangely touching report on eccentricity, and on the lives of those Kötting holds most dear. The director manages to mesh documentary, avant-garde aesthetics (found footage, time-lapse photography) and family adventure movie, exploring matters that divide and unify three generations.

7. *Detour* (US 1945, dir. Edgar G. Ulmer)

Ulmer was a production designer for Murnau, Lang, and Lubitsch in 1920s Germany, before joining the great German/Viennese diaspora to Hollywood. In *Detour* he made perhaps the greatest of all B-movies. Downtrodden New York pianist Al Roberts (Tom Neal), hitching to Los Angeles where his girlfriend is a waitress, accepts a ride from an affable playboy who then suffers a fatal heart attack. Fearing he'll be accused of murder, Roberts takes the man's clothes, wallet, and vehicle. His next mistake is to pick up a strange woman (Ann Savage), who coolly asks him, 'What did you do with the body?'

Shot in six days and hampered by clumsy in-camera optical effects, *Detour* is still a triumph of style over budget, infusing the road movie with shades of film noir (the femme fatale, flashback, voice-over). At 68 minutes the picture moves at a clip, yet mines a deep well of nihilism. Its cult status was sealed after Neal was convicted of murdering his third wife.

6. *The Straight Story* (US 1999, dir. David Lynch)

Usually associated with sexual aberration, unrestrained violence and twisting narrative, David Lynch took a straightforward approach to this engaging true-life tale of elderly Alvin Straight's journey from Laurens, Iowa, to reconcile with his ailing brother in Mt Zion, Wisconsin. Since Alvin is unfit for car travel, he undertakes the journey in an idiosyncratic vehicle: a tooled-up motor-driven lawnmower. The digressions and eccentric character interludes common to the genre are all present here, as Alvin suffers an early mechanical breakdown and interacts with various misfits en route. There are also flashes of comic brio to underscore the absurdity of his endeavour: the best a dramatic tilt from the mower up to the clouds, as if Alvin's vehicle were about to zoom into the distance, but swiftly descending to reveal he has travelled but a single yard.

5. *Mad Max 2 / The Road Warrior* (Australia 1981, dir. George Miller)

For the follow-up to his surprise debut hit George Miller was armed with an increased budget and a newly famous Mel Gibson. Underpinned by a cruel Aussie humour, *The Road Warrior* careens towards a brilliantly mounted chase sequence that constitutes its entire last third, Miller paying homage to the speeding locomotive of Buster Keaton's *The General* (1927).

In a post-apocalyptic wasteland, ex-highway patrolman Max Rockatansky (Gibson) has become a drifter, scavenging for petrol. Falling in with an idealistic clan under threat from marauding desert warriors, Max offers to help the tribe transport a tanker full of petrol to the coast where the promise of a new life awaits. Miller creates an impressive post-industrial futureworld, and his vision of man's addictive need for ever-more scarce gasoline has remained eerily prophetic. The cars and motorcycles are familiar from the highways of the early 1980s but in line with the film's auto-fetishism receive DIY makeovers. The most fearsome has a bumper of two steel posts to which enemies can be strapped, and made to die first in the event of collision.

4. *Y tu mamá también* (Mexico 2001, dir. Alfonso Cuarón)

As youths Alfonso Cuarón and his scriptwriter brother Carlos shared ownership of a car they called Betsabé. As film-making collaborators they merged the road movie with a frank coming-of-age drama. Prominent amongst the film's many pleasures is the poignant interplay between another pair of real-life childhood friends, Gael García Bernal and Diego Luna. They play buddies journeying across Mexico towards a famous coastal beauty spot, joined along the way by Luisa (Maribel Verdú), an older, sexually experienced woman who decides to teach the teenage boys about love and life. Director Cuarón was returning to Mexico after a sojourn in Hollywood. And in charting a geographical journey (from the sprawling city to a mythical paradise) alongside an emotional journey (from adolescence to adulthood), he offered an allegory for Mexico itself.

3. *Radio On* (UK/West Germany 1979, dir. Chris Petit)

A striking debut, *Radio On* offers a hymn to the clear highway, ruefully aware that, in England at least, the road fast runs out. While employed as film editor of London's *Time Out*, Petit charmed Wim Wenders into involvement as co-producer, and his debt to Wenders's own Euro-road movies is clear.

A young man (David Beames) drives to Bristol to investigate the death of his brother. En route he encounters others as rootless as himself: an army deserter from Northern Ireland; a German woman looking for her lost child (Lisa Kreuzer, on loan from Wenders); and a garage mechanic (Sting, in an effective cameo). The film offers a compelling, even mythic vision of an England stricken by economic decline, uncertain of its place or future. Photographed in luminous monochrome and driven by a new wave soundtrack of *Low*-era Bowie, and Kraftwerk, Petit's debut echoed punk culture's austere aesthetic, its sense of faltering communication and lurking disenchantment.

2. *Kings of the Road* (West Germany 1976, dir. Wim Wenders)

Wenders took to the road with a handful of actors, a small crew and a few completed script pages. He wrote overnight, and if inspiration didn't flow they didn't shoot the next day. Starting with the character of a self-sufficient projector repairman servicing rural cinemas, *Kings of the Road* evolved into an analysis of the relationship that develops between Bruno (Rüdiger Vogler), and a suicidal linguist, Robert (Hanns Zischler), as they travel in Bruno's truck along the border roads. Lonely and introspective, the pair tentatively bond over their love of pop records, but are unable to totally escape their longing for the company of women.

Low on dramatic tension, the film's documentary aesthetic is loaned a lyrical quality by Robby Müller's sumptuous monochrome photography. The obsessions Wenders earlier exhibited came to fruition here: language, Germany's past, the dominance of American culture, and pop music. 'My life was saved by rock and roll' reads a salient graffito.

1. *Two-Lane Blacktop* (US 1971, dir. Monte Hellman)

Universal Studios thought they had a hit to cash in on the cult of *Easy Rider*. Monte Hellman, fresh from making enigmatic westerns for Roger Corman, was preoccupied by man's search for identity in an existential landscape. Critics weren't keen, audiences left cold. But today *Two-Lane Blacktop* is considered a Road Movie classic.

The Driver (James Taylor) and the Mechanic (Beach Boy Dennis Wilson) trek across the American south-west in their finely tuned, primer-grey '55 Chevy, occasionally competing in drag races. They barely speak, other than on mechanical matters, or in aphorisms ('You can never go fast enough'). Their relations suffer once they allow a female hitcher into their circle, then accept a challenge from a Pontiac-driving braggart (the incomparable Warren Oates) to race from Oklahoma to Washington D.C. Ostensibly a racing film, but haunted by images of desolate highways, *Two-Lane Blacktop* suggests the utter meaninglessness of motion in a nation where everyone is lost. Its final image is of the celluloid flipping out of the projector and igniting, as if road movies had finally crashed and burned. And yet Hellman had actually reinvigorated the genre.

12

Sex, Drugs and a Little Bit of Rock 'n' Roll

MIKE FIGGIS: A Surprising Intimacy – Ten Films that Have Interesting Sensuality

PAUL DALE: Once More With Feeling – The Ten Most Convincing Sex Scenes Not in a Porn Film

GEOFFREY MACNAB: The Prying Dutchman – The Ten Most Gratuitous Uses of Sex and Nudity in the Oeuvre of Paul Verhoeven

RICHARD T. KELLY: Heroic Doses, Hellish Descents – Ten Very Bad Trips, Man

MATT THORNE: Make Mine a Double – The Ten Best Screen Drunks

RICHARD T. KELLY AND NEV PIERCE: Thank You for Smoking – Ten Movies that Made Cigarettes Look Cool

JASON WOOD: The Ultimate Performance – Ten Great Acting Turns by Rock Stars and Other Musicians

A Surprising Intimacy

Ten Films that Have Interesting Sensuality

MIKE FIGGIS

Sex is very difficult to translate into cinema. It's not enough to just film it, because that only deals with the surface of sex (and that's why porno is so abysmal). A number of films that have been touted as groundbreaking in recent years have all (for my money, at least) been noticed because there was *actual sex on screen*, like a porno but 'meaningful'. But in fact they are 'like porn' inasmuch as not a lot else is going on; and, when it comes down to it, just a bit of penetration is as boring as watching stock-car racing.

So I've put together a list of the films that I find to have had some small measure of success in dealing with sex. They seem to fall into one of two categories. One is where the actors seem to mean it – as in, they look at each other and have feelings for each other, be they tender, violent, even detached. The second version is where the director manipulates the film in the edit, to create an erotic ambience.

10. *Peeping Tom* (GB 1960, dir. Michael Powell)

Powell's film is still pretty weird and still ahead of its time (see page 231). Like Polanski's *Repulsion* it taps into sexual nerves usually ignored by film-makers.

9. *Mulholland Dr.* (US 2001, dir. David Lynch)

Lynch is very sexual and not at all shy in how he does it. The scene where Naomi Watts masturbates but we can hear that she is dry (and that it is painful) is both erotic and tragic – and that is what is so interesting about Lynch's vision. Also, the scene in *Blue Velvet* (1986) where Kyle MacLachlan watches as Dennis Hopper abuses Isabella Rossellini is amazing – of course, by putting Kyle in there as the watcher Lynch allows us the audience to watch with him. I'd say Lynch is the most adult of the film-makers on this list.

8. *Jag är nyfiken – en film i gult / I Am Curious – Yellow* (Sweden 1967, dir. Vilgot Sjöman)

The scandal that surrounded this film at the time of its release and the subsequent battles in the US Supreme Court make it the film equivalent of *Lady Chatterley's Lover*. It's a remarkable film, way ahead of its time and the lead actress Lena Nyman is superb as she cuts a swathe through bourgeois Stockholm in the early sixties. The sex in it is very realistic.

7. *Once Upon a Time in America* (US 1984, dir. Sergio Leone)

There's a scene where Robert De Niro and his gang are robbing a jewellery place and the owner's wife (Tuesday Weld) gets turned on by the criminality of it all and demands to be serviced while the robbery continues.

6. *Le Train* (France 1973, dir. Pierre Granier-Deferre)

This is a really strong film. I haven't seen it for a while but I recall a scene where the leads Jean-Louis Trintignant and Romy Schneider have sex in a train in the dark, surrounded by other people. They're both fleeing from the Nazis in France, he's married and she's a Jewish refugee. This is another category of its own: forbidden sex, crazy sex, can't-keep-your-hands-off-each-other-despite-knowing-it-can-never-work-out sex.

5. *The Misfits* (US 1961, dir. John Huston)

Huston is not famous for depictions of sexuality, and it's rumoured that he had little patience for Marilyn Monroe in this, her last completed picture. But there is a scene which is deeply erotic – Monroe is playing a bat-and-ball game in a bar. As she hits the ball in time her ass moves provocatively, and a cowboy can't resist spanking her – Monty Cliff then punches him out, but for a moment there is sexual anarchy.

4. *The Man Who Fell to Earth* (US/GB 1975, dir. Nicolas Roeg)

This could just as easily have been *Performance* or the celebrated scene between Julie Christie and Donald Sutherland in *Don't Look Now*. Roeg uses the camera and then the edit to create sexual tension. The opening of *Performance* where James Fox is having rough sex with a former Miss World (Anne Sydney) is erotic – it contains the threat of violence. In *The Man Who Fell to Earth* there is a scene early on where Rip Torn has sex with a student of his: the cutting is amazing and the girl (an unknown) is very sexy, the whole both urgent and surprising.

3. 'The Tide', from the portmanteau *Contes immoraux* (France 1974, dir. Walerian Borowczyk)

This is a short film about a sexual encounter between teenage cousins on a seaside holiday in France. It is witty and ironic and sexy. Like many a good film-maker Borowczyk realizes that ironic dialogue is the key to cinematic eroticism. It's somehow necessary to use this device to take us out of the perversity of being present in the intimate act of two persons: we perhaps need a level of theatricality in order to feel comfortable. Interesting sociological moment when the girl is naked: her huge bush dates the film more than would any flared trouser-leg.

2. *Ai No Corrida / In the Realm of the Senses* (Japan 1976, dir. Nagisa Oshima)

Oshima's film created quite a stir when it came out. I saw it at a festival in France and was shocked. But I was also entirely affected by it, and I can't recall having such an experience since. The actors are amazing, and the way they relate to each other sums up the problems of the porn industry for me. In porn the actors don't relate, they don't look at each other and they make silly noises while they're doing the business. In the Oshima film the intimacy of the two actors is amazing and entirely believable. Like Truffaut's *Woman Next Door* it places sex into a very doom laden environment. There's nothing chirpy or jokey about either film: sex=passion=death.

1. *Week End* (France 1967, dir. Jean-Luc Godard)

Has the best sex scene in film history for my money. There is no sex, just a very bourgeois woman describing a threesome in the most offhand manner – a kind of Godardian comedy sketch based perhaps on Georges Bataille's infamous novel *The Story of the Eye*. (Of course Bergman's *Persona* also has a very erotic scene where there's no visual depiction, merely a verbal description of a sexual encounter on a beach somewhere.) But what's interesting about *Week End* is that despite the shallowness of the couple, the text is still sexy – or maybe this says something more about me than about the film . . .

Once More With Feeling

The Ten Most Convincing Sex Scenes Not in a Porn Film

PAUL DALE

Raw sex no longer sells cinema tickets. It's arguable whether it ever did. The last film with 'realistic' sex scenes to make good money was in fact anything but: the excremental phony-X-certificate *Come Play with Me* was a huge come-on of a movie that played at the Classic Moulin cinema in Soho for almost four years on the boast that it contained genuine coitus, when in fact it contained less of same (and more innuendo) than your average *Carry On* film. It sometimes seems that the public likes the promise of sex but not the delivery. Good, convincing sex scenes outside of porn are an art, to be savoured for their rarity, naturalism, and detail. As Billy Joel said: 'There's nothing better than good sex. But bad sex? A peanut butter and jelly sandwich is better than bad sex.' Here are ten movie sex scenes that really deliver.

10. *Le Diable au corps* / *The Devil in the Flesh* (France 1947, dir. Claude Autant-Lara)

But allow me to start with the abstract and get more graphic from there. Based on Raymond Radiguet's scandalous novel about infidelity, adultery and death in First World War France, this now hard-to-see film carries with it all the shocking (for the time) sexual potency of the book. This being the late 1940s, of course, there are no sex scenes but in leads Gérard Philipe and Micheline Presle (the underage student and the older married woman caught up in sexual obsession) Autant-Lara had found two Gallic mini-cauldrons of boiling passion. At those moments where we assume sex is happening, he employs metaphors of ejaculation – church bells slow down, the end of war is celebrated prematurely. *The Devil in the Flesh* is a masterpiece of poise and sexual suggestion.

9. *The Brown Bunny* (US 2003, dir. Vincent Gallo)

Vincent Gallo is Bud Clay, a professional motorcycle rider who is heading from New Hampshire to California so he can race again. Along the way he has sex with lots of needy ladies but there is only one old love who really knows how to please him. Gallo's much-derided male-fantasy ego-trip may actually be better than we deserve for indulging his unique declamatory talents for so long, but there is something about the final oral sex scene that is hard to forget. Shot using remote cameras in a smallish room, the scene is both relentless and oddly loving and compelling. Chloë Sevigny, an old friend of Gallo's and one of the few who seems to have stayed on the right side of him, has claimed that the scene was not simulated but real. Whatever the truth it is a benchmark in childish cinematic misogyny (her character's name is even Daisy for chrissakes) and believable blowjobs.

8. *9 Songs* (GB 2004, dir. Michael Winterbottom)

Where does one start with Winterbottom's depiction of a modern romance based solely on hardcore sex and going to gigs by rubbish indie bands in Brixton? There is certainly a lot of sex to choose from as Matt (Kieran O'Brien) and his big cock penetrate waif-like Lisa (Margot Stilley) over and over again. (What a trial.) But the sequence that really stands out is the one in which – late on in the film when their clearly shallow relationship is already in decline – Lisa takes herself off to the bedroom and masturbates using a small vibrator. After a while Matt follows her and watches from the bedroom door. But Lisa seems to be less masturbating than exorcizing some deep sexual demon. She twitches and turns before climaxing. Matt, depressed, returns to the kitchen. It is a scene that all too clearly illustrates the ennui and loveless sexual abyss into which the passage of time will often push couples.

7. *Intimacy* (France/GB 2000, dir. Patrice Chéreau)

Probably the nastiest and definitely the seediest contender on this list is Chéreau's sordid middle-class fuckfest in which Jay (Mark Rylance) and Claire (Kerry Fox) meet up every Wednesday afternoon for a bit of anonymous non-verbal sex. Things begin to unravel however when they start the small talk. All the sex scenes in this drama based on stories by Hanif Kureishi are explicit and allegedly performed for real by the two brave leads, but the scene in which Fox gets carpet-burn while being taken from behind in the filthy London flat is quite jaw-dropping.

6. *Shortbus* (US 2006, dir. John Cameron Mitchell)

There are so many great sex scenes to choose from in Mitchell's fearless and very funny farce (a love hymn to his beloved Manhattan) but the one that really takes the soggy biscuit comes right at the beginning of the film, where one of the subsidiary characters blows his own bone, i.e. leans forward and sucks his beef-stick dry – if you catch my drift? It's an awesome feat with which to open a movie about the shenanigans of an underground New York sex salon; one only equalled by porcine degenerate Ron Jeremy in the much-celebrated 1981 skin flick *Lips*, also starring Vanessa Del Rio.

5. *Caligula* (Italy/US 1979, dir. Tinto Brass)

All hail Brass, the demented Italian who gave us the fascistically perverse *Salon Kitty* and this bizarre fusion of historical epic and soft-core porno. Produced by *Penthouse* magazine CEO Bob Guccione and first scripted by Gore Vidal (who then disassociated himself and spoke witheringly of 'Tinto Zinc'), *Caligula* attempts to tell the shocking and tragic tale of the extravagant, eccentric, depraved and despotic Roman emperor. If Brass had been allowed to edit the film *Caligula* could have been something really quite interesting. It was, however, producer Guccione and legendary but hardly inspired Italian editor Nino Baragli who took that duty upon themselves. The result is fragmented and messy (as Guccione tries to insert as many shots as possible of his 'Penthouse Pets' into the orgy scenes). There are, however, some surprisingly effective and convincing sequences in the film, particularly that where Caligula (Malcolm McDowell), Caesonia (Helen Mirren), and Drusilla (Teresa Ann Savoy) have sex, for it includes inserts of a lesbian tryst shot by Guccione. This footage replaces shots that made the scene necessary for plot reasons (the original script had various court members looking through the peephole, thus explaining the close-ups of the moon face in the bedroom), as well as a different lesbian act featuring the ladies-in-waiting, shot by Brass.

4. *Dogme number 2: Idioterne / The Idiots* (Denmark 1998, dir. Lars von Trier)

Sex and 'spazzing' Danish style. Trier's tale of group sex and bizarre forms of gestalt therapy in a Copenhagen suburb was one of the big censor-baiting causes célèbres of the 1990s and it's not difficult to see why. The gang-bang scene in which assorted members of the commune access their 'inner idiot' by behaving like a group of lubricious loons (or randy Rain Men) is quite something to behold, erect penises and all.

3. *La Vie de Jésus* (France 1997, dir./scr. Bruno Dumont)

The film that is often credited as the first containing real sex to appear in British cinemas (though 'British cinemas' is a broad term, here denoting a two-week run at London's ICA). French auteur Dumont's account of the life of an unemployed epileptic finch-fancier in an impoverished lowland area of France contains a scene where the two non-professional actors, David Douche and

Marjorie Cottreel, appear to be having real sex in a field. There is an unmistakable veracity to the scene that, in terms of depictions of dyspeptic youth, has been rarely bettered. But stunt genitals were employed for the actual penetration, and sadly the film did nothing for the careers of the two courageous performers who seem never to have worked again. Douche was recently reported to be living rough in Lille.

2. *Red Road* (GB 2006, dir. Andrea Arnold)

There's nothing like a good old-fashioned Scottish thriller featuring ginger sex and surveillance cameras. Arnold's astounding Glasgow-set tale of vengeance contains one of the great modern-day sex scenes. When Jackie (Kate Dickie) gets into a bedroom with jailbird Clyde (Tony Curran) in a high-rise flat on the run-down Red Road scheme, sparks fly in one of the most graphic and violent sex scenes ever committed to celluloid. Everything looks so real but was apparently all simulated between the two Scottish actors, who are not only good friends but trained together many years before. Apparently even the oral sex sequence is fake: a grapefruit was placed between Dickie's legs for Curran to lick out.

1. *Ai No Corrida / In the Realm of the Senses* (Japan 1976, dir. Nagisa Oshima)

And of course the number one spot goes to Oshima's masterful portrait of torrid love between master and servant in 1936 Japan. Based (like many of Oshima's previous films) on an actual sensational event, the film is about love, death, power, and the rise of militant Japanese nationalism. It also features a veritable Kama Sutra of sexual positions and acts (horizontal, vertical; him on top, her on top; vaginal sex, anal sex, oral sex; lesbian sex, group sex, sado-masochistic sex; masturbation; tasting of genital fluids and so on) all of which are convincing and highly eligible for this list. But the gong has to go to a scene banned by the Japanese censor until 2001. Early in the film Sada (Eiko Matsudo) is propositioned by an impotent old man. She responds by flaunting her pubic hair; he desperately masturbates himself but his penis remains limp. At the time the film was made Japanese censorship laws allowed graphic representations of violence (including rape) yet forbade the display of sexual organs and pubic hair. This taboo originated in the Meiji era and was connected to the campaign to be accepted by the Western powers as a modern civilized state. (Prior to the so-called Meiji Restoration, the pornography industry flourished in both literature and art.) So in one wholly incontrovertible move Oshima used a flaccid cock as a weapon of attack on the old men in the government censorship offices who designated pubic hair 'obscene' throughout the twentieth century. It's a Protest (Non-)Wank, one that was to influence the reshaping of Japan's censorship laws over the next thirty years. For which, Oshima *sensei*, we salute you.

The Prying Dutchman

The Ten Most Gratuitous Uses of Sex and Nudity in the Oeuvre of Paul Verhoeven

GEOFFREY MACNAB

'There is a fear about sex in motion pictures,' Paul Verhoeven once remarked, 'as if sex would undermine morality.' In his work Verhoeven has always tried to play on this fear. He orchestrates his sex scenes with the same fetish for detail and ballyhoo that Busby Berkeley used to bring to his dance numbers. They are his trademark.

We're not talking Russ Meyer here. Verhoeven is a ferociously intelligent and serious film-maker. He graduated from Leiden University with a doctorate in mathematics. As he has frequently acknowledged, he is a child of his times. 'We grew up in the 1970s where there was absolute sexual freedom in our artistic world,' he told one journalist. 'There was no AIDs, the pill had just come in, women were autonomous, and we all had fun.'

His early Dutch films reflect this sense of counter-culture liberation. In Hollywood, though, the sex has proved more problematic. One of the great pleasures in following his US career has been in watching the free-thinking Dutchman wrestling with the hypocrisy and prurience of the studio system. Violence presented no such difficulties: Robocop could kill indiscriminately without the censors blinking. Sex was something else. Amazingly, *Basic Instinct* was given an 'R' rating but Verhoeven enjoyed no such luck on *Showgirls*, which received the dreaded NC-17 tag that stopped it from being shown in mainstream cinemas, but not from being roundly ridiculed.

No one would deny Verhoeven his sex scenes. That is not the reason for this list. Instead, below, we pick up on moments when the sex is thrown in, almost like a nervous tic: when it really has little to do with the main action . . .

10. Gina Gershon and Elisabeth Berkley examine each others' chests: *Showgirls* (US 1995)

Sometimes Verhoeven doesn't even need to show the sex. It's the smutty dialogue that really zings here. Gina Gershon and Elisabeth Berkley are making small-talk at lunch. 'You have great tits,' Gershon proposes. 'They're really beautiful. I like nice tits. I always have. What about you?' 'I like having nice tits,' Berkley replies. 'How do you like having them?' 'What do you mean?' 'You know what I mean.' 'I like having them in a nice dress.' It's worth remembering that screenwriter Joe Eszterhas used to be paid millions of dollars for providing Verhoeven and cast with lines such as these.

9. Kevin Bacon cops a feel: *Hollow Man* (US 2000).

If you are invisible, you ought to be allowed a good grope. Such is the philosophy that appears to run through Verhoeven's foray into the world of H.G. Wells. Kevin Bacon is the scientist who turns psychotic once he has managed to make himself invisible. There is an air of inevitability about the scene in which he uses his undetectable hand to fondle a woman's breast. This wasn't something you ever found Claude Rains resorting to in James Whale's 1933 stab at *The Invisible Man*.

8. The feather duster: *Wat Zien Ik / Business is Business* (Holland 1971)

Verhoeven's debut feature is a bawdy drama set inside a brothel. The director isn't making a social realist drama about the plight of prostitutes. The tone here is closer to that of 1970s sitcom. While he might hint at the squalor and difficulty of his protagonists' lives, he can't resist throwing in some bizarrely comical sex scenes. Consider the sequence with the feather duster. One client, dressed as a maid, fails to clean up properly. There is only one thing for it – he needs to be thrashed. This is not the glossy, hi-tech sex we know from *Basic Instinct*. As filmed by Verhoeven and cinematographer Jan De Bont, it is like an out-take from *The Benny Hill Show*.

7. The chicken dance: *Wat Zien Ik / Business is Business* (Holland 1971)

And then this, surely the strangest scene in the entire Verhoeven *oeuvre*. A client turns up at the brothel with a briefcase full of feathers. Soon, he is pretending he is a cock chasing two chickens round the room. The problem is that the chickens (who are dressed in nothing but feathers) go 'peep' instead of 'cluck'. The man's farmyard fantasy is ruined by their choice of noise. The scene ends with the women evicting the man and throwing his feathers after him.

6. The fake moustache et al.: *Turks fruit / Turkish Delight* (Holland 1973)

This is Rutger Hauer in Robin Askwith mode. Early in the film, Hauer (playing a mercurial artist with a manic sex drive) goes on a romantic rampage. Stung by the end of his relationship with Monique van de Ven, he embarks on a one-man quest to seduce all the women in Amsterdam. He jumps in their cars, accosts young mothers and generally hurls himself at everyone he sees. Not only do we have a pram being rocked by one of Hauer's conquests in rhythm with their love-making; in one ill-judged moment, we see Hauer use a pair of scissors to cut himself off some pubic hair and then hold it beneath his nose as if it were a Hitler moustache. Later, the hapless Hauer gets his penis caught in his zip. Given that *Turkish Delight* turns into a terminal illness love story, the bawdy gags with which Verhoeven opens the movie seem utterly incongruous.

5. The medical check-up: *Keetje Tippel / Katie Tippel* (Holland 1975)

This is Verhoeven's stab at a nineteenth-century costume drama. It comes complete with bonnets and brooches and Dickensian-like street scenes. The subject is the plight of poverty-stricken country workers forced to move to the big city. Among them is the beautiful blonde Katie (Monique van de Ven). When she falls ill with consumption, the doctor needs to examine her – and so, it seems, does Verhoeven. For no very good reason, van de Ven plays the scene naked. The doctor is prurient and manipulative – but so is the director.

4. Sharon Stone uncrosses her legs: *Basic Instinct* (US 1992)

When Verhoeven dies, this is the cinematic moment that all his obituary writers will turn to first. It is shot in expressionistic, sub-Hitchcock-style with heavy use of chiaroscuro. Michael Douglas and various pot-bellied cops are lurking in the shadows interviewing icy blonde Sharon Stone. She is toying with them, smoking (even though this is forbidden) and making provocative remarks about her hobbies (which seem to begin and end with sado-masochistic sex). Then comes what we latterly might call the Britney Spears moment: as the cops begin to look more and more clammy and agitated, the thighs beneath Stone's ultra-short skirt suddenly part, briefly laying bare the bull's-eye. Gratuitous? Maybe, maybe not, but you can't help thinking it's a pity that a film-maker as brilliant as Verhoeven will forever be remembered for this one sneaky peek.

3. Carice van Houten dyes her pubic hair: *Zwartboek / Black Book* (Holland 2006)

'I'm from Holland and so I'm used to that nudity stuff,' actress Carice van Houten told the press of her role as Rachel, the femme fatale/Anne Frank figure in Verhoeven's Second World War film. Even so, the scene with the paintbrush comes as a surprise. Rachel has to keep her Jewish identity secret and to convince the Nazis that she is the nearest thing to Marlene Dietrich they'll find in the Hague. Cue the dye. You have the sense that this is a self-referential joke and that Verhoeven is simply trying to remind the audience of a certain moment in *Basic Instinct* . . .

2. Sex in the window: *Soldaat van Oranje / Soldier of Orange* (Holland 1977)

We're in England, 1939. Heroic toff Rutger Hauer is meeting the Dutch Queen-in-exile and telling her of his plans to go back to the Netherlands as part of the resistance to the Nazi invasion. This is a dialogue-heavy sequence that plays out in a leafy English garden. The Queen informs Hauer that 'aristocracy belongs in the past' and that 'the true nobility are the resistance fighters'. It's all very earnest, which is no doubt why Verhoeven throws in a cut-away to a couple (Jeroen Krabbé and Susan Penhaligon) making love in an upstairs window. Hauer shuffles awkwardly, trying to keep the Queen from looking upward. Just why they've chosen this particular moment to prance around naked in the full view of Her Majesty is anyone's guess.

1. Sex in the hay: *Soldaat van Oranje / Soldier of Orange* (Holland 1977)

Holland is being invaded by the Nazis. As they march through the countryside, the Dutch troops hear from an escaped lunatic that there are German paratroopers in the vicinity. They go to investigate and discover a bare-buttocked couple making love in a haystack. This early scene is in the spirit of Dick Emery. What is Verhoeven telling us? That farmworkers and peasant girls had more on their minds than resisting the enemy? That Dutch soldiers are peeping toms? Or was it simply that Verhoeven felt that the narrative would flag unless there was a sex scene every twenty minutes?

Heaven Must be Missing an Angel: Ten Otherworldly Girls, p 193

Heroic Doses, Hellish Descents

Ten Very Bad Trips, Man

RICHARD T. KELLY

'The poet makes himself a seer', declared Rimbaud, 'by a long, prodigious and rational disordering of the senses. He reaches the unknown and even if, terrified, he ends up by losing the meaning of his visions, at least he has seen them!' That sounds like the stuff of drama, doesn't it? Hallucinogenic drugs became the subject of much concerted thought and abuse in the 1960s, and naturally burrowed their way into movies too. But in films as in life, how seriously should we take the claims of those who urge 'experimentation' with drugs so strong that they carry a weapons-grade? The guru Terence McKenna made himself fashionable by talking up the idea of the 'heroic dose'. But Terence Stamp maybe put it best when he observed that one really only has to take acid once to get the picture: the rest is mere indulgence. These ten movies are a weird bunch, some with moments of savage irreality that could have you groping for the comfort-blanket. Yet strangely, they nearly all make the same essential point: just say no.

10. Paul Groves (Peter Fonda) in *The Trip* (US 1967, dir. Roger Corman)

Two years before *Easy Rider* changed everything, *The Trip* first brought together Fonda, Jack Nicholson (who wrote the earnest script) and Dennis Hopper (in the first of his many biodegradable druggy roles). Commercials director Fonda is suffering through his divorce from lovely Susan Strasberg, so psychologist friend Bruce Dern proposes a soothing LSD experiment at his place in the Hollywood Hills. 'I'm gonna be here, man, trust me,' he stresses. Soon Fonda is joyfully holding up an orange and crying, 'Oh, it gives off an orange cloud of light that just *flows* . . .' His trouble begins when he hallucinates Dern's death and flees down into the freakshow of Sunset Boulevard. *The Trip* is a timepiece, boldly edited, but slackly imagined, full of silly steals from *The Seventh Seal* and light bouncing off bare breasts in a rock club. To his credit, Corman did the research prior to shooting, studiously tripping on Big Sur beach.

9. Joe Buck (Jon Voight) and Ratso Rizzo (Dustin Hoffman) in Midnight Cowboy (US 1969, dir. John Schlesinger)

This is something of a cheat, in that Joe is the one who inhales, at some free Greenwich Village loft party he and Ratso have crashed; and he finds himself enjoying pretty much the whole loud freaky light-show experience. But consequently the ailing Ratso is unable to talk to him or understand him in turn. Thieving salami from the free buffet, he's observed in the act by some dazed but supercilious hippy chick. Worse, other such chicks want to paw him as if he were a small crippled animal. In other words, one man's high times may be nothing but a heavy downer for a friend who's straight and hating it.

8. Bill Lee (Peter Weller) and Joan Frost (Judy Davis) in Naked Lunch (GB/Canada 1992, dir. David Cronenberg)

'I suffer from sporadic hallucinations,' mutters Weller in his best William Burroughs voice. 'Join the club,' murmurs Davis, playing a version of Jane Bowles. The two have met in Interzone, a kasbah of the mind, and Weller is itching to crack out his new drug of choice, the black meat of the giant centipede. Cronenberg believed his Naked Lunch 'was like Burroughs and myself fusing in the telepod of The Fly'. What's lost is Burroughs's aggressive homosexuality, with Cronenberg channelling his own erotic imagination into typewriters that are hallucinated as talking insects. To wit: as Weller and Davis lose themselves in the black meat and each other, a nearby writing machine turns weirdly fleshly, exposes an orifice, sprouts a phallus, then becomes a spiny legless pink-buttocked thing that joins the couple in writhing on the floor.

7. Hunter S. Thompson (Johnny Depp) in Fear and Loathing in Las Vegas (US 1998, dir. Terry Gilliam)

Given the fertile source that was Thompson's much-loved semi-fiction, this could have been the Citizen Kane of trip movies.

Depp and Benicio del Toro certainly look devoted to the spirit of derangement ('Here's your half of the sunshine acid'). But Gilliam, like Cronenberg, seems to have no real interest in psychedelic drugs, and the movie falls apart in freak-out scene after freak-out scene. The first – the duo's epic check-in at the Mint Hotel in Vegas – is much the best. 'There is no way of explaining the terror I felt . . .' runs Depp's muttered voice-over, and we're right with him in his sweaty close-ups, his listing POV, the dread things he thinks he's overhearing (' . . . waitress about sixteen years old, they chopped her goddamn head off'). Hilariously, amid the mayhem, Gilliam throws in one cold objective view of Depp babbling away at the desk clerk. The fun only stops when the director takes Thompson too literally, placing his boys in a hotel bar seemingly packed with big, vicious, rutting lizards.

6. Jacob Singer (Tim Robbins) in *Jacob's Ladder* (US 1990, dir. Adrian Lyne)

From the writer of *Ghost* and the director of *Fatal Attraction* comes – nothing you would ever pay to see, right? Yet *Jacob's Ladder* was always considered a great unfilmed script, and finally emerged as one of those hellish movies that bait you to decide which bits of them are *not* savage chemical-soaked nightmares. We're fairly sure something terrible happened to Tim Robbins in Vietnam. But he seems to have a life in the present: a postman, married for the second time. The worst bit – until things get really dreadful – is when he attends a lively house party and encounters a palm-reader: 'You have a very strange line. No, it's not funny. See, according to this you're already dead.' That would unnerve anyone, but as Robbins stumbles through the dark and deteriorating throng he starts to see the beating of leathery wings, under-cranked heads gnashing their teeth at him, and his wife being evilly raped by some horned and tailed monstrosity.

5. Sonny (Gary Stretch), Soz (Neil Bell) and Herbie (Stuart Wolfenden) in *Dead Man's Shoes* (GB 2004, dir. Shane Meadows)

Ex-squaddie Richard is back in town (Matlock, Derbyshire, to be precise) and shadowing a crew of drug-dealing louts, giving them the creeping fear that he intends to inflict something awful upon them – commensurate with how they once abused his mentally impaired kid-brother. The menace takes shape as we watch Richard mulling over a thieved sheet of acid tabs ('I'm gonna give 'em a super-duper fookin' dose. I'm gonna send 'em to space, man'). Then the crew find their members turning up butchered, and the survivors seek refuge in a safe-house, arming themselves with crossbows and swords. But Richard is already there and has emptied all that acid into the kettle from which the lads top up their Pot Noodle snacks. Soon they're cramming into the toilet, avidly cleaning the kitchen, maniacally lifting weights – tripping their little heads off. They get so sweaty and woozy and helpless that they (and we) almost forget that Richard is still in the house, waiting, with a pistol and a knife and a suitcase stuffed full of something yet more horrendous.

4. Donna Hayward (Moira Kelly) in *Twin Peaks: Fire Walk With Me* (US 1992, dir. David Lynch)

Donna is determined to prove her friendship to troubled Laura Palmer (Sheryl Lee): also that maybe Laura isn't such a bad girl as she thinks, nor Donna quite so good. They pick up two burly dudes in the Bang-Bang Bar and then it's off to some hell-pit club, a barn with bare bulbs and fluoro-strip flicker, the music (a cello and drums) too loud to let you hear yourself think. So Donna simply isn't paying attention when her bottle gets spiked in a game of pass-the-beer. When all the girls in the place start peeling their clothes off, Donna is in a poor place to resist. Only a late attack of conscience ('Donna, not you!') compels naked Laura to rescue her semi-ravished friend. In the aftermath Lynch gives us a grim dolly over a sticky barroom floor, a cemetery of butts and bottles, then we find Donna back on her couch, bundled up in a dressing gown, shaking her head. 'How did I get back to my house?' Ah, the solace of poor recall.

3. Professor Eddie Jessup (William Hurt) in *Altered States* (US 1980, dir. Ken Russell)

When Professor Jessup's new girlfriend Emily (Blair Brown) notes the funny face that he pulls at the height of their shared pleasure and so ventures to ask him what he's thinking about in the moment . . . well, she asked for it. 'Christ, blood, the crucifixion,' he pants distractedly, like this ought to be obvious. Jessup lost his religious faith after his father's death, but he's seeking something better to put in its place. In short, this is not a man who needs to ingest great swallows of peyote with Hichi Indians or spend hours in a sensory deprivation tank, hallucinating 'like a son-of-a-bitch'. The odds would propose some sort of regression to a primordial state, and sure enough Jessup is soon running with wild dogs and killing deer with his bare hands. Russell's trip-imagery perhaps looks a little florid to a sober eye, but should not be viewed by anybody temporarily on vacation from their right mind.

2. Billy (Dennis Hopper), Captain America (Peter Fonda), Karen (Karen Black) and Mary (Toni Basil) in *Easy Rider* (US 1969, dir. Hopper)

The sixties were headed for the out-door anyhow but *Easy Rider* slammed it shut. 'Just shut up and take it' is Hopper's charming inducement to the girls he and Fonda have dragged along to a New Orleans cemetery: hardly the most affable start to a groovy trip, nor the ideal place for it. And it soon becomes a bad scene for all concerned, Basil getting naked, Black distressed, Hopper drunk and Fonda quite sick. The camera only does what passed for *vérité* trippiness in those days – twisting POVs and fish-eye lenses. But Hopper's blink editing is brave and striking, and it was a smart move to cross-cut the early bourbon-swigging euphoria and clammy sex with the later despair and tears. That day-and-a-half's shooting was fraught for everyone but especially Fonda, whom Hopper urged to release suppressed feelings about his mother's suicide. 'You're such a fool, mother', Fonda weeps, 'and I hate you so much' – more than we need to know.

1. Chas Devlin (James Fox) in *Performance* (GB 1970, dir. Donald Cammell & Nicolas Roeg)

Bad craziness at 81 Powys Square, Notting Hill Gate. Gangland enforcer Chas is holed up in bohemia, hiding from his vengeful boss Harry Flowers. He wants to get out of the country, but reclusive rock star Turner (Mick Jagger) wants to get him out of his head. So Turner's delicious handmaiden Pherber (Anita Pallenberg) slips Chas two-thirds of a big psilocybin mushroom, and soon this hardcase is commenting on the prettiness of an inlaid table and the heat of a candle ('I've never seen that sort before'). 'He's on his way, that man,' observes Turner. 'You've poisoned me!' is Chas's angry cry on learning he's been medicined. 'Ooh, he's on a bummer,' frets Turner. But Chas gets into the ride, even while Turner is burbling passages from Borges and Pherber is trying to seduce him with playful androgynous talk he finds unmanly. His big treat is to watch the stupendous dancing of Lucy (Michèle Breton) and Jagger's blinding performance of 'Memo From Turner'. All things considered, you mightn't even call it a bad trip – were it not that, come the bleary dawn, Chas is so minced he makes a phone call that leads Flowers' goons to the door of number 81. Comedowns should be about tea and sympathy, not escorted drives to one's own execution.

Make Mine a Double

The Ten Best Screen Drunks

BY MATT THORNE

Although Hollywood (at least in public) grows ever more puritanical, onscreen drinking has yet to face the same opprobrium as onscreen smoking. Los Angeles may be a town where hotel mini-bars have warnings against the carcinogenic properties of alcohol, but Hollywood directors still usually give alcoholic detectives at least a shot at redemption. There's no doubt that times have changed since the golden age of William Powell and Myrna Loy as Nick and Nora, the alcoholic couple at the centre of the *Thin Man* films. But then it's not so long ago that Nicolas Cage got the Oscar for playing a drunk in *Leaving Las Vegas*. Here, then, are my Top Ten favourite celluloid soaks.

10. Martha (Elizabeth Taylor) in *Who's Afraid of Virginia Woolf?* (US 1966, dir. Mike Nichols, scr. Ernest Lehman from the play by Edward Albee)

Lest this list seem depressing at face value, it's important to remember that in movies, as in life, alcoholics can be funny. Drunks can be the comic relief in westerns or war stories, or they can allow the screenwriter to voice painful truths that sober people would never risk saying. Among the best examples of the latter category is Elizabeth Taylor's Martha in Nichols's film of Albee's play. Everyone in the picture (Taylor and Richard Burton, George Segal and Sandy Dennis) is perfectly cast, and while how much you enjoy it will depend on your taste for domestic bickering, it offers a great illustration of how self-degradation can sometimes be the only way to get to the heart of a matter.

9. Wanda Wilcox (Faye Dunaway) in *Barfly* (US 1987, dir. Barbet Schroeder, scr. Charles Bukowski)

Bukowski has always been taken more seriously by musicians and film-makers than by literary critics. Perhaps it's because he was such a brilliant embodiment of everything Hollywood celebrities and pop stars like to believe about writers and writing. He's been played onscreen by Mickey Rourke and Matt Dillon among others, but perhaps the best performance in a Bukowski-inspired picture comes from Faye Dunaway as Wanda in Barbet Schroeder's *Barfly*. Unlike most women in these sorts of films – who either stand by their man, abandon him, or are sucked unwillingly into their alcoholism – Wilcox is every bit the equal of 'Henry Chinaski' (Rourke), determined to remain on the stool alongside him through any number of LA's dive bars.

8. Roger Wade (Sterling Hayden) in *The Long Goodbye* (US 1973, dir. Robert Altman, scr. Leigh Brackett, from the novel by Raymond Chandler)

Among the late Robert Altman's unusual achievements was managing to make films that (sometimes simultaneously) seemed both stunningly misanthropic and yet fully sympathetic to all kinds of human frailty. The latter quality clearly extended to his treatment of his actors, especially when it was good for the film. When Sterling Hayden showed up drunk on the set of *The Long Goodbye*, Altman realized this was perfect for Hayden's role as the blocked writer Wade, and managed to extract one of the best performances the actor ever gave (though it's said that Hayden could remember nothing of the work he had done by the following day).

7. Withnail (Richard E. Grant) in *Withnail & I* (GB 1987, dir./scr. Bruce Robinson)

Now that Bruce Robinson's debut feature is a canonized Cult Classic, it's more difficult to appreciate just what a peculiar film it is. If Robinson has never come close to repeating the achievement (although his fiction is good, and *How to Get Ahead in Advertising* is a guilty pleasure), it's not really his fault: Withnail lurches woozily from one unlikely scene to another, but perfectly in keeping with its crapulous heroes. It's hard to work out why the whole is so charming: whether it's because of the student humour, the dozens of memorable lines about alcohol, or the way it all feels so *defiant*. But it's a delicious and much-commented on irony that one of the most towering of all screen drunks (Richard E. Grant) is teetotal in real life.

6. Ben Sanderson (Nicolas Cage) in *Leaving Las Vegas* (US 1995, dir. Mike Figgis, scr. Figgis, from a novel by John O'Brien)

I was in two minds about including *Leaving Las Vegas*, partly because it seems to me one of the weaker films in Figgis's otherwise extraordinary *oeuvre*; and also because it marks the point after which Nicolas Cage stopped being one of America's most interesting actors and became the country's least interesting action hero. But I include it here for several reasons: John O'Brien, who committed suicide two weeks into production, contributed source material in the form of a novel so strong it was inevitable a film would have some dramatic power; to me Elisabeth Shue is every bit as good as Cage is bad; and also because for all its flaws, it does say something important about how many struggling artists (Cage plays a screenwriter) give up the artistic struggle to seek oblivion through the bottle

5. Don Birnam (Ray Milland) in *The Lost Weekend* (US 1945, dir. Billy Wilder, scr. Wilder & Charles Brackett from a novel by Charles R. Jackson)

No list of cinema's greatest lushes would be complete without this man. One of the hardest-hitting films on this list, *The Lost Weekend* follows Milland's Birnam through a four-day bender. This is the one that most alcoholics think gets closest to the possible horrors of the drinking life, and it has a psychological realism absent from many films that tackle this difficult subject. This is about hidden bottles and broken promises, and although Wilder sweetens the pill by giving Ray a girlfriend in the shape of Jane Wyman (married to Ronald Reagan in real life at the time), this feels less like a cop-out than a deliberate attempt to reveal the charm of an alcoholic.

4. Nadia Gates (Kim Basinger) in *Blind Date* (US 1987, dir. Blake Edwards, scr. Dale Launer)

Like Daryl Hannah, Kim Basinger is one of those big, spacey blondes that Hollywood never knew quite how to handle, with directors tending to cast her as an alien or, in *Blind Date*, an out-of-control alcoholic. Bruce Willis plays Walter Davis, a typical 1980s workaholic yuppie, who is advised by the late Phil Hartman that if he gives Basinger's Nadia Gates alcohol, she will become wild and out of control. What starts off as a sexy version of *Gremlins* duly turns into every man's worst nightmare.

3. Ray (Ray Winstone) in *Nil by Mouth* (GB 1997, dir./scr. Gary Oldman)

This is the truly ugly side of alcoholism. To date, the only film that Oldman has directed (or indeed written), it drew on his working-class London childhood to present a hellish portrait of family life, Winstone playing a brutal husband-and-father (with whom he worryingly shares a first name). I don't know what Winstone did to Oldman or his contemporary Tim Roth (who cast him as a baby-rapist in *The War Zone*), but they gave him the two darkest roles of his career, which is saying something for the star of *Scum* (1979). Booze is so central in Ray's life (he's constantly sat looking sweaty in pubs and clubs) that he could never consider 'cutting back'. Oldman, who has suffered his own alcohol problems, always makes the pub scenes feel authentic. Those scenes where Winstone abuses wife Kathy Burke are only bearable if you imagine the jokes they would have made in breaks between filming.

2. Joe Clay (Jack Lemmon) in *Days of Wine and Roses* (US 1962, dir. Blake Edwards, scr. J.P. Miller)

This picture is about not knowing you're an alcoholic . . . until the party's over. Distinct from contemporary films such as *Leaving Las Vegas* this is not about alcoholism as heroic self-destruction ('I'm going to drink myself to death!') but about the role booze plays in certain professions, especially for those close to the entertainment industry. Jack Lemmon plays a PR guy who is always trying to make life exciting, and in doing so, gets his fragile wife (played by Lee Remick) addicted to alcohol. It may seem like favouritism to have two Blake Edwards films in this list, but more than any other director, from *The Party* onwards, he is without equal at staging scenes of manic socializing. Throughout his career he also took some deserved pot-shots at the entertainment industry, and this is the best example of same.

1. Elwood P. Dowd (James Stewart) in *Harvey* (US 1950, dir. Henry Koster, scr. Oscar Brodney)

Has there ever been a more charming alcoholic? Elwood P. Dowd is one of Stewart's stranger creations, a man convinced that he has a six-foot rabbit pal named Harvey. While everyone around him worries that his boozing has made him mad, he insists that he is merely misunderstood. The film is about tolerance, but not of the modern politically correct kind: it's about the importance of avoiding intervention in happy people's lives, even if they suffer from delusions or are self-destructive. Although it has a 'family film' premise, this is one of the most adult films ever made. Unless, of course, Harvey is real.

Thank You for Smoking
Ten Movies that Made Cigarettes Look Cool

RICHARD T. KELLY AND NEV PIERCE

A 2003 study by the *Lancet* medical journal warned that teenagers are significantly more likely to try their first cigarette as a result of exposure to cinema. Movies, after all, are very good at depicting nicotine-fiends as chic, tough, or rebellious – and conversely rather shy of conveying the stench of the ashtray, the yellowing of teeth and the cancerous blackening of lungs. But the appeal was not invented out of nothing. Something about smoking *is* cool, and it *is* sexy. You can't blame it on Big Tobacco, any more than you can convince teenagers they won't live for ever. For elders, there's an existential shade to smoking fags, what Richard Klein in his book *Cigarettes are Sublime* calls the 'painful pleasure that arises from some intimation of eternity'. Moreover: 'Smoking', observes Christopher Hitchens, 'is, in men, a tremendous enhancement of bearing and address and, in women, a consistent set-off to beauty'. Yes, that more or less summarizes The Case For. But these ten movies are objects given in evidence. (RTK)

10. Ed Crane (Billy Bob Thornton) in *The Man Who Wasn't There* (US 2001, dir. Joel Coen)

Thornton stopped smoking after shooting this movie. He'd spent twenty years suckling at the nicotine teat, but the chain-inhaling required to play taciturn barber Crane almost amounted to self-asphyxiation. He was admitted to hospital for nine days with bronchitis, and drop-kicked the butts on release. So – in case you didn't know – Smoking is a Bad Thing. But here it looks so glorious. As lensed by Roger Deakins, virtually every frame is fugged, Thornton's lip constantly dangling a filter-less Death Stick – a bygone age evoked, of Monty Clift and Bogie and believing cigarettes could be good for you. The Coens' mid-life crisis masterpiece looks beautiful, but the sweetest thing for film-makers criticized as relying on style is that substance abuse perfectly spotlights the theme: a man's quietly desperate search for meaning before being 'smoked' into the next life. 'Maybe there I can tell her . . . all those things they don't have words for here . . .' (NP)

9. Philip Marlowe (Humphrey Bogart) and Vivian Sternwood (Lauren Bacall) in *The Big Sleep* (US 1946, dir. Howard Hawks)

Everybody knew Chandler's novel was a tough, twisty story to get right on screen. Hawks shot his stab at it in 1945 but it sat on the shelf awhile in the post-Second World War backlog, during which 'Bogie and Bacall' became hot stuff in Hawks's *To Have and Have Not*, and then married. *Sleep* began to look a little tepid, twenty-year-old Betty Bacall having not quite clicked with her new hubby on this occasion. Hawks the master tinker-man knew he had to inject something. Presto, he and his writers came up with a glistening nightclub scene where the two leads sit and trade innuendoes about riding – horses, that is. 'I like to see them work out a little first,' Hawks has Bacall say. 'See if they're front-runners or come from behind . . . A lot depends on who's in the saddle.' And what provides the touch of atmospheric dressing for all this erotic lather? That's right, swathes and plumes of sweet cigarette smoke. (RTK)

8. Tyler Durden (Brad Pitt) in *Fight Club* (US 1999, dir. David Fincher)

How did Brad Pitt prepare to play the thrift-store chic guru-cum-Anti-Christ of the best movie of 1999? 'I upped my smoking to two packs a day.' Everyone took *Fight Club* way too seriously. 'It was more deeply rooted in Monty Python than it was in, you know, *Failsafe*,' says Fincher, who allowed Pitt to play with the absurdity of being the men-want-to-be-him, women-want-to-be-with-him alpha-male movie star. Strutting, cocky, sly – and, yes, smoking – he's so cool and seductive that *Fight Club* was accused of a fascistic extolling of Tyler's tear-it-down mentality. The cigarette is one of Tyler's essential props – harnessing generations of too-cool-for-school outsider iconography, while being essentially stupid and destructive; appropriate, as you come to realize (perhaps after more than one viewing) he's not the messiah, he's a very naughty boy. (NP)

7. Jake Gittes (Jack Nicholson) in *The Two Jakes* (US 1990, dir. Nicholson)

Nicholson's commitment to smoking is as deep on screen as it is in life, but it probably needed Nicholson the director to give the actor full licence to explore his *grand amour*. *The Two Jakes*, Robert Towne's sequel to *Chinatown* and Nicholson's third try at the helm, was ill-starred, Towne having bailed as director rather than try to get a performance out of Robert Evans as Jake number two. Rancour attended both men's departures, and the script Nicholson shot was lacking a final act, but then he was evidently less interested in plot than in period and mood, and a sort of towering wistfulness, sufficient to permit lines like 'You can't forget the past any more than you can change it.' Peggy Lee's rendition of 'Don't Smoke in Bed' sets the languorous tone from the credits. It's 1948, a brightening LA of prosperity and thickening midriffs. Gittes had a good war and now plays a lot of golf. But an old line of work – a divorce case – reopens old wounds. Jake becomes a gumshoe again. For this, he needs a lot of cigarettes, and by god he gets through them, manfully if regretfully. (RTK)

6. J.J. Hunsecker (Burt Lancaster) in *Sweet Smell of Success* (US 1957, dir. Alexander Mackendrick)

'Match me, Sidney.'
    It's the greatest line in screenwriting.
    'Match me, Sidney.'
    It points to character, theme and story.
    'Match me, Sidney.'

Tyrannical columnist Hunsecker tops a character assassination of obsequious PR Sidney Falco (Tony Curtis) by demanding a light. Falco declines to battle wits ('Not right now JJ'), but swallows all pride and sparks the cig. Yes, there's little cool about Hunsecker, just the cheap allure of power. He's a warped hack using his position to hurt and destroy. But Falco's every bit as amoral, and everything – cigarettes, sets, the brutish angles of Hunsecker's glasses – looks superb in the smoke-gauzed black and white of Sandy Mackendrick's portrait of huckstering media culture. Fifty years later it's still an accurate picture, only the power has shifted from journalist to publicist and now it's film PRs – many of whom don't care about movies any more than they do about, say, tractors – who can humiliate the opposition. 'You're dead, son. Get yourself buried.' (NP)

5. John and Miriam Blaylock (David Bowie and Catherine Deneuve) in The Hunger (US 1983, dir. Tony Scott)

If your pleasure and purpose in life is sucking the blood out of ripe youths, why would you waste a moment sucking on evil high-tar cigarettes? Well, probably for the same reason that you walk around a nightclub wearing vintage sunglasses – because it looks cool. Tony Scott's debut feature about vogueish Manhattan vampires showed off a wealth of stylistic tics and hip-abstract touches carried over from advertising, but time has not been kind to Scott's choice of motifs (doves and billowing curtains) or music (Bauhaus, Lakmé by Delibes). Even today, though, Bowie and Deneuve look fantastic, not least when they're flaring up their smokes with an old burnished Ronson petrol lighter. Deneuve set some kind of mid-career benchmark for her beauty here, though amazingly she was to carry on surpassing it. (RTK)

4. Sam Rothstein (Robert De Niro) in Casino (US 1995, dir. Martin Scorsese)

Robert De Niro always smokes as if his life depends on it. And there's no greater icon for dislocated young men than the guy behind Johnny Boy, Travis Bickle and Jimmy Conway. But while

Taxi Driver's gun-wielding 'You talking to me?' mirror scene may be the most memorable De Niro moment, it was seeing him chaining it amid the razzle-dazzle of Las Vegas as casino honcho Rothstein that reduced this eighteen-year-old student journalist to posing in front of the looking glass, mimicking that squinty cig-suck and satisfied smirk. At least a Camel is friendlier than a Magnum .44 . . . On the gaming floor Rothstein is a man in complete control, drawing on his tar-wand as if it's a power source; but smokers know there are tabs of pain, too – when it's merely a desperate crutch as things fall apart. Nicotine is key to the story in *Casino*: once Rothstein starts using a cigarette-holder, you know he's done for. (NP)

3. Dallas 'Dally' Wilson (Matt Dillon) in *The Outsiders* (US 1983, dir. Francis Ford Coppola)

Had your correspondent been born thirty years earlier, this entry would be about James Dean in *Rebel Without a Cause*, his pack of smokes every bit as vital to his get-up as the classic red windcheater and Levi's. But we're talking here about the early 1980s, when Matt Dillon was the cool ruler, and no-brainer casting as doomed bad boy Dally in Coppola's film of S.E. Hinton's school-age classic. The dumb and swaggering Dally is actually a hard kid to like, and yet uptown girl Cherry (Diane Lane) is seen to fall for him, just as Lane did for Dillon off-camera. And no youth ever looked better than Dillon when introduced to us leaning-to and lighting up a 'cancer-stick' outside a diner. 'What you wanna do?' asks Ponyboy (C.Thomas Howell). 'Nothing legal man, let's get out of here.' Stationed in Tulsa, Oklahoma, Coppola shot *The Outsiders* back-to-back with a second Hinton adaptation, the moodier *Rumblefish*, and in that one Dillon had to play second fiddle as the dim-bulb brother of Mickey Rourke, another top-drawer smoker. Dillon could at least console himself that he had the best cheekbones. He still does. (RTK)

2. James Bond (Sean Connery) in *Goldfinger* (GB 1964, dir. Guy Hamilton)

Obviously. (NP)

1. The Film Star (Peter Falk) in *Der Himmel über Berlin* / *Wings of Desire* (1987, dir. Wim Wenders)

Damiel (Bruno Ganz) is the angel who ghosts unseen around gravely black-and-white Berlin, observing human affairs sympathetically, but longing to take part, to assume the true privilege of feeling. Straying on to a film set around dawn he senses a certain sympathy in an American movie actor (Falk) loitering by the coffee stand. In fact, Falk knows Damiel is there, for he was quite possibly once an angel himself. 'I wish I could see your face, just look into your eyes and tell you how good it is to be here,' Falk grins. 'To smoke, have coffee. And if you do 'em together, it's *fantastic*.' A godly sentiment, and if you don't get it then you've been reading the wrong list. (RTK)

The Ultimate Performance

Ten Great Acting Turns by Rock Stars and Other Musicians

JASON WOOD

I've been fascinated by the intersection between music and movies for as long as I can remember. Perhaps the keenest object of my obsession has been the casting of figures from the music world in acting roles. A sometimes felicitous union between performers keen to prove that they are multi-talented, reach new audiences or just fan their egos, and film-makers keen to harness a little charisma and perhaps crowds, the origins of this cultural coalition stretch right back to Louis Jordan and Bessie Smith. Finding particular favour in the fifties and sixties with Elvis Presley and Cliff Richard, the practice has continued with mixed results to the present day. An Alan 'Fluff' Freemanesque countdown of what I consider to be ten very good character performances by a musical figure (hence none of the great band flicks such as Slade in *Flame*), this list is damned from the outset by what even I consider to be notable omissions. No Tina Turner in *Mad Max Beyond Thunderdome* and no David Essex in *That'll Be the Day*. There's also no Bob Dylan in

Pat Garrett and Billy the Kid but that's easy to explain. There are very few rules when it comes to movies and musicians, except the one that says that Dylan, like Prince, can't act.

10. P.J. Harvey as Magdalene in *The Book of Life* (US/France 1998, dir. Hal Hartley)

Jesus (Martin Donovan) shows up in New York on the last day of the century with his assistant, Magdalene (Harvey, in her sole acting venture). Sent by his father to perform the Last Judgement and initiate the end of the world, he is having second thoughts about destroying mankind. Commissioned as part of a series of films about millennial anxiety, *The Book of Life* allowed Hartley to fully embrace the aesthetics of digital film-making. Hartley had used one of the West Country singer's tracks on the soundtrack to *Amateur*; this film allowed for a closer collaboration, with the director receptive to the intense Catholic imagery in Harvey's songs of tortured love. Magdalene even mimes to one of Harvey's compositions in a record store.

9. Nick Cave as Maynard in *Ghosts . . . of the Civil Dead* (Australia 1988, dir. John Hillcoat)

They met when Hillcoat directed a number of Cave promos, but this brutal prison drama marked the Aussie duo's first collaboration for cinema. Co-written by Cave, this uncompromising work featured his first and best character performance as the psychopathic inmate Maynard. Unfolding in flashback to detail the events that necessitated a lockdown after the prisoners had rebelled against the institution's regimented sadism, the film makes few concessions to commercial considerations and refuses to establish a fully sympathetic character. The stark cinematography further enhances the nihilistic streak. Shorn of his trademark crow black mane, Cave effectively conveys the sense that Maynard is one of the last people on earth that you would want to be stuck in a cell with. Hillcoat and Cave have collaborated on subsequent occasions, most notably on the acclaimed outback western *The Proposition* (2005). Sadly, Cave remained off screen.

8. Frank Sinatra as Frankie Machine in *The Man with the Golden Arm* (US 1955, dir. Otto Preminger)

Based on the novel by Nelson Algren, this was the first major Hollywood film on heroin addiction, and aroused more controversy when Preminger announced that he was prepared to release the film without the sanction of a Hays Production Code seal. Old Blue Eyes excels as an illegal poker dealer and recovering heroin addict who yearns to become a jazz drummer. A searing drama which candidly portrays the harsh realities of addiction – Sinatra's cold turkey scene is especially memorable – the film's authenticity is underpinned by Sinatra's tender rapport with Kim Novak as his enigmatic mistress. An Academy Award winner two years earlier for *From Here to Eternity*, Sinatra lost out this time round to Ernest Borgnine in *Marty*.

7. Jimmy Cliff as Ivanhoe 'Ivan' Martin in *The Harder They Come* (Jamaica 1972, dir. Perry Henzell)

The first independent feature produced in Jamaica, *The Harder They Come* presents a hard-edged story of poverty, crime, and outlaw culture that plays like a West Indian corollary to the classic gangster films of the 1930s and 1940s whilst also looking forward to the black urban dramas of the early 1990s. Even though singing sensation Cliff had never acted before, he's thoroughly convincing as the tough-as-nails country boy who rises up the charts on the strength of his criminal record. Rough around the edges, Henzell's approach effectively captures the harsh reality of Kingston street life and is similarly spot on in its re-creation of the shady business dealings that characterized the Jamaican music industry; a scene in which Ivan is offered a mere 20 dollars by a record producer to cut his first single being allegedly based on Cliff's formative experiences. A performer of depth and vitality, Cliff is also the star of the film's superlative soundtrack, contributing, amongst others, the hymnal *Many Rivers to Cross*.

6. Tom Waits as Zack in *Down by Law* (US 1986, dir. Jim Jarmusch)

One of the few contemporary musicians to have sustained a genuine acting career (Kris Kristofferson and Cher – yep, Cher – being the others), Waits's origins as an actor began through his association with Coppola. In his first starring role, *Down by Law* casts him as Zack, a New Orleans DJ framed by the local police. Zack finds himself sharing a cell with a motor-mouth Italian (Roberto Benigni) and a pouting pimp (Lounge Lizard John Lurie, making this a two-for-one entry) before the unlikely trio put aside their simmering antagonism to escape across a Southern bayou. A characteristically esoteric combination of comedy, buddy movie and offbeat prison drama, *Down by Law* is driven by the director's interest in American culture colliding with a foreign element. That the theme is particularly realized here is largely down to the chemistry between the leading players. Waits would offer a reprisal of his role – albeit on air only – in *Night on Earth* (1991).

5. Tupac Shakur as Bishop in *Juice* (US 1992, dir. Ernest R. Dickerson)

Shakur's scintillating acting debut, *Juice* offers a convincing and despairingly authentic depiction of inner city life as commonly experienced by young black Americans. The tale of four friends bonded by a love of music and a desire to escape the endless cycle of poverty and violence, it showcases an outstanding quartet of relatively unknown actors. Shakur just about shades the honours, capturing the escalating psychosis that results from his character's destructive and increasingly insatiable thirst for money and power. One of numerous movies dealing with the consequences of black-on-black violence in the early nineties, the film proved Shakur's stepping stone to international stardom – he remains one of the biggest recording artists of his generation – and further critical acclaim for performances in *Poetic Justice* (1993, dir. John Singleton) and *Gridlock'd* (1997, dir. Vondie Curtis-Hall). Murdered in a gang-related shooting outside a Las Vegas motel, Shakur didn't live to see the latter film's release.

4. Deborah Harry as Nikki Brand in *Videodrome* (Canada 1983, dir. David Cronenberg)

After a cameo in Amos Poe's *The Foreigner* (1978) and a more substantial role in Marcus Reichert's *Union City* (1980), Blondie's Debbie Harry, pin-up-girl of the New York New Wave scene, found her metier in Cronenberg's mind-and-flesh-altering *Videodrome*. James Woods stars as Max Renn, a sleazy cable-channel boss whose search for an intense new show leads him to an underground broadcast that seems to present real-life sexualized torture, even murder. When Renn sets out to track down the source of this delightful entertainment, his thrill-seeking girlfriend Nikki (Harry) volunteers herself as bait. In taking on the role of a dead-eyed attention-seeker with a mile-wide masochistic streak (stubbing out cigarettes on her breasts a particular speciality) Harry made flesh a million unspoken male fantasies, even going a little further out there than most would have thought necessary. Though she never topped her work here, she nevertheless became a reliable character actor, contributing to *Hairspray* (dir. John Waters, 1988) and *Heavy* (dir. James Mangold, 1995).

3. Mick Jagger as Turner in *Performance* (GB 1970, dir. Donald Cammell & Nicolas Roeg)

Few directors have a better track record at working with musicians than Roeg. He even got a superb performance out of Art Garfunkel in *Bad Timing* (1980). For *Performance* he and Cammell deliberately drew on Jagger's pop persona, coaxing something rather complex out of 'Old Rubber Lips': a fascinating and contradictory blend of arrogance, androgyny and washed-up artistry. 'You'll look funny when you're fifty' sneers Chas prophetically. This kaleidoscopic masterpiece left Warner Bros so unimpressed by its immersion in the counter-culture that they shelved it for two years. Jagger would never look so comfortable on screen again (Tony Richardson's *Ned Kelly*, 1970 being a particularly awkward watch) – so establishing, alongside the efforts of Bowie, the popular perception that musicians couldn't act . . .

Capital Offences: Ten Places You Wouldn't Expect to Find a Severed Head, p 203

2. David Bowie as Thomas Jerome Newton in *The Man Who Fell to Earth* (US 1976, Nicolas Roeg)

A daring exploration of science fiction as art form, a formally bold study of alienation, and a caustic critique of capitalist society. And yet debutant actor Bowie, arriving on location in New Mexico with a shock of orange hair, saw it as a straightforward love story; he also claims never to have read the script. He plays an alien tasked to save his dying planet from drought, who crash-lands on Earth and uses his superior intelligence to build a vast business empire. Harnessing Bowie's otherworldliness and androgynous, futuristic pop persona, Roeg was vindicated in his instinct that the star, then at the height of his creative powers, would be perfect as the fallen angel figure – references to Icarus abound – ultimately undone by earthly temptations. Repeatedly asked if it was wise to cast someone who had never acted, Roeg responded by asking if it wasn't a form of acting when Bowie played live to vast audiences night after night? Bowie's subsequent acting career has been much derided, with the singer himself describing *Just a Gigolo* (dir. David Hemmings, 1979) as 'all my Elvis Presley movies rolled into one'. But there have been bright spots: Scorsese's *The Last Temptation of Christ* (1988, a last-minute replacement for Sting pop pickers) and Nikola Tesla in *The Prestige* (dir. Christopher Nolan, 2006). See also page 109.

1. Dexter Gordon as Dale Turner in *'Round Midnight* (US/France 1986, dir. Bertrand Tavernier)

A Parisian bebop aficionado (François Cluzet, playing a character based on real-life enthusiast Francis Paudras) befriends an ex-pat American jazz musician (saxophonist Dexter Gordon) and attempts to save him from self-destruction in Bertrand Tavernier's beautiful jazz homage. A fictional figure inspired by the lives of Bud Powell and Lester Young, with his struggles with alcoholism and depression Gordon's Dale Turner sails close to his own life experiences. Gordon's fascinating history and magnetic screen presence lends the film a sobering authenticity (other jazz musicians such as Herbie Hancock and Bobby Hutcherson also feature in the cast), combining with Tavernier's obvious attentiveness to the visual – the blue palette evokes countless Blue Note sleeves – and aural textures of the milieu to present perhaps the finest evocation of jazz on screen. Widely seen as an epitaph to a musical form that was considered on the brink of extinction, the film's understated melancholy is further teased out by an exemplary soundtrack supervised by Hancock. Gordon's compelling performance came just four years before his death and garnered an Academy Award nomination.

13

The Grown-Up Arts

Older Forms and Their Impact on Film

GEOFF ANDREW: The Painter's Painter as Director – Ten Films Somehow Related to the Paintings of Diego Rodríguez de Silva y Velázquez (1599–1660)

PAUL FARLEY: 'My Man John Keats Said That!' Ten Great Uses of Poetry at the Movies

IAN CHRISTIE: Based on the Movie – The Ten Best Stories or Novels about Cinema

MATT THORNE: Never Trust a Screenwriter – Ten Loose Adaptations

The Painter's Painter as Director

Ten Films Somehow Related to the Paintings of Diego
Rodríguez de Silva y Velázquez (1599–1660)

GEOFF ANDREW

When inviting me to contribute to this book, Richard T. Kelly said
he was hoping for some 'offbeat' lists. I was reminded of an earlier
invitation, odd enough in itself. In 2006 I received an email from
London's National Gallery, proposing I deliver a lecture on
'Velázquez and the Cinema' to coincide with an exhibition devoted to the Spanish artist. A joke, surely? I love Velázquez's work but
am no expert on him, or on any other painter. But the proposal
was serious – and intriguing. Velázquez died more than two centuries before cinema came into being, so what relationship could
there possibly be between his work and the movies?

Any decent director pays great attention to composition,
colour, lighting, camera movement; images tell stories, create
moods, express emotions and ideas. That's what Velázquez was
doing, too. So in the end my lecture was not about individual
shots that reminded me of particular paintings, but about the relationship between image and narrative: how that relationship
functions in Velázquez's paintings, and how it functions in the
cinema of certain auteurs. I included clips from a dozen or so
movies in the lecture. Here are ten.

10. *Pierrot le Fou* (France/Italy 1965, dir. Jean-Luc Godard)

Godard's movie kicks off with a quotation from a book about
Velázquez being read out loud to a small girl by Jean-Paul
Belmondo while he's in the bath. But I must confess I'm unable to
see the relevance of this allusion to the rest of the movie.

9. *Viridiana* (Spain/Mexico 1961, dir. Luis Buñuel)

Velázquez's use of ordinary folk in paintings such as *The Forge of
Vulcan* or *Joseph's Coat Brought to Jacob* always reminded me of
Italian realist film-making, especially late Pasolini – those youth-

ful torsos! But it was his conjoining of a well-oiled peasantry and a mythic subject normally associated with high culture in *The Feast of Bacchus* (*The Drunks*) that made me think of the beggars' orgy in Buñuel's film, performed mostly by real down-and-outs to the strains of the 'Hallelujah Chorus', with one shot that is a bawdy, blasphemous parody of *The Last Supper*.

8. *Conte d'hiver* / *A Winter's Tale* (France 1992, dir. Eric Rohmer)

In paintings such as *Kitchen Scene with Christ in the House of Martha and Mary* and *The Fable of Arachne* (*The Spinners*), Velázquez used images-within-the-image to allude to existing traditions of storytelling and painting. Rohmer frequently references the arts and philosophy in his films; *Pauline at the Beach*, for example, has its young heroine sleep beneath a painting by Matisse, whose sunny Mediterranean palette influenced Rohmer's choice of costumes and props for the film. Perhaps the most affecting example is the scene when the heroine of *A Winter's Tale* – believing against the odds that her long-lost dream-lover will some day reappear – starts sobbing at a performance of Shakespeare's play of the same name, when a seemingly dead queen is miraculously revived by sheer force of love and faith.

7. *Citizen Kane* (US 1941, dir. Orson Welles)

Look closely at the paintwork for the costumes in royal portraits such as *Philip IV of Spain in Brown and Silver* or *Infanta Margarita in a Blue Dress*, and you'll find squiggles, dots and dashes, rather than properly detailed renditions of embroidered patterns. This is a technique of suggestion; long before the Impressionists, Velázquez knew the spectator's imagination would do some of his work for him in terms of completing the image. Now look at Welles's masterpiece – the scene, for example, where Kane talks to Susan Alexander as she's poring over her jigsaws in Xanadu's cavernous great hall. See how little of the room is really there; Welles used black velvet drapes, low lighting, a few carefully placed props and echoing voices on the soundtrack to suggest size and opulence. We fill in the gaps.

6. *The Long Goodbye* (US 1973 dir. Robert Altman)

A memorable scene in Altman's Chandler adaptation has Roger Wade ask Marlowe to leave him alone with his wife Eileen; clearly anxious about what her volatile husband will do, Eileen suggests the private dick stick around, so he goes off to smoke a cigarette on the beach. We then see and hear the couple arguing indoors, behind the window of their Malibu home; at the same time we see Marlowe evading the waves on the shore, reflected in that same window. Altman disorients us with the superimposed images, using the confusing profusion of perspectives to make us think more deeply about what we're actually seeing; he's also drawing attention to the artifice of film-making itself. Wasn't Velázquez doing much the same thing in *Kitchen Scene with Christ in the House of Martha and Mary*, *The Fable of Arachne*, or *Las Meninas*?

5. *El Sol del membrillo* / *The Quince Tree Sun* (Spain 1991, dir. Victor Erice)

Las Meninas – that endlessly fascinating, puzzling portrait of the Infanta, her courtiers, and Velázquez himself, all looking at . . . what? Who? – brings us to the heart of the matter. As a student in Madrid, Erice went regularly to look at Velázquez's most intriguing masterpiece in the Prado, and later planned to make a film inspired by the painting, its creation and its relevance to the modern world. Sadly, for reasons too complex to go into here, the film was never made, but many of its themes found their way into this, his superb semi-documentary study of the painter Antonio López at work in his garden. In *An Old Woman Cooking Eggs* and *The Fable of Arachne* Velázquez attempts to depict the passing of time; but as López discovers in his efforts to achieve an accurate portrait of his ever-maturing quince tree, painting can do no more than *suggest* time's passing. We needed cinema, with its illusion of movement created by the succession of 24 frames per second, for duration to be properly conveyed by an art form. Erice explores this discrepancy between Lopez's medium and his own, while including compositions and changes in perspective indicative of his profound knowledge of *Las Meninas*.

4. *Sommaren med Monika* / *Summer with Monika* (Sweden 1953, dir. Ingmar Bergman)

It was actually Erice who suggested I look at a scene towards the end of Bergman's film, where Monika, sitting smoking in a bar, suddenly turns her gaze directly to the camera and stares defiantly, as if challenging us to judge her for her treatment of her lover and child. Leaving aside the ancient tradition whereby comedians address or look to the audience to enlist our sympathy, this is probably the first instance in a film of the invisible relationship between the spectator and a screen character being openly acknowledged; it disrupts the illusion of reality, reminding us of our own creative role in the process whereby a film's meaning is constructed and understood. In Velázquez's *Las Meniñas*, *The Surrender of Breda* or *La Tela Real*, people also look at us rather than at the 'action' depicted in the paintings; in *Infante Baltasar Carlos in the Riding School*, a dwarf not only looks at us but points at Baltasar as if reminding us we should concentrate on the prince, not his courtiers.

3. *Caché* / *Hidden* (France/Austria 2005, dir. Michael Haneke)

Bergman acknowledged the relationship between spectator and subject – but what of the creator? Velázquez inserted himself into *Las Meniñas*; he's taking a pause from painting to look at us – or at the King and Queen of Spain, whom we see reflected in a mirror at the back of the room on view, and whose point of view (outside of the painting) we are sharing. Dizzying self-referential stuff; perhaps the closest filmic equivalent is the start of *Hidden* – where we first think we're watching a house, and then are made aware by off-screen voices and a rewind effect that we're watching a *videotape* of that house, recorded in the past but now being watched by the very people we've just seen leaving the house. Those people then ask each other who could have filmed the house and where the camera was positioned. Questions the film never answers. But of course someone *did* film the house: it was Haneke, creator of *Hidden* and its characters, and of the film within that film. He may not be visible, but he's very much present.

2. *Bad ma ra khahad bord / The Wind Will Carry Us* (France/Iran 1999, dir. Abbas Kiarostami)

In the films of Kiarostami one often finds a surrogate for the director; this film, about a documentarist travelling from the city to a remote village in the hope of filming an arcane funeral ritual, is merely the most obvious example. But it is also a film in which many of the characters are unseen – most notably the old woman whose death the documentarist awaits, and a gravedigger who almost dies when the hole in which he's working caves in. *Las Meninas*, as we've noted, also has its unseen characters – the King and Queen. Both Kiarostami and Velázquez are creating 'meaning' partly through the interplay between what is visible and what is kept hidden.

1. *Sang sattawat / Syndromes and a Century* (Thailand 2006, dir. Apichatpong Weerasethakul)

I saw this film shortly before giving my lecture, and was struck by a scene in which doctors discuss the illness of a young patient. Suddenly, without provocation, one turns away from her colleagues to look directly towards the camera, and stares at us while the others continue talking. That even an experimental Thai film might echo Velázquez's work was not my only interesting discovery; I also realized that most of the clips I'd already chosen were linked in that they dealt one way or another with death: that unavoidable fact of life that people often prefer to forget about.

Film records time's passing: death's unstoppable approach. The quotation in *Pierrot le Fou* cites the morbid atmosphere of the Spanish court in which Velázquez worked; I was reminded of Erice's words about a certain tradition in Spanish painting, with its 'idea of the light that is extinguished, of death'. Velázquez's extraordinary final painting of Philip IV of Spain shows a fifty-year-old, with heavy, sagging flesh and tired eyes, saddened by numerous deaths in his family. The 'painter's painter', like our best film-makers, knew that the greatest of all life's mysteries cannot simply be ignored; even if it isn't always visible, it's always there, with and in us all.

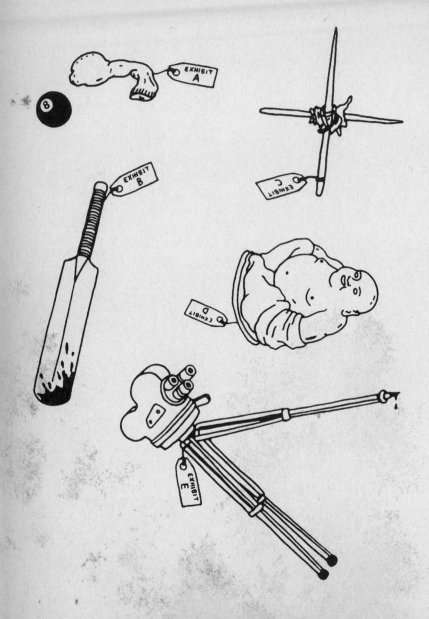

Rope, Dagger, Revolver? Too Easy: Ten Improvised/Unlikely Weapons, p 227

'My Man John Keats Said That!'

Ten Great Uses of Poetry at the Movies

PAUL FARLEY

In Martin Amis's short story 'Career Move', poets are flown across the pond first class to LAX by producers keen to develop their latest treatment for 'the sonnet', while the poor novelists make do with living in ashtrays and sending their work off to the 'little magazines'. The inversion is hilarious, and sad. But cinema hasn't excluded the poem. The upstart medium takes it wherever it can find it, and screenwriters and directors have managed to incorporate verse in many different dimensions. Poetry can be found right at the iconic heart of cinema, from Coleridge at the gates of Kane's Xanadu to 'The Hollow Men' in Colonel Kurtz's subfusc jungle outpost. It can linger, diffused and hanging in the air 'like sea mist or incense', as David Thomson said of Welles's *Othello*; or it can come through in strange, unexpected bursts like the car radio of Cocteau's *Orphée*. This is a relationship at least as old as the talkies: let me count the ways . . .

10. Alexander Pope in *Eternal Sunshine of the Spotless Mind* (US 2004, dir. Michel Gondry)

Cinema, like the novel before it, has often drawn on the vast archive of poetry to come up with an arresting title for a movie. *Paths of Glory* (1957, Stanley Kubrick) is all the more resonant once we know they 'lead but to the grave' in Thomas Gray's *Elegy*; *Splendor in the Grass* (1961, Elia Kazan) relies on a central, vital airing of William Wordsworth's *Ode: Intimations of Immortality*; Powell and Pressburger's romance *I Know Where I'm Going* (1945) uses the first line of a popular Scottish ballad; even *Gone With the Wind* (Victor Fleming, 1939) comes to us from a poem by Ernest Dowson (*Non sum qualis eram bonae sub regno Cynarae*), via Margaret Mitchell's novel. In the end, though, I went for Gondry's film on memory. Scriptwriter Charlie Kaufman happily came upon the title late in the day, using *Bartlett's Quotations* just as the character of Mary (Kate Winslett) happens upon Alexander Pope's *Eloise to Abelard* on screen, and the resonance with a character who has visited Lacuna Inc to have her memories removed is affecting: 'How happy is the blameless vestal's lot! / The world forgetting, by the world forgot. / Eternal sunshine of the spotless mind! / Each prayer accepted, and each wish resigned.'

9. Emily Dickinson in *Seabiscuit* (US 2003, dir. Gary Ross)

The poem used ceremoniously in a film connects our flickering world to a much older one. There's something intimate, and almost primal, about the lone lyric voice being raised above the gathered silence. Film-makers have sometimes framed the spoken poem beautifully: the most noticeable piece of invention in John Huston's otherwise faithful version of Joyce's *The Dead* (1987) is the addition of a character, Mr Grace, who reads Lady Gregory's version of 'Donal Og', an eighth-century Irish poem – 'the snipe was speaking of you in her deep marsh' – unforgettably; *Four Weddings and a Funeral* (Mike Newell, 1994) did wonders for sales of W.H. Auden after John Hannah's recitation of 'Funeral Blues' (though poets might think it bad form to 'crack' the way Hannah, understandably, does on 'I thought that love would last for ever: I was wrong': you don't get high on your own supply). Having first considered trying a verse of his own, writer Richard Curtis must be glad he went with Wystan. But *Seabiscuit* wins it by a nose. Toby Maguire's recitation at the dinner table of Emily Dickinson's 'We never know how high we are . . .' casts a long shadow through the film, acquiring weight and gradually defining the character he plays, jockey Red Pollard.

8. The absence of Plath in *Sylvia* (GB/US 2003, dir. Christine Jeffs)

There have been plenty of poetry biopics, but here's one that relies mostly on a resonance in this compiler's imagination, outside of any critical estimation. *Sylvia* is notable for its absence of poetry. Gwyneth Paltrow plays the ill-fated Sylvia Plath, and a pre-Bond Daniel Craig is Ted Hughes, but none of Plath's poetry features in the movie because permission was never granted to use it. I always conflate this blank space with a story told by the poet Hugo Williams, who, returning home one evening, found his street in North London was being used as the location shoot for *Sylvia*, and that the terrible winter of 1962/63 was being re-created using a shredded white paper snowstorm. This is a kind of poetry.

7. e.e. cummings in *Hannah and Her Sisters* (US 1986, dir. Woody Allen)

When words fail us, poems can articulate desire. In the movies, it's no different. Michael Caine's wooing of Barbara Hershey – his sister-in-law – in Allen's film is thoroughly bookish, conducted through the medium of a collection by cummings. In a New York bookstore he implores and insists she accept the volume, and directs her to a single page number, and the poem 'somewhere I have never traveled, gladly beyond . . .' The verse is introduced like a catalyst, setting off the slow burn of a reaction and understanding as the two are drawn towards one another, working in voice-over and as text in a title panel: 'nobody, not even the rain, has such small hands'.

6. W.B. Yeats in *84 Charing Cross Road* (GB/US 1987, dir. David Hugh Jones)

I chose this because of the way another bookish affair – this time conducted by transatlantic letters between Anthony Hopkins (in London) and Anne Bancroft (in New York) – uses a poem to postulate something more complicated than desire: a deep-seated longing, tenderness and regret. Hopkins and Bancroft are due to meet in the flesh after their long exchanges, but her cancellation leads to a let-down, and his suddenly moving reading of Yeats's 'He Wishes for the Cloths of Heaven': 'Tread softly because you tread on my dreams' is just so quietly devastating here.

5. John Keats in *White Men Can't Jump* (US 1992, dir. Ron Shelton)

'*A thing of beauty is a joy forever*. My man John Keats said that.' So a fan applauds the game of basketball in a Los Angeles park by quoting from *Endymion*. The riposte, 'Shut your anorexic tapeworm-having overdosed Dick Gregory Bahamian-diet-drinking ass up!' is a kind of poetry, too. The way shooting hoops becomes a context in which the demotic can accommodate such shifts in register is funny and arresting, and the speed of the court banter proves – to paraphrase Frost, speaking of another court game – how it's so much less fun with the net down.

4. Robert Frost in *Telefon* (US 1977, dir. Don Siegel)

Robert Frost is so present in the American imagination that Anthony Jr. in *The Sopranos* can struggle over 'Stopping by Woods on a Snowy Evening' for his homework. I can think of at least three instances of Frost on film. Is that 'Nothing Gold Can Stay' we hear in *The Outsiders* (Francis Ford Coppola, 1983)? I think it is. In *Down by Law* (Jim Jarmusch, 1986), Roberto Benigni asks his fellow jailbirds 'Do you like Bob Frost?' and the film takes 'The Road Less Traveled' to its visual heart. But Siegel's *Telefon* uses Frost chillingly: 'Stopping by Woods on a Snowy Evening' is the trigger that will thaw deep-cover Soviet agents from their 'sleep' in the US: a KGB agent (Donald Pleasence) only has to pick up the phone and whisper the final stanza: 'The woods are lovely, dark, and deep, / But I have promises to keep, / And miles to go before I sleep, / And miles to go before I sleep.'

3. 'John Lillison' in *The Man with Two Brains* (US 1983, dir. Carl Reiner)

What about bad poetry in the movies? In Alan Rudolph's *Choose Me* (1984), Keith Carradine plays a man who never tells lies, but asks us to believe he has photographed covers for *Life* magazine, flown jets and spied in Soviet Russia. At a bar, a female customer reads him some of her doggerel, and asks him what he thinks: 'It's great.' She then – fatally! – asks him what he *really* thinks: 'Okay, it sucks. I think you stole it.' His criticism is all the more devastating when he discloses that he once taught poetry at Yale. But Steve Martin's Dr Michael Hfuhruhurr takes the honours, quoting from the work of one John Lillison ('England's greatest one-armed poet'): 'O pointy birds, o pointy pointy / Anoint my head, anointy-nointy' (which Martin quoted again in *LA Story*). Martin's curse on faithless wife Kathleen Turner – 'Into the mud, Scum Queen!' – is also a kind of poetry.

2. Robert Browning in *The Sweet Hereafter* (Canada 1997, dir. Atom Agoyan)

Sometimes, a poem or poet is so unexpectedly crucial and central to a film's very being – Jim Jarmusch's *Dead Man* (1995) sets one 'William Blake' down in the American West; *Kiss Me Deadly* (Robert Aldrich, 1955) holds Christina Rossetti's sonnet 'Remember' up to the light as a clue; in *Wit* (Mike Nichols, 2001) John Donne works like a kind of metaphysical counterpoint to the very physical travails of Emma Thompson. I chose Atom Agoyan's film in the end, though. Fourteen children die when a bus crashes into a frozen lake, and Sarah Polley's long voice-overs from Robert Browning's 'The Pied Piper of Hamelin' have us wondering where we, and the characters, are being led. One of those instances where film casts a rich new light on a poem, while a poem modulates and adds new dimensions to what we're seeing on screen: a powerful synthesis.

1. Andrew Marvell in *A Matter of Life and Death* (GB 1946, dir./prod. Michael Powell/Emeric Pressburger)

'But at my back I always hear / Time's wingèd chariot hurrying near . . .' And sniggers. I remember watching this at the ICA in London a few years ago and blushing in the dark – which seemed suddenly full of stifled laughter – as David Niven's stricken air-man (who is also a published poet) plummets earthward in his burning Lancaster, reciting Raleigh – 'I'd rather have written that than have flown through Hitler's legs' – and Marvell ('Andy Marvell, what a marvel!') But I love it: what an opening! Niven's radio soliloquy – though we soon realize Kim Hunter is listening too, back on *terra firma* – needs this urgent concision: why not reach for a poem when you're falling from the skies? It stands as a metaphor for poetry in film: such an economy of means can be crucial, and useful, and doesn't burn as many precious seconds of screen time. Marvell's 'To His Coy Mistress' also foreshadows what's to come, unspooling brilliantly through later scenes: Niven will find himself trapped inside frozen moments – 'deserts of vast eternity' – unable to connect with Hunter, joined only by a heavenly emissary 'starved of Technicolor'. But he ultimately, and movingly, wins back 'world enough and time' in which to consummate the affair and live his life.

Based on the Movie

The Ten Best Stories or Novels about Cinema

IAN CHRISTIE

Considering how many writers have lived off or close to film-making, the quantity of high-quality fictional writing about the film industry doesn't seem overwhelming. The most obvious reason may be that many of the aforesaid writers had bad experiences, ranging from failing to earn what they hoped, to seeing their efforts discarded or mangled. So the embittered or phlegmatic scriptwriter is a stock figure of twentieth-century literary biography, from Faulkner and Fitzgerald to Elmore Leonard. Most of the fiction on this list turns out to be by writers who already had first-hand experience, or would later be drawn into the cinema. In general I've tried to keep Europeans in the picture in a genre often seemingly dominated by American writers, also to avoid mere cynicism (as in Budd Schulberg's *What Makes Sammy Run?* and Evelyn Waugh's *Vile Bodies*), preferring instead stories that try to reach into the mystery of why movies are so compelling, considering how unrewarding and tedious their making can be.

10. Peter Handke, *Short Letter, Long Farewell* (1972)

Cheating a bit, perhaps, but this terse, haunting novel by the writer of two of Wim Wenders's best films, *The Goalkeeper's Fear of the*

Penalty and *Wings of Desire*, imagines a journey across America by a European whose bearings are all derived from movies – at one point he compares seeing the 'real' Lauren Bacall on stage in New York with the memory of her in *To Have and Have Not*. Then in the final pages, he is reunited with the wife who left the original 'short letter', they arrive in Los Angeles and – astonishingly – meet John Ford, spending an idyllic day with the great man. Magic.

9. Nathaniel West, *Day of the Locust* (1939)

The original disenchanted scoop on Tinseltown. West portrayed Hollywood in the 1930s through the eyes of a young scenery painter, hired fresh from Yale and dropped into the small town that Hollywood then was. The world he discovers is anything but glamorous, full of disappointment and discontent, which finally erupts into a riot that mirrors the apocalyptic painting he has been working on. In a final real-life twist, West was killed in a motor accident the day after Fitzgerald died.

8. F. Scott Fitzgerald, *The Last Tycoon* (1941) and the Pat Hobby Stories (1939–40)

It may be cheating to include both Fitzgerald's last, unfinished novel and the brief magazine stories he wrote to stay alive while working on the novel, but taken together they surely provide the best evocation of the rackety world of Hollywood's golden age. His tycoon was based on Irving Thalberg, MGM's boy-wonder head of production, who Fitzgerald memorably described as the only man to understand 'the whole equation' of Hollywood – a phrase since borrowed by David Thomson. But alongside the pathos of the novel, the 'Pat Hobby' stories about a broken-down script hack have a cheeky un-self-pitying quality that captures the raffish side of studio life.

7. Luigi Pirandello, *Shoot!* (1915)

The view from the cameraman, and a devastating glimpse into the melodramatic world of the diva on and off screen in early Italian cinema. Even before his breakthrough with *Six Characters in Search of an Author*, Pirandello was preoccupied with reality not being what it seems, or at least how it's usually shown. In this first great novel about the cinema, he's fascinated by the relationship between what's recorded and what's really happening, as observed by the impassive Serafino Gubbio who just keeps turning the handle. (Newly available in a version by the great Proust translator C. K. Moncrieff.)

6. William Boyd, *The New Confessions* (1987)

An extraordinary feat of synthesis and sheer chutzpah. Boyd weaves together parts of the biographies of a dozen or more film-makers to create a fictitious career that stretches across most of the century of cinema, ranging from filming on the Western Front to the same 1920s Berlin film-world cinema that fascinated Isherwood and Roszak, then on to London and eventually Hollywood, before the McCarthy Blacklist intervenes, and sends his hero into exile in Europe. 'John James Todd' becomes cinema's and the century's Everyman – so much that today you could almost expect to find him on the Internet Movie Database.

5. Alberto Moravia, *A Ghost at Noon / Il Disprezzo* (1954)

The ultimate writer's complaint about movie-making, although with redeeming irony. Moravia's novel is set in the Roman film world of ancient-world muscle man epics, and has certainly suffered from being eclipsed by Godard's masterly, yet irreverent, film adaptation, *Contempt* (1963). This is doubly ironic, since it's the story of a writer who believes his wife despises him because he has prostituted himself to film-making. But even if Godard added new layers to the original, Moravia's novel remains the source of an intriguing psychological study of the mixed motives involved in selling one's soul to the movies.

4. Vladimir Nabokov, *Laughter in the Dark* (1932–8)

Forget Tony Richardson's updated Swinging London film of Nabokov's great novel about illusion and self-deception, originally set in the 1920s Berlin that Nabokov knew as an exile from Russia. When an art connoisseur falls for an usherette, they spend a lot of time slumming in Berlin cinemas, while the connoisseur pursues his idea of turning great paintings into animated films. One of the few novels that revels in the illicit pleasure of sneaking off to the cinema, while also celebrating the elusive dreams that cinema can offer to philistines and aesthetes alike.

3. Christopher Isherwood, *Prater Violet* (1945)

Young Christopher has been hired to work on the script of an operetta film set in Old Vienna, being made in London by a Great European Director (based on Berthold Viertal), while Austria is falling under the Nazi shadow. From the high farce of Imperial Bulldog Pictures mismanaging their production to a grim reflection on the tragic mismatch between art and life, this is surely the ultimate novel about movie-making. It's also the source of some immortal quotes: 'You have never been inside a film studio . . .? It is unspeakable.' Director to writer: 'We are like two married men who meet in a whorehouse.' And: 'All politicians are amateurs. It's as if we'd handed over the studio to the publicity department.'

2. Rudyard Kipling, 'Mrs Bathurst' (1904)

One of the very first stories to deal with the fascination of watching films and one of the weirdest, written by Kipling after he'd seen the impact of films on sailors and troops going to South Africa during the Anglo-Boer War. In the story, some old hands recall how an early 'actuality' film showing an everyday scene at Paddington Station became an obsession for a ship's stoker, who insists he knows a woman in the crowd, and she's searching for *him* . . .

1. Theodore Roszak, *Flicker* (1991)

Roszak's admittedly bizarre novel about the search for a legendary and apparently demonic director from the German Expressionist cinema of the 1920s is something of a cult, and perhaps great literature. Yet somehow it seems to penetrate close to the heart of the weirdness of taking movies more seriously than life – and in doing so lines up disconcertingly with the new Gothic fiction of the Templars, Cathars, Grail etc. But it's also cinema-literate in a way few novels are, with a central character who's a critic and rep cinema programmer, apparently based on the early Berkeley career of Pauline Kael, and it conveys a vivid, almost palpable, sense of how compulsive and dangerous cinema can be that remains unique.

Never Trust a Screenwriter

Ten Loose Adaptations

MATT THORNE

If I was in charge of the film industry I would ban any screenwriter adapting a novel from making any changes to the plot. In fact, my ideal film adaptation of a cherished novel would just be an actor reading from the text: an audio-book, with an accompanying visual image. So much nonsense is spoken about how important it is to 'throw out the book' when you're making a film, when in fact some of the best adaptations are the most faithful. But here is a list of loose adaptations that work: examples of screenwriters taking their source material and doing something different with it. In every case, the film might not be the same as the book, but it is at least of equal merit.

10. *Nothing but Trouble* (US 1991, dir./scr. Dan Aykroyd)

A rare example of film sampling, this: not so much a loose adaptation as an (unacknowledged) riffing and variation on the 1954 Gene Kelly classic *Brigadoon* – except that Dan Aykroyd (who wrote, directed and stars in the film as a pair of giant babies and a centuries-old judge) has chosen to combine family comedy with a strange parody of *The Texas Chainsaw Massacre*. Aykroyd acknowledges the inspiration of rap in the film by casting all the members of 1980s outfit Digital Underground (including the late Tupac Shakur, in his first onscreen appearance) alongside the gruesome trio of John Candy, Demi Moore and Chevy Chase.

9. *Howard the Duck* (1986, dir. Willard Huyck, scr. Willard Huyck & Gloria Katz, based on the comic books by Steve Gerber)

As with the other most famous flop films (*Heaven's Gate, Ishtar*) of the era, *Howard the Duck* has aged well. But I include it here as an example of how protective the comics community can be when a much-loved title makes it to the big screen. Legendary comics writer Alan Moore has been so disappointed by the adaptations of his work (including *From Hell, Constantine, The League of Extraordinary Gentlemen* and *V For Vendetta*) that he no longer accepts money from Hollywood, giving it all to the artists instead. *Howard the Duck* has very little connection to its source material, but for non-comic fans it offers an amusing parody of 1980s family films, along with the pleasure of watching the sometimes sanctimonious Tim Robbins being really silly.

8. *Der Amerikanische Freund / The American Friend* (Germany 1977, dir. Wim Wenders, scr. Wim Wenders from the novel *Ripley's Game* by Patricia Highsmith)

Highsmith wasn't the first author to be upset by the choice of actor to play a treasured protagonist (Ian Fleming, remember, didn't have any time for Sean Connery). But she may have had the biggest cause for complaint: could anyone other than Wim Wenders have cast Dennis Hopper as Tom Ripley? Credit to the enigma of Highsmith's creation: it's hard to imagine any other character who could be portrayed on screen by actors as diverse as Hopper, Matt Damon, John Malkovich, Alain Delon and Barry Pepper. Yet Wenders's film is the best Highsmith adaptation, and his best film, a hypnotic thriller that expertly combines art-movie existentialism with genuine suspense.

7. *Salò, o le 120 giornate de Sodoma* (Italy/France 1975, dir. Pier Paolo Pasolini, scr. Pier Paolo Pasolini & Sergio Citti, from the novel by the Marquis de Sade)

While it seems unlikely that Pasolini's final film will ever be entirely domesticated, it no longer has quite the shock value it once did. As Sade himself is increasingly tamed as a figure in films such as Philip Kaufman's *Quills*, so *Salò* begins to crop up in incongruous places (it was even a midnight movie at my local multiplex). And Pasolini's argument that his scenes of coprophilia were a comment on processed food no longer seem so outrageous after *Fast Food Nation*'s assertion that everyone has to eat a little shit now and again.

6. *Hearts in Atlantis* (US 2001, dir. Scott Hicks, scr. William Goldman from the novel by Stephen King)
5. *The Door in the Floor* (US 2004, dir. Todd Williams, scr. Todd Williams from the novel by John Irving)

Stephen King and John Irving are friends, have done literary events together, and have more in common than some readers might imagine. These two adaptations take an identical approach: rather than squeeze a 600-page novel into a two-hour running time, they each concentrate on the first hundred or so pages, and make films out of that. In doing so, these two films (while probably not the best made from either author's work) get closer to the spirit of King and of Irving than more conventional adaptations. *Hearts in Atlantis* stars Anthony Hopkins, and Goldman's script makes deliberate inter-textual reference to an earlier film the two men made together, *Magic* (1978). What's most interesting about this film is that there is no attempt to make it a self-contained piece: viewed without knowledge of the King novel, it makes no narrative sense whatsoever. *The Door in the Floor* is similarly open-ended, but can be taken on its own merits, and is reportedly Irving's favourite film made from his fiction.

4. *Naked Lunch* (US/GB 1991, dir. David Cronenberg, scr. David Cronenberg, from the novel by William Burroughs)

Cronenberg has made several literary adaptations, including another book that many considered unfilmable, J.G. Ballard's *Crash* (1996). *Naked Lunch* is the more interesting adaptation, pushing biographical details about Burroughs to the surface, and truly capturing both the perversity of the writer and the horrors of an outlaw literary life. It came out the same year as *Barton Fink*, a film that has the same nightmarish sensibility and one of the same cast members (Judy Davis): another study of the special horror of life behind a bug-shaped typewriter.

3. *The Osterman Weekend* (US 1983, dir. Sam Peckinpah, scr. Alan Sharp from the novel by Robert Ludlum)

Peckinpah's final film resembles Hitchcock's little-seen *Topaz* (1969) in its filleting of an airport thriller so as to allow the director to pursue favourite themes and attempt compelling set-pieces. TV reporter Rutger Hauer is pressured by CIA man John Hurt into trying to unmask a spy among his circle of friends during a supposedly relaxing weekend stay-over. Completely misunderstood on first release, its recent reappearance on DVD (along with Peckinpah's original cut, preserved on a Betamax tape for over twenty years) reveals the film to be a delirious satire of television and surveillance, best considered alongside the same year's *The King of Comedy* and *Videodrome*. All three films now seem like relics not from the past, but from a creepy alternate reality, where television wasn't largely supplanted by the Internet but became a truly monstrous force.

2. *Short Cuts* (US 1993, dir. Robert Altman, scr. Robert Altman & Frank Barhydt from the writings of Raymond Carver)

The good Altman films start off in exactly the same way as his bad ones: the only way to tell the difference is if you're still watching after an hour. *Short Cuts* is an adaptation of several Carver stories (and a poem), transplanted from nondescript suburbia to LA, and interwoven in such a way that the film owes as much to Altman's past films as Carver's source material. Over three hours in length, it's packed with incredible performances from arguably the best cast Altman ever worked with, including Jack Lemmon (as an absentee grandfather), Chris Penn (as a pool cleaner), and Julianne Moore (as a real redhead).

1. *Adaptation* (US 2002, dir. Spike Jonze, scr. Charlie Kaufman
& Donald Kaufman, from *The Orchid Thief* by Susan Orlean)

The purest expression of screenwriter blues committed to celluloid. It's a Valentine for anyone who has suffered through a
Robert McKee screenwriting course, for any screenwriter forced
to adapt a book they either think is beneath them or just won't
make a good movie (in this case, Orlean's non-fiction *The Orchid
Thief*) and for anyone who thinks that the joke about the actress
so dumb she slept with the screenwriter isn't *that* funny. The
metafictional devices Kaufman uses in his script (appearing in the
film himself, giving himself an imaginary brother, deviating from
the supposed story) had long since grown stale in literature, and
didn't remain fresh in film for long (they'd lost their charm by
2006's *Stranger Than Fiction*) but here seemed a genuine innovation.

14

Craftsmen at Work

Unsung Techniques that Have Transformed Movies

RAFAELA ROMAYA: Credit Where it's Due – Ten Great Opening-
Credit Sequences

EDWARD LAWRENSON: Perpetual-Motion Men – Ten Bravura
Long Takes

MARK SALISBURY: Gonna Fly Now – Ten Cool Steadicam Shots

IAN CHRISTIE: 'Checking the Gate' Is for Wimps – Ten Great
Films that Didn't Use a Camera (or, at Least, not the Film-
maker's Camera)

EDWARD LAWRENSON: It's Not Over 'til We Say it's Over – Ten
Brave Uses of Obsolete Technology

IAN CHRISTIE: A Branch of Conjuring – The Ten Best Animated
Films (Excluding Disney)

KALEEM AFTAB: You Have Been Watching . . . Ten Classic End-
Credit Cast Lists

Credit Where it's Due

Ten Great Opening-Credit Sequences

RAFAELA ROMAYA

After the lights go down and the big curtains part, they seize you by the lapels from the first few frames. They make you forget your bucket of popcorn. They light your way into the dreamtime of celluloid, dissolving the humdrum day outside, a liminal zone between the Street and the Main Feature. Oh, and they tell you who's in the movie. (Also, for multiplex viewers, whether you're in the right auditorium . . .)

I'm talking about the opening credits, of course. While fulfilling their main function as a set of acknowledgements, they can also engage, entertain, and arouse the promise of pleasures to come. Not to be confused with the opening sequence (that's a different list), credits offer a wealth of opportunity for directors and designers alike, in that short window between the start of the film and the film starting. Some directors take credits very seriously; others run out of money and opt for classy (cheap), no-frills, white-on-black numbers. Woody Allen seems to favour the latter course as a matter of taste.

Whether – like Allen's character in *Annie Hall* – you can't bear to enter the cinema knowing that you've missed them; or whether they represent just a few moments of grace for the taco-toting shufflers among you – who am I to say? But one thing we can agree on is that there have been some very striking credit sequences in film history, and that credits have become an increasingly important and elaborate part of film-making. Audiences have long since come to expect more from the start of a film than just a bare-chested guy with a gong and some basic info. To demonstrate the abundance of creative talent, experimental techniques and aesthetics used to encapsulate, prepare and précis a movie, I present this highly biased selection, limited to just one entry per designer/director. My Top Ten exposes only a fraction of what is now a considerable canon of title sequences, highlighted by the quality of those omitted: *Dr Strangelove*, *Superman*, *To Die For*, *Catch Me if You Can* or all those slick Bond sequences blending a seductive cocktail of guns and girls, now synonymous with the 007 brand.

10. *The Fearless Vampire Killers or Pardon Me But Your Teeth are in my Neck* (US 1966, dir. Roman Polanski. Titles by André François)

This most definitely doesn't suck. It gets the mix of chuckles and chills going for Polanski's comedy-horror right from the outset: even the MGM lion transforms into a green cartoon vampire. The ghoul sprouts fangs from which a drop of blood falls and runs through the entire handwritten sequence. As the credits scroll, the blood seamlessly morphs into a flying bat, squirting droplets and blood-red lips – in all, a humorous yet spooky sequence fit to sink your teeth into. (*Enough vampire gags, thanks – Ed.*)

9. *The Great Ziegfeld* (US 1936, dir. Robert Z. Leonard)

William Powell, who played Florenz Ziegfeld Jr. in this Oscar-winning biopic, said, 'He was financially impractical but aesthetically impeccable.' Befitting the great showman's extravagant life, this sequence was the most expensive of its day – costing 10,000 dollars alone – and literally highlighted how vital titles were beginning to be considered to a movie's showcasing. In an age before CGI, the credits lavishly acknowledge the whole crew in life-size electric-lights mounted on scaffolding: the camera carefully pans round to frame, however briefly, each and every one.

8. *Bande à part* (France 1964, dir. Jean-Luc Godard)

From the 'Golden Age of Hollywood' to the 'Golden Age of Titles'. The 1960s were a revolutionary period in movie credits: not just in Hollywood, but for European and underground films too. Chopping faster than a sushi chef, the editor almost creates a strobe effect here, flashing between full-frame images of the film's trio of misfits – streetwise crooks Arthur (Claude Brasseur), Franz

(Sami Frey) and Odile (Anna Karina, Godard's beautiful wife and muse at the time) – nicely in-sync with the soundtrack. Contrasting typography allows each letter of the main title to gradually appear. Look how these black and white credits set the film's tempo; they still set the heart racing in anticipation.

7. *King of Comedy* (US 1982, dir. Martin Scorsese, title design by Dan Perri)

As Godard once said, 'Photography is truth. And cinema is truth twenty-four times a second.' This sequence freeze-frames obsessive celebrity stalker Masha (the comedienne Sandra Bernhard) with her hands glued to the inside of a car window in the pop of a flashbulb, while delusional stand-up comic Rupert Pupkin (Robert De Niro) peers in. The credits run their course in this frozen single frame, possibly reflecting the very fleeting nature of the fame that Pupkin so desperately craves.

6. *Scorpio Rising* (US 1963, dir. and titles by Kenneth Anger)

'What fools these Mortals be!' is PUCK Film Production's motto. Here, the underbelly – or, at least, a belly – of America's milieu of biker culture is revealed. After the most virile of signs – a red scorpion motif zooms into frame and then fades out – an engine revs for the bare-chested leather-clad biker on whose jacket the titles are physically pierced in metal studs. Anger manages to synthesize a whole style, an aesthetic, with a kind of brilliant DIY economy all too rare in an age of squeaky clean, clear-cut fonts and thumping, monolithic titles.

5. *The Thomas Crown Affair* (US 1968, dir. Norman Jewison, title design by Pablo Ferro Films)

Split screen with sex appeal: this pioneering title montage of seductive private eye Vicky Anderson (Dunaway) and millionaire playboy Thomas Crown (McQueen) cut a six-minute sequence down to forty seconds. Tinted sub-frames and frequently changing position and scale, set to the Oscar-winning song 'The Windmills of Your Mind', results for the viewer in a jacked-up sense of urgency and tension about the heist movie to come. Viewed today, it almost seems to exude the very essence of the late 1960s.

4. *Ed Wood* (US 1994, dir. Tim Burton, title design by Robert Dawson/Paul Boyington/Cinema Research Corporation)

In the opening sequence Criswell asks: 'Can your heart stand the shocking facts about Edward D. Wood Jr.?' Thanks to the credits the answer is a resounding Yes. These titles pay tribute to Ed Wood's film *Plan 9 from Outer Space* (frequently cited in 'Worst Film of All Time' lists) using a pastiche of that film's title sequence in particular, and honouring the B-movie in general, being replete with dry ice graveyards and animated octopuses fighting off Tupperware flying saucers. (Are those the strings?). The titles transcend imitation though by creating a sequence in which the elements are so lovingly faithful to the genre. And the audience are in on the joke from the word go.

3. *To Kill a Mockingbird* (US 1962, dir. Robert Mulligan, title design by Stephen Frankfurt)

'You never know someone', Atticus Finch tells feisty tomboy Scout, 'until you step inside their skin and walk around a little.' This sequence does just that, giving us an insight into the world of young Jem and his sister Scout through his most cherished possession. The camera seamlessly pans over the contents of a cigar box filled with childish trinkets and keepsakes – a watch, a figurine, pennies and marbles. A childish hand makes a crayon rubbing of the movie's title. Highly regarded among designers as a model of accomplishment, this sequence beautifully melds all the elements of film together: live action, music, sound effects, typography and illustration.

2. *Se7en* (US 1995, dir. David Fincher, title design by Kyle Cooper/RGA/LA)

Radical at the time of its release, this 'mini-movie' transports one straight into the mind of the film's protagonist, serial murderer

'John Doe' (who will be tardy about revealing his face). The virtuoso sequence gives oblique and harsh hints at a hidden and terrible private activity going on in our midst. Layered images of the killer meticulously preparing his journals and razoring his fingerprints, distressed credits gouged into the celluloid, and an edgy remixed Nine Inch Nails track ('You Bring Me Closer to God') create a cinematic equivalent to nails being scratched down a blackboard. A paradigm shift for 1990s design, Se7en spawned a thousand imitations, and Cooper was hailed as the new Saul Bass. But there's only one Saul Bass. To wit:

1. *Psycho* (US 1960, dir. Alfred Hitchcock, title design by Saul Bass)

'No One . . . BUT NO ONE . . . Will be Admitted to the Theatre After the Start of Each Performance of Alfred Hitchcock's *Psycho*' demanded Hitchcock. Acting as an abstract overture to this groundbreaking thriller, the titles' pulsating visual rhythm is all clean economy and design elegance, but seems to manifest fracture and disjointedness: vertical bars fluctuate like a sound level meter, stabbed by Bernard Herrmann's lacerating Stravinskyesque score. The strings move from melodrama to shrieking; horizontal bars suggest shutter-blinds, tempting voyeurism. The very typography unsettles: language is slashed and broken, a foreshadowing of the state of mind we will encounter – homicidal peeping tom Norman Bates – and as the abstract shapes of the credits fade, their sinister energy seems to bleed into the fabric of the city . . .

Perpetual-Motion Men

Ten Bravura Long Takes

EDWARD LAWRENSON

Filming sequences in long, unbroken takes is often a cinematic equivalent of extreme sports. It takes a supremely confident director to stage a long sequence in real time (often simultaneously overseeing complex camera moves) without the safety-net provision of fixing the footage in the editing suite. A minute's worth of continuous action can require days of preparation, and it takes only a tiny thing – a camera jamming, an actor fluffing his lines – to foul up all that work. Now that computer-generated imagery can simulate all manner of elaborate camera movements, we should commemorate those film-makers who made minimum recourse to post-production trickery. Celebrating directors for whom 'Cut' was a dirty word, these are our Top Ten instances of single and continuous shots. The criteria forbid sequences shot with a Steadicam, which warrant their own entry a few pages ahead.

10. *Persona* (Sweden 1966, dir. Ingmar Bergman)

In a film remarkable for its austere, unflinching close-ups of faces, there is a bravura tracking shot around the mid-point, following the two lead actresses along an otherwise empty beach. The movie is a dark, psychologically rich study of the relationship between a celebrated actress (Liv Ullmann) and the nurse (Bibi Andersson) caring for her after her breakdown, and this sequence comes after a violent confrontation between the two women. Gliding quickly over an ashen beach and wiry outcrops of scrub, to the sound of breaking waves from the cold grey sea in the background, the camera tries to keep pace with Ullmann as she stomps away from Andersson. Using what seems a small railway line's worth of camera track, this long, seemingly effortless speeding camera movement lets some air – albeit of a chilly, desolate variety – into this most claustrophobic of chamber pieces.

9. Four-fifths of *Five* (Iran/Japan 2003, dir. Abbas Kiarostami)

Subtitled 'Five Long Takes Dedicated to Yasujiro Ozu', Kiarostami's *Five* is a suitably minimalist tribute to the pared-down elegance of the Japanese master. The movie comprises five wordless shots, filmed on digital video: a piece of driftwood tossed about by incoming tide; a crowd of people traversing a seafront esplanade; some dogs on a beach; a flock of ducks waddling across the screen; and the reflective play of moonlight on the surface of a pond (actually a composite of

different shots, merged together during post-production, and therefore disqualified from this list). Seemingly unmediated ten-minute-
plus long slices of happenstance – video art for the webcam generation – these strangely compelling vignettes in fact required some
subtle manipulation from Kiarostami. If nothing else, the fourth
instalment is the finest example of duck choreography in cinema.

8. *Eternity and a Day* (Greece/France/Italy/Germany 1998, dir.
Theo Angelopoulos)

In tandem with his cinematographer Yorgos Arvanitis,
Angelopoulos is among the finest exponents of long-take cinema
today. Filming his actors in striking, constantly shifting tableaux,
usually against the landscape of his native Greece, his camera-work
is sinewy, elegant, breathtakingly precise. The closing sequence of
Eternity and a Day is a typically bravura example. Moving from the
interior of the ailing hero's home through the window to the sea outside, the sequence required over twenty people to open a false wall
through which the camera passed. To actor Bruno Ganz's objections
that he found it difficult to perform this emotionally intense scene
with so much commotion, Angelopoulos said: 'Listen, you're the
actor, not me. Imagine nothing's happening.'

7. *Offret / The Sacrifice* (Sweden 1986, dir. Andrei Tarkovsky)

Swedish intellectual Alexander (Erland Josephson) makes a pact
with God to renounce his material goods so as to avert a nuclear
apocalypse. Waking up the morning after the deal, Alexander
calmly constructs a pyre of dining chairs in his living room and
sets fire to his two-storey wooden house. In a stunning six-minute
long shot, Tarkovsky (and *Persona* cinematographer Sven
Nykvist) watch from a sorrowful distance as flames engulf the
house, gracefully tracking across the puddled grassland in the
foreground as Alexander scurries away from his distraught family.
In the first attempt to film this scene, the camera jammed – one
of the perils of long-take film-making that is excruciatingly
detailed in the documentary *Directed by Andrei Tarkovsky*.
Resisting calls to edit the footage together, the director had his

crew rebuild the house over some days, and then set fire to it again.

6. *Professione: Reporter / The Passenger* (US 1975, dir. Michelangelo Antonioni)

In the final scene the journalist-hero Locke (Jack Nicholson) is assassinated by African revolutionaries as he lies on his hotel bed. It's an occasion for one of Antonioni's most celebrated shots: a seven-minute take in which the camera slowly seems to move through the iron grille of Nicholson's hotel window to perform a steady circling move in the courtyard outside, so capturing the arrival of the assassins and, soon after, of the police who discover Locke's corpse. Antonioni observes the action of this sequence at an imperious remove, making at once a display of his masterly control and a brand of existentialism so exquisitely chilly that even death is something that happens off screen.

5. *Wavelength* (US 1967, dir. Michael Snow)

A landmark film of late-sixties experimental cinema, *Wavelength* begins in the empty room of a New York apartment, the fixed camera facing two tall windows between which a photograph is pinned to the wall. Slowly, almost imperceptibly, Snow zooms into the picture; an oscillating, high-pitch electronic wail accompanies the movement, gifting it a sense of eerie foreboding, as Snow distorts the image by placing coloured filters on the lens. The gradual, snail's-pace action of the zoom is strangely absorbing, so much so you might fail to notice the appearance of a male figure who enters the room and promptly collapses on the floor, possibly dead. A work about the allure of form and aesthetic processes rather than conventional narrative, *Wavelength* makes a poor kind of murder mystery, but hovers as an influence on the closing death scene of *The Passenger*.

4. *Empire* (US 1964, dir. Andy Warhol)

In July of 1964 Warhol trained a static camera on the Empire State Building and filmed continuously between eight o'clock in the evening to the small hours of the following morning. Although technically not a single shot in its eight-hour-plus entirety – Warhol had to allow for short breaks to change the film reel – the film is the most extreme example of the exacting demands single-take cinema can make of its viewers. If the glamour and celebrity buzz of Warhol's artworks owed something to Hollywood, this is a film whose very stillness aspires to the condition of a painting. But stay with it long enough and you'll see the slow darkening of night. It is, Warhol said, something to watch 'to see time go by'.

3. *Sunrise – A Song of Two Humans* (US 1927, dir. F.W. Murnau)

In 1926 William Fox – he of the Fox Film Corporation – invited German master Murnau to the US. Having impressed Fox with his 1924 *The Last Laugh*, Murnau was given rare freedom to make a film of his choosing. The result, *Sunrise*, marked a high point of silent cinema. Among the many remarkable sequences was a single one-and-a-half minute shot that accompanies the hero (George O'Brien) through misty marshland for a late-night tryst with his lover (Margaret Livingston). Mounted on a track set into the studio ceiling, the camera – operated by Karl Struss – follows O'Brien through a vast interior set, passing through smoky wisps, dense masses of branches and tall grass, over a fence, and then briefly pans away from O'Brien to provide his point of view as he pushes aside more plant life to reveal Livingston, statuesque in front of a *trompe l'oeil* moon. Months after *Sunrise* opened the talkies were introduced, but it would be years before they matched the expressive peaks achieved here.

2. *Touch of Evil* (US 1958, dir. Orson Welles)

In its celebrated three-minute-plus opening shot, *Touch of Evil* begins on the close-up of a bomb. The camera then follows the shadow of the man holding the device as he runs to a parked car and plants the timed explosive in its boot; swoops up over a nearby rooftop as a couple get into the car and drive away; tracks the vehicle through a wide street that quickly fills with pedestrians; picks out for our attention the newlywed heroes played by Charlton Heston and Janet Leigh; stops at the US-Mexico border control for a brief dialogue scene between Heston, the guard and the doomed occupants of the car (who have now pulled up alongside the couple); and then sweeps into Heston and Leigh embracing as the automobile drives off. 'Do you realize I haven't kissed you in over an hour?' says Heston, charmingly. Boom! A virtuoso example of Hitchcock's contention that ticking time-bombs can only be suspenseful plot devices when the audience has foreknowledge of their existence, this painstakingly prepared sequence had to be filmed several times because, according to Welles, the border guard kept fluffing his lines.

1. *Soy Cuba* (USSR/Cuba 1964, dir. Mikhail Kalatozov)

Telling the story of the Cuban overthrow of the Batista regime, *Soy Cuba* is a triumph of long-take cinema. It is a film whose best sequences are marked by fluid, dynamic movements from handheld wide-angle close-ups to vast crowd scenes: in the best revolutionary tradition, individual action is inextricably linked to collective endeavour by Kalatozov's roaming camera-work. But the standout moment is Kalatozov's giddy, single-take condemnation of Western consumerism. Opening on a band playing jazz on top of a hotel roof in Havana, the camera mingles among bikini-clad female contestants of a beauty contest, then drops down a couple of floors past the onlooking rich tourists, to focus on one sunbather as she walks over to the roof-top pool and takes a swim, followed underwater by the camera itself. *Soy Cuba* so impressed Martin Scorsese – whose Steadicam work on *GoodFellas* recalls Kalatozov's movie – that he co-sponsored its US re-release in 1995.

Gonna Fly Now

Ten Cool Steadicam Shots

MARK SALISBURY

Essentially a stabilizing mount that isolates the movement of the camera from that of its operator, the Steadicam enables travelling shots that are both fluid and flexible without the need to lay yards of dolly-track. Over the last thirty years it has released film-makers to be bolder, more inventive and more audacious in their camera movement. First employed by Hal Ashby in his 1976 *Bound For Glory* (though John Avildsen's *Rocky*, shot later, reached cinemas first), Steadicam is now a staple of movies, TV shows and sports broadcasts, its floating motion and flexibility exploited most zealously by directors such as Scorsese and De Palma. The latter is arguably the master of the tool, transforming his movies, good, bad or indifferent, into cinematic events by virtue of technical acumen. The only inspired moments in his otherwise mediocre *Mission to Mars* are two Steadicam shots that comprise the opening-title sequence, introducing the main cast in a stylishly efficient piece of storytelling. Elsewhere, the Steadicam can be deployed to suggest a director's third-person omniscient consciousness, or a first-person point of view. It's a device that in the right hands can produce results that are stunning, profound or just very cool. Here are ten of the best.

10. *Raising Cain* (US 1992, dir. Brian De Palma)

De Palma's demented tale of multi-personalities features an astonishing four-minute sequence following Frances Sternhagen's doctor in a bad wig ('I look like a transvestite'), Gregg Henry's police lieutenant and another officer as they walk along the station's corridors, down several flights of stairs, out into the lobby, then into a lift, before finally they emerge in the morgue to view a dead body, as Sternhagen outlines the bonkers plot and Henry pulls and nudges her this way and that.

9. *Serenity* (US 2005, dir. Joss Whedon)

Buffy the Vampire Slayer creator Joss Whedon employed the Steadicam for his feature directorial debut, using it to prowl the corridors of the creaky titular spaceship and introduce us to all eight members of the Serenity crew as they bicker, fight, and make preparation for a (potential) crash-landing on a far-off planet.

8. *The Bonfire of the Vanities* (US 1990, dir. Brian De Palma)

The opening of De Palma's meek, misguided adaptation of Tom Wolfe's satirical bestseller is a four-and-a-half minute Steadicam shot that begins with a limo entering an underground garage, out of which emerges drunken tabloid journalist Peter Fallow (Bruce Willis). We follow him as he hops on a golf-cart and is whizzed along a tunnel before stumbling onward through a kitchen and into a lift (in which he flirts with a young lady and chomps on poached salmon), then out on to another level, where his shirt is removed and he's dressed in a clean bow-tie and tux, before finally emerging on to the grand Winter Garden at the World Financial Centre, where a reception is being thrown in his honour.

7. *Boogie Nights* (US 1997, dir. Paul Thomas Anderson)

Anderson's exploration of the ups and downs of the porn scene in LA's San Fernando Valley during the late 1970s and early 1980s owes much to Robert Altman, though the three-minute Steadicam shot that begins the film is more *un hommage* to a similar moment in *GoodFellas*. Beginning with the Steadicam operator on a crane, the shot starts with a close-up of a neon sign bearing the film's title, before tilting up and then back down to follow a car arriving at a nightclub across the street. As Burt Reynolds and Julianne Moore exit the car, the operator hops off the crane and follows this pair into the Hot Traxx nightclub whereupon we meet owner Luis Guzmán, step on to the dance-floor with Don Cheadle and John C. Reilly, and whiz around with Heather Graham's Roller Girl, before the camera comes to rest on Mark Wahlberg's busboy and porn-star-in-the-making, the one and only Dirk Diggler.

6. *Carlito's Way* (US 1993, dir. Brian De Palma)

De Palma manages to wrestle not one but two extended sequences into this picture. Both are part of an extended chase sequence as Al Pacino's Carlito, freed from jail on a technicality and intent on carving out a law-abiding future, finds that going straight ain't so easy. The first sequence lasts around two minutes as Carlito is pursued on to a subway platform, Pacino running alongside an approaching train. As the train stops, the camera hops on board with Pacino, then out on to the platform, then back on to the train – finding the fidgety, nervous Carlito as he tries desperately to evade capture. The second shot takes place in New York's Grand Central Station where Carlito has been cornered by three armed goons, and the camera dogs Pacino as he evades capture, then leaves him on the first floor and riding the escalator down to ground level where the bad guys are waiting – before following them back up the escalator.

5. *Raging Bull* (US 1980, dir. Martin Scorsese)

An elegant Steadicam shot in glorious black and white, wherein the camera picks up De Niro's Jake La Motta in his pre-fight basement dressing room, going through a last-minute workout with Joe Pesci, then follows him along a corridor, past a number of adoring fans, up some stairs, and through into the auditorium itself where a crowd of 3000 spectators are waiting. As La Motta steps into the ring for his bout against middleweight champion Marcel Cerdan, the camera rises into the air, with the Steadicam operator hopping on to a crane. According to editor Thelma Schoonmaker, Scorsese's favourite take of the scene was ruined by a camera fault, but the shot we get to see was at least the next best.

4. *The Player* (US 1992, dir. Robert Altman)

Altman's vicious Hollywood satire begins with an eight-minute shot that moves in and out of offices on a studio lot as a series of screenwriters pitch ridiculous movies (among them Buck Henry offering his concept for 'The Graduate Part 2') and studio detective Walter (Fred Ward) talks with two others about famous 'long shots' in film history, referencing the six-and-a-half-minute opening of Orson Welles's *Touch of Evil* and a scene in Bertolucci's *The Sheltering Sky*.

3. *Snake Eyes* (US 1998, dir. Brian De Palma)

Another bravura stroke from De Palma who begins this Atlantic

City-set thriller with what appears to be a stunning twelve(!)-minute shot – actually around eight takes spliced together with invisible wipes. We begin outdoors on a rain-lashed reporter before the camera pulls back and pans over to a TV monitor showing fast-talking cop Rick Santora (Nicolas Cage), then travels with him as he paces around a hotel/casino complex prior to a heavyweight title fight; visits various guest rooms; tries to place a bet; moves down an escalator; roughs up Luis Guzmán; talks on his cellphone; chats up the round-display girl; and finally heads ringside where, eventually, the US Secretary for Defense will be assassinated in front of hundreds of witnesses.

2. *GoodFellas* (US 1990, dir. Martin Scorsese)

Scorsese's gangster epic is remembered for much – the violence, the performances, the general cinematic brilliance – but the moment where the Steadicam follows Ray Liotta and Lorraine Bracco as they enter the Copacabana is possibly the most celebrated of all. A three-minute piece of pure cinema, much imitated but rarely bettered, the shot begins with Henry and Karen outside on the street as he hands his car keys to the valet. We follow them as they bypass the queue and walk down some side-stairs, the camera gliding into this world as Henry shows off his exalted status to Karen, and she (and consequently we, the audience) get to witness his wiseguy world first-hand. They stride down a long hallway, into and out of the kitchen, before emerging, finally, into the Copacabana itself where a table is whisked out especially for them and placed right beside the stage where Bobby Vinton is singing. Talk about class.

1. *Russkiy kovcheg / Russian Ark* (Russia/Germany 2002, dir. Aleksandr Sokurov)

Sokurov's sublime accomplishment stands not only as the longest continuous take in the history of cinema, but as a piece of art itself. Shot in a single 96-minute take using a DV camera mounted to a Steadicam, this is bravura film-making of the highest order, a breathtaking experience gliding back and forth through time, and through some thirty-three rooms of the Hermitage Museum in St Petersburg, encountering around 2000 costumed actors and extras, and even a full symphony orchestra, with Tilman Büttner's camera less an observer and more an actual participant in the action, peering into windows, moving among the artworks. Sheer genius.

'Checking the Gate' Is for Wimps

Ten Great Films that Didn't Use a Camera (or, at Least, Not the Film-maker's Camera)

BY IAN CHRISTIE

It was Hollis Frampton, a disciple of Ezra Pound and friend of Carl Andre (of the notorious Tate 'bricks' sculpture), who once described film as 'a means of modulating a standardized light beam' as it passes through a projector. Normally, this modulation re-creates whatever was photographed on the original of the film – but not always. There are a select number of films that reach the projector without having passed through their maker's camera, and such are the concern of this list.

As you might expect, there are two main types of camera-less film: works that might be labelled 'avant-garde', and forms of documentary that are built entirely from previously existing film (hence that caveat about 'not the film-maker's camera'). Sometimes they overlap, as in artists' 'found footage' work. None is likely to feature on any other Top Ten list, but here they can compete happily among themselves, shedding light on the outer limits of what we might call Cinema.

One entry, Kubelka's *Arnulf Rainer*, will have to stand in for a cluster of 'flicker films', made from completely blank frames arranged in rhythmic order, which would include such masterpieces as Tony Conrad's *The Flicker* and Paul Sharits's *Ray Gun Virus*. Also missing – because I always contrived to avoid subjecting myself to it – is Anthony Scott's ultimate found-footage compilation *The Longest Most Meaningless Movie in the World*, which reputedly ran for five hours at the London Arts Lab in 1968 (or even eight days, according to another account – which must then qualify it for a future list of longest films?). Ah, those were the days . . .

10. *The Story of the Unknown Soldier*, 1932, Henri Storck

Politicians pontificate, but ordinary citizens still die in spite of their good intentions. The message of Belgian pioneer Storck's bitter little satire on plans to 'outlaw war' is a topical today as it was in 1932, when he took newsreel of the 1928 Kellogg-Briand pact and wove it into an angry, yet often witty, polemic against the warmongers waiting in the wings. The film's indictment hit home, getting it banned in France, and probably ensuring it's never had the reputation it deserves abroad.

9. *Horror Film No.1*, 1971, Malcolm Le Grice

No, it's not really a horror movie in any familiar form of the genre; indeed it's not even a movie in the conventional sense of the word. Back in the glory days of British experimental film-making, 'expanded cinema' meant making the 16mm projector the star of the show, or even using a bunch of them together in a gallery space. Le Grice created a series of such 'expanded' pieces, and for this one, stripped to the waist, he would perform a shadow-play in the superimposed beams of several projectors running tinted film-loops. The effect is part-Victorian parlour show and part genuinely spooky performance, with a skeleton image nodding to the Phantasmagoria tradition.

8. *A Movie*, 1958, Bruce Conner

One of the earliest, and still the best, artist's 'found footage' film. Plundering news film and pulp fiction, Conner created a rapid-fire collision between the most diverse images imaginable. It's often been imitated, not least by Conner himself, but rarely to such ecstatic effect. As cowboys, Indians, deep-sea divers and strippers hurtle past, we realize there is an underlying theme to all this kaleidoscopic imagery: it's our civilization, obsessed with sex and death, heading towards oblivion.

7. *Arnulf Rainer*, 1958, Peter Kubelka

Named after the Austrian abstract painter, after fellow-Austrian Kubelka had failed to make a documentary about him, this small but perfectly formed work uses just black and white clear frames arranged in rhythmic patterns, with a matching soundtrack of 'white noise' and silence, to create an experience of pure cinema. Ideally, it should be seen on a vast screen, played at full blast, and the effect is overwhelming – not just the physical impact of flickering light and on-off sound, but the sense of elemental drama. As Kubelka would say, it's not *about* something – it *is* something: light, darkness, thunder, silence, taking us back to cinema as it might have been experienced in a prehistoric cave.

6. *Begone Dull Care*, 1949, Norman McLaren and Evelyn Lambert

There aren't many films that have been compared to Jackson Pollock or Willem de Kooning, but McLaren and Lambert's hand-painted fantasia, accompanying three short jazz numbers by Oscar Peterson, has been more than once. Compared with Lye's ground-breaking *Colour Box* and McLaren's own earlier *Dots*, this is more refined and eventually more frenetic: a continuous improvisation that perfectly matches Peterson's music, with an astonishing repertoire of lines, squiggles, inscriptions, mould, dirt, washes – yes, it really is like action painting or, more precisely, abstract expressionism in film.

5. *The Fall of the Romanov Dynasty*, 1927, Esfir Shub

A simple enough idea and one since used in almost every tele-documentary, but the Russian editor Esfir Shub was the first to weave newsreel and home-movies film into a full-scale historical chronicle. Alongside flashier celebrations of the tenth anniversary of the Bolshevik Revolution, by Eisenstein and others, Shub told the story of the last years of the Tsars entirely through film shot of and for them. The result is surprisingly restrained, even elegiac, and it was hailed as a model of how film could become the new history. But the real pay-off came decades later, in compilation films such as Mikhail Romm's *Ordinary Fascism* and the work of Marcel Ophüls.

4. *Film in Which There Appear Edge Lettering, Sprocket Holes, Dirt Particles, Etc*, 1966, Owen Land (formerly George Landow)

You can't say you haven't been warned. For four minutes, you do indeed see the above, as part of what seems to be a Kodak test leader repeating in an endless loop, complete with grinning peroxide model. Doesn't sound appealing? But it is, just as much as anything else by avant-garde film's greatest punster and satirist. All of Land's (as he mysteriously renamed himself) films are parodies of instructional films, documentaries, abandoned scraps, but transformed by a keen intelligence that wants to question our normal experience of viewing, and maybe send us spinning off into some kind of spiritual awakening. One of Landow's films is actually about a man having an epiphany while watching an avant-garde film in a Midwestern arts centre – and his longest features two pandas discussing Freud's marriage-broker jokes. But *Film in Which . . .* is the nursery slope.

3. *Rose Hobart*, Joseph Cornell, 1936

Reclusive American surrealist Joseph Cornell had an oblique relationship to movies. Almost none of those credited to him were actually shot by him. Instead, he preferred to commission others to shoot them for him, or, as in this case, to edit his own film from a routine Hollywood melo, *East of Borneo*. Intrigued by the minor actress Rose Hobart, Cornell focuses almost exclusively on her, sacrificing the plot for a dreamy hymn to movie star glamour. Cornell's cut-up, shown in slow-motion to the accompaniment of some Brazilian records that he found in a junk shop, and through a tinted filter, is one of the Surrealist protests against banal cinema. Dream, or better still, make your own film!

2. *Colour Box*, Len Lye, 1935

The first, or at least the earliest surviving, 'direct' film and still the most mesmerizing. New Zealand-born painter and sculptor

Len Lye took up film after he reached London in the late 1920s, and immediately began experimenting. *Colour Box* exploited the new technologies of synch sound and colour to produce, literally, a moving painting, set to an infectious Cuban-style dance number. Lines and shapes painted directly on to the filmstrip pulsate and ripple, interrupted only briefly with an advertising message from the Post Office, which was enough to get the film widely distributed in cinemas (so making it probably the most widely seen of all experimental films) and to launch Lye on a career in which he managed to get sponsors to pay for many of his gloriously insouciant experiments. (His later *Free Radicals*, scratched directly on black leader film in 1958, could also figure in this list.)

1. *Mothlight*, Stan Brakhage, 1963

Surely the unchallenged greatest film ever made without a camera? Using neither found footage nor painting or scratching, Brakhage became fascinated by the idea of projecting moth-wings and other once-living material on to the screen, by sandwiching this in a clear strip and then producing a negative from the result. On screen, it's a rapid fluttering image that's hard to interpret, lacking the usual coordinates of the frame. But the film really comes into its own when looked at by hand against the light, and you can see what's mummified within the filmstrip. Most films make little sense viewed this way, but *Mothlight* actually makes more sense, or at least more beauty, outside the projector.

'It's Not Over 'til We Say it's Over

Ten Brave Uses of Obsolete Technology

BY EDWARD LAWRENSON

Cinema is art. It is big business. But it is also a technology, a constantly evolving, highly industrial blend of chemical processes, optical engineering and software development. The Lumière brothers were inventors before they were film-makers. And for many directors, pushing the expressive capabilities of cinema goes hand in hand with innovating existing film-making techniques. From Orson Welles's pioneering work with deep focus on *Citizen Kane* to Steven Spielberg's computer-generated dinosaurs in *Jurassic Park*, the most admired directors are often cinema's most tireless R&D specialists.

But what of film-makers who choose to stick by technology from the medium's past? In the exhaustive, ever-onward quest for novelty, the decision to use devices or processes that have fallen out of fashion can exploit cinema's in-built obsolescence to wonderful effect. Retrieving a now discarded technology can be *un hommage* to film history. Or it can simply be a deliciously contrarian gesture of cinematic Ludditism. These are the ten best examples to my mind.

10. *Bram Stoker's Dracula* (US 1992, dir. Francis Coppola)

An early scene takes place in a Victorian fairground, an apt setting for a movie steeped in filmic magic tricks that stretch back to cinema's beginnings as a carnival attraction. In particular, Coppola's use of matte shots – whereby fantastic locations such as Dracula's castle, painted on to glass screens, were combined in camera with live-action footage – use a technique pioneered in the medium's birthing years. Classing matte paintings as a variation of pre-cinema 'stage-craft', Coppola said that it was 'appropriate to make our films with the cinema effects of 1900', contemporaneous with Stoker's novel. Lending the film the feel of a bloodstained storybook, the revival of this century-old visual device made for a film that subtly subverted the fad for CG-enhancement then taking hold in Hollywood.

9. *Why Didn't Anybody Tell Me it Would Become this Bad in Afghanistan* (Netherlands 2006, dir. Cyrus Frisch)

The first feature to be entirely shot on a camera-phone employed technology that was relatively new at the time of its 2006 production. But Cyrus Frisch's decision to film much of this 70-minute drama (about a Dutch soldier returning from the Afghanistan conflict) on the low-resolution settings of his mobile phone (a Sharp 903, to be precise) must number as one of the more perverse acts of resistance to technological progress. Filmed mostly in an Amsterdam flat, this is a film of woozy, washy imagery often stretched to the point of abstraction. Watching it blown up on the big screen, even Frisch admitted to the occasional headache.

8. The Wallace & Gromit films (dir. Nick Park)

Using stop-motion techniques that date back to the first years of cinema, Park's Aardman-produced Wallace & Gromit films are a striking anachronism in an era of computer-generated animation. Having originally opted for Plasticine as his preferred medium because the materials for traditional Disney-style cell animation were too expensive, Park has stuck to this hand-crafted, solidly three-dimensional form with a determination that echoes the Lancastrian doggedness of his two heroes. When Aardman – in the last of their collaborations with US studio DreamWorks – produced their first CG feature *Flushed Away*, it was widely deemed a flop.

7. The *oeuvre* of Harry Smith

Much like his work in musicology (notably the landmark 1952 collection of 'lost' roots music, *Anthology of American Folk*) Harry Smith's film-making drew heavily on the art form's past, resurrecting and applying anew techniques that had been forgotten for decades. In experimental animations made in the 1950s such as *Heaven and Earth Magic* Smith hand-tinted individual frames of celluloid, a practice that had its origins in the early cinema of Méliès. And in a nod to devices such as magic lanterns that predated cinema, Smith projected images from painted glass slides to frame the animated sequences of his films. A delirious concoction of early cinema technology and nineteenth-century light shows (often played to live improvised jazz) Smith's films were a big influence on sixties psychedelia.

6. *Awesome; I Fuckin' Shot That!* (US 2006, dir. Adam Yauch)

A record of a 2004 Beastie Boys gig at Madison Square Garden, *Awesome; I Fuckin' Shot That!* is the ultimate fan's-eye concert film. The band gave out fifty camcorders to audience members, authorizing them to film what they wanted, and the subsequent movie is mostly compiled from that footage. What's more, the fans were shooting Hi-8, an analogue video format popular with home-movie-makers in the 1990s but noticeably less crisp than the digital-video material shot on stage. The grainy, under-lit results give the movie a bootleg roughness and home-video immediacy. Having dated more quickly than the vinyl technologies of a DJ's decks, Hi-8 was obsolete: the Beastie Boys actually had trouble tracking enough cameras down for the project.

5. *Polyester* (US 1981, dir. John Waters)

'Smelling is Believing' proclaimed the poster for Waters' *Polyester* but it would be wrong to characterize the 'Odorama' scratch-and-sniff cards that accompanied the film's 1981 release as a leap forward for cinematic realism. A suitably kitsch throwback to the Smell-O-Vision gimmicks of William Castle, master of 1960s drive-in cinema, Odorama's ten fragrances included (inevitably) a fart. This particular innovation – thankfully – never caught on.

4. Pixelvision

On the market for only two years in the late 1980s, the Pixelvision PXL 2000 was toy manufacturer Fisher-Price's video-camcorder for kids. Recording black-and-white on to audio cassette, the camera rendered its subject matter into blurry blocks of images. The device was probably too expensive and specialized for children; but video artists responded to the camera's haunting results, and a sub-genre of Pixelvision experimental shorts soon developed. Notable exponents include queer film-maker Sadie Benning (who responded to the format's confessional potential) and the format was even included in a feature when Michael Almereyda used Pixelvision footage in his 1991 film *Nadja*. Originally retailing for 100 dollars, Pixelvision cameras are now highly sought after collectors' items.

3. *The Good German* (US 2006, dir. Steven Soderbergh)

Set in Berlin in the immediate aftermath of the Second World

War, *The Good German* was made to look as if it were a Hollywood studio picture of that period. Predictably Soderbergh opted for black-and-white. But it was his use of other, less obvious techniques from the 1940s that lent his film its striking authenticity. Soderbergh employed back-projection to re-create Berlin exteriors in his LA studio, filming the actors in front of archive footage of the city in a now rarely used process that lent the project a dreamy sense of artifice. And he restricted his choice of lenses to those available in the 1940s, which captured the actors in wider, continuously held shots – an elegant alternative to the choppy, to-and-fro editing between close-ups that is the dominant style today. Were it not for the absence of scratches, and the periodic bursts of sex and violence (deliberately souring the nostalgia), you'd swear you were watching a forgotten gem from the 1940s.

2. *City Lights* (US 1931, dir. Charles Chaplin)

Chaplin, the pre-eminent star of silent cinema, regretted the introduction of synched sound and 'talkies' ('I loath 'em' was his comment). But his most eloquent response was also his most muted: the dialogue-free *City Lights*, made in 1931 with talking pictures by then well established. Using music (partly composed by Chaplin himself) and the occasional sound effect, this comic weepie sees the Little Tramp fall in love with a blind flower-seller. Though not one of his best, the combination of Victorian stage sentimentality and visual slapstick is characteristically Chaplinesque. Released only four years after *The Jazz Singer*, *City Lights* feel like the embers of a fading art.

1. *Lumière and Company* (France/Denmark/Spain/Sweden 1995)

To mark the centenary of the Lumière brothers' public presentation of their first films, forty directors were asked to make short films with an original camera as used by the French inventors (lovingly restored by Philippe Poulet). The likes of Wim Wenders, Spike Lee and Zhang Yimou were all restricted to a single take of around fifty seconds. The various contributions ranged

from doodles (Abbas Kiarostami filmed an egg frying) to ambitious, large-scale endeavours: David Lynch's nightmarish vignette
made use of five different sets, all connected by a 100-foot track
on which the Lumière's *cinématographe* was pushed. The results play
a little like science fiction. Focused on contemporary subject matter,
yet unnaturally aged by the smoky, flickering patina of the Lumière
technology, these fascinating fragments feel like the dispatches of a
late-nineteenth-century documentarian on 1990s society.

A Branch of Conjuring

The Ten Best Animated Films (Excluding Disney)

IAN CHRISTIE

It's not that the works of Disney wouldn't be in any animation
fan's Top Ten. The problem is how *many* Disney films would have
to be there, crowding out other deserving entries. So why not
imagine a separate Disney domain, where half a dozen *Silly
Symphonies*, *Skeleton Dance*, *Steamboat Willie*, *Snow White*, *Dumbo*,
bits of *Fantasia*, *Bambi*, *Toy Story 2* and all the rest can slug it out?
Then we can get on with the truly impossible task of rating the
whole history of graphic cinema or animation, which has for too
long languished in the margins of most filmgoers' (and critics')
awareness.

There are, of course, some problems of definition. And with
CGI playing an ever-greater part in supposedly 'live-action' film-
making, it's a moot point whether indeed the majority of films
won't soon have to be ranked as 'animation'. But maybe that
should be another list: ten best CGI films excluding *Star Wars* and
its immediate kin?

Back in Animation proper, there is still a major distinction
to be made between 'flat' 2D work and 3D puppet- or object-
animation, which reaches back to the very earliest years of
making magic on the screen. For that's what animation is really about: making inanimate things come alive. It's a branch of
conjuring, which is no doubt why there are qualities of cheeki-

ness, showmanship and mystery about the best animation. But so much to choose from! Animation is truly international in a way that live-action cinema hasn't been for decades: small countries (as well as large ones) that have been left behind by Hollywoodization still have as much chance of producing great animation as the usual big players. And by sticking to films proper, I've dealt with the problem of what to do about such brilliant TV series as *The Simpsons*, *Futurama*, *Family Guy*, *South Park* . . .

10. *South Park: Bigger, Longer and Uncut* (US 1999, dir. Trey Parker)

. . . but as the title boasts, this really *is* a film, and one which goes to lengths that had critics' jaws littering the preview theatre floors. All the familiar *South Park* characters and deadpan shock tactics are present, but taken to lengths of sublime scatological excess. Apart from grotesquely holding Canada responsible for the moral corruption of its big neighbour, the film rises to Miltonic heights (depths?) with its central conceit of an infernal affair between Satan and Saddam Hussein that threatens hell on earth for aeons. Given a bigger screen than usual, Parker and Co. rise to the occasion with a terrifying escalation of their normal assault on American innocence.

9. *Allegretto* (US 1936, dir. Oskar Fischinger)

Originally made to be used in one of Paramount's big musicals, which was then switched to black-and-white, this became probably the finest free-standing display of 'abstract' animation, using colour and recorded music when these were still quite new. Fischinger had made a name for himself in Germany with pioneering experiments with 'motion painting', but it was a cigarette advertisement, with goose-stepping ciggies, that recommended him to Hollywood. Although his dealings with the studios, and especially with Disney, never worked out, America allowed him to reach the dizzying heights of *Allegretto*, with its pulsing lozenges and radiating circles.

Heroic Doses, Hellish Descents: Ten Very Bad Trips, Man, p 291

8. *Street of Crocodiles* (GB 1986, dir. the Brothers Quay)

Puppets coming to life is one of the oldest stories in the haunted cupboard, but with the Quays' nocturnal and decidedly sexual world of reanimation it took a number of new twists – including an amazing sequence of self-turning screws that would deserve a place on its own. Finding a match for their surreal worldview in Bruno Schultz's text (though freely departing from it), the Quays produced what is probably their most complete vision of a world of objects brought to life by the magic of cinema, plenty of smoke and mirrors, and spittle.

7. *Duck Amuck*, (US 1953, dir. Chuck Jones)

When push comes to shove – as it often did in the knockabout world of Tom and Jerry, Bugs Bunny and Daffy Duck – there *has* to be a Chuck Jones in any animation Top Ten (and there should be a Tex Avery too, but this will have to stand for the pair). So how to choose? In *Duck Amuck*, Daffy has to contend with an off-screen animator who quick-changes his costume and even takes away his backgrounds, leaving him to thrash around in the virtual space of the empty screen. What this lacks in the sheer malice that motivates many great Hollywood 'toons, it makes up by harking back to the earliest days of film cartoons, which show the figures coming to life 'out of the inkwell'. Here, though it's more a case of Daffy triumphantly resisting all attempts to wipe him out.

6. *Fétiche / The Mascot* (France 1933, dir. Wladyslaw Starewicz)

Russian émigré Starewicz is probably the puppet animator most revered by later exponents of this genre, which is no guarantee of how well his films stand up today. While some are sentimental and others quite nasty in their attitudes, *The Mascot* strikes a fine balance between true sentiment – a young girl is about to lose her toy dog, who decides to find a gift for her – and a truly depraved Parisian cabaret that houses a witches' sabbath which could still give lessons to today's animators out to shock. Bones, vegetables, debris of all kinds, Satan himself – all are brought to vivid life with a brilliantly evocative soundtrack.

5. *The Little Island* (GB 1958, dir. Richard Williams)

Canadian-born Williams' fable about the human condition once enjoyed a reputation as animation's boldest attempt to be taken seriously, with the Big Allegory. Then it dropped out of fashion, as its creator became better known for a string of even more ambitious epics, mostly unfinished, and finally the 'toon side of *Who Framed Roger Rabbit?* But his debut remains amazing: like *Gulliver's Travels* or *Candide*, it translates big ideas – Goodness, Beauty and Truth – into unforgettable characters; in this case blobs that get out of hand and threaten nuclear Armageddon. Amazing drawing, too.

4. *Moznosti dialogu* / *Dimensions of Dialogue*, Czechoslovakia 1982, dir. Jan Svankmajer)

Not a film to watch before or after eating! After one head composed of utensils devours another made from fruit and vegetables, a series of such emblematic heads, inspired by the eccentric Mannerist painter Arcimboldo, continues the process of reckless consumption. Next comes sexual union and finally – well, there's no point in spelling out the message of Czech Surrealism's star pessimist. Before Svankmajer turned to feature-length films, combining live-action with animation, his no-budget shorts made under conditions of extreme political repression were a startling proof of the power of art to protest.

3. *A Grand Day Out* (GB 1989, dir. Nick Park)

Is it just nostalgia to still regard Nick Park's original Wallace and Gromit outing as the best, unsurpassed even while budgets have spiralled? Of course not. The soul of Aardman lay in Peter Lord's skeletal *Morph*, *Creature Comforts* and the wonderfully varied early work, including what began as Park's student film. The humour of *A Grand Day Out* is less calculating than its successors, and the premise of a trip to the moon in search of cheese more naively dotty than later attempts to stretch the narratives. Back to basics – and Wensleydale!

2. *Spirited Away* (Japan 2001, dir. Kayao Miyazaki)

Purists might argue that *Princess Mononoke* has a greater range than the feature which swept Miyazaki and Studio Ghibli to worldwide recognition; and pedants might point out that Disney had a hand in this . . . but I'm standing firm on its inclusion. The adventures of little Chihiro in a haunted bathhouse of the gods draws on all the intrepid heroines of past fairytales in a story of astonishing virtuosity with some moral depth. This (along with *Toy Story 2*) is what you'd show a sceptic to prove that animation can still scale the heights.

1. *The Tale of Tales* (USSR 1979, dir. Yuri Norstein)

This may be the 'official' Best Animated Film of All Time (according to various animation festival polls), but that's no reason not to agree it really is. After an apprenticeship in the Soviet animation industry during the 1960s and 1970s, Norstein poured much of his own experience growing up during and immediately after the Second World War into this poetic multi-layered fable. The central character may be a little wolf, but this is far from a cuddly toy story. It ranges from the pain of losing so many husbands and sons during the war, to a sunlit world of myth, which may be the source of all art and storytelling. In the end, it seems to be about almost everything, but in a beguiling, mysterious way that even puzzled the original scriptwriter, Lyudmila Petrushevskaya, when she saw what Norstein had made of her outline.

You Have Been Watching . . .
Ten Classic End-Credit Cast Lists

KALEEM AFTAB

It's an argument that may be heard emanating from at least one couple near the end of any film: Should we stay for the credits? This

was never an issue until the 1970s, when it became standard practice to put the credits at the back and not the front, and for anyone
remotely attached to the film to be thanked therein. (By the way:
thanks, Ma and Pa.) Naturally, some film-makers are desperate to
make the end-reel more interesting. The likes of Jackie Chan or
Todd Philips add out-takes or bloopers; *Ferris Bueller's Day Off* lays
on an extra special scene. Indeed the post-credit scene of *X-Men 3*
resuscitates a character previously killed off. But by far the classiest
and least intrusive method of making sure everyone lingers for at
least part of the credits is the happy compromise whereby the actors
are given an extra moment in the sun, their credit appearing over
a visual reminder of their performance. This has the added bonus of
helping out those audience members who spent the last twenty
minutes worrying over who that actor was, having forgotten his/her
character name. All that then remains is a prayer that the people
sitting in front of you will choose to stay seated or otherwise leave
the auditorium promptly, rather than standing up and loitering in
your line of vision for the next five minutes . . .

10. *The Great Escape* (US/West Germany 1963, dir. John Sturges)

The one everyone remembers when it comes to the combo of
actor, character and image. First we read 'This film is dedicated to
the fifty. THE END.' Cut to images of the fourteen principal cast
members as seen in the movie: over each of these, in capitals, the
name of the actor, below which is written 'as' and the name of the
character, with their nickname in quotation marks. Naturally it
ends on the high-spot of STEVE McQUEEN as Hilts 'The Cooler
King', a designation that would also be correct if it simply said
'The King of Cool'.

9. *Citizen Kane* (US 1941, dir. Orson Welles)

No one could begrudge this very good picture running on a little, and so a title-card proclaims 'Most of the principal actors in
CITIZEN KANE are new to motion pictures. The Mercury
Theatre is proud to introduce them.' The salutation is reinforced
by acknowledging the actors whilst replaying a line spoken by

each (or in one instance an audible sigh). Niftily, the credit for Everett Sloane and William Alland shows both actors in the frame, and as Sloane speaks his name appears only to be replaced when Alland jumps in to ask a question. Taken together, the selected lines provide a nice overview of the movie, ending on the assertion, 'I think it would be fun to run a newspaper . . .'

8. *Arthur and the Invisibles* (France 2006, dir. Luc Besson)

Watching Besson's adaptation of his own children's book, it's easy to forget how many stars he has brought together to voice the animated characters, since (unlike those folk at Pixar) he hasn't designed the CGI-rendered characters to resemble the actors who voice them (apart from David Bowie as the wizard Maltazard). So each character takes an onscreen bow and as they walk across screen the name of the voice-over artist appears (be it Madonna, Robert De Niro or Chazz Palminteri). Of course the reason for the physical dissimilarity is that the film was always going to be dubbed into French too, whereupon a French-speaking soundalike is sometimes engaged: thus does rapper Rhoff do the substitution for Snoop Dog's rhymes.

7. *Starsky & Hutch* (US 2004, dir. Todd Phillips)

It was American TV cop shows above all that really went to town on showing the faces of actors as they were credited. Usually the programme makers popped this in at the start rather than the end of the show. But in Todd Phillips's broad comic reinterpretation of *Starsky & Hutch*, the visual credits were saved as the *pièce de résistance*. Of course, like the TV show, the roll-call ends on the iconic Huggy Bear, here played by Snoop Dog, who's becoming quite a regular on this list.

6. *Once Upon a Time in the Midlands* (GB 2002, dir. Shane Meadows)

Meadows enters this list with a bid for the most surprising actor-credit of all, though its effect may be wasted on viewers outside the UK, Darlington and Middlesbrough in particular. In classic western style we're watching the names and faces of the actors flash up on screen, until halfway through we're offered an image of two clowns who appeared in a single scene, somewhat extraneous to the great scheme of the movie. Unmasked, however, they are revealed to be the comic duo Vic Reeves and Bob Mortimer, a pair of clowns playing clowns.

5. *Coming to America* (US 1988, dir. John Landis)

The multifarious talents of Eddie Murphy and his old pal Arsenio Hall are on display throughout the movie as the duo take on various roles apiece: Murphy even plays the only white guy. This prowess is then celebrated in the credits as both actors hog the billings, their various creations acknowledged as either Murphy or Hall, again and again. To be fair, the device is successfully kept within the bounds of being funny rather than tiresome. Of course director Landis was only sharpening credit-making skills he had previously displayed on *The Blues Brothers* (1980).

4. *Chariots of Fire* (GB 1981, dir. Hugh Hudson)

Cast your mind back to this Oscar-winner and the first image that reliably comes to mind is men running on a beach in slow-motion to the music of Vangelis. Hudson replays and exploits its iconic qualities for his end credits. As the men pound their way down the sand Hudson pans across their faces and individually credits the four actors who play athletes: Nigel Havers, Ian Charleson, Ben Cross and Daniel Gerrol.

3. *M*A*S*H** (US 1970, dir. Robert Altman)

It wasn't until post-production that Altman added in the camp loudspeaker announcements that shaped his episodic narrative. In keeping with Altman's playful use of sound and dialogue, the concept was extended to the end credits, with nothing written but the loudspeaker announcing, 'Tonight's movie has been M*A*S*H*' and running through a cast-list that begins with

Donald Sutherland and ends on Bobby Troop. Troop then ends the wheeze by shouting, 'This goddamn army!'

2. *The List of Adrian Messenger* (US 1963, dir. John Huston)

The main point of interest in Huston's lark of a film is the actor-billing. The tagline was 'Five Great Stars Challenge You to Guess the Disguised Roles They Play!' The stars in question were Tony Curtis, Burt Lancaster, Robert Mitchum, Frank Sinatra and Kirk Douglas, playing multiple roles. The disguises are great and it's only in the credits that unmasking occurs. The gimmick has since begot a mystery greater than that which was central to *Adrian Messenger*'s lacklustre plot. In Jan Merlin's fascinating *Shooting Montezuma*, a thinly disguised book about the making of Huston's movie, Merlin claims to have played at least one of the masked characters himself, and that it was only when Huston was shooting the unmasking scenes that the likes of Sinatra and Lancaster appeared on set.

1. *Around the World in 80 Days* (US 1956, dir. Michael Anderson)

Just in case you'd forgotten what had happened over the course of this epic Best Picture Oscar winner, the great Saul Bass was called in to design the end-titles. He made a six-minute film-within-a-film, imaginatively titled 'WHO WAS SEEN IN WHAT SCENE . . . AND WHO DID WHAT'. The characters are represented by animated versions of themselves, ranging from playing cards to bicycles: a clock is David Niven's face and a piano stool is Frank Sinatra. There were forty-four cameo appearances to acknowledge in all, and it's all brought off in chronological order and a myriad of colour, following the action precisely as it has taken place on screen. Some guy, that Saul Bass . . .

15

Strange, the Power of Cheap Music

(With Apologies to Noël Coward)

MAVIS CHEEK: Oh-So-Stirring Stuff – Ten Embarrassingly Sentimental Film Scores that Make My Spine Tingle (Despite Being a Rational Sort in All Other Respects)

GEORGE PELECANOS: Ten Movie Soundtrack Cues that Are on My iPod (Not All of Them Westerns)

Oh-So-Stirring Stuff

Ten Embarrassingly Sentimental Film Scores that Make My Spine Tingle (Despite Being a Rational Sort in All Other Respects)

MAVIS CHEEK

10. *Gone With the Wind* (US 1939, dir. Victor Fleming)

How my heart turned over when I first saw Vivien Leigh stand against an angry sky and vow that she would go to Tara and never be hungry again! Oh that profile, oh those bravely tattered clothes. It was 1959, I was nine years old, and as Max Steiner's fabulous score echoed around the walls of the Rialto, Raynes Park, my soul cried out that I too would never be hungry again, and I too would go to Tara. Not that I ever had been hungry before, nor that I knew what Tara was, exactly. At that tender stage in my development the film left me slightly confused – but I sure knew what that music meant. It meant suffering bravely borne, it meant losing love (my mother had the hots for Leslie Howard so I was prepared to believe he was handsome; though to me he looked old and a bit thin on top). It meant, above all, that you could yield to the feelings the music drew out of you, and allow yourself to cry. After all, your mother was crying too. The music was Vivien, *you* were Vivien, who was also Scarlett, and very possibly you were Tara, too. For the rest of the movie, whenever the music played, that bursting-heart phenomenon chased away all rationale: lovely, lovely self-indulgence in the austere late fifties. Just sing a note or two of *Gone With the Wind* and the world was a braver place. Just sing a note or three and you, too, could believe that Vivien and her Mammy really did make a fabulous outfit from an old pair of green and gold curtains. La-la-la-la. La la la la . . .

9. *Death in Venice* (Italy 1971, dir. Luchino Visconti)

Dirk Bogarde told the story of how Visconti sat him in a launch on the Grand Canal and told him that, as the boat went under the

Rialto bridge – or maybe it was the Accademia – he should just stand up and look about him. He duly did so, in his full nineteenth-century Thomas Mann kit, moustachioed, the sunlight glinting off his round spectacles. His face was a smiling mask of inscrutability: not surprisingly, as Bogarde had no idea what he was supposed to be thinking, or that Visconti was going to superimpose Mahler's orgasmic Fifth Symphony over the moment. Up came those passionate, soaring notes as Bogarde made his pact with Venice, beauty, and death. I nearly choked at this point, and the intake of breath in the right-on Renoir Cinema was absolutely palpable as the music blasted us all out of our nice, controlled, art-cool and thrust us into a rampant thrill zone. How many babies were made that night in Hampstead, I wonder? The fusion of Venice, Bogarde, Visconti and Mahler stirred the loins. No wonder that on a private screening of the film, one of the movie moguls watching leapt up and asked who wrote the music. On being told it was Gustav Mahler he immediately ordered the studio to sign him up . . . Watch, listen and yield. Again and again.

8. *Brief Encounter* (GB 1941, dir. David Lean)

I do not like Rachmaninov. I do not care for his over-romantic, sentimental surges. I can say, with pride, that I do not have one bit of Rachmaninov in the house. Except, except . . . on my video of *Brief Encounter*, wherein David Lean takes every opportunity to use Rachmaninov's very horrible Concerto No. 2 to very dreadful effect. Not a dry eye in the house. Every time. He plays it when poor Laura flees from the possibility of illicit sex in a borrowed flat; he plays it at the end when Laura and Alec wait at Milford Junction for Alec's train to come and take him away to Africa (Africa!) never to be seen again – and in comes Dolly, crashing about with her silly English vowels and bringing her friend called Rachmaninov, to talk away their precious last few minutes and swamp it with violins. It all works so cruelly well: the wild strings illuminating the doomed lovers' wild (yet suppressed) emotions. And yes – there's the train pulling out, with Alec sitting in it, and Laura suddenly leaping out of the station buffet with

Rachmaninov hot on her heels – to watch the love of her life from the platform as he slowly rattles away . . . 'Cue violins' was never more appropriately said. Well, after that he's everywhere, Rach, including on the wireless when Laura is safely and purely back at home with her husband, the poor chap. He doesn't seem to hear what's behind Rachmaninov as he sits quietly doing the crossword. And we, like poor Laura, must sit there and suffer and soar with it, too.

7. *King of Kings* (US 1961, dir. Nicholas Ray)

Imagine, if you will, a row of cinema seats occupied by a dozen pre-pubescent girls who are out on a school trip to see the new film about Jesus in which you actually see Jesus up close, far away, and somewhere in the middle. He is no longer a back view, or a shadow, or even just a bit of lightning on the mountainside – no, this is a real Jesus, looking just as if he has stepped out of a Sunday-school print.

Even more amazingly, this Jesus who walks and talks and eats and everything is played by an actor whom you have only seen playing cowboys up until then: Jeffrey Hunter. The row of pre-pubescent girls yawns a bit in the first scenes – after all, they know the story, the manger, the three kings et cetera et cetera. And there is old John the Baptist banging on about the coming Messiah and stuff. And then, lo! A man appears and looks down on John the Baptist with the bluest eyes in the whole world. Right up close, we look into those eyes, bluer than it is possible to have blue eyes and not be . . . Yes! It is Jesus. And we girls are deeply moved in our row of seats, and deeply confused, because we have all fallen in love with Jesus. With Jesus! And just at that very moment a heavenly choir and some heart-stirring, earth-moving music starts up and the row of us girls is completely and utterly sunk. It is all the fault of Miklós Rózsa who wrote the score for the film, with such heart-twisting verve that we can't get it out of our minds. It is synonymous with love and Jesus and such odd feelings – certainly not religious – that stir in the strangest of our private places as we watch those blue eyes and listen to those shocking chords. We are in the Gaumont Cinema in South Wimbledon and it has never seen anything like this. Nor have we. Or heard anything, either.

Of us all Jeannette Reynolds is the only one rich enough to buy the LP of the music, so we all spend most afternoons after school round at her place playing it and crying a bit and just imagining Jesus and Jeffrey, Jeffrey and Jesus, and thinking, Master, we are yours.

6. *The Magnificent Seven* (US 1960, dir. John Sturges)

Well, if it was confusing to see a cowboy playing Jesus, how much more odd was it to see the King of Siam suddenly bestride a horse and ride over the hill with six other gun-toting, tall-hat-wearing cowboys? And did it matter? No. And why? Because the music that accompanied him and his pals was so glorious that you forgot 'Shall We Dance?' and wanted to Ride Out instead – for the music took you to a place apart from ordinary, mortal westerns and made your heart fairly sing whenever you saw the seven of them ride forth. It was the music for heroes, and every young girl wanted a hero. What Elmer Bernstein did with the music for *The Magnificent Seven* was take the Wild West out of the cowboys and replace it with something grand and imposing and almost spiritual – as if – in cowboy terms – he wanted to reprise his theme from *Exodus*. I was no western fan – girls just weren't – but this movie has stayed close to my heart for those glorious moments when the theme would play (the *Calvera*, Bernstein grandly called it), and breasting the hill would be those seven avenging horsemen – doing good in the saddle, righting wrongs in the one-horse towns and generally showing you that whenever that music played, God was on your side.

5. *Elvira Madigan* (Sweden 1967, dir. Bo Widerberg)

After seeing this movie where the doomed lovers hold hands and run through a field of corn with the sun shining behind them – the world in soft-focus, Elvira wearing a pale, diaphanous gown and her be-ribboned hair flowing free in the breeze – well, the sixties were never the same again. Gone was the healthy cynicism of my political youth, replaced by an overwhelming desire to be dressed in white and running through a field with someone sensitive and gorgeous like Elvira's soldier lover (it was all right, he'd given up the army). And this seditious romanticism was less the fault of director Widerberg than his choice of the slow movement from Mozart's most sublime piano concerto, No. 21, which he juxtaposed with the slo-mo lovers, thereby stitching you up completely. Elvira was sublime and it was one of the saddest, most beautiful moments I ever experienced in the cinema (I was, after all, a teenager). So powerful was the image and its effect on the nation's young women (and the rush on buying Laura Ashley frocks in Elvira-style) that we all went around for weeks attempting to look and feel like Elvira – with ruffled hems and lace-up boots and ribbons in our hair. The Mozart concerto sold out in all the shops and became ever after known as 'Elvira Madigan'. How Wolfgang Amadeus would have loved that . . .

4. *The Dam Busters* (GB 1955, dir. Michael Anderson)

Pre-Suez of course. And significantly the only scenes I remember of this film are the ones where the aeroplanes return from their successful bombing mission and Eric Coates's 'Dam Busters March', designed to stir the hearts of even the most committed Labour voter in 1955, belts it out as they make their fine and British way home. It went deep into the psyche of patriotism and – though I have never seen the movie again – every time I hear the music I'm right back there in the one-and-three's in the Rialto, feeling completely proud of something but I know not what. An experience almost certainly to be filed under the heading of *Beyond the Fringe*'s 'Son, you have been born British and have therefore won first prize in the lottery of life . . .'

3. *Reach for the Sky* (GB 1956, dir. Lewis Gilbert)

This is a companion musical memory to *The Dam Busters* for its patriotic nerve. When Douglas Bader straps on his tin legs

and gets into his little aeroplane and flies off up into the sky to
become a Battle of Britain Ace – to the sound of John
Addison's heroic flying music, well – I was right up there with
him and breaking out in a sweat of painful pride. It is the music
of inspiration – though I don't think I really wanted to be a
pilot – but with those stirring notes under my belt I sure came
out blinking into the sunlight wanting to do *something*. You
just wanted to cheer to the music – some in the cinema did.
Douglas Bader, what a hero, what a moment when he leads the
victory fly-past over London in 1945 and up comes that music
again. Stirs the blood, stiffens the sinews, brilliant, brilliant,
brilliant. I remember being very disappointed some years later
when I saw a photograph of the real Bader and he looked nothing like Kenneth More. Up until then I thought that all battles in the air involved loud music and handsome men.
Movies!

2. *Robin Hood, Prince of Thieves* (US 1991, dir. Kevin Reynolds)

Now comes the truly embarrassing bit, for I cannot claim to
have been a child, pre-teen or teen-proper when this one hit
me between the eyes. How unfortunate to see this movie just
at a point in my own life when I was deeply in love and therefore longing to inspire the same emotions as in the movie's
theme song in the man in my life . . . so many of us women did,
so many of us were disappointed. And how much more unfortunate that Bryan Adams decided to write such a grindingly
sentimental success for this movie which it seemed to be de
rigueur to go and see. With the impossibly slender and beautiful Mary Elizabeth Mastrantonio as Maid Marian the outing
did absolutely nothing for one's ego. Nevertheless, 'Everything
I do (I do it for you)' left not a dry eye in the house. At the end
of the film, rather than a stampede for the door, most of the
audience stood and listened to this stunning piece of schmaltz
as once, long ago, they stood for the National Anthem. My
only excuse is that it obviously did something very, very profound to women's psyches because it topped the pop charts for

sixteen weeks, the longest stint in history. I rest my case. Oh, except to say that many years later I found out that the one moment in the movie that made me forget my lover for a picosecond and concentrate on Kevin Costner – to whit, the moment Marian espies him naked in the water – *it was not Kevin Costner's bum*, but a stand-in's. How absurd, how coy, how low was that?

1. *Henry V* (GB 1944, dir. Laurence Olivier)

Well, of course, when Olivier gave William Walton the brief to write the music for this, the most excitingly filmed bit of Shakespeare ever, it was a case of two gigantic egos in synch, and they matched one another to perfection. The Crispin's Day speech explodes into Walton's score as a very orgasm of heroism ('We few, we happy few, we band of brothers'). In other words, lest the combined talents of Shakespeare and Olivier have failed to arouse you, here's William Walton to shore you up and make your heart fair burst to be English (and sod the French). I love this movie: Kenneth Branagh's version, though a brave failure, wasn't a patch on it (how could you have a King of England with no lips?). Olivier's *Henry V* will never, ever be surpassed, and the music makes that a certainty. Olivier's genius was not only in making the movie and starring in it – but in the choice of Walton, a man even more ruthlessly dedicated to his art than Larry. When he saw this commission he saw God. Lady Walton tells the story of how, when they met, William proposed to her quite baldly and with the proviso that there must be no children. And when she became pregnant, and went to him, he told her to have a termination (nothing must get in the way of the great man) which she did. But she couldn't stop crying. In the end William told his wife that she could choose either the tears or him but she couldn't have both . . . She dried her tears and they lived in harmony ever after. Appalling. But it does not detract one jot from this most famous and successful and spine-tingling of film scores. Whoever said geniuses must be kind?

Ten Movie Soundtrack Cues that Are On My iPod (Not All of Them Westerns)

BY GEORGE PELECANOS

As much as I love rock and soul, I find myself listening to movie soundtrack cues on my iPod more often than any other type of music. I could have gone exclusively with westerns here. But I am trying to broaden my horizons.

10. *Vertigo* (US 1958, dir. Alfred Hitchcock): 'Scene d'Amour' by Bernard Herrmann

As Scottie (James Stewart) waits in a neon-drenched hotel room for Madeleine/Judy (Kim Novak) to emerge from the bathroom wearing the hair, clothing, and make-up of his deceased lover, Herrmann slowly takes us into the most romantic sex-and-death theme ever committed to film. For the impatient, I should say that Novak walks into the room – like a big blonde cat, feral, lovely, and braless – at the 3:38 mark. After Hitch split with Herrmann his films were never again this beautiful or disturbing.

9. *Miller's Crossing* (US 1990, dir. Joel Coen): 'Main Theme' by Carter Burwell

Lyrical, with a touch of Irish instrumentation reflecting the ethnic origin of its gangster characters, the music plays over the credit sequence and a long tracking shot through the woods where Bernie Bernbaum (John Turturro) will eventually beg for his life, asking Tom Reagan (Gabriel Byrne) to 'look into his heart'. The Coens' best film, Burwell's best score.

8. *Assault on Precinct 13* (US 1976, dir. John Carpenter): 'Main Title' by John Carpenter

A handful of notes on a synthesizer, a cheesy drum machine, and it sounds like the director recorded it in his basement. Still, try to forget it. By the time the cop and the con walk side-by-side out of the war zone after the final battle, the theme pulsating into the end credits, this will be permanently burned into your head.

7. *Zulu* (GB 1965, dir. Cy Enfield): 'Zulu', by John Barry

Men who have sat through this film multiple times (yes, we are legion) can sing the theme note for note. I watched *Zulu* with my son when he was very young, and during the last assault he turned to me and said, 'Who are we supposed to be rooting for, Dad?' 'It's complicated,' I replied.

6. *Dead Presidents* (US 1995, dir. Albert Hughes & Allen Hughes): theme by Danny Elfman

The great title theme to the almost-great blaxploitation from the twisted Hughes brothers. Images of legal tender set on fire appear over the credits as the pounding, dramatic music rocks the house. After this, the movie couldn't have lived up to the expectations the music created. But they gave it a good try.

5. *Where Eagles Dare* (US 1968, dir. Brian G. Hutton): score by Ron Goodwin

Martial theme for a completely ridiculous, rousing war film based on an Alistair MacLean novel. I saw this with my father as a boy, and the music has haunted me since. A glassy-eyed Richard Burton looks bored, mows down scores of Nazis, kicks ass atop a cable car, and doesn't seem to know or care that a young Clint Eastwood is stealing his stardom and the film. The perfect cure for a Saturday morning hangover.

4. *Hour of the Gun* (US 1967, dir. John Sturges): score by Jerry Goldsmith

One of the most underrated westerns of the sixties, this is Sturges's second retelling of the Wyatt Earp myth, describing the bloody aftermath of the OK Corral gunfight, and its cost. The final scene between Wyatt (James Garner) and Doc Holiday

(Jason Robards) hits like a punch in the heart. So does Goldsmith's score.

3. *Two Mules for Sister Sara* (US 1970, dir. Don Siegel): 'Main Theme' by Ennio Morricone

Acoustic guitar, Jew's harp, fiddle, a heavenly choir, penny-whistle, and something like the bleating of a cow are a few of the elements present in this bit of genius from Morricone. An Eastwood/Siegel/Budd Boetticher collaboration that should have been better, but has its moments. Watch it for the score.

2. *Bullitt* (US 1968, dir. Peter Yates): 'Changing Gears' by Lalo Schifrin

As a Mopar and a Ford prepare to duel it out on the streets of San Francisco, Schifrin's swinging arrangement creates tension and anticipation over the rumble of muscled-up engines and the fastening of a seatbelt clicked into place. Then Peter Yates delivers the greatest car chase ever filmed. This was the first song I played in my new Mustang GT, purchased last summer. Try to keep your foot off the gas.

1. *The Magnificent Seven* (US 1960, dir. John Sturges): score by Elmer Bernstein

From opening to closing credits, this is the one – the perfect marriage of music to image. The Phoenix Symphony performance on the Koch label, conducted by James Sedares, was Bernstein's preferred recording. 'Now we are seven.'

16

Location, Location, Location

Where it Happens, Why that Matters

GEOFFREY MACNAB: Escalating Genius – The Ten Best Uses of Steps or Staircases

MATT THORNE: No One Under 21 Admitted – Top Ten Movie Nightclubs I Wish Were Real

DANNY LEIGH: This is Not America? – Ten Great American Movies Made by Non-Americans

Escalating Genius

The Ten Best Uses of Steps or Staircases

GEOFFREY MACNAB

Stairways stand for so much in cinema. They are showcases, obstacles, markers of envy, aspiration or decline; playthings for kids, bridges between heaven and earth, excuses for pratfalls; sites for chases or swordfights, symbolic routes into the unconscious, or glorified props in Gothic horror movies. They can be descended in regal pomp or mounted in furtive terror. They can be treacherous or liberating. They can stand for modernity, or for the inescapable past. Inventive directors love to use them. With low-angle shots, you can create giants. With high-angle shots, you can show people scurrying away like rats. They are just far more dramatic than any mere stretch of level ground.

10. James Cagney dies on the steps of the church at the end of *The Roaring Twenties* (US 1939, dir. Raoul Walsh)

Cagney went to some truly memorable movie ends: trussed up and posted through the door in *The Public Enemy* (1931), sent squawking to the gas chamber in *Angels With Dirty Faces* (1938). None of his exits, though, was as poignant as those death-throes in Walsh's *The Roaring Twenties*. After the war-hero turned bootlegger is shot, he lurches through the snow, making it as far as the church. He tries to clamber up, but his energy is going. He falls down dead. 'What was his business?' a cop asks. Gladys George, the gangster's moll cradling his corpse, signs him out with the immortal line: 'He used to be a bigshot.'

9. Meeting Bela Lugosi in *Dracula* (US 1931, dir. Tod Browning)

Browning realized that staircases can't be beaten when it comes to making slow and dramatic entrances. Thus Lugosi's Count: we see him in his cape, walking as if in a trance down the dilapidated stone staircase of his Transylvanian manor. He is holding a candle.

His hair is slicked back. He has the demeanour of a Hungarian waiter. 'I am . . . *Dracoola*,' he intones in that eccentric voice. 'I bid you welcome.'

8. Bobby Henrey peering at the adults in *The Fallen Idol* (GB 1948, dir. Carol Reed)

As if to signal the gulf that separates the adult world from that of the ingenuous young Philippe (Henrey), Carol Reed constantly shows the boy peering at his elders through the bannisters of the long, winding staircase at the French Embassy in London where his parents work. The very first shot finds him occupied thus, and the key moments of the film take place on that staircase. It's down same that the butler's wife falls after losing her footing, thereby convincing the boy that he has witnessed a murder, perhaps committed by his beloved Baines the butler (Ralph Richardson).

7. Arbogast descending the staircase in *Psycho* (US 1960, dir. Alfred Hitchcock)

The killing of Detective Arbogast (Martin Balsam) has an unsettling dream-like quality. We see him walking slowly up the stairs from a high angle. When he reaches the top, a door cracks open, *somebody* steps out, and suddenly he is stabbed repeatedly and falls backward in prolonged slow motion. Gravity seems to be suspended. It is as if he is floating downward with his arms flailing. He could almost be drowning. Only Hitchcock could manage to make a violent slasher scene seem so perversely poetic.

6. A stairway to heaven in *A Matter of Life and Death* (GB 1946, dir. Michael Powell)

Squadron Leader Peter Carter (David Niven), a freak survivor when his Lancaster bomber is shot down, is called before a celestial court to appeal for the right to live. Linking Heaven and Earth is a giant escalator. We're never quite sure whether the stairway to heaven is Peter's hallucination, since he's under anaesthesia. With its depiction of Heaven in monochrome and Earth

in Technicolor, the film teeters on the edge of kitsch. It's the
sheer scope of the visual imagination of Powell and Pressburger
that makes the storytelling compelling. The court-case ends with
the judge and advocates descending to Earth down the escalator
to quiz Carter about whether he really loves June (Kim Hunter),
the young American radio operator. If you want to show what it
is like when young lovers are separated against their will, where
better than on an escalator?

5. The Odessa steps sequence in *Battleship Potemkin* (USSR
1925, dir. Sergei Eisenstein)

Courtesy of the second most-celebrated sequence in cinema history, we're hurled pell-mell into the midst of revolutionary history, and an infamous tsarist massacre. The Odessa townsfolk, who
have been supporting mutineer seamen, are fleeing down the
steps. The czar's soldiers open fire. The corpses mount. A child is
killed. A mother gathers him up in her arms and marches back up
the stairs to confront the soldiers. A woman is shot and releases
her hold on her pram, which starts to clunk and hurtle downward.
What makes the scene so dynamic and so affecting is the montage: the way Eisenstein switches from wide shots to close-ups.
The out-of-control pram stands for the helplessness of the victims
as they struggle down the seemingly interminable set of steps.

4. John Garfield, Hades-bound in *Force of Evil* (US 1948, dir.
Abraham Polonsky)

This is a film about betrayal. Joe Morse (Garfield) has abandoned
his principles to become a lawyer for the mob. His brother Leo
(Thomas Gomez) gave up his chance to become a lawyer so Joe
could get ahead, but now Joe has taken a wrong turn. Leo has
been left to eke out an existence as a small-time operator in the
numbers racket. But Joe fails to protect Leo when he falls foul of
the mob, and Leo is murdered. It is at this point that Joe's guilt
becomes all-consuming.

In the dawn light, we see him descending a vast set of steps. He
is heading toward the river but it is as if he were descending into

Hades. 'I just kept going down and down,' he tells us in his fatalistic voice-over. 'It was like going to the bottom of the world to
find my brother.' It is a melancholy, doom-laden sequence. With
each step downward, the tone of the storytelling becomes yet
darker. For a brief moment – adding to the mythic resonance – he
appears to be the only man in New York City. Eventually, he finds
his brother's corpse on the rocks by the Hudson, '. . . where they
had thrown it away like an old dirty rag that nobody wants.'

3. Laurel and Hardy try to deliver a piano in *The Music Box* (US
1932, dir. James Parrott)

Call it a one-gag film, but that one gag works beautifully. Laurel
and Hardy's Oscar-winning short is Hollywood's version of the
Myth of Sisyphus. Stan and Ollie have to deliver a huge piano to
an apartment at the top of a flight of steps. (The film was shot on
location in Silver Lake, Los Angeles.) Whenever the piano is
hoisted to the top, it comes sliding down again. The two removal
men, like overgrown kids in their boiler-suits and top hats, keep
getting agonizingly close to completing their chore, but that just
makes their continual failures all the more funny and affecting.
The harder they struggle, the angrier their customer, Professor
Theodore Von Schwratzenhoffen, becomes. But with a name like
that he was bound to be angry.

2. Agnes Moorehead has a hysterical fit on the stairs in *The
Magnificent Ambersons* (US 1942, dir. Orson Welles)

The staircase in the Amberson mansion is used both as a symbol
of their magnificence and as a portent of the family's disintegration. In an early sequence we see Georgie Minafer (Tim Holt) in
his white tie, swollen with self-importance, escorting the beautiful Lucy (Anne Baxter) up the steps during a lavish party. Later,
when the family's fortune has dissipated, it is on the same steps
(now shrouded in shadow) that the bitterest encounters of the
film take place. In one of the grimmest scenes, we see Aunt Fanny
(Agnes Moorehead) railing against Georgie and finally admitting
her love for Eugene Morgan (Joseph Cotten), a love she knows

never stood any chance of being requited given Eugene's love for Georgie's mother. 'Oh I was a fool!' she laments. 'Eugene never would have looked at me, even if he'd never seen Isabel.'

1. Barbara Stanwyck descends the stairs in *Double Indemnity* (US 1944, dir. Billy Wilder)

Phyllis Dietrichson (Stanwyck) is first spotted by insurance man Walter Neff (Fred MacMurray) at the top of the staircase of her LA home. Her hair is immaculately coiffed but she is wearing nothing more than a towel. 'If you wait till I put something on, I'll be right down,' she purrs. Cue one of the most erotically charged descents of a staircase in movie history. It's a foot fetishist's delight. Wilder's camera hones in on Stanwyck's shapely ankles and high-heeled shoes as she comes down the steps. Eventually, the camera pulls back to show her in full frame, still ostentatiously buttoning her blouse. It's those ankles which stick in Neff's mind as he is drawn into Dietrichson's murderous web. Wilder even throws in a second sequence of Stanwyck coming down the steps, this time in a new pair of black high heels. As Neff puts it: 'I had a lot of stuff lined up for that Thursday afternoon including a trip down to Santa Monica to see a couple of live prospects about some group insurance, but I kept thinking about Phyllis Dietrichson and the way that ankle of hers cut into her leg.'

No One Under 21 Admitted

Top Ten Movie Nightclubs I Wish Were Real

MATT THORNE

Very few films manage to get nightclubs right. Whether it's Michael Douglas grooving under disco lights in his V-neck sweater (*Basic Instinct*, in case you could forget), or the tendency to cut to a honking saxophone, or the way that the people dancing never seem to be quite in synch with the music – 'club' scenes are, even more so than sex scenes, almost always an embarrassing interruption of the action. The exceptions to this rule are therefore to be cherished. Here's a list of ten highly diverse movie nightspots that, if they actually existed, I would definitely consider visiting.

10. 'Torchy's' in 48 HRS (US 1982, dir. Walter Hill)

'Not a very popular place with the brothers,' announces Eddie Murphy's parolee Reggie Hammond as he enters a redneck bar after accepting a bet from Nick Nolte's mean cop Jack Cates. Amazingly, Hammond then very coolly succeeds in making everybody *else* in the place feel uncomfortable. This ten-minute scene made the film, and Murphy's name. But lest it seem that I'm championing intolerant redneck joints, I should point out that Torchy's is a nightclub that appears under different guises in several of director Walter Hill's films (for instance, it's a stripclub in 1984's *Streets of Fire*), and the 'Torchy scene' is always the high-light of the movie. Besides, I like the name.

9. 'Bob's Country Bunker' in The Blues Brothers (US 1980, dir. John Landis)

This movie was another playground favourite among my particular generation, and the most-recited line was the exchange between Elwood Blues (Dan Aykroyd) and Claire, a patron of the country bar ('What kind of music do you usually have here?' 'Oh, we have both kinds. Country *and* Western.') With the subsequent arrival of 'alt-country', and the critical reclamation of Johnny Cash, Willie Nelson et al., this line has since lost a lot of its humour; and in any case it's harder now to understand why people ever thought that porkpie-hat-and-shades-wearing white blues revivalists represented an acceptable face of modern music. If Bob's Country Bunker did exist, I'd be there with the rednecks throwing bottles at Dan Aykroyd's head.

8. 'The Blue Oyster Bar' in the first four Police Academy films (US 1984–7)

Ask the 1980s generation to name one famous movie nightclub

and it's quite possible the first they'll mention is The Blue Oyster. Quite why this location should be so memorable is a mystery. It only appears in the first four entries to the *Police Academy* series (before the recruits begin their overseas adventures), and is a gay club filled with men dressed up in Kenny Everett-style leathers and Village People costumes. These patrons lie in wait for unsuspecting heterosexuals to enter the bar, only to then force them into dancing a close tango called 'El Bimbo'. It's hard to remember why this was so hilarious (it happens twice in the first film, and at least once in the next three sequels). But really it would be good if this bar were real, so I could trick someone into going there and finding out.

7. Various clubs in the *Blade* Trilogy (US 1998–2004)

I won't claim that the *Blade* films – a series of comic-book adaptations starring Wesley Snipes as a leather-clad vampire hunter – are great art, but all three work as repositories of the best then-current trash culture. From Kool Keith on the soundtrack to Parker Posey at her most throwaway, the set-dressing is all fine-tuned for connoisseurs of junk. Among the many things that make the films so entertaining are their set-piece nightclub scenes: every club in this trilogy seemed realistic and current in a way few other films manage. Okay, so they might be full of *vampires*, but the details are right.

6. 'Eve's' in *Choose Me* (US 1984, dir. Alan Rudolph)

Several Rudolph films have nightclubs that could have made it on to this list, but I'm going to go with Eve's because it is the quintessential 1980s cinema singles bar. Everything about this film comments on promiscuity and the single life, and we learn that even the owner of the club (an ex-hooker played by the ever-fragile Lesley Ann Warren) bought it because it was named for another woman called Eve and not her. *Choose Me* is driven by longing, expressed through radio-call-in loneliness, sad soul, jazz and reggae songs, and the pick-up lines of Keith Carradine as an escaped mental patient. Films present us with alternative lives, and in those lives just as this one we need somewhere to go to meet potential partners. And pick-up joints don't come better than Eve's bar.

5. The 'Terminal Bar' in *After Hours* (US 1985, dir. Martin Scorsese)

Scorsese may have eventually won his Oscar for *The Departed*, but my favourite of his films is among his most underrated: the black comedy *After Hours*, in which Griffin Dunne's decision to try his luck with a girl in a coffee-shop (Rosanna Arquette) leads to his getting trapped all night in New York's SoHo district. It's a film filled with unlikely bars and nightclubs, any of which could have made this list (such as Club Berlin, where they have 'Mohawk Night' – guess what happens to Dunne – and a lonely woman living in the basement). But I'll plump for the Terminal Bar, staffed by John Heard in the most sympathetic role of his career as a kindly bartender who will do anything to keep his patrons happy, even immediately after being informed of his girlfriend's suicide.

4. The club in *Werckmeister Harmonies* (Hungary 2000, dir. Béla Tarr)

The Hungarian Tarr is seen by some as a depressing director, but most of his films have a humorous element, even if only in the way they inspire a profound feeling of 'How is he getting away with this?' As with many art-house directors, Tarr has his characters go to bars and clubs to escape their desperate lives, and among the most amusing is the club at the beginning of *Werckmeister Harmonies*, where János Valuska persuades the patrons to act out a solar eclipse, several drunkards then playing the sun, moon and earth. It would be fun to go to a club where this sort of thing goes on, and the owner gets rid of you by shouting, 'Get out of here, you tubs of beer!'

3. 'The Power and the Glory' in *Twin Peaks: Fire Walk With Me* (US 1992, dir. David Lynch)

David Lynch's films always do something miraculous with music, whether it's managing to make Beck sound cool for the first time in his career (on the soundtrack of *Inland Empire*) or helping German industrialists Rammstein achieve breakthrough success via their churning contributions to the music of *Lost Highway* (1997). Lynch's nightclub scenes usually feature a strange combination of metal, jazz and 1950s standards, but by far the best is The Power and the Glory club in the *Twin Peaks* feature film *Fire Walk With Me*. This is a place where people go to get truly wasted, and where strong drink, drugs and sex are freely available. Serial killers and psychos from the nearby woods mix with experimenting teenagers, and everyone gets something from the exchange. If the Power and the Glory did exist, you might never leave.

2. The cocktail lounge of the Beverly Hills Hotel in *American Gigolo* (US 1980, dir. Paul Schrader)

Gigolo caught the time perfectly upon its release, but it also seems to improve with age. Undoubtedly some of the clubs in the film now look a bit silly, with one key scene between the upscale hustler Julian Kay (Richard Gere) and his erstwhile pimp Leon (Bill Duke) taking place in a venue that oddly resembles *Police Academy*'s Blue Oyster Bar (see above). But the minimal salmon-red-lit lounge where Gere first meets Lauren Hutton is everything that a club should be. Like nearly every other interior in the movie, it was purpose-built on a Paramount sound-stage by the legendary designer Ferdinando Scarfiotti. *American Gigolo* no doubt influenced more than a few real-life American clubs as the 1980s wore on, but really they should have just pinched Scarfiotti's blueprints and replicated this place exactly.

1. The 'Korova Milk Bar' in *A Clockwork Orange* (GB 1971, dir. Stanley Kubrick)

For a reclusive man, Stanley Kubrick was good at coming up with depictions of highly desirable clubs. The jazz bar where Nick Nightingale plays in *Eyes Wide Shut* looks like a very pleasant spot of an evening (all the more extraordinary for being shot in London's somewhat faded Madame JoJo's). But nothing can rival the Korova Milk Bar. I myself am lactose-intolerant, but even I would consider dropping by this stunning venue for a nightcap of milk plus vellocet or synthemesc or drencrom. In fact, and inevitably, several New York clubs have tried to imitate the Korova, right down to its naked mannequin tables, but no imitation could hope to capture quite the sense of excitement and menace in the 'real' thing, with its pop art decor and scary patrons.

This is Not America?

Ten Great American Movies Made by Non-Americans

DANNY LEIGH

Much like the oddity of the current British monarchy in its derivation from the Bavarian Saxe-Coburgs, it's always been one of the ironies of Hollywood that an industry so definitively American has relied on foreigners for its directors – from the earliest days of the studios, the figures calling 'Action!' were as likely to be sons of Tblisi (Rouben Mamoulian) or Whangaroa, New Zealand (Rupert Julian), as Brooklyn or Pittsburgh. Over time a further irony revealed itself – that among the vast range of movies made by non-Americans, many of the most emblematic portraits of American life have been made by those same directors.

Hence this list – but I should say in advance that any number of wonderful films have been omitted here, not for any lack of greatness, but simply for not quite having the same sense of an entire national identity being held under a magnifying glass. Among them (to name but the most obvious examples) you can count Billy Wilder's *Some Like it Hot*, Milos Forman's *One Flew Over the Cuckoo's Nest* and – most grievous for me personally – Charles Laughton's *Night of the Hunter*. The ghost of Robert Mitchum will, I'm certain, shortly be laying a tattooed hand on my shoulder . . .

10. *Mildred Pierce* (US 1942, dir. Michael Curtiz)

The legend goes that Curtiz (born Manó Kertész Kaminer to a

Jewish family in Budapest) never entirely mastered the English language, despite more than three decades in Hollywood: David Niven's autobiography *Bring on the Empty Horses* was named after Curtiz's demand for riderless horses on the set of 1936's *The Charge of the Light Brigade*. Still, having learned his craft in his native Hungary, he swiftly came to terms with the Hollywood mode of production, his versatility making him a mainstay of the studio system. Yet he also had gimlet eye for the character of his adopted homeland – and so it proved with his adaptation of James M. Cain's 1941 novel, and its waspish portrait of a downtrodden single mother's transformation into prosperous restaurateur. With the pursed Joan Crawford in the title role, Curtiz's film was suffused in Americana, from the noir-ish opening on Santa Monica pier to Mildred's ferreting away of her waitressing tips in the homespun Glendale Savings and Trust, her rise to wealth forever soured by her dreadful, grasping daughter Veda – walking proof of the fallacy that America was ever a classless society.

9. *Midnight Cowboy* (US 1969, dir. John Schlesinger)

Of all the downcast American cinema in that curdled period when the sixties bled into the seventies, perhaps the most iconically grim was *Midnight Cowboy* – an autopsy of dreams in a squalid New York, made by John Schlesinger, a middle-class Londoner whose earliest professional experience had come as an actor with the Colchester Repertory Company. And yet a raw authenticity seeped from every frame of Schlesinger's account of the travails of Texan hustler Joe Buck and bronchial conman Ratso Rizzo (Jon Voight and Dustin Hoffman). Partly that was a result of the film having been shot entirely on location, and partly it came from Waldo Salt's pungent script – but it also grew out of cares taken in depicting the resonance of Voight's cowboy get-up, Ratso's relative non-existence in a country of winners, and the pair's ill-fated journey from the verminous East Village to cloudless Miami.

8. *Paris, Texas* (West Germany/France/GB 1984, dir. Wim Wenders)

Born in Düsseldorf in the months after the end of the Second World War, Wenders was raised amid what he calls the 'Americanization of Germany', immersed in the cultural colonization of its music and its movies. As such, it was perhaps inevitable that he would eventually cross the Atlantic to the home of his formative influences. *Hammett* and *The State of Things* (both 1982) proved not the most fulfilling American ventures, before a collaboration with playwright Sam Shepard really planted Wenders on American soil. Opening with Harry Dean Stanton (looking, as always, like a one-man American Gothic), emerging parched and wild-eyed from the desert to search for his lost family, *Paris, Texas* often seemed as much about its vistas of sun-blasted roads and lonely gas stations as it did the shambling figure whose melancholic Odyssey reached its conclusion in (where else?) a strip joint. Wenders's film never quite lost the tinge of European otherness: its very title reflects bi-continental origins and it's tempting to see Stanton's estranged wife Natassja Kinski as the director's onscreen surrogate. But this was a film steeped in America, from the first mournful notes of Ry Cooder's score.

7. *Fury* (US 1936, dir. Fritz Lang)

A director with less integrity than Lang could have been tempted to offer something in the way of soft soap after arriving in America from Hitler's Germany (where he had reputedly been offered the post of head of the German state film studio UFA by Goebbels, in the same breath as being told his masterful *The Testament of Dr Mabuse* was being banned). Lang, however, was nothing if not his own master – and so, for his first Hollywood feature, he made this brutal and brazen denunciation of mob rule. With Spencer Tracy starring as an innocent man arrested for kidnapping, whom twenty-two small-town burghers then attempt to lynch before setting fire to his jail, Lang never flinched in condemning the dreadful juggernaut at the heart of his story: the hate-raddled features of the upstanding citizens hurling lit torches towards their quarry as unfor-gettable as anything the director created in *Metropolis* or *M*. Some may try to claim it as simply an allegory for the traumas then tak-ing place back in Europe – but seventy years after it was made, *Fury* looks a whole lot more literal than that.

6. *The Man With the Golden Arm* (US 1954, dir. Otto Preminger)

Another in the long line of directors who fled Europe in the dark years before the Second World War, the Viennese-born Preminger made a number of films that could be claimed as quin-tessentially American: the woozy *Laura* (1944), for instance, or the caustic *Anatomy of a Murder* (1959). But it was *The Man With the Golden Arm* that brought forth the most vivid account of the dapper, swaggering post-war US. Following the struggle of hep-cat drummer and sometime junkie Frankie Machine to shrug off the monkey on his back, the film's touchstones of jazz, addiction and poker would only grow more and more resonant in the country's self-mythology, while Elmer Bernstein's score soon became sonic shorthand for the American underbelly.

5. *Deliverance* (US 1972, dir. John Boorman)

Springing from that home of British film-making Shepperton, John Boorman decamped to Los Angeles in 1967 to make *Point Blank* with Lee Marvin. By the time he came to *Deliverance*, he seemed to have a gut understanding of the American psyche not generally available to residents of the south-westerly suburbs of London. Revelling in the eternal tension between soft-handed urbanites and insular country folk, Boorman carried that univer-sal dynamic into the uniquely American context of the back-woods of Georgia, creating a nightmare of national identity that was, tellingly, instantly embraced in the US itself. Although the horror movie would shortly annex the concept of prissy city-dwellers terrorized by hillbillies (*The Texas Chainsaw Massacre* et al.), *Deliverance* should always stand as the definitive account of America's terror of its own scenic interior.

4. *All That Heaven Allows* (US 1955, dir. Douglas Sirk)

Sometimes a stranger's gaze is the most acute of all – and few eyes
have been as sharp as Sirk's, born in Hamburg to Danish parents,
whose career in Germany ended when he fled from Hitler to the
US in 1937. While it was only years after his retirement that
their excellence was recognized, the string of gorgeous melodra-
mas that he directed in the 1950s – dismissed as sudsy fripperies
at the time – proved the era's most discreetly radical films. *All
That Heaven Allows* is, perhaps, the finest of them. Visually, its
lush wash of Technicolor seduces as it dazzles, the perfect reflection of prosperous, post-war American society (compare Sirk's
movies with the austere black-and-white-British cinema of the
same period) – and yet behind the curtain, the scene is a little
less appealing. And behind the curtain was always where Sirk
was busiest, showing us a welter of ambiguity beyond the white
picket fences, thirty years ahead of David Lynch's *Blue Velvet*.
Here, the insight was enabled by the illicit May–September
romance between genteel widow Jane Wyman and rough-hewn
gardener Rock Hudson – a plotline Sirk used to spotlight the
shortfalls and compromises of every character on screen, their
lives hemmed in by class and convention.

3. *Sweet Smell of Success* (US 1957, dir. Alexander Mackendrick)

A qualified entry to the list, given that the director of this brilliantly scabrous movie was born in Boston, albeit to Scottish parents. But he was raised in Glasgow, then went on to make some
of British cinema's best-loved films for Ealing Studios (among
them *Whisky Galore!* and *The Ladykillers*). It wasn't until the mid-
fifties (and his own mid-forties) that Mackendrick returned to the
US, following an offer from producers Hecht-Hill-Lancaster to
direct an adaptation of Shaw's *The Devil's Disciple*. Once that project fell through, however, his US debut would be this blistering
account of the machinations of low-life press agent Sidney Falco
as he toadies to demonic columnist J.J. Hunsecker. Years before
the PR industry became inescapable, the film peered in disgust at
a Manhattan of unrestrained ambition, shysterism and back-

scratching, exposing for ever the reality behind New York's feral glamour. *Sweet Smell of Success* was not a film without precedent – despite their apparent joviality, Mackendrick's Ealing comedies always had an eyebrow raised at human behaviour – but its sheer corrosive honesty was all but unique.

2. *Repo Man* (US 1984, dir. Alex Cox)

For all the free-floating weirdness of the US in the early 1980s, only one film truly captured the lunacy of the 'It's Morning in America' era, and that film was *Repo Man*. All the more remarkable, then, that this nigh-on perfect movie was not only a debut feature, but one made by a gangling twenty-nine-year-old from the Wirral. Alex Cox, a graduate film student at Bristol University, decamped for the balmier climes of UCLA film school at the end of the 1970s. And it was Los Angeles with its looping freeways and lack of any real centre that provided the setting for the story of Otto (Emilio Estevez), a 'white suburban punk' who falls in with a firm of repo men – semi-legal, philosophically inclined goons charged with repossessing the cars of defaulting debtors. Cox not only displayed a premonitionary awareness of many of the themes that would fixate us in later years (conspiracy theories, corporate branding, 'the lattice of co-incidence'), he captured an America that a lot of its citizens weren't yet familiar with: one where the evangelical preachers had moved out of the pulpit and on to TV, and middle-class Black Flag fans rebelled by running out on sushi bills.

1. *Chinatown* (US 1974, dir. Roman Polanski)

Water rights and moral rot – the twin foundations of modern California, according to *Chinatown*. While drawing inspiration from the vintage Hollywood tropes of *The Maltese Falcon*, and being based (to some extent) on the Owens Valley water wars of the teens and 1920s, the movie nonetheless reeked of the America of the early 1970s. For a start, there was the presence behind the camera of the French-born Pole Polanski, who had, of course, lost his wife Sharon Tate to the Manson family in 1969 –

the event that more than any other ended the frolics of American hippiedom. (Perhaps understandably, it was Polanksi who pushed for the film's indelibly downbeat ending.) More tellingly still, its portrait of corruption – both political and personal – spoke directly to a country then reeling from Watergate and Vietnam. The sociopath Noah Cross (John Huston) is symbolic of the men who made modern America in their image. Could there be a bleaker conclusion than the sight of his grand-daughter being driven away by the monstrous Cross, he feigning concern over her welfare? 'Forget it, Jake,' Jack Nicholson's stunned private eye J.J. Gittes is told. 'It's Chinatown.' But for Polanski, Chinatown was LA, LA was California – and California was the entire US.

17

Cinema Will Eat Itself

Loving Acts of Self-reference

DAVID THOMPSON: Ten Great Films Watched by Characters in Great Films (So Making an Indelible Impression)

JAMES MOTTRAM: A Two-For-One Offer You Can't Refuse – The Ten Most Diverting Films-Within-Films

Ten Great Films Watched by Characters in Great Films (So Making an Indelible Impression)
DAVID THOMPSON

Any movie-maker who places his or her characters in a cinema to watch a film that then changes their lives is taking a serious risk. For one thing, it smashes our illusion as viewers that the lives of the people we are watching are far too rich and exciting for them to waste time at the movies. It also suggests that the film we have paid to see is just as illusory as the one the characters are seeing. And, worst of all, we might find we wish we too were watching that film instead of the one we find ourselves sitting through. (A friend of mine cites the experience of *Vertigo* as glimpsed in *Twelve Monkeys* . . .)

But quoting movies within movies remains an irresistible plot device for certain screenwriters and directors, and has been around since the birth of the medium. In 1901 R.W. Paul showed a country bumpkin running scared from the screen image of a steam locomotive coming towards him (so consolidating the urban myth that virgin audiences scattered when Lumière's train entered the station). Today we're more likely to observe characters catching an old movie on television, such as *The Quiet Man* in *E.T.* or *It's a Wonderful Life* in *Gremlins* – neither of which qualify for the list for that reason. And one of the best scenes I know involving a cinema audience – Anthony Asquith's stunning silent *Cottage on Dartmoor* – has to be excluded because we never actually see the film on the screen, only reactions on the watching faces.

The titles in the list below are included because the film being watched has such a rapturous effect on its audience that the scene simply couldn't be excluded, or the image left to our imagination. Sometimes the films quoted are very rarely screened, and for many it will be their only chance to see even a glimpse of them. Others are more familiar, iconic even. Today, going to a cinema or watching a film being projected is dangerously becoming a nostalgic act in itself, as was so treacly underlined in *Cinema Paradiso*.

But I don't believe an image on a miniature portable screen will ever have the impact of one greater in size than the spectator, in which you can immerse yourself in every sense. And it's just that delirious power I think all the pictures below truly celebrate.

10. *The Last Picture Show* (US 1971, dir. Peter Bogdanovich)

Like many of the generation of American film-makers who emerged in the seventies, Bogdanovich was keen to express his cinephilia at every opportunity. In his debut *Targets* (1968), he cast Boris Karloff as an ageing horror-movie star made to appear alongside his screen self in the Roger Corman production *The Terror* (1963). Bogdanovich also acted in the film, declaring that all the great movies had already been made. But in his adaptation of Larry McMurtry's novel about a fading Texas town, dead-end lives were beautifully echoed in the closing of the local picture house which is playing Hawks's *Red River*, from which we see the rousing cries that begin the cattle-trek. Everything is in beautiful black-and-white, of course.

9. *Show People* (US 1928, dir. King Vidor)

Vidor's comedy about Hollywood is a droll look at the cult of celebrity, in which a Southern ingenue forsakes her gift for slap-stick comedy to become a new Garbo, until true love shows how much she has misjudged her talent. The stars are now more famous for their off-screen lives: Marion Davies as the mistress of William Randolph Hearst (made to suffer for the allusion made to a tender part of her in *Citizen Kane*), and William Haines black-listed by Hollywood for his open homosexuality. In *Show People* the two attend a preview of their first comic effort together, and a star is born. But Davies insists on staying for the main feature, which turns out to be a swashbuckler made two years earlier by Vidor called *Bardelys the Magnificent*. This is now a 'lost film', and we see a fragment of the only scene in the film Vidor would ever talk about, a romantic tryst in a boat gliding under weeping wil-lows, all of which was entirely improvised on location.

Make Mine a Double: The Ten Best Screen Drunks, p 296

8. *Intervista* (Italy 1987, dir. Federico Fellini)

When he ran out of other subjects, Fellini never seemed to have any trouble looking inwards, making autobiographical fantasies that would integrate the film-making process into their ragged narratives. In *Intervista* he reunites the two stars of his most notorious film, *La Dolce Vita* – a crumpled Marcello Mastroianni and a giantesque Anita Ekberg – and makes them watch their younger selves on an improvised screen, once again at play in the Trevi fountain. It's both a shocking and touching sight to witness the passing of time on these two icons from a former age.

7. *Au Revoir les Enfants* (France 1987, dir. Louis Malle)

In what proved to be arguably Malle's finest film, he told the autobiographical story of his childhood during the Occupation, when he witnessed the Gestapo's arrest of a Jewish boy in his class at school. In one scene the schoolboys are treated to a screening of Chaplin's *The Immigrant*. They laugh heartily at the gags involving the turbulent sea journey, but then fall silent at the sight of the Statue of Liberty. In particular Jean, the Jewish boy being protected by the school, sees for himself the path to freedom and security denied to him by history, one that will be for ever closed off by the end of the film.

6. *The Smallest Show on Earth* (UK 1957, dir. Basil Dearden)

The film that has for ever created the image of the 'fleapit cinema', the type of emporium rendered defunct by television and now utterly divorced from anyone's idea of a place of escape. One night, the young couple who have inherited the decrepit Bijou find the ageing staff indulging in a nostalgia trip, Peter Sellers projecting a silent film accompanied by Margaret Rutherford on the piano. What's curious is the choice of film, Cecil Hepworth's 1922 remake of his earlier hit, *Comin' Thro' the Rye*. Hepworth once ran a thriving studio in Walton-on-Thames, but refused to change his ways in the face of Hollywood and was actually bankrupted by this last gasp of English pastoralism. Today a print exists

in the National Film Archive, minus its last reel, and few have
seen it outside of Dearden's comedy, in which the old-timers
watch it with tearful regret.

5. *Mes petites amoureuses* (France 1975, dir. Jean Eustache)

Eustache, whose awkward career ended in early suicide, followed
his post-1968 intimate epic *La Maman et la Putain* with this semi-
autobiographical account of adolescence in provincial France. The
delicate, natural colours of Néstor Almendros's photography are in
sharp contrast to what the film's protagonist experiences in the cinema – an early scene from Albert Lewin's magnificent Technicolor
folly *Pandora and the Flying Dutchman*. The sight of Ava Gardner
lying on her back, her face in giant close-up, with a diminutive,
ineffectual Nigel Patrick standing in the distance, makes a huge
impact on the dreamy boy – as it did on this spectator at the time
of the film's release, when Lewin's work was hard to see.

4. *Sunset Boulevard* (US 1950, dir. Billy Wilder)

'I am big. It's the pictures that got small.' So protests Gloria
Swanson, once a genuine silent-movie star, now playing an insane
mirror-image of herself in Wilder's bitter requiem to old
Hollywood. To remind herself of past glories, she screens *Queen
Kelly*, a film Swanson starred in and produced, and was directed
by the great Erich von Stroheim, now reduced to screen cameos
like his role as her chauffeur in *Sunset Boulevard*. Swanson
released the film in a truncated version in 1929, but then with-
drew it from the public gaze, so this was the only sight of it we
were privileged to have until a few decades ago.

3. *Sullivan's Travels* (US 1941, dir. Preston Sturges)

This is the one about Joel McCrea as the director of hit comedies
who wants to make his big social statement – a film to be called
O Brother, Where Art Thou?, which, of course, years later was
made by the Coen brothers (sort of). McCrea's determination
leads him to get a taste of the rough life, eventually landing him

on a chain-gang where the only relief from unrelenting misery is a movie show. And when his fellow prisoners laugh their heads off at a Mickey Mouse cartoon, he naturally sees the error of his ways. I saw this film when I was very, very young, and for years I didn't even realize it was a comedy – I only remembered the dark scenes.

2. *Vivre sa Vie* (France 1962, dir. Jean-Luc Godard)

Some might say Godard has made an entire career out of visual and verbal quotation – in the case of *Nouvelle Vague*, he claimed himself that all the dialogue was lifted. In *Les Carabiniers*, he had a character so excited by the flickering image of a woman taking a bath he goes up to the screen for a better look. But no scene has been more affecting than Anna Karina as the doomed prostitute in *Vivre sa Vie* watching the intense close-up of Falconetti in Dreyer's *La Passion de Jeanne d'Arc*, and shedding her own tears to match those of the tormented saint being told about her imminent execution. The silence observed (screenings of silent films at the Cinémathèque Francaise, the temple of the *nouvelle vague*, were always *sans musique*) only adds to the intensity of the moment.

1. *The Spirit of the Beehive* (Spain 1973, dir. Victor Erice)

Erice's magnificent film on the traumas of the Civil War (made at a time when this was still a dangerous subject in Franco's Spain) sees the world through the eyes of little girl Ana, who is so overwhelmed by seeing James Whale's *Frankenstein* that she confuses the reality of a wounded Republican soldier on the run with the doleful countenance of Boris Karloff's tragic monster. Unforgettable.

A Two-for-One Offer You Can't Refuse
The Ten Most Diverting Films-Within-Films

JAMES MOTTRAM

Don't expect cinematic gold in the selection of ten that follows: this list comprises movies that are glimpsed or extracted as discrete works within the fiction of a larger film, but which have no existence outside of that film. All of these mini-movies are deliberately inferior to the framework of the 'host' film that supports them, quite possibly for no reason other than to ensure the ego of the 'real' director remains properly inflated: for as David Thompson has noted, it would be an awful thing were the audience to prefer the shorter effort. The ordering of the ten is designed to reflect which of these invented movies best show up the folly that film-making can so often become.

10. 'Co-Ed Frenzy' in *Blow Out* (US 1981, dir. Brian De Palma).

In De Palma's reworking of Antonioni's *Blow Up* John Travolta plays a sound recordist who gathers atmospheric effects, screams and suchlike for low-grade horror pictures – such as the one that opens *Blow Out*. 'Co-Ed Frenzy' is like a bad version of *Halloween*. A cheeky nod to a genre of which De Palma's 1976 hit *Carrie* was at the centre, it comes complete with heaps of gratuitous nudity. We are with the POV of a knife-wielding killer as he enters a girls' college dorm to find his victim in – where else? – the shower. And yet the joke backfires, for the clumsy voyeurism on show only serves as a reminder of De Palma's own lurid style of directing when properly on duty.

9. 'Home For Purim' in *For Your Consideration* (US 2006, dir. Christopher Guest)

At the core of Christopher Guest's comedy about what happens when a low-budget film begins to garner Oscar buzz is 'Home For Purim', a 1940-set melodrama about the Pischers, a Jewish family from Georgia. As we discover, the clan's matriarch Esther (played by Marilyn Hack, an over-the-hill actress last heard voicing a cartoon character called 'Pimples') is terminally ill and the Pischers realize this may be the last time they celebrate the festive Purim holiday together. An 'extraordinarily poorly written movie', according to Guest, but only made more so when the studio head (Ricky Gervais) asks if its 'Jewishness' can be toned down.

8. 'Stab' in *Scream 2* (US 1997, dir. Wes Craven)

Opening the sequel to Craven's modern horror classic, 'Stab' is an adaptation of 'The Woodsboro Murders', journalist Gale Weathers's account of the events in the original *Scream*. Smartly reprising *Scream*'s first murder wherein Drew Barrymore's luckless victim was gutted 'like a fish' by the ghost-mask-wearing killer, the excerpt from the gratuitous Hollywood version sees Heather Graham, a poor-man's Drew if ever there was one, in the victim role. Furthering its self-reflexive nature, Tori Spelling is cast as the 'Stab' version of principal *Scream* character Sidney, thus making true Sidney's prediction in *Scream* that, knowing her luck, the *Beverly Hills 90210* star would wind up playing her in a movie.

7. 'O Brother, Where Art Thou?' in *Sullivan's Travels* (US 1941, dir. Preston Sturges)

More a treatment-within-a-movie, we never discover much about pompous director John Sullivan's intended picture other than its title and his stated intention that it will be 'a commentary on the human condition', and thus a radical about-turn from the musicals on which he's built his career. Doubtless Preston Sturges revelled in taking a swipe at the social-realist pictures of the time, while simultaneously hailing the healing powers of the lighter fare for which he was renowned. For as he makes Sullivan come to realize, 'There's a lot to be said for making people laugh.'

6. 'The Dancing Cavalier' in *Singin' in the Rain* (US 1952, dir. Stanley Donen & Gene Kelly)

At the heart of Hollywood's most enduring musical is a wretched-looking swashbuckler that, mid-production, is changed from a silent to a talkie after the success of *The Jazz Singer* shakes up the industry irreparably. But when test audiences guffaw at Lina Lamont's squeaky voice and co-star Don Lockwood's terrible improvising in a romantic clinch (a parody of silent icon John Gilbert), it's then improbably turned into a musical-comedy: 'The Dancing Cavalier'! Almost certainly a reference to 1928 silent

The Cavalier, notable only for the addition of several poorly dubbed songs to cash in on the advent of sound, one thing's for sure: it's no *Singin' in the Rain*.

5. 'The Orchid Thief' in *Adaptation* (US 2002, dir. Spike Jonze)

Charlie Kaufman's brilliant script about a tortured screenwriter – himself, no less – hired to adapt Susan Orlean's 1998 bestseller about a maverick Florida orchid collector offers a fresh take on the whole movie-within-a-movie concept. As the real Kaufman puts it, 'You're watching a movie he's writing as he writes it', with scenes from Orlean's book intercut with Charlie's struggle to realize them. By the final act, with the conclusion to 'The Orchid Thief' cramming in sex, car chases and guns – all the 'movie shit' that the noble Charlie despises – his script has undergone an all-too-familiar adaptation, morphing into a 'Hollywood product' at the expense of its artistic integrity.

4. 'The Purple Rose of Cairo' in *The Purple Rose of Cairo* (US 1985, dir. Woody Allen)

John McTiernan's *The Last Action Hero* (1993) had a boy getting sucked into a movie, but only served to prove that Woody Allen had done things the right way round in his Depression-era comedy that sees a character called Tom Baxter literally step out of a film and off a movie screen, into the life of movie-loving housewife Cecilia (Mia Farrow). His act is less surprising given that the film in question is a featherweight black-and-white romantic adventure about a bored playwright who brings Baxter's explorer back to New York for 'a madcap Manhattan weekend'. His departure stalls the picture, the rest of the characters unable to finish the story without him, but this feels like nothing short of a mercy killing.

3. 'Meet Pamela' in *Day for Night* / *La Nuit Américane* (France/Italy 1973, dir. François Truffaut)

Winner of the 1973 Oscar for Best Foreign Film, Truffaut's affectionate valentine to the madness that is movie-making gently sent up his own work with 'Meet Pamela'. Truffaut emphasized the point by playing the film's director Ferrand, his project proving to be an overwrought melodrama about an illicit love affair between an English bride and her new French father-in-law. Certainly it doesn't shape up as the masterpiece Ferrand hoped for: as he puts it, 'Shooting a movie is like a stagecoach ride in the Old West. At first you hope for a nice trip. Soon you just hope to reach your destination.'

2. 'Habeas Corpus' in *The Player* (US 1992, dir. Robert Altman)

'No stars, no Schwarzenegger, no pat Hollywood ending,' says screenwriter Tom Oakley. 'This is an American tragedy.' But by the time Altman's savage Hollywood satire concludes with the ending of 'Habeas Corpus' screened for executives, Oakley's story of an innocent woman going to the gas chamber has been mangled in the studio mill. With Julia Roberts 'cast' in the central role, her character moments from death, there is a reprieve. In bursts her beloved, played by Bruce Willis, who hacks through the glass chamber with an axe. 'What took you so long?' says she. 'Traffic was a bitch,' he quips. The perfect Hollywood pay-off.

1. 'Living in Oblivion' in *Living in Oblivion* (US 1995, dir. Tom DiCillo)

The ultimate film about the frustration of film-making, DiCillo's comedy also summed up just how bad American independent movies can be. Although we're never given a clear idea of the subject of the picture we see being made, the main scene shown to us is a dream sequence that feels like it never made the final cut of *Twin Peaks*. In a red room the famished bride-to-be Nicole is circled by Tito, a dwarf holding an apple that she is unable to reach. 'Is that the only way you can make this a dream? Put a dwarf in it?' rages Tito at the director. 'The only place I've seen dwarves in dreams is in stupid movies like this!'

18

Spoiler Alert!

Narrative Turns, Stings and Endings

MATT THORNE: Heeeere's Mommy! – Ten Great Twists in the Tail

RICHARD T. KELLY: Judas Kisses – Ten Terrible Betrayals

DANNY LEIGH: Commended to Heaven – Ten Great Funerals

GEOFFREY MACNAB: The Wind Blows Where It Will – Ten Wholly Unexpected 'Grace Notes'

ANTHONY QUINN: The Ten Best Movie Endings

Heeeere's Mommy!

Ten Great Twists in the Tail

MATT THORNE

There's no Oscar for Best Twist. And though a script with a twist can make a good calling-card for a screenwriter, only M. Night Shyamalan has tried to make a whole career out of surprising his audience thus. Robert Zemeckis (who made a twist-picture of his own, *What Lies Beneath*) used to argue in interviews that most American audiences hate to be surprised, and would rather know exactly what's going to happen in a film before they see it. Whether this is true or not, it's a good deal harder to hide a good twist these days, what with so many amateur internet movie reviewers – not to mention trailers that seem increasingly to reveal the whole plot. I will try to leave the mystery intact in the following list of favourites.

10. *Angel Heart* (US 1987, dir. Alan Parker, scr. Alan Parker, from the novel *Fallen Angel* by William Hjortsberg)

Undeniably a travesty of Hjortsberg's novel, Parker's film scrapes on to the list for sheer camp appeal as much as anything else (and in spite of such insanely obvious winks as naming its private-detective protagonist 'Harry Angel', and his saturnine employer 'Louis Cyphre'). Mickey Rourke and Robert De Niro turn in outrageously hammy performances, and it's hard to discern whether anyone on set was taking the venture seriously. But this is an essential aspect of the twist film: a few may make it into the canon, but mostly the genre is one of guilty pleasures, the sorts of films that make you smile when you think about them later.

9. *Society* (US 1989, dir. Brian Yuzna, scr. Rick Fry & Woody Keith)

The DVD of this film has a truly disgusting cover: the face of a rich libertine emerging from the backside of someone else's body. But

when the film was first released theatrically it worked so well precisely because it looked like an average 1980s teen flick. 'Star' Billy
Warlock was a bland youth known from TV's *21 Jump Street* and
Baywatch, director Brian Yuzna was a largely unknown quantity,
and the original glossy poster (a leggy female behind a mask) suggested that while the picture might offer a satire on personal image,
it was unlikely to achieve great depth. Indeed, for the first hour
Society seems to be about not much more than a paranoid teenager's
fear that he doesn't fit in with everyone around him. When he finds
out precisely why, the film turns out to be a sick masterpiece,
among the most subversive Hollywood releases of all time.

8. *The Crying Game* (GB 1992, dir/scr. Neil Jordan)

A film that has become so firmly a part of cinema history that it
could conceivably be parodied in sketch shows for ever, *The
Crying Game* is included here for the quality of the twist rather
than the film itself. Twist films are like jokes: if the construction
isn't perfect, it doesn't work. For that reason they rarely stand up
to more than a second viewing. Neil Jordan's film, which begins
as a psychological thriller about a conscientious IRA volunteer
(Stephen Rea at his least annoying) does go on to something
interesting about gender identity, but for most viewers it's about
one shock moment (in the same way *Basic Instinct* can be reduced
to the interrogation scene alone).

7. *Unbreakable* (US 2000, dir/scr. M. Night Shyamalan)

As mentioned above, Shyamalan has made his career out of twist
pictures, each more ludicrous than the last. For some *The Sixth Sense*
is his only good movie, but I guessed that twist from looking at the
poster, so it didn't work for me. *Unbreakable* is no masterpiece, but
the twist (which was borrowed for the US TV hit *Heroes*) does manage to surprise, and unlike the later *Signs* or *The Village* feels like the
result of careful construction rather than narrative desperation. It's
also the closest Hollywood has come to a grown-up superhero film,
and has an expertly judged performance from Bruce Willis as the
seemingly average man who discovers he's invincible.

6. *The Usual Suspects* (US 1995, dir. Bryan Singer, scr.
Christopher McQuarrie)

Singer's decision to waste his career on average superhero films
has taken the shine off his earlier work, including *The Usual
Suspects* and the underrated *Public Access*, but no list of best twists
would be complete without this influential thriller. The film's big
question: Who is Keyser Soze? And how does he fit into the elaborate criminal conspiracy retold by Verbal Kint (Kevin Spacey) to
a pair of gullible cops? What's great about this twist is that not
only does it utterly destroy everything that's gone before (so that
almost any interpretation of the action can be justified) but that
it does so in a satisfying way. It's a small screenwriting miracle –
not just the utilization of an unreliable narrator in a cinematic
context, but a liberating deconstruction of conventional narrative expectation.

5. *The Game* (US 1997, dir. David Fincher, scr. John D.
Brancato & Michael Ferris)

The jury's out on Fincher. Does 2007's *Zodiac* mark a return to the
form of *Se7en*, *The Game* and *Fight Club* or is it another disappointment like *Panic Room*? The man himself is oddly dismissive of much
of his own work, including *The Game*, my favourite of his films,
which he reckoned to be nothing more than an average episode of
the *Twilight Zone*. Similar to John Fowles's *The Magus*, this is an
example of storytelling as a grand joke, a god-game where minted
financier Nicholas Van Orton (Michael Douglas) is made to suffer
by the malevolent CRS company, allegedly a corporate entertainment firm engaged on his behalf as a birthday gift from black-sheep
brother Conrad (Sean Penn). The ending is so outrageous that it
takes several viewings before it makes sense, and emerges as the
only way to conclude such a brilliantly executed joke.

4. *April Fool's Day* (US 1986, dir. Fred Walton, scr. Danilo
Bach)

It may seem perverse to place a seemingly undistinguished slasher movie so high in this list, but what initially seems like just another routine frightener based around a scary date in the calendar (cf. *Halloween* or the *Friday the 13th* series) is revealed in its final minutes to be something else entirely. Deborah Foreman plays both party-host Muffy and her homicidal twin sister Buffy, as a group of friends get together to celebrate her April-first birthday only to find themselves massacred one by one. The clue is in the title, but as the various victims get up and wipe the fake blood from their bodies, revealing themselves to be unharmed, the filmmakers both satirize the whole notion of slasher films and succeed in making something far more disturbing.

3. *Das Cabinet des Dr. Caligari* (Germany 1920, dir. Robert Wiene, scr. Hans Janowitz & Carl Mayer)

Every film that ends with its protagonist in an insane asylum owes a debt to this silent movie. 'And then I woke up and it was all a dream . . .' may be an ending detested by many viewers but it's one that Hollywood continues to use as a get-out-of-jail card. (It's also been used in TV programmes from *Dallas* to *Buffy the Vampire Slayer* to recent hit *Lost*.) But as well as originating the device, Wiene's film uses it brilliantly, a (literally) nightmarish tale of madness, murder and (temporary) redemption through love as a seemingly deranged doctor wreaks havoc in a German mountain village.

2. *Spoorloos / The Vanishing* (Netherlands/France 1988, dir. George Sluizer, scr. Sluizer and Tim Krabbé from his novel *The Golden Egg*)

We return to the chief problem with a list of Top Twists, namely that it's hard to discuss the films without giving away what makes them great. If you haven't yet seen any of these ten, ignore the descriptions and rent the films straight away. But be warned, for those of a certain sensibility *The Vanishing* is the most frightening film ever made. The story of one man's test to see whether he can perform an act of true evil so as to balance out a good deed features an ordinary villain far more chilling than hammy old Hannibal Lecter. Life's final twist, of course, is death, and whatever (if anything) comes afterward. The best twists play on that fear, and the final moments of Sluizer's one masterpiece remind the viewer that there's one thing worse than being buried . . .

1. *Psycho* (US 1960, dir. Alfred Hitchcock, scr. Joseph Stefano from the novel by Robert Bloch)

The most wonderful thing about Alfred Hitchcock (like William Shakespeare) is that while the whole world recognizes his genius, there are still moments of sheer perversity in his work that continue to delight far longer than the efforts of safer talents. It seems extraordinary that a film as playful as *Psycho* – in which Anthony Perkins presides over the Bates Motel, a temporary rest-stop where rest becomes permanent – has become central to the celluloid canon. But its influence is inescapable, and the film's two body-blows (the ostensible heroine's disappearance and the final reveal) remain as glorious as ever, impossible to replicate in any of the film's many sequels, or indeed any of the slasher movies that have tried to ape its brilliance.

Judas Kisses

Ten Terrible Betrayals

RICHARD T. KELLY

Why did Judas Iscariot do it? Because he was fated to? Surely not just for thirty pieces of silver? Out of disappointment, perhaps, in his oddly passive master, or from an envy that curdled into hatred? Maybe the Devil just made him. Or possibly the motives lay deeper still: 'In the lost boyhood of Judas,' wrote George Russell, 'Christ was betrayed.' Whatever moral the fabulists of the Gospels intended us to draw, they certainly laid down a memorable template for the particular drama of one man (or woman) being brutally unfaithful to his or her fellow. These, then, are ten immemorial movie moments of deception, desertion, double-crossing and delivering up of one's friend to the enemy. As to the question of

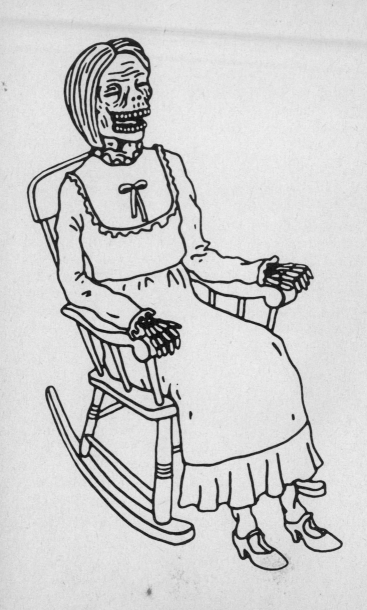

Heeeere's Mommy!: Ten Great Twists In The Tail, p 419

whether said friend actually deserved such a fate – well, that I leave to your own moral accounting.

10. Of each other by Countess Livia Serpieri (Alida Valli) and Lt Franz Mahler (Farley Granger) in *Senso* (Italy 1954, dir. Luchino Visconti, scr. Luchino Visconti, Suso Cecchi d'Amico, Carlo Alianello, Giorgio Bassani, & Giorgio Prosperi, from the novella by Camillo Boito)

'He's a bastard, yes, but I can change him': so runs the timeless female romantic fantasy, which can only be indulged for so long. In Visconti's heady, operatic masterpiece it drives Countess Livia to betray not just her elderly husband but her country – and in 1866 of all moments, as a resurgent Italian nationalism mobilizes against occupying Austria. The tumultuous times fail to register with Livia once she has encountered Austrian lieutenant Mahler after a performance of *Il Trovatore* at La Fenice. He's merely a beautiful shyster, but she can't stop herself falling. After he deserts, she shelters him and steals money meant for Garibaldi's partisans so that he might bribe his way back to civilian life. The reward for her steadfastness will be to stumble upon him cheating on her with a Veronese whore – whereupon the scales fall from her eyes, her own excusable betrayal being to take the matter to Mahler's commanding officer.

9. Of Walker (Lee Marvin) by Mal Reese (John Vernon) and Lynne Walker (Sharon Acker) in *Point Blank* (US 1967, dir. John Boorman, scr. Alexander Jacobs, David Newhouse & Rafe Newhouse, from the novel *The Hunter* by Richard Stark)

Implacable Walker, clacking down endless corridors, fists and Magnum pistol at the ready: he *really* wants the 93,000 dollars he's owed. Is it just the money? Or the size of the wound left in his gut by Mal and Lynne? Shot and left for dead in a squalid stone cell on Alcatraz island, he had time to reflect on the ignominy: betrayed not just by his pal Reese (John Vernon, never to be trusted), and for gambling debts of all the lousy things – but by his faithless, seemingly lovely wife. It's in these flashbacks that we glimpse a lighter side to Walker (and to Lee Marvin), admiring Sharon Acker as she twists her hair in the rain, the two of them breasting the waves on some beach vacation in happier times.

8. Of Han Solo (Harrison Ford) by Lando Calrissian (Billy Dee Williams) in *Star Wars Episode V: The Empire Strikes Back* (US 1980, dir. Irvin Kershner, scr. Lawrence Kasdan & Leigh Brackett)

'I've just made a deal that will keep the Empire out of here for ever.' So the suave Calrissian tells his old pal Solo as they stride the gleaming corridors of the mining colony he manages on 'Cloud City'. Solo is under the impression he's found a sanctuary for himself and his newly beloved Princess Leia, but should he really have expected kindness from a man he has cheerfully described as a 'scoundrel'? In due course a door swishes wide to reveal a gleaming Darth Vader with bounty hunter Boba Fett ('We would be *honoured* if you would join us'). It wasn't until the next film in the series that Solo got rescued while Calrissian redeemed himself by joining the Rebel Alliance, a stroke that probably saved Billy Dee Williams from a lot of abuse at *Star Wars* fan conventions.

7. Of Noodles Aaronson (Robert De Niro) by Max Bercovicz (James Woods) in *Once Upon a Time in America* (US 1984, dir. Sergio Leone, scr. Sergio Leone, Leonardo Benvenuti, Piero De Bernardi, Enrico Medioli, Franco Arcalli & Franco Ferrini, from the novel *The Hoods* by Harry Grey)

'When you've been betrayed by a friend,' says Max, 'you hit back.' Thirty years ago he stole Noodles's sweetheart and his savings; yet Noodles believed Max was dead, as a result of his own botched effort to get his pal arrested and safely off the streets. Now a crooked politician facing disgrace, Max offers Noodles the chance to cut him down and settle the debt. It's a good job that Leone's Jewish gangster epic – brutal and Proustian by turns – dwells on the shared childhoods of these two, or else we would wonder how they ever got friendly. It's the heaviness of Time the enemy that we feel between them more than the onus of friendship – that and the heaviness of De Niro, who went back on the pasta and ice-cream to play pension-age Noodles. Still, in a poignant outcome Noodles spurns the gun and chooses instead to live by his preferred version of events: 'I had a friend, a dear friend. I turned him in to save his life . . . but he was killed. But he wanted it that way. It was a great friendship. It went bad for him, and it went bad for me too.'

6. Of Michel Poiccard (Jean-Paul Belmondo) by Patricia Franchini (Jean Seberg) in *A Bout de Souffle / Breathless* (France 1960, dir. Jean-Luc Godard)

'*Qu'est-ce que c'est, "degueulasse"?*' she asks the policemen as they all stand over Michel's body. His last muttered words were a curse on lousy fate, but the cops have decided the late M. Poiccard was talking about her – Patricia, *l'Americaine*. He watched her on the Champs-Elysées yelling '*New York Herald Tribune!*' and, in his insouciant movie-mad way, chose her to be his moll – after all, she has such a lovely neck. She is clearly the adult of the pair, he the feckless junior; and yet, strictly speaking, he's a crook and a cop-killer. What is she really thinking when she's with him? That she's on an interesting outing? Upon reflection she makes her decision on whether to betray him to *les flics* into a test to determine if she loves him or not: a cold choice, and a rotten shame, for Belmondo and Seberg make such a timelessly beautiful couple that with a happier ending the English title could as easily have been 'Deathless'.

5. Of Michael Corleone (Al Pacino) by Fredo Corleone (John Cazale) in *The Godfather, Part II* (US 1974, dir. Francis Ford Coppola)

In Italian families of multiple brothers it is said to this day: 'There's always a Fredo . . .' By no means a man of action, Fredo Corleone is also sadly deficient as a liar. This much becomes forcibly clear to his 'kid brother' Michael in the surroundings of the sleazy Havana sex club where Fredo leads him and some visiting US senators. As the live show starts, Fredo can't seem to stop himself from blurting out that he was introduced to this joint by Johnny Ola, henchman to Michael's mortal enemy Hyman Roth – and someone he was treating as a stranger earlier that same evening. Per family tradition, Michael succeeds in letting nobody know what he's thinking until the stroke of New Year when he seizes his brother's face: 'I know it was you, Fredo. You broke my heart.' Fredo's subsequent attempts to rationalize his treachery ('I'm your older brother, Mike, and I was stepped over . . . I'm *smart* and I want *respect*') are so pitiful as to stall our sympathies, even though we know Michael's awful intentions.

4. Of Jose Dolores (Evaristo Márquez) by Sir William Walker (Marlon Brando) in *Queimada! / Burn!* (Italy/France 1968, dir. Gillo Pontecorvo, scr. Franco Solinas)

1845, the Caribbean island of Queimada, and lowly bag-carrier Jose Dolores gets off his knees to lead a popular revolt against colonial Portugal. But the hidden author of the uprising is Walker, agent provocateur for the British Admiralty. Having found in Jose a man of unyielding spirit, he further instructs him in generalship: camaraderie blooms over shared swigs from a canteen, and we get the related pleasure of watching charismatic amateur Márquez clashing with Brando at his most exquisitely high-nosed. It is only after Jose has trooped his guerrillas into the capital of the new republic that he sees how Walker serves other, higher powers – Her Majesty, and the big sugar exporters. When Walker returns to Queimada ten years later, now in the pay of the Antilles Royal Sugar Company, Jose is an outlaw. Walker sends messengers to carry Jose a peace-offering canteen. Corpses come back, with a scrawled warning: 'I will drink no more, Englishman.' Though Walker, touchingly, intends to be magnanimous, Jose is resolved to die a martyr, the better to inspire other men of spirit; and one such will be waiting for Walker with a knife as he tries to hasten from the island.

3. Of Rosemary Woodhouse (Mia Farrow) by Guy Woodhouse (John Cassavetes) in *Rosemary's Baby* (US 1968, dir. Roman Polanski, scr. Roman Polanski, from the novel by Ira Levin)

Struggling actor Guy strikes surely the paltriest deal with the devil one could ever envisage: a part on TV's *Miami Beach* is his seeming reward for having leased his wife's womb to the Evil One. Guy would have been a great part for Robert Redford, as was one-time hoped, but it was the unsmiling Cassavetes who wound up playing Mia Farrow's graceless husband. We see the Woodhouses are a little at odds with one another as they move into a subtly menacing old New York apartment building; yet Guy fits right in, even with batty old neighbours Minnie and Roman Castavet. Soon his career is picking up, albeit due to another's misfortune, and Rosemary is pregnant, though she has but half-memories of conception night having been rather hellish. Guy and the Castavets prevail upon her to dump her polite young obstetrician Dr Hill for an avuncular cove called Abe Sapirstein: all in a day's work, we fear, for a coven wishing Satan's spawn into the world . . . and yet the picture is working so well because of Farrow's gamine figure and pale eyes, and Polanski's sharp evocation of the vulnerability of pregnancy. So isn't it possible that Rosemary is just imagining the whole thing? Yes – up to a point.

2. Of Riquet (Fabrizio Rongione) by Rosetta (Emilie Dequenne) in *Rosetta* (Belgium 1999, scr./dir. Jean-Pierre Dardenne & Luc Dardenne)

Possibly the finest film-makers at work today, the Dardenne brothers locate their stories in the unlovely post-industrial outskirts of Liege and hinge them upon huge moral questions. Teenage Rosetta lives on a muddy caravan site with her alcoholic mother. She would like to have a friend, but a job, however lousy, is vital if she's not to be consigned for ever to the underclass. She attracts Riquet, an affable lad with a warm flat and a motorbike, but what she likes best about him is his job at an underpass waffle-stand, where he runs a small scam selling home-cooked wares. In a moment of unbearable tension, Rosetta goes to Riquet's boss, exposes his fiddle, and usurps his place behind the counter. For a while she is happy, feeling she has a place in the world. But each night as she locks up she hears the angry rasp of Riquet's bike in the underpass; and as she trudges home, he dogs her steps, his face a mask of virulence. 'You could say that to betray someone is to kill them – even to kill oneself,' Luc Dardenne once told me in interview. 'And that's the violence of Rosetta's world, that she could even contemplate the question, "Could I – should I – betray my only friend?"'

1. Of Professor Quadri (Enzo Tarascio) by Marcello Clerici (Jean-Louis Trintignant) in *Il Conformista* / *The Conformist* (Italy/France/West Germany 1970, dir. Bernardo Bertolucci, scr. Bernardo Bertolucci from the novel by Alberto Moravia)

He spends much of the movie in the freezing back seat of a sedan, the brim of his fedora low, seemingly trying to disappear into his coat-collar. Film noir is all over *The Conformist*, not least in its flashback structure (devised by editor Kim Arcalli). But the time present is 1938, and civil servant Clerici is an odd recruit to Mussolini's intelligence service: a turning worm who believes he can hide the shame that haunts him (for his childhood killing of a pederast chauffeur) behind some cloak of 'normality'. The mission to which he commits is to abet the 'liquidation' of his former professor, now a Marxist dissident in Paris, whom he must first befriend anew. Yet Marcello seems to know the betrayal will bring doom down upon more than one party ('I confess today for the crime I'll commit tomorrow'). So why does he proceed? He has been seduced, perhaps, by the chilly allure of fascist Rome's imperial-modernist grandeur. But in Paris Quadri's sensuous wife Anna (Dominique Sanda) embodies a different allure. Clerici desires her, while fighting the attraction. She sees through him, while hoping her appeal will be her and her husband's salvation. When she sees Clerici truly – and for the last time – through the window of that sedan on which she hammers hopelessly, we are near to an awful denouement.

On the matter of betrayal, a true-life footnote: the address in Bertolucci's film given as Quadri's (17 Rue St Jacques) was then the real residence of Jean-Luc Godard, who had been Bertolucci's idol since *A Bout de Souffle*. Their friendship cooled around the same time Bertolucci arranged financing for *The Conformist* with Paramount; yet the two made a date in Paris to discuss the finished film. In the event Godard merely left Bertolucci a note, a picture of Mao overwritten with the legend, '*Il faut lutter contre la capitalisme et l'individualité*': proof that life is too short to remain on Godard's good side.

Commended to Heaven

Ten Great Funerals

BY DANNY LEIGH

Executed with sufficient aplomb, the movie funeral can be so much more than a mere plot point – with its time-worn sense of ceremony and overtones of grief and regret, the spectacle of mourners clustered around a bleak graveside should provide the artful film-maker with the perfect union of visual spice and emotional clout. In common with most major religions, funerals are something at which the movies excel – and I hope the list that follows gathers together a goodly number of the most memorable examples.

10. *The Godfather, Part II* (US 1974, dir. Francis Ford Coppola, scr. Francis Ford Coppola & Mario Puzo)

In every end, a beginning – and so it proves with perhaps the most celebrated sequel in film history, as we find ourselves observing a rustic Sicilian funeral, circa 1901. A ragged band of musicians perform a dirge as they make their way across the parched landscape (Coppola's and Puzo's script describes them as emerging 'seemingly from out of hundreds of years of the past'), while a rough coffin is held aloft by the pallbearers, behind it a grieving widow, her arm around a young boy. Then, from some unknown vantage point, there is gunfire – and, as the mourners scatter, screams. Another boy lies dead: Paolo, the widow's eldest son, child of the man whose funeral this was, Antonio Andolini – the father killed by the local Don in the name of an 'insult', the son to prevent him exacting revenge. And now only one son remains, the 'dumb-witted' Vito; timid, near-mute, and nine years old – the child who will, one day, grow up to be Don Corleone.

9. *Brazil* (GB 1985, dir. Terry Gilliam)

'There's been a little complication with my complication,' the luckless Mrs Terrain announces to Sam Lowry (Jonathan Pryce) after her latest disastrous plastic surgery, her grisly decline under the knife a running joke in Gilliam's often uncomfortably prescient satire of a totalitarian Britain. The punchline comes in a gaudy Vegas-style chapel complete with an underlit platform, upon which her gift-wrapped coffin slowly revolves; into this sickly spectacle bursts Lowry, escaping torture at the offices of Information Retrieval. Here he finds his mother in the front row of the mourners, but with *her* various surgeries having transformed her into an Oedipally-charged likeness of Sam's true love. Yet before this psychic violation can even sink in, the funeral is stormed by state troopers, their arrival causing a panicked Sam to dislodge the coffin so that its grim, unrecognizable contents spill on to the floor. Probably the most nightmarish scene on this list, strangely rendered only more so by the fact that it's not actually happening – the whole thing taking place in Sam's imagination as he remains captive at Information Retrieval.

8. *The Third Man* (GB 1949, dir. Carol Reed)

Every funeral needs a corpse; whether it belongs to the name on the headstone is another matter. So discovers the hapless Holly Martins (Joseph Cotten) after his arrival in post-war Vienna 'happy as a lark and without a cent' in Reed's acid interpretation of Graham Greene's screenplay. With the first afternoon of his jaunt to Europe spent in a frostbitten cemetery for the unexpected funeral of his old pal and supposed sponsor Harry Lime, Martins finds a gaggle of haggard mourners around the grave – among them a watchful British intelligence officer (played, without any discernible movement of the lips, by Trevor Howard) and Harry's broken-hearted girl, Anna (Alida Valli). For Holly, who just hours earlier was disembarking a train in the happy expectation of a job with the same friend whose coffin he's now throwing dirt over, this is only the first unpleasant surprise he will suffer in Vienna: by his return to the same graveyard at the end of the film, he will have realized what was really being buried here – friendship and truth.

7. *The Funeral* (US 1996, dir. Abel Ferrara)

The only open-casket affair in our list, the body therein being multi-tasking controversialist Vincent Gallo, cast as Johnny Tempio, the youngest of a trio of gangster brothers in 1930s New York. Having found himself torn between American communism (not always the oxymoron it might appear to modern eyes) and the more worldly appeal of a mobster's life, Johnny has been mown down at the age of twenty-two; now, he's being primped by undertakers in readiness for his last farewell. With the entire film taking place in advance of the funeral itself (the story unfolding in flashbacks throughout), the presence of director Abel Ferrara's flawed modern classic here could be considered something of a cheat – and yet I feel it's not only qualified by title, but by sheer, overwhelming morbidity. With family members tearfully gathered around him, Gallo spends half the movie prone in his coffin as his eyebrows are smoothed, his forehead powdered, and even while being shot twice in his already lifeless corpse. Technically, it may be a lying-in-state more than an actual funeral, but to quibble would surely be to split hairs – and who splits hairs with death?

6. *Santa sangre* (Mexico/Italy 1989, dir. Alejandro Jodorowsky)

The only non-human funeral on the list, courtesy of a film that is *sui generis* in pretty much every other respect too. The deceased is a Mexican circus elephant, fervently mourned by Fenix, the young son of the circus owners. The animal's send-off is, at least, a triumph, as the circus performers conduct the funeral procession through town, each of them dressed in black replicas of their usual costumes, while Fenix's father carries a black-and-white Stars and Stripes ahead of the coffin – and what a coffin! A giant, ornate casket borne on a flat-bed lorry, and thus transported to a ravine that serves as a garbage dump. There, watched by hundreds of dust-caked residents of an adjacent shanty town, the vast coffin is finally released – whereupon, amid mad scenes of jubilation, the shanty dwellers prise it open and then tear apart the beast inside for meat. High above them, Fenix weeps. An extraordinary scene in an extraordinary movie.

5. *Harold and Maude* (US 1970, dir. Hal Ashby)

In a movie made up of equal parts love and death, it seems only fitting that the cross-generational romance at its centre should begin at a funeral. Harold (Bud Cort), the pale young owner of a second-hand hearse, given to staging gory suicides so as to perturb his mother, has fallen into the habit of attending the funerals of strangers – until, at one dreary service in a near-empty church, a birdlike elderly woman takes up position in the pew behind him. There is a sharp *Pssst*; then an ice-breaking offer of liquorice. Soon, a conversation has been initiated, in the course of which it emerges that *neither* of them knew the deceased. After the coffin is hoisted up on its way to the cemetery, Ashby holds a mordant close-up on the 'Permaseal' badge on its lid, and the interlopers – she by now introduced to us as Maude (Ruth Gordon) – loiter a moment outside the church. 'Do you sing and dance?' Maude enquires of Harold, and when he admits he doesn't, she smiles to herself: 'I thought not.' A moment later, she steals the priest's car. Was there ever a more irresistible cue for love?

4. *Kind Heart and Coronets* (GB 1950, dir. Robert Hamer)

Having embarked on his mission to murder the entire D'Ascoyne family and thus ascend to a dukedom, Louis Mazzini (the elegant Dennis Price) has managed only two when he arrives at his second victim's funeral in this, Ealing's blackest and most durable comedy. There, in the ancient country church whose vault has played host to the D'Ascoynes for numberless generations, the disinherited 'poor boy from Clapham' finally sees the rest of the clan – each played, in a still-audacious sight gag, by Alec Guinness. Their presence leaves Mazzini despondent at the scale of the task still ahead of him, but the funeral itself does make his job easier in one respect – so painfully dull is the sermon delivered by Reverend D'Ascoyne that Mazzini immediately identifies the parson as the next of his victims. Unsurprisingly, this is not the last funeral to take place in the film.

3. *Orphans* (GB 1998, dir. Peter Mullan)

If the bulk of Mullan's hugely underrated debut is a prelude to a funeral (as four Glasgow siblings flounder amid ever-mounting chaos the night before their mother is buried), the climax doesn't disappoint. With the roof torn off the church following an aptly biblical storm, prayer books scattered and pigeons cooing from the rafters, the pompously dutiful Thomas (Gary Lewis) takes to the pulpit to give a reading as his brothers and sister, bloody and ashen, belatedly arrive. Finally, wounded brother Michael (Douglas Henshall) staggers to the front of the church, only to collapse from his injuries – but Thomas just keeps reading as his siblings leave for hospital. Then, outside, good son that he is, he demands to act as sole pallbearer. It is, of course, lunacy – Thomas bent double with his mother's coffin on his back, each step a fresh hell, the task leaving him whimpering in agony until, inevitably, he collapses, the other mourners rescuing the coffin, then shuffling on towards the grave with Thomas face down and semi-conscious. Ridiculous, blackly comic and heart-rending: in its portrait of death, *Orphans*' funeral says everything about life.

2. *Le Corbeau* / *The Raven* (France 1943, dir. Henri-Georges Clouzot)

A masterful set-piece in Clouzot's dissection of a small French town rotten to its priggish core, the funeral of 'Patient 13' (a long-term resident of the local hospital) takes place after his suicide –

one triggered by the antics of a mysterious letter-writer who signs their work as 'Le Corbeau' ('The Raven'). With the town under the spell of The Raven's poisonous missives, suspicion falls on Patient 13's nurse, Marie Corbin (the sombre Héléna Manson). In a scene as black-hearted as it is expert, the townsfolk turn out *en masse* for Patient 13's funeral procession, his mother lost in grief behind her veil as, in the wake of her son's coffin, the assembled hypocrites, liars, and adulterers pass by. And then, from among the wreaths, a sheet of paper dislodges itself from that sent by Corbin and flutters gently to the ground – a letter that, one by one, the mourners step around as if it were literally toxic. Finally, however, a young boy picks it up, it is confirmed that it has, of course, been penned by The Raven – and (while we sense that perhaps the unfortunate Mme Corbin is not the guilty party) nothing can prevent the funeral of Patient 13 swiftly descending into a witch-hunt.

1. *Imitation of Life* (US 1959, dir. Douglas Sirk)

The funeral as emotional punch to the gut could surely find no better illustration than here, in director Douglas Sirk's typically subversive scrutiny of race and class in the guise of glossily disposable 'women's picture'. The deceased is Annie Johnson (Juanita Moore), a black woman in 1950s New York whose light-skinned daughter Sarah-Jane has repeatedly rejected her in desperation to pass for white. Dying broken-hearted over her daughter's cruelty, Annie's last wish was for a grand funeral and in death, at least, she is indulged – the service unfolding in a vast church awash with floral tributes, filled with hundreds of mourners and gospel icon Mahalia Jackson in the pulpit singing 'Trouble of the World' ('No more weepin' and wailin' / I'm going home to live with God'). Outside, however, comes the clincher, as the coffin is loaded on to a carriage pulled by four white horses and, through the crowd, a distraught Sarah-Jane rushes up to it, falling upon her mother's casket as she sobs: 'I didn't mean it, Mama. Mama, can you hear me?' Dry eyes? You can forget 'em.

The Wind Blows Where It Will

Ten Wholly Unexpected 'Grace Notes'

GEOFFREY MACNAB

What we're looking for here are moments of magnanimity: instants in movies where characters behave with compassion when you least expect it – miraculously, one might say. This can be as trivial as the offer of an umbrella in a rainstorm. They can also be moments of self-sacrifice through which catastrophe is averted, or scenes in which suppressed emotions finally surface. They can be epiphanies in which couples belatedly realize that they love each other. They are not confined to any one genre or type of protagonist. At their best, these moments have a transcendent quality. For a few seconds, we are removed from the squabbles and conspiracies that make up the film's plot, and we are shown something more profound.

10. The raft scene in *Pat Garrett and Billy the Kid* (US 1973, dir. Sam Peckinpah)

This was a sequence that Peckinpah and his crew shot on their day off, behind the back of the studio. MGM couldn't see the point in a scene that added nothing to the narrative. Garrett (James Coburn) is shown sitting by his campfire at twilight, looking out at the river. He sees a homesteader and his family floating downstream. The homesteader is shooting at a bottle in the water. Garrett, too, begins to shoot at the bottle. The homesteader (a stranger whom we never see again) takes aim at Garrett, who readies himself to fire back. At the final moment, the two men think better of it. It's an ambiguous moment, about camaraderie and the random violence of the west. There is no reason why the two men should be taking potshots at one another. Nor is it easy to explain why their sudden cessation of hostility should seem so moving.

9. The kid falls from the high-rise apartment in *L'Argent de Poche* / *Small Change* (France 1976, dir. François Truffaut)

A mum and her toddler are coming home with their shopping. They stop en route for a chat with a neighbour. The boy, a cute little two- or three-year old called Gregory, empties all the food on the floor. Then, back in his own apartment, he wanders in pursuit of a cat. His mother has lost her wallet and is looking for it on the stairs. The boy plays with the cat on the window ledge. The cat loses its footing and slips. The boy tries to go after it. By now, there is a crowd of worried onlookers at ground level. Sure enough, the boy slips and plummets downward. Nobody catches him. There is nothing to break his fall. By all rights, he should die. Instead, he simply lands with a bump, brushes himself off, smiles winningly and continues playing. The mother sees how far he has fallen and promptly faints.

Truffaut had a famously troubled childhood: in his movies, his anger at the mistreatment of kids and his own affection for them always shine through. This scene is a perfect example of Truffaut using cinema correctively, to temper the cruelty of real life. What makes it all the more surprising is that the film, which is about the lives of a group of kids in a provincial town, is not whimsical or stylized: nobody else here defies gravity.

8. Ronald Colman dies at the guillotine in A *Tale of Two Cities* (GB 1935, dir. Jack Conway)

Dying selflessly on screen is an art at which British actors excel. Ronald Colman has just the right mix of melancholy, self-pity and insouciance as Dickens's jaded London lawyer Sydney Carton, sacrificing himself in the place of a French aristocrat for the sake of the woman he loves: 'It's a far, far better thing I do than I have ever done. It's a far, far better rest I go to than I have ever known,' Colman tells us in that mellifluous voice of his as he prepares to have his head lopped off. The lines are so familiar as to seem instantly corny, but Colman puts them across with such conviction that you buy into the scene in spite of its contrivances.

7. Jon Voight tends the dying Dustin Hoffman in *Midnight Cowboy* (US 1969, dir. John Schlesinger)

Jon Voight's would-be gigolo Joe Buck is naive and narcissistic. That is what makes his solicitude toward his sickly, low-life friend Ratso all the more surprising. In Lewis Milestone's Depression-era *Of Mice and Men*, the giant slow-witted farmhand, Lennie, played by Lon Chaney, dreamed of tending rabbits on a ranch with his friend George (Burgess Meredith). Ratso and Joe yearn to escape their sleazy Times Square existence and start afresh in Florida. The problem is that Ratso is dying. There is something hugely affecting about the way Joe looks after his sweaty, diminutive friend during the long bus ride south.

6. *Mat i Syn / Mother and Son* (Germany/Russia 1997, dir. Aleksandr Sokurov)

Sokurov's *Mother and Son* might best be described as a feature-length grace note. A son tends his dying mother. That's the plot in a nutshell. He carries her and tends her. They talk. He combs her hair. As the mother weakens, we hear the rustling of the trees and see painterly, blurred images of the countryside. What is startling is the intimacy of the relationship between the two: Sokurov captures brilliantly, if obliquely, the strange mix of terror, yearning and grief that the son feels as he watches his mother die.

5. Love redeems Martin Lassalle in *Pickpocket* (France 1959, dir. Robert Bresson)

The solitary pickpocket Michel (Lassalle) is in prison and close to despair. His one friend Jeanne (Marika Green) has stopped visiting him. She looked after his ailing mother, and knows he is a thief. Then, he receives a letter in which she tells him her baby has been ill: she hasn't abandoned him after all. When she visits him again, they embrace through the bars – a scene Bresson shows in big close-up, with Mozart to underline matters. 'Oh, Jeanne, to reach you at last, what a path I had to take.' It's a transcendent moment – the first blast of naked emotion in a film that has been characterized throughout by its detachment. There is an earlier scene in which she embraces him after he confesses his thieving. There, he shirks from her touch. Here, he seeks it.

4. George Sanders and Ingrid Bergman rediscover their love in *Viaggio in Italia* (Italy 1954, dir. Roberto Rossellini)

What causes relationships to end? Most films struggle to convey the many reasons, often banal in themselves, that can provoke the break-up of a marriage. Rossellini's *Viaggio in Italia* was the director's last film with his then-wife, Ingrid Bergman. It was released when the tensions were beginning to show in their marriage – a marriage that had led Bergman to leave Hollywood a few years before. Rossellini depicts the mix of boredom, contempt and irritation with which the husband and wife, Alex (George Sanders) and Katherine Joyce (Bergman), treat one another. Every sigh, sneer and gesture is registered.

The couple are in the hothouse atmosphere of Naples, where they have come to dispose of a dead relative's villa. 'After eight years of marriage, it seems we don't know anything about each other,' Sanders sneers at Bergman. Used to an orderly English gentleman's lifestyle, he is clearly repelled by the chaotic informality and sheer sensuousness of Neapolitan society. As he talks of Italy 'poisoning you with laziness', he drinks too much and flirts with other women. Katherine, meanwhile, is increasingly left on her own. Rossellini fills the film with symbols of death and fecundity. The streets are full of pregnant women. In the museums, there are skulls and crypts. The strangest moment is when Bergman and Sanders come face to face with the remains of a couple who died 2000 years before. A few moments later, they are discussing divorce as they drive through Naples. There is a religious procession and they are caught in the crowds. When she is swept away in the throng and he thinks he is about to lose her, he suddenly realizes that he does still love her. Their reconciliation is like something out of a Roman or Greek myth – and it is all the more affecting because it is so abrupt and unexpected.

3. The miracle in *Ordet / The Word* (Denmark 1955, dir. Carl Th. Dreyer).

A religious fanatic and misfit steps up to the coffin of his sister-in-law, who has just died in childbirth. He whispers in her ear and she comes back to life. As the producer and screenwriter James Schamus once observed of Dreyer, 'his goal was to create a crisis of signification, of the way we understand the world, and to give us [a] brief, sometimes very traumatic opening into what is outside our own understanding.' The miracle of *Ordet* is just such an opening. If you approach the scene with even the slightest scepticism, it will seem absurd. Give into it, though, and you'll find it both mysterious and hugely moving.

2. The sportswriter offers the ageing movie star shelter in *Veronika Voss* (West Germany 1982, dir. Rainer-Werner Fassbinder)

Fassbinder is often thought of as a trenchant satirist and polemicist, probing away relentlessly at social and sexual hypocrisy in post-war Germany. Strangely, given his reputation, the most resonant moments in his films are often those that are the quietest and gentlest. He throws in scenes of tenderness when we least expect them, showing people in adverse circumstances behaving (at least fleetingly) with decency and consideration. There is a beautiful moment early in *Veronika Voss* when sportswriter Robert Krohn (Hilmar Thate) spots Veronika (Rosel Zech) in the rain. The once-famous movie star from the 1930s is cold and distressed. Robert offers her the use of his umbrella. 'Umbrella . . . and protection,' she says to him, as if he is a knight who has come to save her from the dragon. At this point, we begin to hear Peer Raben's lilting, elegiac music on the soundtrack. *Veronika Voss* delves into some murky areas. It is a film about drug addiction, about the poisonous legacy of the Nazi era and about the self-pitying narcissism of its Dietrich-like leading character. This is the one scene in which Veronika achieves a kind of innocence.

1. John Wayne decides not to kill Natalie Wood in *The Searchers* (US 1956, dir. John Ford)

We first see Ethan Edwards (Wayne) riding out of the landscape. Even before the massacre of his brother's family that turns him into a vengeful near-psychopath, it is apparent that he is an Ahab-like loner, an old Confederate who still hasn't come to terms with the end of the American Civil War. *The Searchers* follows Ethan on his quest to track down Scar, the Comanche chief behind the massacre. Ethan's niece Deborah survived it, only to be raised by the Comanches as one of their own. His other niece Lucy was raped and killed. Moreover, Ethan and his brother's wife – Debbie's mother – clearly harboured a suppressed love. The idea that Debbie might now be one of Scar's squaws is therefore doubly anathema to the cowboy-turned-vigilante. Ethan's racism is self-evident. 'I could mistake you for a half-breed,' he sneers at his nephew Martin Pawley (Jeffrey Hunter). He considers any white who lives with the Comanches as less than a human being.

It is Ethan's utter malevolence that makes the film's finale so moving. The Comanche camp has been breached and Scar killed. Debbie flees. We see Ethan gallop after her, bearing down. We know he hates her for having gone over to the other side: we fully expect him to rip her to shreds. Just when the act of violence that will damn him until eternity seems inevitable – Ethan swoops down and lifts her into his arms. 'Let's go home, Debbie,' is all he says, but it is arguably the most affecting moment in any Ford movie – perhaps even in cinema.

The Ten Best Movie Endings

ANTHONY QUINN

Endings are, arguably, the most important aspect of a movie's narrative apparatus. The final minutes, or seconds, form the most immediate basis on which an audience, emerging from the dark, will judge the success or failure of the story they've been involved in. We have a natural human desire for resolution – 'closure', in modern parlance

– and we will be more inclined to forgive a movie its other short-comings if it manages to astound us, or move us, or choke us, with a great ending. David Mamet, who's written plenty of endings in his time both for plays and films, puts it like this: 'Turn the thing around in the last two minutes, and you can live quite nicely. Turn it around again in the last ten seconds and you can buy a house in Bel Air.'

The great ending is an extraordinarily difficult thing to pull off. Film-makers by and large want to fulfil their audience's expectation, and the safest way to achieve that is with a happy ending. These tend to be unmemorable: the boy gets the girl, the soldier makes it home, the cop catches the killer, the sporting legend proves he's the best after all. As Pauline Kael once wrote, 'the motive power behind much of our commercial entertainment is: Give the public a happy ending so they won't have to think about it afterwards.' The real challenge is to give an audience something that confounds rather than reassures, something that turns expectation on its head yet makes perfect sense. It's a challenge some of the most accomplished film-makers have flubbed: think only of the third and final instal-ment of the *Lord of the Rings* trilogy, *The Return of the King*. Peter Jackson naturally wanted a grand conclusion to his epic, and had sev-eral opportunities to ring the curtain down with appropriate gravitas. Sadly, like a chronic gambler who doesn't know when to quit, he just kept on raising – and finished up with a full-house of duff endings: a textbook lesson in how not to do it.

The list below is a highly partial and non-definitive selection of endings that are remarkable either for an element of surprise or else for the way the final moments elegantly dovetail with the moods and themes the movie has been exploring. It might only be a few words, or fleeting images, or even a freeze-frame, but each of them impresses for its absolute and immutable rightness. It will also remind us that the great endings are not, usually, happy endings.

10. *The Taking of Pelham One Two Three* (US 1974, dir. Joseph Sargent)

This so-so group-in-jeopardy thriller stars Walter Matthau as a New York Transit Authority chief forced to deal with a crisis: a subway train has been hijacked and its passengers held to ransom. The gang, led by a somewhat mechanical Robert Shaw, have already executed two hostages, and Matthau has the job of negotiating with them. In the course of their fraught exchanges via radio Matthau can hear that one hijacker (Martin Balsam) has a heavy cold, and occasionally interrupts his boss with a loud sneeze. 'Gesundheit!' says Matthau distractedly. Cut to the movie's endgame: all the hijackers are dead, apart from Balsam, who has somehow escaped with the loot and hastily hidden it in his kitchen. Matthau and his partner arrive to interview him – a standard suspect because he's actually a subway train driver – and seem to have drawn a blank: Balsam claims to have been home with a cold all day, so he couldn't have been hijacking a train. Matthau is out the door and mentally striking this suspect off his list when, suddenly, Balsam sneezes. Gesundheit! Matthau's head pokes round the door again – he's busted. A superb final twist: it deserves that house in Bel Air.

9. *North by Northwest* (US 1959, dir. Alfred Hitchcock)

William Goldman has said he doesn't know of a 'more adroit' ending to a film than this. Cary Grant is hanging perilously on to the edge of Mount Rushmore, while his lady, Eva Marie Saint, is hanging on to him. Martin Landau, the subvillain, stands a few feet away, holding a statuette that contains top-secret microfilm that would endanger America if it fell into enemy hands. He walks over to the dangling man and, instead of helping him up, grinds his shoe down on Grant's hand. It looks all over for our hero. The scriptwriter, Ernest Lehman, has an escape of his own to make here, and yet, as Goldman expresses it, the following occurs:

'(a) Landau is made to cease and desist.
(b) Grant saves himself.
(c) Grant also saves Eva Marie Saint.
(d) The two of them get married.
(e) The microfilm is saved for America.
(f) James Mason, the chief villain, is captured and handed over to the authorities.
(g) Grant and Saint take a train ride back east.'

The Wind Blows Where It Will: Ten Wholly Unexpected 'Grace Notes', p 437

Can you guess how long it takes Hitchcock and Lehman to tie up these narrative ends? Goldman has timed it for us: 43 seconds. No, I couldn't believe it either, until I watched the film again. Not a great ending, perhaps, but a marvel of efficiency.

8. *Don't Look Now* (GB 1973, dir. Nicolas Roeg)

This is the ending as unrepeatable shocker. Donald Sutherland and Julie Christie, grieving the death of their young daughter, repair to off-season Venice and try to forget. They are approached by a blind woman who has clairvoyant messages of danger, apparently delivered by the ghost of their dead child. But what is the danger? Nicolas Roeg creates an ominous, disorientating pattern of flashbacks, echoes and colours around the couple's troubled sojourn while Venice, almost incidentally, becomes the scene of several unexplained murders. The closing minutes find Sutherland caught between hope and dread, pursuing a red-coated apparition through the dank alleys and courts of the eerily empty city. Finally, breathless, he catches up with his quarry, and offers gentle words of reassurance: 'I'm not going to hurt you.' Too right: the hooded figure in red turns round to reveal a dwarfish face of unutterable malignity, and a knife is suddenly slashing at Sutherland's jugular. He collapses, dark gouts of blood pouring from his neck. Death in Venice, only this time with horror instead of seedy pathos.

7. *The Long Good Friday* (GB 1980, dir. John MacKenzie)

Bob Hoskins, as bantam East End gangster Harold Shand, has come to the Savoy Hotel hoping to finalize details of a business partnership with an American mobster. But the Americans are getting out of there, spooked by an Easter weekend of carnage and mayhem that eclipses the St Valentine's Day Massacre, all of it traceable to Harold's vendetta with Irish Republicans. Disgusted with such pusillanimity, Harold storms out, though not before delivering a great (if ungrammatical) putdown: 'The Mafia? I've shit 'em!' He then emerges on to the hotel's circular concourse and climbs into his limo – which suddenly accelerates away. His

own driver is gone, replaced by a man whose hooded eyes are
reflected in the rear-view mirror, while another (a fresh-faced
Pierce Brosnan) trains a gun on him from the passenger side. It's
the IRA, whose tenacious reach Harold has consistently, and
hubristically, underestimated. John MacKenzie's camera fixes on
him in the back seat, and as Francis Monkman's busy, brassy score
kicks in, we watch a grim rictus settle on Harold's face that seems
to pass through anger, to resignation, to a sort of rueful admiration
for his nemesis. For another iconic gangster face that closes a
movie there's De Niro staring up from his opium dream in *Once
Upon a Time in America*. But I think Hoskins just shades it.

6. *The Private Life of Sherlock Holmes* (GB 1970, dir. Billy Wilder)

I owe my love of this movie to the novelist Jonathan Coe, who
wrote an excellent essay on it for *Cahiers du cinéma*. Billy Wilder
and I.A.L. Diamond wrote more famous endings (to *Some Like it
Hot*, to *The Apartment*) but none more moving, I think, than the
epilogue to their Holmes pastiche, a film whose charm must be
weighed against its unevenness – great tranches of it were inexplicably lost. The second half concerns a shaggy-dog story in
which Holmes (Robert Stephens), on a mission in Scotland, pretends to be married to a woman (Genevieve Page) who is later
unmasked as a German spy. The final scene has Watson (Colin
Blakely) reading a letter which reports that she has been executed by firing-squad, though a postscript adds that the woman had
lived her last months as 'Mrs Ashdown', the name Holmes
assumed when they pretended to be man and wife. Holmes, broken by this belated revelation, bids Watson prepare his needle –
only cocaine can salve him – while Miklós Rózsa's beautiful and
melancholy violin concerto mourns in the background. There is
a level of pathos here one would not usually associate with the
great detective – or, indeed, with this great director.

5. *The Conversation* (US 1974, dir. Francis Ford Coppola)

This could be a companion piece to *Chinatown*, resonating as it

does with contemporary American crises: the curdling of idealism, the fear of conspiracy and an intuition that the bad guys are
getting away with it. Gene Hackman has never been better than
as Harry Caul, a professional wire-tapper who steals privacy for a
living and whose latest assignment seems to have endangered the
lives of an innocent couple. Coppola's masterstroke was to hinge
the plot on the misinterpretation of a single line ('He'd kill us if
he got the chance') but it is Hackman's presence that reverberates
in the film's devastating coda: double-crossed by his paymasters,
he now knows that *he* is under surveillance, and has torn up the
walls and floors of his apartment in search of the elusive bug. Our
last sight of him, blowing on a saxophone amid the ruins of his
home, is a picture of pure loneliness, and a chilling physical
metaphor: a man who has stripped down his life to the core and
found absolutely nothing.

4. *The Third Man* (GB 1949, dir. Carol Reed)

Screenwriter Graham Greene torments Holly Martins, the
naive American protagonist played by Joseph Cotten, from the
moment he arrives in the rubble-strewn desolation of post-war
Vienna to attend the funeral of his friend Harry Lime. Martins,
a hack writer of pulp westerns, finds himself blanked by the
locals, patronized by the urbane British major (Trevor Howard)
and duped by the very man (Orson Welles) he believed to be
cold in his grave. At one point he is even bitten by a parrot.
But Greene saves his most poignant humiliation until the very
last scene. Having attended Harry's funeral (his real one, this
time) Martins waits for Harry's actress girlfriend (Alida Valli)
in the hope of sparking a reconciliation, and perhaps even a
romance. Valli walks towards camera down an avenue lined
with cypress trees – and passes right by him, without so much
as a glance, while Anton Karas's famous zither score keeps up a
mocking jauntiness. Holly's last illusion, that this woman might
have cared for him, lies shattered. Robert Altman liked this
ending so much he paid homage to it at the conclusion of *The
Long Goodbye*.

3. *Casablanca* (US 1942, dir. Michael Curtiz)

It would be a kind of churlishness not to include this. Curtiz's wartime melodrama has lines in it so terrible even the cast would break up with laughter, yet it remains as fond and familiar to us as a comfortable old sofa. The trick of this ending is to give the audience what it wants, but not in the way it expects. Bogart, as the defiant lone-wolf Rick, has already proven himself a romantic by helping a young woman escape Casablanca and the corrupting grasp of Captain Renault; but who on earth could have anticipated the last-gasp nobility of his handing Ilsa, the woman he loves, back to her freedom-fighting husband Lazlo? Having tied up the romantic narrative, Rick then opens up a new political front by shooting dead Major Strasser and converting the cynical Renault to patriotism. 'Round up the usual suspects . . .' What nerve! As Rick and Renault slope off into the fog we seem to be witnessing not just the start of a beautiful friendship but a stirring alliance that will, hell, alter the whole course of the Second World War.

2. *Chinatown* (US 1974, dir. Roman Polanski, scr. Robert Towne)

'Forget it, Jake, it's Chinatown.' One of the most quoted lines in cinema snaps the lock shut on one of its most perfect plots. Yet the key line is the one Jake Gittes first uses to head off Evelyn Mulwray's question about what he used to do as a policeman in Chinatown: 'As little as possible,' he deadpans, later repeating the words (though they're not in the published screenplay) as he looks horror-stricken upon Evelyn's corpse and realizes his own implication in her doom. The lieutenant on duty, Escobar, who has a previous history with Gittes, overhears the line and says, 'What's that?' Incandescent with rage – 'As little as possible' evidently encapsulates police procedure in Chinatown – Escobar orders Gittes to clear off. 'Go home, Jake – I'm doing you a favour.' Slowly, Jake and his associates turn away, the camera rises and the sad trumpet theme fades in. Screenwriter Robert Towne argued bitterly with Polanski over this ending, after the latter insisted that Evelyn should die and the satanic Noah Cross escape justice. Polanski got his way, and Towne got the Oscar for Best Screenplay.

1. *The Wild Bunch* (US 1969, dir. Sam Peckinpah)

A whole movie about endings: Peckinpah's ageing outlaws, on the run through Mexico in 1913, have reached the end of the line, and have gone down in a savage, apocalyptic gun-battle (itself a shocking new departure in screen violence). Robert Ryan has unholstered his friend William Holden's gun for the last time, and now sits in front of the shattered fortress. Edmond O'Brien, the only other survivor, tells him there's only one more fight left – the Mexican Revolution. 'It ain't like it used to be,' he grins, 'but it'll do.' They don't care about the cause, they just want to keep moving. As the two men ride off, laughing together, Peckinpah does one more startling thing: he elides their laughter into a montage of the dead members of the Bunch – Holden, Ernest Borgnine, Warren Oates, Ben Johnson, Jaime Sanchez – whose own laughing faces fade in and out to the tearful chorus of 'La Golondrina'. Paul Schrader called it 'one of the strongest emotional kickbacks of any film', and this from a writer who knew an emotional kickback when he felt one. To have switched from appalling carnage to this moving, elegiac salute to the killers is a transition only Peckinpah, one feels, could have finessed. It's a great ending to one of the greatest American movies.

19

And Finally

With Compliments of the Season

GRAHAM FULLER: Deck the Halls with Bladeless Razors – Ten
Christmas Movies to Save Us All from Satan's Power

Deck the Halls with Bladeless Razors

Ten Christmas Movies to Save Us All from Satan's Power

BY GRAHAM FULLER

A nostalgified panacea of pine, tinsel, and tintinnabulation? Or a black hole of loneliness, bitterness, and melancholy? Films about Christmas, wholly or partially, have straddled both polarities over the years, producing a surprising number of classics. In compiling this list, I hummed and hahed over Terry Zwigoff's *Bad Santa* (2003), starring Billy Bob Thornton as a misanthropic crook who poses in the red suit and white beard to get at a department store's Christmas takings. It's a superbly cynical comedy, but to have included it would have been disingenuous: at the time of writing, there is a remote chance that my six-year-old will suspend disbelief in Santa Claus for one more Christmas.

I regret, too, the omission of Wong Kar-wai's *2046* (2004), in which Mr Chow (Tony Leung) dines with his landlord's lovelorn daughter (Faye Wong) on Christmas Eve and persuades her to phone her Japanese boyfriend. As Nat King Cole's 'The Christmas Song' fades out, Chow watches the girl chatting away and reflects, in the retrospective voice-over, that many people need comfort on Christmas Eve, and that he didn't mind there was none for him. It's just a touch of Christmas in a romantic reverie – but sometimes a touch is all you need.

Sublime stocking-fillers: *Meet Me in St Louis* (1944), *Fanny and Alexander* (1983), *The Dead* (1987), *Tim Burton's The Nightmare Before Christmas* (1993), *The City of Lost Children* (1995)

Spartan fare to savour: *Metropolitan* (1990), *A Midnight Clear* (1992)

Overcooked chestnuts: *A Miracle on 34th Street* (1947), *White Christmas* (1954), *How the Grinch Stole Christmas* (2000), *Love Actually* (2003), *The Polar Express* (2004), *The Family Stone* (2005)

Best Nativity: *Monty Python's Life of Brian* (1979)

Best motto: 'You can't fool-a me. There ain't no Sanity Clause!'
(Chico Marx in *A Night at the Opera* [1935])

10. *Christmas Holiday* (US 1944, dir. Robert Siodmak)

Jilted by his fiancée on Christmas Eve and grounded in New Orleans,
a soldier takes a nightclub chanteuse (Deanna Durbin) to midnight
Mass. He is moved by her tears, and she tells him of her undying love
for her husband (Gene Kelly) – a psychotic racetrack hustler with
slippery charm and an over-affectionate mother (Gale Sondergaard)
– who breaks jail even as they talk. Casting against type was never
more effective than in Siodmak's supremely perverse noir, adapted by
Herman J. Mankiewicz from a Somerset Maugham novel. Kelly's performance laid down the blueprint for Robert Walker in *Strangers on
a Train* and Robert De Niro in *The King of Comedy*, and Durbin looks
as fragile as a glass bauble on a Christmas tree.

9. *Swiss Miss* (US 1938, dir. John G. Blystone)

There are movies about Christmas that lose nothing from being
watched out of season. There are movies *not* about Christmas that
sparkle the most when watched in December. There are people of
my intimate acquaintance who find it impossible to get through the
holiday without Mr Laurel and Mr Hardy. The duo's twee
Christmas movie *Babes in Toyland* pales beside the inspired Alpine
nonsense of *Swiss Miss*, in which Stan and Ollie play American
mousetrap salesmen in cheese-laden Switzerland and Ollie falls in
love with an opera singer masquerading as a chambermaid. A gorilla, far from home, interferes with the boys' attempt to carry a piano
across a rope bridge (a nod to *The Music Box*). A St Bernard refuses to give up its brandy to Stan. But no matter! The hapless one
resigns himself to plucking a chicken, whereupon the snowstorm of
falling feathers prompts the dog to do its duty, effecting Stan's
instant inebriation. That's Christmassy enough for this list.

8. *The Man Who Came to Dinner* (US 1942, dir. William Keighley)

National radio celebrity Sheridan Whiteside (Monty Woolley)

breaks his hip entering the home of the Stanley family in Ohio and convalesces there over Christmas, terrorizing his hosts (Billie Burke, Grant Mitchell), his nurse (Mary Wickes), and his secretary (Bette Davis), whose love life he attempts to sabotage. This Warner Bros. adaptation of Kaufman and Hart's Broadway cocktail has lost none of its kick over the years, not least because director Keighley stood back to let the verbal vitriol drip. The acidulous Whiteside is Kaufman's and Hart's tribute to the critic Alexander Woollcott, who considered playing the character on stage; Ann Sheridan, Reginald Gardiner and Jimmy Durante drop in to spoof Tallulah Bankhead, Noël Coward and Harpo Marx respectively. The mad aunt (Ruth Vivian) is ostensibly the nineteenth-century murder suspect Lizzie Borden in disguise. Delicious.

7. *The Magnificent Ambersons* (US 1942, dir. Orson Welles)

Fleetingly, Welles's butchered masterpiece offers the finest evocation of Christmas past. On a country outing following 'the last of the great long-remembered dances', George (Tim Holt) and Lucy (Anne Baxter) embrace when their sleigh crashes in the snow, and they, Isabel (Dolores Costello), Eugene (Joseph Cotten), and the others in the party go home in Eugene's 'horseless carriage', singing 'The Man Who Broke the Bank at Monte Carlo'. Using real snow, Welles created his winter wonderland in the Union Ice Company refrigeration plant in downtown LA; the chill air enabled him to capture the actors' and horses' 'white' breath, which contrasts with the automobile's black exhaust smoke. As pretty and fake as a Christmas card, the sequence is often compared with a Currier & Ives lithograph, but it is tinged with foreboding. Welles ended the epiphany with an iris shot of the happy group disappearing into the distance, a metaphor for the end of the Amberson era.

6. *Comfort and Joy* (GB 1984, dir. Bill Forsyth)

Disc jockey Dickie Bird (Bill Paterson), recently dumped by his girlfriend, is solaced by the part he plays in ending Glasgow's 'Ice Cream Wars', though Bill Forsyth's film plays down the actual violence (which resulted in six killings). Forsyth anoints the urban setting with typical Shakespearian magic – the spectral lights and nursery jingles of the mirage-like ice-cream van and the pixieish presence of Claire Grogan usher the film into faerie. As with *Local Hero*, Forsyth doesn't diminish ruefulness with sentiment. But Dickie's healing has begun, and though he winds up alone in his studio on Christmas Day, there are listeners out there who need him.

5. *The Night Before Christmas* (US 1941, dir. William Hanna & Joseph Barbera)

Though this is one of the more benign Hanna–Barbera cartoons featuring Tom and Jerry, it has its moments of friction – and the Yule atmosphere is exquisite. Jerry is tempted out of his hole by a slice of cheese, thoughtfully wrapped and served on a mousetrap by Tom, and explores the glistening cornucopia beneath the Christmas tree, where war inevitably ensues. Having paid a painful penalty for puckering up under the mistletoe, Tom then ejects his tiny nemesis through the mailbox into a blizzard, only to have a Scrooge-ian crisis of conscience and so brings him inside to thaw out on the hearth. The message, of course, is peace and goodwill to all mice, though one may safely assume that hostilities were resumed on Boxing Day.

4. *A Christmas Story* (Canada 1983, dir. Bob Clark)

'A crummy commercial? Sonofabitch,' fumes nine-year-old Ralphie (Peter Billingsley), disappointed by the Ovaltine slogan he's decoded from Radio Orphan Annie's secret message. Culled from Jean Shepherd's novel *In God We Trust: All Others Pay Cash*, Bob Clark's Rockwellian portrait of Christmas in 1940s Indiana focuses on Ralphie's Machiavellian ploys to lay his hands on a Red Ryder Carbine Action Range Model Air Rifle. The film succeeds because it never gives in to sappiness. Not the least of the film's joys is its bored and dyspeptic Santa, dispatching Ralphie with a boot as his malevolent elves look on. Billy Bob Thornton presumably took notes.

3. *The Apartment* (US 1960, dir. Billy Wilder)

Wilder's masterpiece could top any number of lists – The Ten Most Bacchanalian Workplace Movies, say, or The Ten Most Sordid Winners of the Academy Award for Best Picture. It's about a lowly Manhattan insurance clerk, C.C. Baxter (Jack Lemmon), who climbs the corporate ladder by lending his apartment key to the company philanderers, even as he falls for the elevator girl Fran Kubelik (Shirley MacLaine), who's sleeping with his married boss Sheldrake (Fred MacMurray). The delights include Baxter straining spaghetti through his tennis racket and shaving with a bladeless razor; Miss Olsen (Edie Adams), another discarded Sheldrake mistress, calling up his wife to blow the whistle; the incredulity of the doctor (Jack Kruschen) who thinks Baxter, his neighbour, is a playboy; and Baxter's tryst with the booze-befuddled pick-up (Hope Holiday) who recites, "Twas the night before Christmas and all through the house/ Not a creature was stirring. Nothin'. No action. Dullsville. You married?' Like Baxter, I fell in love with 'Kubelik' (as the office lechers call her) and years later I informed Miss MacLaine of same in an interview. She did not respond.

2. *Scrooge* (GB 1951, dir. Brian Desmond Hurst)

Charles Dickens would have admired Alastair Sim's performance in this unimprovable adaptation of *A Christmas Carol*. 'He is of the sneer, sneery; of the growl, growly,' he might have written. 'The Americans have their Wayne and their Welles, we have our Sim and our Sim.' Sim's tortured performance and his terrifying visions are complemented by the Gothic mise-en-scène and C.M. Pennington-Richards' near-expressionistic black-and-white cinematography; Ernest Thesiger, a veteran of James Whale's *The Old Dark House* (1932) and *A Bride of Frankenstein* (1935), surely revelled in his role as the undertaker. Marley's ghost is played by Michael Hordern and George Cole (Sim's adopted son) is the young Ebenezer. But Sim towers over the tale.

1. *It's a Wonderful Life* (US 1946, dir. Frank Capra)

James Agee commended Capra's classic as 'one of the most efficient sentimental pieces since *A Christmas Carol* [1938]'. Only a
Scrooge – or a Mr Potter (Lionel Barrymore) – would deny
George Bailey (James Stewart) a guardian angel and the joyous
resolution in which he is saved from ruin by the Bedford Falls
community he has so conscientiously served. The film has myriad
pleasures: George and Mary Frances (luminous Donna Reed)
singing 'Buffalo Gals' and talking 'medieval' as they walk home
from the dance, and the subsequent loss of her robe; their sharing
of the phone receiver that glues them together; the impromptu
honeymoon arranged for them by Bert and Ernie; flirty Violet
(Gloria Grahame) promenading down main street; George calling Clarence (Henry Travers) 'bub', and yelling with joy when
he's told that his mouth's bleeding.

But as a film about an ambitious man worn down by disappointment and the shortcomings of small-town existence, *It's a
Wonderful Life* becomes more troubling as the years go by: it's hard
to imagine that George's kids, when fully grown, didn't recall the
Christmas Eve when he so brutally bawled them out. (Anthony
Mann's 1950s westerns similarly picked up on the Stewart persona's repressed rage.) The noir dream that results from George's
crack-up has a dark and terrible poetry: it partially inspired David
Thomson's novel *Suspects*, the most incisive commentary on a
film that is often misunderstood as a celebration. 'Zuzu's petals'
preserve it from tragedy.

Acknowledgements

Special thanks are owed to Geoff Andrew and *Time Out*, as Geoff originally commissioned Ethan Coen and Joel Coen's list of 'dream remakes' to accompany his interview with the brothers for *The Ladykillers* (2004) in *Time Out* (London); and to *Interview* magazine (Brant Publications, Inc.), as Graham Fuller's Christmas movie list is inspired by 'Have Yourself a Movie Little Christmas', a piece Graham published in *Interview* in December 1990.

In terms of the making of this book, the editor must express extreme gratitude to all of its ingenious and industrious contributors; to Andrew Rae for his inimitable artwork, and to Darren Wall for the overseeing of design elements; to John Grindrod, Rachel Alexander, Bomi Odufunade, Andrew Benbow and Matthew de Ville for their creative input; and most especially to Lucie Ewin, for marshalling the whole project through its stages of production.

RTK

Film Noir: The Encyclopedia
Alain Silver, Elizabeth Ward,
James Ursini, and Robert Porfirio

978-1-59020-144-2
$45.00 HC

Film Noir is the acknowledged bible of the genre, unsurpassed in
its erudition, range, and authority since its first publication in 1979.
For the first time, this classic of film reference receives a total updating
and revision. With entries for now over 500 American and international films, more than 500 evocative stills and other photos, and in-depth
analysis of the elements of the genre, this all new edition is surely
the last word on the noir film.

"If anyone is ever going to solve the mystery of noir's intense but
fairly short-lived dominance of our screens, it will have to be Silver
and Ursini, who have written many invaluable books on the subject."
—Richard Schickel, *Los Angeles Times*

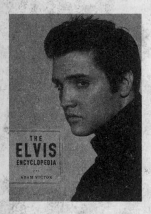

The Elvis Encyclopedia
Adam Victor

978-1-58567-598-2
$65.00 HC

By combining obsessive research with absorbing writing, Adam Victor, author of the bestselling *The Marilyn Encyclopedia*, sifts through the competing versions of events throughout Elvis's life and traces a young man's path to immortality.

"The book is lavishly and lovingly illustrated."
—*New York Times Book Review*

The Marilyn Encyclopedia
Adam Victor

978-1-58567-188-5
$35.00 PB

Through astute research and crisp writing, Victor traces Marilyn's inexorable path to iconhood, creating a compelling anatomy of fame in our century. The book also includes a bibliography, list of fan clubs, web sites, and hundreds of photos and illustrations, many of them rare, some simply never seen before. Marvelously stylish and incomparable in scope and depth, *The Marilyn Encyclopedia* will satisfy even her most ravenous fans.

Casablanca: Script and Legend
Howard Koch

978-0-87951-319-1
$19.95 PB

This volume contains the complete screenplay as well as a behind-the-scenes look at how the Oscar-winning movie was made, by screenwriter Howard Koch.

OTHER TITLES OF INTEREST

Choking on Marlon Brando
Antonia Quirke

978-1-59020-054-4
$13.95 PB

Choking on Marlon Brando is moving and hilarious, a bittersweet and endearing story of a woman who can't draw the line between her live life and the art she loves.

Raymond Chandler's L.A.
Elizabeth Ward and Alain Silver

978-0-87951-351-1
$23.95 PB

This evocative and elegant book juxtaposes excerpts of Chandler's tough, cynical prose with black-and-white photographs of the city he described as "no worse than others, a city rich and vigorous and full of pride, a city lost and beaten and full of emptiness."

St. Trinians: The Entire Appalling Business
Ronald Searle

978-1-58567-958-4
$29.95 HC

"Before *St. Trinian's* was a big-screen movie, it was a series of Charles Addams-esque cartoons by Ronald Searle ... *St Trinian's: The Entire Appalling Business* collects Searle's strips in a handsome hardcover package that is an absolute delight." —BoingBoing.net